Praise for

Conservatism: A Rediscovery

"With this astonishing book, Yoram Hazony takes uncontestable leadership of postliberal conservatism, becoming not only its most important public intellectual, but also its passionate prophet. *Conservatism: A Rediscovery* is the book we have long been waiting for: a compelling critique of where the right went wrong and how it can create a vital new public philosophy by reinvigorating old truths. An unusually compelling mix of history, political science, cultural analysis, religious wisdom, and personal testimony, Hazony's instant classic is not just the voice of a new conservatism; it is also the voice of an old civilization whose clarion call proclaims hope and sounds the way out of the contemporary West's dark wood."

— **Rod Dreher,** senior editor at *The American Conservative* and author of *Live Not by Lies*

"*Conservatism: A Rediscovery* is a fascinating, erudite, and mind-opening work—historically adept, philosophically vital, and clearly written. It's a must-buy and a must-read for anyone who thinks deeply about liberty, responsibility, and community."

— **Ben Shapiro,** host of *The Ben Shapiro Show* and editor emeritus of The Daily Wire

"Steeped in history, framed with well-defined concepts, and presented in crystal clear prose, Hazony's powerful vision of conservatism for the twenty-first century is capable of steering the ship of state out of our present perils."

— **R. R. Reno,** editor of *First Things* and author of *Return of the Strong Gods*

"Libertarians are used to arguing against those who praise government in the name of 'progress' and for the sake of their own power. But the more intellectually forceful challenge to libertarianism comes not from progressives but from conservatives. Yoram Hazony provides that challenge in this lucid exposition of a tradition of conservative nationalism that begins in the Old Testament and passes through George Washington and Alexander Hamilton to our own moment."

— **Peter Thiel,** author of *Zero to One*

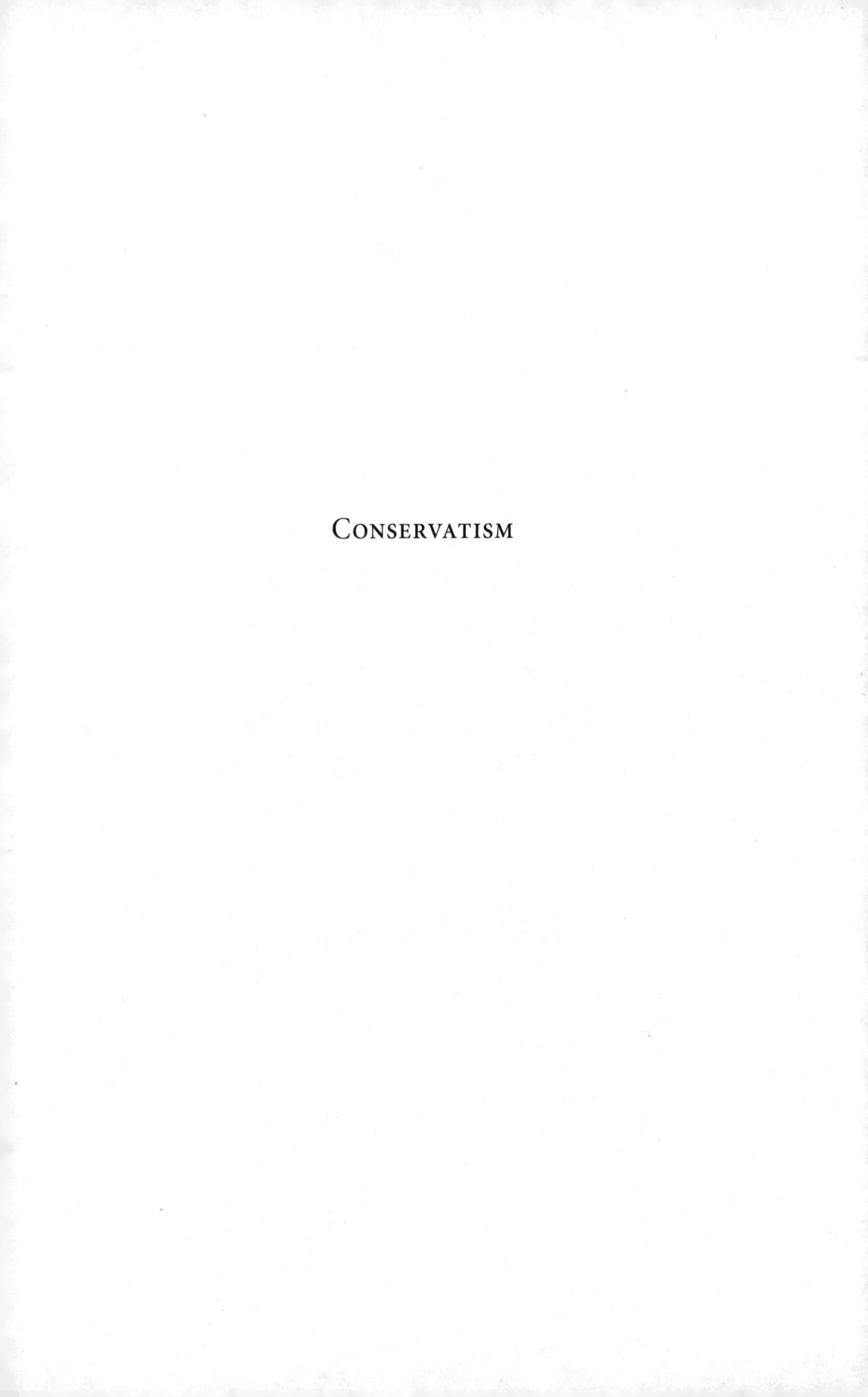

Conservatism

CONSERVATISM

A Rediscovery

Yoram Hazony

Regnery books may be purchased in bulk at special discounts for sales promotion, corporate gifts, fund-raising, or educational purposes. Special editions can also be created to specifications. For details, contact the Special Sales Department, Regnery, 307 West 36th Street, 11th Floor, New York, NY 10018 or info@skyhorsepublishing.com.

Regnery® is an imprint of Skyhorse Publishing, Inc.®, a Delaware corporation.

Visit our website at www.regnery.com.

Please follow our publisher Tony Lyons on Instagram @tonylyonsisuncertain.

10 9 8 7 6 5 4 3 2 1

Library of Congress Cataloging-in-Publication Data is available on file.

Cover design by John Caruso

Paperback ISBN: 978-1-68451-589-9
Hardcover ISBN; 978-1-68451-109-9
eBook ISBN: 978-1-68451-110-5

Printed in the United States of America

Dedicated with love to
Isaac and Linda Hazony

Contents

Introduction

Is Conservative Revival Possible?

For three generations, Western nations have lived in the shadow of the World Wars. The depths of the trauma have never been fully examined, nor its consequences entirely mapped. But we know that within a few years after the end of the Second World War, political life in these countries underwent an unprecedented revision. By the 1960s, the old Protestant nationalism that had animated the generation of Franklin Roosevelt and Dwight Eisenhower had been set aside, and Enlightenment liberalism became the new framework within which American political life was conducted. America was given what was, in effect, a new liberal constitution that guaranteed the civil liberties of blacks and other minorities, but also banned prayer and Bible-reading from the schools and lifted earlier legal restrictions on divorce, pornography, immigration, and abortion. Academics and intellectuals even gave a new name to the regime—which they now called "liberal democracy."[1]

In the decades that followed, many Americans and Europeans came to believe that in liberalism, they had discovered the final political theory: a regime so obviously desirable that competition among political ideologies had in effect come to an end. Soon, liberalism would be adopted by all nations. The reign of liberal ideas would last forever.

No one believes this anymore.

Five years of political upheaval—from 2016 to 2020—was all it took to shatter the hegemony of Enlightenment liberalism. Suddenly, the conflict among competing political visions was fiercely alive once more.

On the one hand, the appeal of a revived nationalist conservatism was given dramatic expression by the 2016 election of Donald Trump's "America First" administration in the United States, by Britain's departure from the European Union, and by the rise of nationalist conservative governments in Eastern Europe, Italy, India, Brazil, and other countries.

At the same time, an updated Marxism (calling itself "Progressivism," "Anti-Racism," or "Woke") launched an astonishingly successful bid to seize control of the institutions that had been, until only recently, responsible for the development and circulation of liberal ideas in America, Britain, and beyond. Indeed, by the summer of 2020, most of the important news media, universities and schools, big tech and other major corporations, and even the government bureaucracy and the military had adopted a policy of accommodating the new Marxism and advancing its agenda.

Meanwhile, in 2018, a rising China anointed the chairman of the Communist Party, Xi Jinping, ruler for life. Persecution of religious and political dissidents followed, reaching a climax with the effective annexation of Hong Kong, until recently a symbol of Enlightenment liberalism in Asia, in 2020. These events put an end to the long-standing myth that economic prosperity would bring a liberal political order to China. Instead, Americans abruptly found themselves facing the bleak reality of an imperialist China pursuing an increasingly credible campaign to overthrow the liberal Western nations as the dominant power in world affairs.[2]

The hegemony of liberal ideas, which was supposed to last forever and to be embraced by all nations, has come to an end after only sixty years.

What will happen next?

Many commentators have compared the crumbling of the liberal regime in America to Weimar Germany in the decade before Hitler's rise to power.[3] And indeed, on the far reaches of the political right, new racialist movements (calling themselves "white identitarians") have begun to press their claims, while an assortment of other radicals have taken to mentioning the advantages of dictatorship. So far, these views have remained without much influence. But the collapse of institutional liberalism and an ascendant Marxism could change that, providing fuel for a reaction drawing on authoritarian precedents from the last century.

Yet despite these grim historical parallels, America may have the resources to overcome these challenges. Many Americans still possess a strong intuitive commitment to the Anglo-American constitutional tradition. This includes the great majority of nationalist conservatives who supported the Trump presidency. To be sure, their insistence on the centrality of the nation in political life means that they oppose many aspects of the liberal consensus of recent decades—including large-scale immigration; the offshoring of American manufacturing capabilities to China in the name of free trade; the empowerment of international bodies such as the UN, EU, and WTO at the expense of independent national states; and wars aimed at bringing liberalism to the Middle East. They propose government action against the progressive cartels that dominate big business, the media, universities, and schools, and they seek policy changes that may assist in reversing the dissolution of the family and the decline of religious tradition. But nationalist conservatives support a democratic regime and peaceful transitions of power, as well as customary Anglo-American protections for property rights, freedom of speech, and free exercise of religion. These characteristics make national conservatism a powerful force with great potential for political revival and restoration in the coming years, whether on its own or in alliance with anti-Marxist liberals. In fact, with the collapse of liberal hegemony in America, nationalist conservatism offers the best hope for restoration of political stability and health.

But there are also significant difficulties standing in the way of any kind of revived political conservatism in the English-speaking world right now. In this regard, two things especially stand out.

First, many of today's "conservatives" know very little about what it would take to actually conserve anything—that is, to propagate beneficial ideas, behaviors, and institutions across generations. It is true that Cold War conservatives accomplished crucial things: Intellectuals such as William F. Buckley Jr. and political figures like President Ronald Reagan in the United States and Prime Minister Margaret Thatcher in Britain led the effort to defeat Soviet Communism abroad and socialism at home, a struggle that reached its successful conclusion in the late 1980s. More recently, British conservatives succeeded in restoring the national independence of their country as well. These are resounding historical achievements, not to be taken for granted.

Yet during these very same years—when American and British conservatives frequently held positions of power in every branch of government, appeared often in the major media, and wrote many bestselling books—the political and religious traditions that had granted stability and continuity to these countries for centuries were being severely damaged or overthrown entirely. This shocking destruction of the Anglo-American cultural inheritance has involved the suppression or stigmatization of many of the most important ideas and institutions around which life in Britain and America had been built, including God and Scripture, nation and congregation, marriage and family, man and woman, honor and loyalty, the sabbath and the sacred, among others. This has been possible, in no small part, because with each new step in this ongoing cultural revolution, self-proclaimed "conservatives" have been found who were willing quickly to pronounce the battle lost and to encourage their colleagues to accept the new order and move on. This is not only due to excessive political pragmatism or weakness of character, although these have played a role. There is also, at this point, an astonishing degree of ignorance. Many well-intentioned conservatives really do not know, anymore, why one would need to preserve and strengthen these things.

Which brings us to the second remarkable fact about contemporary conservatism: the extraordinary confusion over what distinguishes Anglo-American conservatism from Enlightenment liberalism (or "classical liberalism" or "libertarianism" or, for that matter, from the philosophy of Ayn Rand). Indeed, for decades now, many prominent "conservatives" have had little interest in political ideas other than those that can be used to justify free trade and lower taxes, and, more generally, to advance the supposition that what is always needed and helpful is a greater measure of personal liberty. And if anyone has tried to point out that these are well-known liberal views, and that they have no power to conserve anything at all, he has been met with the glib rejoinder that *What we are conserving is liberalism*, or that *Conservatism is a branch or species within liberalism*, or that *Liberalism is the new conservatism.*

For the most part, these comments are made out of ignorance, although on rare occasions it does seem as though there may be other motives involved. At any rate, it is now clear that this confusion concerning the content and purposes of political conservatism has paralyzed the conservative impulse in the English-speaking world, rendering it weak and ineffective. For the truth—which at this point cannot be repeated frequently enough—is that Enlightenment liberalism, as a political ideology, is bereft of any interest in conserving anything. It is devoted entirely to freedom, and in particular to freedom from the past. In other words, liberalism is an ideology that promises to liberate us from precisely one thing, and that thing is conservatism. That is, it seeks to liberate us from the kind of public and private life in which men and women know what must be done to propagate beneficial ideas, behaviors, and institutions across generations and see to it that these things really are done.

To the extent that Anglo-American conservatism has become confused with liberalism, it has, for just this reason, become incapable of conserving anything at all. Indeed, in our day conservatives have largely become bystanders, gaping in astonishment as the consuming fire of cultural revolution destroys everything in its path.

So that I should not be misunderstood, I must emphasize that the liberty of the individual is a fine thing, both good in itself and worthwhile for its beneficial effects, when taken in the right proportion. It has, and will always have, an important place in a broader theory of political conservatism.

But under the present conditions of permanent revolution and cultural devastation, the most important thing to remember about individual liberties is that, in and of themselves, they have no power to make anything stable or permanent. This is why the great triumph of liberal ideas after the Second World War has left nothing stable and permanent in its wake. Even its most important achievement—the desegregation of the American South and the putative end of racially based laws and social norms in America—now seems to have been achieved superficially, without arriving at a settlement that could endure the test of generations.

If we care about making anything stable and permanent, we must have other tools at our disposal besides the lists of individual freedoms and proscribed forms of discrimination that liberals have been so busy compiling and attempting to impose on the world since the 1940s.

We must have other tools at our disposal, and these will have to be conservative tools, not liberal ones.

However, to have such conservative tools at their disposal, democratic nations will have to let go of their postwar obsession with liberalism. They will have to turn to other, older philosophies, which are concerned with how things are propagated in time, and to learn from them again. Indeed, if a conservative politics is to play a significant role in democratic nations again, conservative ideas, behaviors, and institutions are going to have to be rediscovered. This will involve rediscovering the *history and philosophy of conservatism*, both of which have by now been largely forgotten. And it will mean rediscovering the *practice of conservatism*—which is not only the practice of *conservative government* but also, especially, the practice of being a *conservative person* and leading a *conservative life.*

Is it possible for a society whose traditions have grown so faint to revive them? Is it possible for individuals who have grown up in a liberal society obsessed with personal freedoms to become strong conservative men and women and to do what a conservative calling demands of them?

I believe it is possible because I have seen it happen many times over the course of my life. It is possible for individuals to discover that they have been on the wrong course, repent, and set out on a new and better course. And this is possible, too, for families and congregations, tribes and nations.

In fact, the sudden rise of the new Marxists presents an opportunity for a conservative revival unlike any we have seen in our lifetimes. To be sure, we are witnessing a spectacular and horrifying historical event. The potential for tragedy is obviously very great. But the extremity of this event can permit a process of rethinking that has been impossible until now. Many will now find that they are ready for the rediscovery that I have described: the rediscovery of a conservative life.

An important principle of Anglo-American conservative thought is this: *When faced with the disastrous consequences of a particular course of action, we must retrace our steps and restore, as much as possible, the conditions that existed prior to setting out on this course.* This is what happened in 1660, when Matthew Hale proposed the restoration of the English monarchy. It is what happened in 1787, when George Washington proposed the restoration of the forms of the traditional English constitution in America. It is what happened in 1863, when Abraham Lincoln proposed that the evil of slavery, that unspeakable digression from the course of English constitutional history, would be abolished. America and Britain have arrived at another such juncture, and they will have to retrace their steps and return to their historic path.

If such a repentance, and such a return to the right path, has taken place time and again in history, why should it not be attempted again? There is nothing to be lost in making the attempt—and everything to be gained by it.

In the political arena, *conservatism* refers to a standpoint that regards the recovery, restoration, elaboration, and repair of national and religious traditions as the key to maintaining a nation and strengthening it through time. In this book, I will be concerned primarily with one conservative political tradition, that of *Anglo-American conservatism.*

This is a tradition already powerfully described by John Fortescue in the fifteenth century, by Richard Hooker in the sixteenth century, and by John Selden, Matthew Hale, and others in the seventeenth century. But it is most familiar to us today for the crucial role it played in the revolutions of the late eighteenth century—when this conservative tradition was upheld by statesmen such as Edmund Burke in Britain and by the Federalist Party of George Washington, John Jay, John Adams, Gouverneur Morris, and Alexander Hamilton in America. This Anglo-American conservatism continued to be an important strand in the politics of the English-speaking peoples into the twentieth century. And it is crucial to us now because it holds the key to understanding what made these nations strong and successful both in political affairs and in almost every other matter.

I will occasionally use the term *national conservatism*, which is associated with the American statesman Daniel Webster, to describe Anglo-American conservatism where it has placed an especial emphasis on national independence and on the loyalties that bind the nation's constitutive factions to one another.[4] There is a certain redundancy built into this expression because Anglo-American conservatism has long placed the idea of the *nation*—at first the English nation, and later the British and American nations—at the center of political life. But the "nationalist" aspect of Anglo-American conservatism does become more pronounced during periods when the integrity of the nation is directly challenged by an excessive internationalism, localism, or individualism. This was the case, for example, when England was threatened with absorption into the Spanish Empire in the 1580s, when the Americans sought to establish themselves as a single independent nation in the 1780s, and with the rise of internationalist utopianism in the 1910s. In the same way, the conservative movement in America and Britain after the mid-2010s is rightly called a "nationalist" conservatism, since it seeks to return the national interest, or the common good of the nation, to the center of political discourse, after decades in which the freedom of the individual became the overriding principle in all spheres of life.[5]

For those who have not come across my work before, it may be relevant to say a few words about how I came to think about this subject.

I grew up in a liberal college town, Princeton, New Jersey; and I studied at two liberal universities, Princeton and Rutgers. But my father's house was steeped in the sense that the society around us had veered off course. In the evenings, my father and I would watch the 10:00 p.m. news together on a New York station, Channel 5, WNEW. Each night, the broadcast included a live debate about national affairs between two local Jewish personalities, the conservative Martin Abend and the liberal Sidney Offit. (It is rumored that these Abend-Offit debates were the inspiration for the legendary "Point, Counterpoint" sketches with Dan Aykroyd and Jane Curtin on *Saturday Night Live.*)[6]

My father never failed to side with Martin Abend in these debates. He thought Sidney Offit didn't have any idea what was involved in maintaining a nation, and that he consistently advocated a loosening of what my father called America's "moral fiber"—that thing which holds people together as a nation, prevents them from harming themselves and others too badly, and gives them the strength to band together and defeat adversity of every kind. The Roman Empire had fallen, my father said, because it had lost its internal unity, and with it the ability to continue fighting. The United States, he said, was headed in the same direction. Without a restoration of its "moral fiber," America wasn't going to make it.

I thought my father was right then, and I still think so now.

My father had been trained as a physicist. He had strong opinions about almost everything reported on the nightly news. But he didn't read books or magazines about political matters, and he didn't suggest that I read any myself. It was my Uncle Dov and Aunt Rina, living in Cleveland, who bought me a subscription to *Commentary* magazine when I was fifteen years old. That same year, I asked the rabbi of our synagogue, Melvin Glatt, if he would allow me to join his Talmud class for adults. These were slender threads, but in following where they led, I began what has turned out to be a lifelong project of rediscovering two important traditions—Anglo-American conservatism and the Jewish biblical and rabbinic tradition—and restoring them to their proper weight and significance in my own life and in the lives of others.

The most important influence on my road to a conservative life was that of my Uncle Isaac and Aunt Linda. After finishing high school, I went to Israel for a year, where I spent my sabbaths and holidays with them and with their children, Meir, Racheli, Shlomi, Rivkaleh, Zehavaleh, and Reuven. I cannot imagine where I would be if my aunt and uncle had not opened their home to me, and to a young woman named Julie whom I met in college, and to so many of our friends from Princeton. This book is dedicated to them in gratitude and love.

My wife Yael and I have done everything together since we met a few weeks after starting college in 1983. The story of my coming to a conservative life is inseparable from who she was and is. I have said a bit more about her in the personal recollections included in the last part of the book. Those who want to know more about Julie and me are welcome to skip to the end.[7]

In what follows, I will share with you some of what I have learned from many years of studying and thinking about Anglo-American conservatism. I offer a picture of what political conservatism is and what it is for. My aim is to help the reader understand what a conservative revival, so badly needed right now, would entail. In other words, my aim is to give conservatives a clear sense of what their responsibilities are.

At the same time, I am hopeful that this book will be useful for anti-Marxist liberals. It is liberalism, after all, that has failed so spectacularly in recent years. I suspect that more than a few liberals will be interested in knowing why.

This book is divided into four parts:

Part One: History, written with the historian Ofir Haivry, offers an introduction to Anglo-American conservatism as a historical phenomenon. Chapter 1, "The English Conservative Tradition," traces the emergence of conservative political theory in the works of great conservative statesmen and thinkers such as John Fortescue, Richard Hooker, John Selden, Matthew Hale, and Edmund Burke. This chapter presents early English conservatism as arising out of a struggle to defend political traditionalism and empiricism in the face of three competing theories: (i) the royal absolutism of the Stuarts, (ii) Puritan revolution, and (iii) rationalist liberalism.

Chapter 2, "American Nationalists," describes the revival of the Anglo-American conservative tradition in the United States in the 1780s. This chapter describes the Federalist Party of George Washington, John Jay, John Adams, Gouverneur Morris, and Alexander Hamilton as the force that actually established America as a cohesive and independent nation. This party was the forerunner of today's nationalist conservatives, developing a political program based on the existence of a distinct American nation of British heritage, the continuity of the traditional British constitution and common law in America, a strong national government, economic nationalism, a nationalist immigration policy, alliance with Britain, and an alliance between religion and state. The American Federalist Party was also a political home for opponents of slavery. Bitterly opposed to Jeffersonian liberalism, America's early nationalist conservatives paved the way for Henry Clay's Whigs and the Republican Party of Abraham Lincoln.

Part Two: Philosophy provides the theoretical foundations for understanding the historical British and American conservatism described in Part One. In Chapter 3, "The Conservative Paradigm," I describe the premises that underpin conservative philosophy, showing why loyalty, hierarchy, honor, cohesion, and constraint are crucial for a realistic understanding of human nature and human societies, and how these things permit ideas, behaviors, and institutions to propagate across generations. I also examine how the liberal political framework systematically blinds its adherents to these crucial aspects of political reality.

In Chapter 4, "God, Scripture, Family, and Congregation," I discuss a number of institutions of the Anglo-American conservative tradition. I argue that Anglo-American conservatism cannot be upheld without recognizing their centrality, and recommend revising our assessment of their nature and significance in light of the conservative paradigm presented in the preceding chapter.

In Chapter 5, I discuss "The Purposes of Government" as these are understood in the Anglo-American conservative tradition. This is a tradition that sees the *national interest* or the *common good* as irreducible to a single principle such as individual liberty. Instead, a balance among various principles—I suggest nine such principles—is needed to understand what government is for and what it should do.

Part Three: Current Affairs turns to the condition of Anglo-American conservatism in our generation and to the tasks that lie ahead. Conservatives face a triple challenge today: They must fight an aggressive new Marxist movement at home and deter an imperialist China abroad, while at the same time freeing themselves from the shackles of liberal dogma. In Chapter 6, "Liberal Hegemony and the Cold War Conservatism," I discuss the causes of America's transition from Christian democracy to liberal democracy in the decades following the Second World War, and I examine the relationship between liberals and conservatives within William F. Buckley Jr.'s coalition of Cold War conservatives. Focusing on the thought of Russell Kirk, Friedrich Hayek, Leo Strauss, and Frank Meyer, I argue that although this Cold War coalition was successful in its struggle against Communism abroad and socialism at home, it also did much damage to the conservative element in American politics. By "fusing" together a public liberalism with a private conservatism, Cold War conservatives set a course that, within a generation, had removed almost everything that wasn't strictly derived from liberalism from the political agenda of the American right, and had cemented this "conservatism" into place as a bulwark helping to prop up the hegemony of liberalism throughout the democratic world.

In Chapter 7, "The Challenge of Marxism," I examine how the liberal hegemony in America destroyed itself and paved the way for an updated Marxism—a process that reached a dramatic climax in 2020 with the triumph of a racialist "woke" ideology in big business, the media, the universities, and government bureaucracy. A return to a society that is capable of constraint and conservation would mean the abandonment of the 1960s-era theory of liberal democracy, and the adoption of a political standpoint that should be called *conservative democracy.* I describe this form of government in Chapter 8, "Conservative Democracy."

In **Part Four: Personal**, which consists of Chapter 9, I provide "Some Notes on Living a Conservative Life." This chapter includes autobiographical material and a discussion of the conservative revival at Princeton University when I was a student there during the 1980s. I have decided to include this material because it sheds light on two subjects not much discussed today:

First, I think it is worth revisiting the connection between Ronald Reagan and Margaret Thatcher and the nationalist and religious conservatism of those years. Today Reagan and Thatcher are often described as if their principal concern were economic liberalism. But many of us, including the circle that founded the university's conservative student publication, *The Princeton Tory*, were animated primarily by the traditionalist, nationalist, and religious aspects of the Reagan-Thatcher movement. In this chapter, I describe how I understood this connection then, emphasizing the crucial role played for us by writers such as George Will (then an eloquent defender of precisely those nationalist conservative views that he now opposes), Irving Kristol, and Dennis Prager.

Second, and more important, I think it may be helpful to use my own experiences—including my marriage to Julie and the birth of our first daughter while we were still students—as a basis for discussing the relationship between conservative political ideas and a conservative life. A large part of the damage that has been done to political conservatism since the 1960s has been due to the acceptance, by conservatives, of the liberal myth that politics can address itself to the public sphere alone, while avoiding having a significant influence on our private lives. As a result, many young people now mistakenly believe that it will do no great harm if they continue to lead a dissolute, liberal life in private while expressing conservative opinions in their public activism (where it "really matters"). This is a destructive view and a false one.

In university, my friends and I didn't just become a local chapter for disseminating general ideas of a conservative character. We wanted to become conservative people, leading a conservative life. In fact, many of us did just that. I've told a part of that story here. Perhaps knowing something about my experiences in those days can be useful to those—both young and old—who are considering taking up a conservative life at this time.

In this book, I have made the case for Anglo-American conservatism as I understand it. And I have contrasted this kind of conservatism with what I see as its principal rivals in the democratic world today: Enlightenment liberalism and a renewed Marxism. I know that some readers will feel that I should have made room to discuss additional intellectual trends that have bearing on my subject. For example, there are many writers who believe that conservatism should be based on something like the Catholic natural law teaching, itself a form of philosophical rationalism. Because of the interest in this philosophical tradition among my friends and colleagues, it would perhaps have been helpful to include a chapter stating why I am not an adherent of the rationalist natural law teaching of Thomas Aquinas. But I have not done so, not for lack of interest but because the book is already long enough, and an adequate treatment of this question would have taken me too far afield. I hope to address this important question on another occasion.

Similarly, the liberalism I discuss in this book is the Enlightenment liberalism that became the dominant political paradigm in America and Europe after the Second World War and continues to strongly influence political affairs to this day. I know that in academia, especially, there are those who have criticized the Enlightenment rationalism upon which liberalism was originally founded, and who do not see it as a suitable basis for their own liberal views. In fact, many scholars consider liberalism as having moved beyond Enlightenment rationalism by the mid-1990s. For this reason, some of my liberal colleagues may feel that my criticism of Enlightenment liberalism in this book amounts to "beating a dead horse."

Here I must disagree—for the simple reason that this horse is still very much alive. Despite the severe blows it has sustained in recent years, a large and vocal contingent of politicians, academics, and journalists continues to defend 1960s-style Enlightenment liberalism in the public sphere. Enlightenment liberalism remains a powerful paradigm, and throughout the democratic world, many still regard it as the only viable alternative to neo-Marxism and authoritarianism. This suggests that liberal political theory has not yet broken with Enlightenment rationalism to the extent that many academics suppose. But this, too, is, a subject that I will have to leave for another time.

Part One

History

Chapter I

The English Conservative Tradition

1. *What Is Conservatism?*

A *conservative* is a traditionalist, a person who works to recover, restore, and build up the traditions of his forefathers and to pass them on to future generations. *Political conservatism* is a political standpoint that regards the recovery, restoration, elaboration, and repair of national and religious traditions as the key to maintaining a nation and strengthening it through time. This means that political conservatism is not, like liberalism or Marxism, a universal theory, which claims to prescribe the true politics for every nation, at every time and place in history. There can be a political conservatism in Germany or Russia, in China or Arabia, and the conservatives of these nations may be very different in their views from those that we find in the English-speaking countries. And this is as it should be. For while there are certainly principles of human nature that are true of all men, and therefore natural laws that prescribe what is good for every human society, nevertheless, these principles and laws are the subject of unending controversy. This is because the great variety of human experience, and the weakness of the operations of the human mind that are used to generalize from this experience, are such as to produce endless variation in the ways we describe man's nature and the laws that are conducive to his good. In these matters, each nation and tribe tends to believe that it knows what is best, in keeping with its own experience and its own unique way of understanding things. And so the conservatives of each nation and tribe will have views of their own, which will be similar to the views of conservatives from another nation or tribe only in a limited degree.

My concern in Chapters 1–2 of this book is not, therefore, to say anything about the generality of mankind, or to attempt to construct some kind of universal conservative theory. Rather, I would like to understand the emergence and principles of a single conservative worldview, that of the *Anglo-American conservative tradition.* This tradition is important to the English-speaking peoples because it is the key to understanding what made these nations powerful and successful, both in political affairs and in almost every other matter. And it is important to other nations that have been influenced by the British and the Americans in various ways.

The emergence of a distinctive Anglo-American conservative tradition can be identified with the words and deeds of a series of towering political and intellectual figures, among whom we can include Sir John Fortescue, Richard Hooker, Sir Edward Coke, John Selden, Edward Hyde (Earl of Clarendon), Sir Matthew Hale, Sir William Temple, Jonathan Swift, William Murray (Lord Mansfield), Sir William Blackstone, Josiah Tucker, and Edmund Burke in Britain; and George Washington, John Jay, John Adams, Gouverneur Morris, and Alexander Hamilton in America. Living in different periods, these individuals nevertheless shared common ideas and principles and saw themselves as part of a common tradition of English, and later Anglo-American, constitutionalism. Scots such as David Hume, Adam Smith, and Adam Ferguson and French-speakers such as

Montesquieu and Vattel obviously contributed much to this tradition as well.[1]

A political-traditionalist outlook of this kind was regarded as commonplace in both England and America up until the French Revolution, and only came to be referred to as "conservative" during the nineteenth century, as it lost ground first to liberalism and then to Marxism. Because the word *conservative* dates from this time of decline, it is often wrongly asserted that those who defended the Anglo-American tradition in the period after the French Revolution—men such as Burke, Adams, and Hamilton—were the "first conservatives."[2] But one has to view history in a peculiar and distorted way to see these men as having founded the tradition they were defending. In fact, neither the principles they upheld nor the arguments with which they defended them were new. They inherited their ideas from earlier thinkers and political figures such as Fortescue, Hooker, Coke, Selden, Hale, and Blackstone. These men, the intellectual and political forefathers of Burke, Adams, and Hamilton, are *conservatives* in the same way that John Locke is a *liberal*. In their day, the term was not yet in use, but the ideas it designates are easily recognizable in their writings, their speeches, and their deeds.

Where does the tradition of Anglo-American conservatism begin? Any date one chooses will be somewhat arbitrary. Even the earliest surviving English legal compilations, dating from the twelfth century, are recognizable as forerunners of this conservative tradition. But I will begin on what seems indisputable ground—with the writings of Sir John Fortescue, which date from the late fifteenth century. Fortescue occupies a position in the Anglo-American conservative tradition somewhat analogous to Locke's in the later liberal tradition: Although not the founder of this tradition, he is nonetheless its first truly outstanding expositor, and the model in light of which the entire subsequent tradition developed.

2. *John Fortescue and the Birth of Anglo-American Conservatism*

The civil war now known as the Wars of the Roses consumed England's leadership and wealth for more than thirty years, until it was finally brought to an end by the rise of Henry VII and the House of Tudor in 1485. Sir John Fortescue had served for almost two decades as chief justice of the King's Bench, the English Supreme Court, when he was deposed, together with the royal family, in 1461. Thereafter, he went into exile with the court of the young prince Edward of Lancaster, the "Red Rose" claimant to the English throne, who had escaped to France to avoid capture by the "White Rose" King Edward IV of York. Fortescue appears to have been named chancellor, or prime minister, of this government in exile.

While in France, Fortescue composed several treatises on the constitution and laws of England, whose purpose was to explain why the English form of government, now threatened with extinction, was worthy of preservation by a new generation whose memory of its splendor was fast receding. Foremost among these works was a small book entitled *In Praise of the Laws of England.* Although it is often mischaracterized as a work on law, anyone picking this book up will immediately recognize it as an early great work of English political philosophy. Far from being a sterile rehearsal of existing law, it is written in dialogue form—between the chancellor of England and the young prince he is educating so that he may wisely rule his realm—and offers a theorist's explanation of the reasons for regarding the English constitution as the best model of political government known to man. (Those who have been taught that it was Montesquieu who first argued that, of all constitutions, the English constitution is the one best suited for human freedom may be surprised to find that this argument is given clear and compelling expression by Fortescue nearly three hundred years earlier, in a work with which Montesquieu was probably familiar.)

Fortescue wrote in the decades before the Reformation and was a firm Catholic. But every page of his work breathes the spirit of English nationalism—the belief that through long centuries of experience, and thanks to a powerful ongoing identification with Hebrew Scripture, the English had succeeded in creating a form of government more conducive to human freedom and flourishing than any other known to man. According to Fortescue, the English constitution provides for what he calls "political and royal government," by which he means that English kings do not rule by their own authority alone (that is, "royal government"), but together with the representatives of the nation in Parliament and in the courts (that is, "political government"). In other words, the powers of the English king are limited by the traditional laws of the English nation in the same way—as Fortescue emphasizes—that the powers of the Jewish king in the Mosaic constitution in Deuteronomy are limited by the traditional laws of the Israelite nation.[3] This is in contrast with the Holy Roman Empire and with France, which were governed by Roman law, and therefore by the maxim that "what pleases the prince has the force of law," thus allowing absolute government.[4] Among other things, the English law is described as providing for the people's representatives, rather than the king, to determine the laws of the realm and to approve requests from the king for taxes.[5]

In addition to this discussion of what later tradition would call the separation of powers and the system of checks and balances, Fortescue also devotes extended discussion to the guarantee of due process under law, which he explores in his discussion of the superior protections afforded to the individual under the English system of trial by jury, with its rejection of torture in judicial proceedings.[6] Crucially, Fortescue consistently connects the character of a nation's laws and their protection of private property to economic prosperity, arguing that limited government bolsters such prosperity, while an absolute government leads the people to destitution and ruin. In another of his writings, *The Difference Between an Absolute and a Limited Monarchy* (also known as *The Governance of England*, ca. 1471), he starkly contrasted the well-fed and healthy English population living under their limited government with the French, whose government was constantly confiscating their property and quartering armies in their towns—at the residents' expense—by unilateral order of the king. The result of such arbitrary taxation and quartering is, as Fortescue writes, that the French people have been "so impoverished and destroyed that they may hardly live.... Truly, they live in the most extreme poverty and misery, and yet they dwell in one of the most fertile parts of the world."[7]

Like later conservatives, Fortescue does not believe that either Scripture or human reason can provide a system of laws suitable for all nations. We do find him drawing frequently on the Mosaic constitution and the biblical "Four Books of Kings" (I–II Samuel and I–II Kings) to assist in understanding the political order and the English constitution. Nevertheless, Fortescue emphasizes that the laws of each realm reflect the historic experience and character of each nation, just as the English common law is in accord with England's historic experience. Thus, for example, Fortescue argued that a nation that is self-disciplined and accustomed to obeying the laws voluntarily rather than by coercion is one that can productively take part in determining the way it is governed. This, Fortescue proposed, was true of the people of England, while the French, who were of undisciplined character, could be governed only by the harsh and arbitrary rule of absolute royal government. On the other hand, Fortescue also insisted, again in keeping with biblical precedent and later conservative tradition, that this kind of national character was not set in stone, and that such traits could be gradually improved or worsened over time.[8]

Fortescue was eventually permitted to return to England, but his loyalty to the defeated House of Lancaster meant that he never returned to power. He was to be chancellor of England only in his philosophical dialogue in *In Praise of the Laws of England.* His book, however, went on to become one of the most influential works of political thought in history. With the accession of Henry Tudor VII to the throne, it became a kind of Tudor manifesto circulating in a small number of copies. First printed in the reign of Henry VIII, Fortescue's *In Praise of the Laws of England* spoke in a resounding voice to that period of heightened nationalist sentiment, in which English traditions, now inextricably identified with Protestantism, were pitted against the threat of invasion by Spanish-Catholic forces aligned with the Holy Roman Emperor.[9] In this environment, Fortescue was quickly recognized as England's most important political theorist, paving the way for him to be read by centuries of law students in both England and America and by educated persons wherever the broader Anglo-American conservative tradition struck root.

3. *Richard Hooker and Protestant Conservatism*

In the 1530s, King Henry VIII led his people in what became the first modern movement for national independence. Regarding themselves as restoring England's ancient freedom, Henry and his advisers cut the ties that bound the English government to the pan-European bureaucracy of the pope and the German emperor, established the king as the head of the Church of England, translated the Bible into English, and dissolved the monasteries that were seen as hotbeds of papist sentiment.[10] Henry's campaign for English independence was followed by aggressive Protestant reforms under the brief rule of his son Edward VI; and then by a desperate attempt to lead the country back into Europe's Catholic political and religious order by Henry's daughter Mary, whose husband, Philip II of Spain, regarded himself as divinely appointed to return England to obedience.

The stability, strength, and cohesion of Britain as an independent, Protestant nation was secured during the forty-five-year reign of Henry's daughter Elizabeth, who ascended to the throne in 1558. It was Elizabeth who eventually defeated Philip's armada and attained a religious "settlement" that established the Anglican church, while tolerating Catholics and Protestant dissenters as long as they remained discreet in their practices. Yet Elizabeth's remarkable achievements were threatened by Protestant radicals, who chafed at her willingness to offer Catholics a degree of accommodation and at her nationalist religious policies which stubbornly refused to conform the Church of England to internationally accepted standards for what reformation should look like.

It was under these conditions that Richard Hooker, a minister to the English legal profession as master of the Temple Church until 1591, took it upon himself to present a theoretical framework for the independent national state that had emerged in England under the Tudors, while at the same time seeking to limit the autocratic tendencies that accompanied their struggles to secure the nation against foreign invasion and internal dissolution. The result was one of the most remarkable works of modern political theory, his eight-volume *Of the Laws of Ecclesiastical Polity*. Among its achievements was its theory of political conservatism, which defended a vision of national particularism within the context of the effort to secure general political, religious, and moral norms.

In disputing the radical proposals of his Puritan opponents, Hooker argued that almost any order is better than no order at all, and that the burden of proof was on those who proposed to abandon existing custom. Moreover, it is not enough to show that a proposed reform would be better in the abstract, because real human beings respond poorly to sudden social and legal changes. As Hooker wrote: "When the people see things suddenly discarded, annulled, and rejected that long custom had made into matters of second nature, they are bewildered, and begin to doubt whether anything is in itself naturally good or evil, rather than being simply whatever men choose to call it at any given moment.... Thus, whenever we change any law, in the eyes of the people it cannot help but impair and weaken the force that makes all laws effectual."[11] He therefore concludes, "If the newer laws are only slightly more beneficial, we should generally conclude that to endure a minor sore is better than to attempt a dangerous remedy."[12]

But of course, the political order Hooker sought to defend—an independent nation and an independent church—was itself the product of the dramatic changes undertaken during Henry's reign. Thus, while arguing forcefully against undertaking revolutionary change in the name of abstract theories, Hooker refused to treat the existing order as sacrosanct: Laws are "instruments to rule by, and... instruments must always be designed not merely according to their general purpose, but also according to the particular context and matter upon which they are made to work. The end for which a law is made may be permanent, but the law may still need changing if the means it prescribes no longer serve that end."[13] This conservative view of political order diverged sharply from that of Hooker's Puritan opponents, who sought to bring down the current regime and to replace it with a perfected political order that they believed could be directly derived by reasoning from Scripture.[14]

The crux of Hooker's debate with the Puritans was thus a disagreement about epistemology: Protestant radicals believed that by their understanding of nature and revelation, they had attained certain knowledge of God's will, which applies in all times and places. Hooker, on the other hand, remained deeply skeptical as to what human beings can know with certainty. He excoriated those who believed that they had put their finger on the "cause of all the world's ills"[15] and had "a comprehensive solution to all these problems."[16] In the end, the statesman must proceed with humility, attempting to gain guidance from the sources available to him and proceeding in "whichever way greatest probability leads."[17]

These considerations brought Hooker to a defense of established laws and customs, which he regarded as an expression of accumulated experience gained over many lifetimes. Of course, ancient beliefs and customs may be mistaken. But they are far less likely to steer us wrong than judgments that have become fashionable only recently. As Hooker puts it, we may not "lightly esteem what has been allowed as fit in the judgment of antiquity, and by the long continued practice of the whole Church; from which unnecessarily to swerve, experience has never as yet found it safe."[18]

It is this suspicion of claims to universally valid knowledge that leads Hooker to nationalism. Where we are unable to obtain certainty by examining nature and revelation, the best way to proceed is by experiment, with each nation maintaining its own customs and practices until a repair is obviously required. Such a procedure will not please the revolutionaries, who insist that all questions have certain and universally valid answers. But it will uphold laws and a way of life that is suited to the history and character of a particular people. Indeed, in their agitation for the English to embrace the ways of the other reformed churches in Geneva or the Netherlands, the Puritans were committed to as rigid an internationalism as the Catholics,[19] whereas the Church of England, as a national church, could accept that different practices are appropriate for different countries. As Hooker put it:

> [The Puritans] have not yet proved that just because foreign churches have done well, it is our duty to follow them,

> or that we must forsake our own course (otherwise well suited to us) just because it differs from that of other churches.... These churches surely cannot think that they have discovered absolutely the best ceremonies that the wit of man could ever devise; rather, if they recognize that they are naturally partial to their own ceremonies simply because they are their own, it is only fair for them to recognize that we too will be partial to our own. Thus we are released from the burden of being forced either to condemn them or imitate them.... This we can do without in any way criticizing our reformed brethren abroad; on the contrary, we approve their practices as well as our own.[20]

This argument follows Fortescue in recognizing that the laws and customs suitable to one nation may not be appropriate for another. But Hooker goes a step further, rejecting the Puritan claim that we can bring peace among nations by adopting a universal political theory. On the contrary, the Puritan pursuit of a single international church meant that "each church, if it found it differed in any way from its neighbors, could hardly help but accuse them of disobeying the will of Christ."[21] It was just this kind of intolerance of diverse customs that had set Europe "aflame with conflict in all its leading nations at once."[22] Indeed, it was precisely the moderation and self-restraint of the English church that had brought peace to the land:

> [God] used His providential hand to restrain the eager affections of some, and settle their resolutions on a more calm and moderate course, so that it might not happen in England as it has in many other wide and flourishing dominions—that is, that one part of the people should become enraged, and

> act as only desperate men do, seeking only the utter oppression and extinction of their adversaries.[23]

Hooker's impact on the conservative tradition has been vast. He provided the theoretical underpinnings for the moderate, skeptical, and tolerant nationalism that has become one pillar of Anglo-American conservatism, and he exerted great influence, as well, on the theory of a balance of powers among the king, Parliament, and Church as discussed in Book VIII of his *Laws*. A generation later, Hooker's students in Parliament would ally themselves with John Selden in his clashes with King James I over the character of the English constitution.

4. The Greatest Conservative: John Selden

I turn now to the decisive chapter in the formation of the modern Anglo-American conservative tradition: the great seventeenth-century battle to defend the traditional English constitution against three different ideological opponents: (i) the political absolutism of the Stuart monarchs, (ii) the growing strength of the Puritan revolutionaries, and (iii) the first advocates of what we know as Enlightenment rationalism. This part of the story is dominated by John Selden, perhaps the most important figure in Anglo-American conservatism.[24]

In 1603, Queen Elizabeth died childless and was succeeded by her distant relation, the king of Scotland, James Stuart. The Stuart kings had little patience for English theories of a balanced constitution as described by Fortescue and Hooker. In fact, James, himself a thinker of some ability, had four years earlier penned a political treatise of his own in which he had explained that kings rule by divine right and that the laws of the realm are, as the title of his book suggested, a *Basilikon Doron* (Greek for "Royal Gift").[25] In other words, the laws are the king's freely given gift, which he can choose to make or revoke as he pleases. James was too prudent a man to openly press his absolutist theories on his English subjects, and he insisted that he meant to respect their traditional constitution. But the English, who had bought thousands of copies of the king's book when he ascended to their throne, were never fully convinced. Indeed, the policies of James and, later, his son Charles I constantly rekindled suspicions that the Stuarts' strategy was a creeping authoritarianism that would eventually leave England as bereft of freedom as France.

When eventually this question came to a head, most members of the English Parliament and common lawyers proved willing to risk their careers, their freedom, and even their lives in the defense of Fortescue's "political and royal rule." Among these were eminent names such as Sir John Eliot and the chief justice of the King's Bench, Sir Edward Coke. But in the generation that bore the full brunt of the new absolutist ideas, John Selden stood above all others. The most influential common lawyer of his generation, he was also a formidable political philosopher and polymath who knew more than twenty languages. Selden became a prominent leader in Parliament, where he joined the older Coke in a series of clashes with the king, in which Parliament denied the king's right to imprison Englishmen without showing cause, to impose taxes and forced loans without the approval of Parliament, to quarter soldiers in private homes, and to wield martial law in order to circumvent the laws of the land.

In 1628, Selden played a leading role in drafting and passing an act of Parliament called the Petition of Right, which sought to restore and safeguard "the divers rights and liberties of the subjects" that had been known under the traditional English constitution. Among other things, it asserted that "your subjects have inherited this freedom, that they should not be compelled to contribute to any tax . . . not set by common consent in Parliament"; that "no freeman may be taken or imprisoned or be disseized of his freehold or liberties, or his free customs... but by the lawful judgment of his peers, or by the law of the land"; and that no man "should be put out of his land or tenements, nor taken, nor imprisoned, nor disinherited nor put to death without being brought to answer by due process of law."[26]

In the Petition of Right, then, we find the famous principle of "no taxation without representation," as well as versions of the rights that would eventually be enumerated in the Third, Fourth, Fifth, Sixth and Seventh Amendments of the American Bill of Rights—all declared to be ancient constitutional English freedoms and unanimously approved by Parliament. Although not mentioned in the Petition explicitly, freedom of speech had likewise been reaffirmed by Coke as "an ancient custom of Parliament" in the 1590s and was the subject of the so-called Protestation of 1621 that landed Coke, then seventy years old, in the Tower of London for nine months.

In other words, Coke, Eliot, and Selden risked everything to defend the same liberties that we ourselves hold dear from the encroachment of an increasingly authoritarian regime. But they did not do so in the name of liberal doctrines of universal reason, natural rights, and "self-evident" truths. They explicitly rejected these doctrines because they were conservatives, not liberals. Let us try to understand this.

Selden saw himself as an heir to Fortescue, and in fact was involved in republishing *In Praise of the Laws of England* in 1616.[27] His own much more extensive theoretical defense of English national traditions appeared in the form of short historical treatises on English law and in a series of massive works (begun while Selden was imprisoned on ill-defined sedition charges for his activities in the Parliament of 1628–1629) examining political theory and law in conversation with classical rabbinic Judaism, of which the most famous was his monumental *Natural and National Law* (1640). In these works, Selden sought to defend conservative traditions, including the English one, not only against the absolutist doctrines of the Stuarts, but also against the claims of a universalist rationalism, according to which men could simply consult their own reason to determine the best constitution for mankind. This rationalist view had begun to collect adherents in England among followers of the great Dutch political theorist Hugo Grotius, whose *On the Law of War and Peace* (1625) suggested that it might be possible to do away with the traditional constitutions of nations by basing the political order solely on the rationality of the individual.[28]

Then as now, conservatives could not understand how such a reliance on alleged universal reason could be remotely workable, and Selden's *Natural and National Law* includes an extended attack on such theories in its first pages. There, Selden argues that everywhere in history, "unrestricted use of pure and simple reason" has led to conclusions that are "intrinsically inconsistent and dissimilar among men." If we were to create government on the basis of pure reason alone, this would not only lead to the eventual dissolution of government, but to widespread confusion, dissention, and perpetual instability.[29] Indeed, following Fortescue, Selden rejects the idea that a universally applicable system of rights is even possible. As he writes in an earlier work, what "may be most convenient or just in one state may be as unjust and inconvenient in another, and yet both excellently as well framed as governed."[30] With regard to those who believe that their reasoning has produced the universal truths that should be evident to all men, he shrewdly warns:

> [Custom] quite often wears the mask of nature, and we are taken in, to the point that the practices adopted by nations,

> based solely on custom, frequently come to seem like natural and universal laws of mankind.[31]

Selden responds to the claims of universal reason by arguing for a position that can be called *historical empiricism*. On this view, our reasoning in political and legal matters should be based upon inherited national tradition. This permits the statesman or jurist to overcome the small stock of observation and experience that individuals are able to accumulate during their own lifetimes ("that kind of ignorant infancy, which our short lives alone allow us") and to take advantage of "the many ages of former experience and observation" which permit us to "accumulate years to us, as if we had lived even from the beginning of time." In other words, by consulting the accumulated experience of the past, we overcome the inherent weakness of individual judgment, bringing to bear the many lifetimes of observation by our forebears, who wrestled with similar questions under diverse conditions.[32]

Yet Selden is unwilling to accept the prescription of the past blindly. He pours scorn on those who embrace errors originating in the distant past, which, he says, have often been accepted as true by entire communities and "adopted without protest, and loaded onto the shoulders of posterity like so much baggage."[33] Recalling the biblical Jeremiah's insistence on an empirical study of the paths of old, Selden argues that the correct method is that "all roads must be carefully examined. We must ask about the ancient paths, and only what is truly the best may be chosen."[34] But for Selden, the instrument for such examination and selection is not the wild guesswork of individuals speculating about various hypothetical possibilities. In the life of a nation, the inherited tradition of legal opinions and legislation preserves a multiplicity of perspectives from different times and circumstances, as well as a record of the consequences for the nation when the law has been interpreted one way or another. Looking back upon these varied and changing positions within the tradition and considering their real-life results, one can distinguish the true precepts of the law from the false turns that have been taken in the past. As Selden explains:

> The way to find out the Truth is by others' mistakings: For if I [wish] to go to such [and such] a place, and one had gone before me on the right-hand, and he was out, [while] another had gone on the left-hand, and he was out, this would direct me to keep the middle way that peradventure would bring me to the place I desired to go.[35]

Selden thus turns to a form of pragmatism to explain what is meant when statesmen and jurists speak of *truth*. The laws develop through a process of trial and error over generations, as we come to understand how peace and prosperity ("what is truly best," "the place I desired to go") arise from adopting one course rather than another.

Selden recognized that in making these selections from the traditions of the past, we tacitly rely upon a higher criterion for selection, a natural law established by God, which prescribes "what is truly best" for mankind in the most elementary terms. In his *Natural and National Law*, he explains that this natural law has been discovered over long generations since biblical times and has come down to us in various versions. Of these, the most reliable is that of the Talmud, which describes the seven laws of the children of Noah prohibiting murder, theft, sexual perversity, cruelty to beasts, idolatry, and defaming God, and requiring courts of law to enforce justice. The experience of thousands of years has taught us that these laws frame the peace and prosperity that is the aim of all nations, and that they are the unseen root from which the diverse laws of all the nations ultimately derive.[36]

Nonetheless, Selden emphasized that no nation can govern itself by directly appealing to such fundamental law, because "diverse nations, as diverse men, have their diverse collections and inferences, and so make their diverse laws to grow to what they are, out of one and the same root."[37] Each nation's effort to implement the natural law is in accordance with its own unique experience and conditions. It is therefore wise to respect the different laws found among nations, both those that appear right to us and those that appear mistaken, for different perspectives may each have something to contribute to our pursuit of the truth. (Selden's treatment of the plurality of human knowledge is cited by Milton as a basis for his defense of freedom of speech in *Areopagitica*.)[38]

Selden thus offers us a picture of a philosophical Parliamentarian or jurist, whose task is constantly to maintain the strength and stability of the inherited national edifice as a whole—but who nonetheless recognizes that he must make repairs and improvements where needed so as to gradually approach, by trial and error, the best arrangement for each nation.

Selden's account of English conservatism was perhaps the most sophisticated ever advanced. But neither his intellectual powers nor his personal bravery, nor that of his colleagues in Parliament, were enough to save the day. By 1642, the Stuarts' absolutism had led to civil war in England and rebellion in Scotland, and finally, in 1649, to a Puritan military dictatorship that not only executed the king but destroyed Parliament and the constitution as well. Selden did not live to see the constitution restored. The regicide regime subsequently offered England several brand-new constitutions, none of which proved workable, and within eleven years it had collapsed.

In 1660, two eminent disciples of Selden, Edward Hyde (afterward Earl of Clarendon) and Sir Matthew Hale, led the restoration of the traditional constitution and the line of Stuart kings.[39]

Clarendon became the first chancellor under the restored Stuart monarchy, while Hale became chief baron of the exchequer and then chief justice of the King's Bench. Hale, whose *History and Analysis of the Common Law of England* (published posthumously in 1713) is the first history of the common law ever written, also wrote a book of *Reflections on Hobbes' Dialogue of the Law*, in which he defended the conservative restoration of the traditional laws of England. As he wrote:

> There are many things specially in laws and governments that mediately, remotely, and consequentially, are reasonable to be approved, although reason does not presently or immediately and distinctly see its reasonableness.... It is a reason for me to prefer a law by which a kingdom has been happily governed for four or five hundred years than to adventure the happiness and peace of a kingdom upon some new theory of my own, though I am better acquainted with the reasonableness of my own theory than with that law.... Long experience makes more discoveries touching conveniences or inconveniences of laws than is possible for the wisest council of men at first to foresee. And that those amendments and supplements that through the various experiences of wise and knowing men have been applied to any law must needs be better suited to the convenience of laws, than the best invention of the most pregnant wits not aided by such a series and tract of experience.... This adds to the difficulty of a present fathoming of the reason of laws, because they are the production of long and iterated experience.... It is not necessary that the reasons of the institution should be evident to us. It is sufficient that they are instituted laws that give a certainty to

> us, and it is reasonable to observe them though the particular reason of the institution appear not.[40]

When the Catholic James II succeeded to the throne in 1685, fear of a relapse into papism and even of a renewed attempt to establish the king's absolute rule moved the rival political factions in Parliament to unite in inviting the next Protestants in the line of succession to take the throne. The king's daughter Mary and her husband Prince William of Orange, the stadtholder of the Dutch Republic, crossed the channel with the support of Parliament to ensure the stability of Protestant England and its constitution. Parliament, having confirmed the willingness of the new joint monarchs to protect the English from "all other attempts upon their religion, rights and liberties," in 1689 established the new king and queen on the throne. The new monarchs, together with Parliament, at the same time ratified England's famous Bill of Rights. This document reasserted the ancient rights invoked in the earlier Petition of Right, among other things affirming the right of Protestant subjects to "have arms for their defense" and the right of "freedom of speech and debates" in Parliament, and that "excessive bail ought not to be required, nor excessive fines imposed, nor cruel and unusual punishments inflicted"—provisions that would later serve as the basis for the First, Second, and Eighth Amendments of the American Bill of Rights. Freedom of speech was quickly extended to the wider public, with the termination of English press licensing laws a few years later.

The restoration of a Protestant monarch and the adoption of the Bill of Rights were undertaken by a Parliament united in its support for the conservative constitutionalism of Selden, Clarendon, and Hale. What came to be called the Glorious Revolution was glorious precisely because it reaffirmed the traditional English constitution and protected the English nation from renewed attacks on "their religion, rights and liberties." With the Puritan dictatorship firmly repudiated, these attacks now came primarily from two directions: from absolutists such as Sir Robert Filmer, whose *Patriarcha* (published posthumously in 1680) advocated authoritarian monarchical government as the only legitimate one, and from radicals such as John Locke, whose rationalist manifesto, *Two Treatises of Government* (1689), responded to the crisis by arguing for the right of the English people to dissolve the traditional constitution and establish a new one in accordance with universal reason.

5. Edmund Burke and the Challenge of Liberalism

During the seventeenth century, English conservatism had become a distinct and coherent political philosophy, standing in opposition to the monarchist absolutism of Stuarts, Hobbes, and Filmer, to Puritan revolution, and to the liberal theories of universal rights advanced by Grotius and then Locke.[41] This conservative view was to remain the mainstream in English political theory and jurisprudence for a century and a half, during which time it was defended by leading intellectuals in works from William Atwood's *Fundamental Constitution of the English Government* (1690) to Josiah Tucker's *A Treatise of Civil Government* (1781). It was the view in which men such as Lord Mansfield, Blackstone, Burke, Washington, and Hamilton were educated—not only in England but in British America, where lawyers were trained in the common law by studying Coke's *Institutes of the Laws of England* (1628–1644) and Hale's *History and Analysis of the Common Law* (1713), and where the law of the land was understood to be the traditional English constitution and common law, amended as needed for local purposes.[42]

Because Locke is today recognized as the decisive figure in the liberal tradition, it is worth looking more carefully at why his political theory was so troubling for conservatives of his day. I have described the Anglo-American conservative tradition as subscribing to a historical empiricism, which proposes that political knowledge is gained by examining the long history of the customary laws of a given nation and the consequences when these laws have been altered in one direction or another. Conservatives understand that a jurist must exercise reason and judgment, of course. But this reasoning is about how best to adapt traditional law to present circumstances, making such changes as are needed for the betterment of the nation, while preserving as much as possible the overall frame of the law. To this I have opposed a standpoint that can be called *rationalist.* Rationalists have a different view of the role of reason in political thought, and in fact a different understanding of what reason itself is. Rather than arguing from the historical experience of nations, rationalists set out by asserting general axioms that they believe to be true of all human beings and that they suppose will be accepted by all human beings examining them with their native rational abilities. From these, they deduce the appropriate constitution or laws for all men.

Locke is often described as an empiricist. But his reputation in this regard is based on his *Treatise Concerning Human Understanding* (1689), which is an influential exercise in empirical psychology.[43] His *Second Treatise on Government* is not, however, a similar effort to formulate a theory of the state from an empirical standpoint. Instead, it begins with a series of axioms that are without any evident connection to what can be known from the historical and empirical study of the state. Among other things, Locke asserts that (i) prior to the establishment of government, men exist in a "state of nature" in which "all men are naturally... in a state of perfect freedom," as well as in a "state of perfect equality, where naturally there is no superiority or jurisdiction of one over another."[44] Moreover, (ii) this state of nature "has a law of nature to govern it, which obliges everyone," and that law is nothing other than "reason," which "teaches all mankind, who will but consult it."[45] It is this universally accessible reason that leads human beings to (iii) terminate the state of nature, "agreeing together mutually to enter into . . . one body politic" by an act of free consent.[46]

From these axioms, Locke then proceeds to deduce the proper character of the political order for all nations on earth.

Three important things should be noticed about this set of axioms. The first is that the elements of Locke's political theory are not known from experience. The "perfect freedom" and "perfect equality" that define the state of nature are ideal forms whose relationship with empirical reality is entirely unclear. Nor can the identity of natural law with reason, or the assertion that the law dictated by reason "teaches all mankind," or the claim that reason is the source of moral and political obligation, or the establishment of the state by means of purely consensual social contract, be known empirically. All of these things are stipulated at the outset, as if a mathematical system is being set out.

The second thing to notice is that there is no reason to think any of Locke's axioms are, in fact, true. Faced with this mass of unverifiable assertions, empiricist political theorists such as Montesquieu, David Hume, Adam Smith, Adam Ferguson, and Edmund Burke rejected Locke's axioms and sought to rebuild political philosophy on the basis of things that can be known from history and from an examination of actual human societies and governments.[47]

Third, Locke's theory not only dispenses with the historical and empirical basis for the state, it also implies that such inquiries are, if not entirely unnecessary, then of secondary importance. For if there exists a form of reason that is accessible to "all mankind, who will but consult it," and that reveals to all the universal laws of nature governing the political realm, then there will be little need for the historically and empirically grounded reasoning of men such as Fortescue, Hooker, Coke, Selden, and Hale. All men, if they will just gather together and consult with their own reason, can design a government that will be better than anything that "the many ages of experience and observation" produced in England. On this view, the Anglo-American conservative tradition—far from having brought into being the freest and best constitution ever known to mankind—is in fact shot through with unwarranted prejudice, and an obstacle to a better life for all. Locke's theory thus pronounces, in other words, the end of Anglo-American conservatism and the end of the traditional constitution that conservatives still held to be among the most precious things on earth.[48]

While Locke's rationalist theories made limited headway in England, they were all the rage in France.[49] Rousseau's *On the Social Contract* (1762) went where others had feared to tread, embracing Locke's system of axioms for correct political thought and calling upon mankind to consent only to the one legitimate constitution dictated by reason.[50] Within thirty years, Rousseau and the other French imitators of Locke's rationalist politics received what they had demanded in the form of the French Revolution, with its universal Declaration of the Rights of Man and subsequent terror for those who would not listen to reason. Terror was soon followed by Napoleon's imperialist liberalism, which brought universal reason and the "rights of man" to the whole continent of Europe by force of arms—at a cost of millions of lives and untold destruction.[51]

In 1790, a year after the beginning of the French Revolution, the Anglo-Irish thinker and Whig parliamentarian Edmund Burke composed his famous defense of the English constitutional tradition against the liberal doctrines of universal reason and universal rights, entitled *Reflections on the Revolution in France* (1790). In a well-known passage of his book, Burke asserted:

> Selden and the other profoundly learned men who drew this Petition of Right were as well acquainted, at least, with all the general theories concerning the "rights of men." . . . But, for reasons worthy of that practical wisdom which superseded their theoretic science, they preferred this positive, recorded, hereditary title to all which can be dear to the man and the citizen, to that vague speculative right which exposed their sure inheritance to be scrambled for and torn to pieces by every wild, litigious spirit.[52]

In this passage, Burke correctly emphasizes that Selden and the other great conservative figures of his day had been quite familiar with the "general theories concerning the rights of men" that had now been used to overthrow the state in France. He then goes on to endorse Selden's argument that universal rights, since they are based only on reason rather than "positive, recorded, hereditary, title," can be said to give everyone a claim to absolutely anything. Adopting a political theory based on such universal rights has one obvious meaning: that the "sure inheritance" of one's nation will immediately be "scrambled for and torn to pieces" by "every wild, litigious spirit" who knows how to use universal rights to make ever-new demands.

Like his predecessors in the English conservative tradition, Burke places the *nation* at the center of his understanding of politics, regarding it as a community projected both backward and forward in time. He views the nation's constitution and laws not as the product of a Lockean moment of consent, but of what is "ten thousand times better" than such consent—namely, the habits of a people as disclosed over centuries. As he put it in a speech before Parliament in 1782,

> A nation is not only an idea of local extent, and individual momentary aggregation, but it is an idea of continuity,

> which extends in time as well as in numbers and in space. And this is a choice not of one day, or of one set of people, not a tumultuary and giddy choice. It is a deliberate election of ages and of generations. It is a constitution made by what is ten thousand times better than choice: It is made by the peculiar circumstances, occasions, tempers, dispositions, and moral, civil and social habitudes of the people, which disclose themselves only in a long space of time.[53]

Burke's concern to understand the circumstances and dispositions of a people over a period of centuries makes him a historical empiricist, and in *Reflections on the Revolution in France* he explicitly declares that construction of a national state is an "experimental science," a body of knowledge that cannot be attained "*a priori*"—that is, by the methods of the rationalists:

> The science of constructing a commonwealth, or renovating it, or reforming it, is, like every other experimental science, not to be taught *a priori.* Nor is it a short experience that can instruct us in that practical science, because the real effects of moral causes are not always immediate; but that which in the first instance is prejudicial may be excellent in the remoter operation.... The science of government being therefore... a matter which requires experience, and even more experience than any one person can gain in his whole life, however sagacious and observing he may be, it is with infinite caution that any man ought to venture upon pulling down an edifice which has answered in any tolerable degree for ages the common purposes of society, or of building it up again without having models and patterns of approved utility before his eyes.[54]

It is often said that Burke's counsel of "infinite caution" amounts to a warning that political change should always be brought about slowly. But this is a mistaken reading of his argument. As we see from this passage, Burke opposes the destruction of institutions that have served "for ages the common purposes of society," because such institutions are "models and patterns of approved utility." Where an institution has already fallen into ruin, Burke has no interest in repairing it only in a gradual manner. Rather, he argues that it should be reconstructed in accordance with models and patterns that have proved themselves. Where possible, this means restoring a national institution to its earlier functionality, as when Parliament intervened to restore the Protestant monarchy during the Glorious Revolution. Where there is no such model or pattern available from the historical experience of the nation in question, Burke advocates seeking "models and patterns of approved utility" in the traditions of other nations, as when the dysfunctional Polish constitution was reformed to more closely resemble the British model.[55] In neither case does Burke praise the repair because it came about slowly.

Burke's objection to the introduction of very general (or abstract) principles into government is that, since they have not been formulated in such a way as to address only the particular grievances at hand, or to make specific improvements, it is impossible to know what one is really doing by adopting them. Men in positions of authority must therefore be alert "to prevent a surprise on their opinions," which results from accepting too general a principle out of a need to make a necessary repair. As he writes:

> Before they listen to even moderate alterations in the government of their country, they ought to take care that principles are not propagated for that purpose, which are too big for their object. Doctrines limited in their present

> application, and wide in their general principles, are never meant to be confined to what they at first pretend.[56]

Here, then, is the manner in which Burke believes that the conservative statesman must go about introducing alterations to the government of his country. It is not the swiftness of the repair that is at issue, but whether principles are adopted "which are too big for their object." The more general and abstract the principle proposed, the more certain one may be that its consequences will not be confined to what has been discussed and foreseen.

This is a powerful argument, directed against the entire project of the universal rights of man that was at the heart of the French Revolution. Burke recognized that its rationalist proponents were "proceeding on speculative grounds," enflaming the passions of the public not with the aim of making moderate alterations to relieve particular hardships and injustices, but in order to promulgate a series of abstract principles whose sweeping consequences no one had yet imagined.[57]

Burke's argument is frequently quoted today by conservatives who assume that his target was Rousseau and his followers in France. But Burke's attack was not primarily aimed at Rousseau, who had few admirers in Britain or America at the time. The actual targets of his attack were contemporary English-speaking liberals, followers of Grotius and Locke—such as Richard Price, Joseph Priestley, Charles James Fox, Charles Grey, Thomas Paine, and Thomas Jefferson. Price, for example, was named as Burke's target in the first pages of *Reflections on the Revolution in France*, and had opened his *Observations on the Nature of Civil Liberty* (1776) with the assertion, "The principles on which I have argued form the foundation of every state as far as it is free, and are the same with those taught by Mr. Locke."[58] And much the same could be said of the others, all of whom followed

Locke in claiming that the only true foundation for political and constitutional thought was precisely in those "general theories concerning the rights of men" that Burke believed would bring turmoil and death to one country after another.

The carnage taking place in France triggered a furious debate in England, pitting supporters of Selden's conservatism (both Whigs and Tories) against admirers of Locke's universal rights theories (the so-called "New Whigs," led in Parliament by Charles James Fox). In this controversy, conservatives insisted that universal rights theories would uproot every traditional political and religious institution in England, just as they were doing in France. It is against the backdrop of this debate that Burke stated in Parliament that of all the books ever written, Locke's *Second Treatise* was "one of the worst."[59]

Burke's conservative defense of the traditional English constitution enjoyed a large measure of success, and it was continued after his death by figures such as George Canning, Arthur Wellesley (Duke of Wellington), and Benjamin Disraeli. This is evident from the fact that institutions such as the monarchy, the House of Lords, and the established Church of England, not to mention the common law itself, were able to withstand the gale winds of universal reason and universal rights, and to this day have their staunch supporters.

6. Principles of Anglo-American Conservatism

As we have seen, the period between John Selden and Edmund Burke gave rise to two distinct and conflicting political traditions in England, conservative and liberal. In the next chapter, I will consider the nature and achievements of political conservatism in America, where it was taken up by the Federalist Party of Washington, Jay, Adams, Hamilton, and Morris. But before turning to the remarkable story of America's nationalist conservatives, it is worth taking stock of what we've learned so far about the Anglo-American conservative tradition from studying its emergence in England.

We can summarize the principles of Anglo-American conservatism, as they appeared in the writings and deeds of the architects of this tradition, as follows:

Principle 1. *Historical Empiricism.* The authority of government derives from constitutional traditions known, through the long historical experience of a given nation, to offer stability, well-being, and freedom. These traditions are refined through trial and error over centuries, with repairs and improvements being introduced where necessary, to maintain the integrity of the inherited national edifice as a whole. Such historical empiricism entails a degree of skepticism regarding the divine right of the rulers, the universal rights of man, and all other abstract, universal systems. Written documents express and consolidate the constitutional tradition of the nation, but they neither capture nor define this political tradition in its entirety.

Principle 2. *Nationalism.* Human beings form national collectives characterized by bonds of mutual loyalty and unique inherited traditions. Nations will have different constitutional and religious traditions due to the diversity of national experience. The Anglo-American tradition is rooted in the ideal of a free and just national state, whose origin is in the Hebrew Bible. This ideal includes a conception of the nation as arising out of diverse tribes, its unity anchored in a common traditional language, law, and religion.[60]

Principle 3. *Religion.* The state upholds and honors God and the Bible, the congregation and the family, and the religious practices common to the nation. These are essential to the national heritage and indispensable for justice and public morals. At the same time, the state offers toleration to religious and social views that do not endanger the integrity and well-being of the nation as a whole.

Principle 4. *Limited Executive Power.* The executive powers of government are vested in a strong, unitary chief executive (that is, the king or president) by the traditional laws of the nation, which the chief executive neither determines nor adjudicates. The powers of the chief executive are limited by the representatives of the people, whose advice and consent he must obtain respecting the laws, taxation, and other crucial matters. The representatives of the people may remove a chief executive where his behavior manifestly endangers the integrity and well-being of the nation as a whole.

Principle 5. *Individual Freedoms.* The security of the individual's life and property is mandated by God as the basis for a peaceful and prosperous society, and it is to be protected against arbitrary actions of the state. The ability of the nation to conduct sound policy depends on freedom of speech and debate. These and other fundamental rights and liberties are guaranteed by law, and may be infringed upon only by due process of law.

These principles can serve as a summary of the Anglo-American conservative tradition that informed the restoration of the English constitution in 1688, as well as the restoration enacted by the American Constitution of 1787. These same principles have continued to underpin subsequent conservative political tradition in Britain, America, and other nations down to our own time.

Consider now how these conservative principles diverge from those of liberalism. The crucial differences between the two traditions can be understood in the following way:

Enlightenment liberalism is a political doctrine based on the assumption that reason is everywhere the same, and accessible, in principle, to all individuals; and that one need only consult reason to arrive at the one form of government that is everywhere the best, for all mankind. It borrows certain principles from the earlier Anglo-American conservative tradition, including those limiting executive power and guaranteeing individual freedoms (Principles 4 and 5 above). But liberalism regards these principles as stand-alone entities, detachable from the broader conservative tradition out of which they arose. Liberals thus tend to have few, if any, qualms about discarding the national and religious foundations of traditional Anglo-American government (Principles 2 and 3) as unnecessary, if not simply contrary to universal reason.

In their effort to identify a form of government mandated by universal reason, liberals have thus confused certain historical-empirical principles of Anglo-American conservatism, painstakingly developed and inculcated over centuries (Principle 1), for universal truths that are accessible to all human beings, regardless of historical or cultural circumstances.[61]

As John Selden put it, they have been "taken in, to the point that the practices adopted by nations, based solely on custom ... come to seem like natural and universal laws of mankind."[62]

CHAPTER II

American Nationalists

The American English, as Burke called them, declared their independence in 1776 and established a unified nation with the ratification of the Constitution of 1787. During the 1780s, two distinct political camps emerged among the Americans.

First, there were those who admired the English constitutional tradition they had inherited, under which Americans had lived and flourished for more than 150 years. Believing that King George III had deprived them of their rights under the English constitution, their aim was to regain them. In the tradition of Coke and Selden, they hoped to achieve a victory against royal absolutism comparable to what the English had achieved in the Glorious Revolution a century earlier. To those of this persuasion, the word *revolution* still retained its older meaning, describing something that "revolves" and finally returns to its rightful place—in effect, a restoration. Alexander Hamilton was among the exponents of this kind of conservative politics, telling the assembled delegates to the Constitutional Convention, "I believe the British government forms the best model the world ever produced."[1]

Second, there were the radicals, liberal followers of Locke such as Jefferson, who despised England and believed—just as the French followers of Rousseau believed—that the dictates of universal reason made the true rights of man evident to all. For them, the traditional English constitution was not the source of their freedoms, but rather something to be swept away by rights dictated by universal reason. And indeed, when the French Revolution came, Jefferson and his supporters embraced it as a direct continuation of what the Americans had started. As he wrote in a notorious letter in 1793: "The liberty of the whole earth was depending on the issue of the contest [in France].... Rather than it should have failed, I would have seen half the earth desolated."[2]

The tension between these conservative and liberal camps finds expression in America's founding documents: The Declaration of Independence, drafted by Jefferson in 1776, is famous for promoting the Lockean doctrine of universal rights as "self-evident" before the light of reason;[3] whereas the Constitution of 1787, drafted at a convention dominated by the conservative party, ended a decade of shocking disorder by restoring the familiar forms of the national English constitution. In accepting it, the Americans gave a strong president, serving as the chief executive, roughly the powers of the British monarch, and balanced these powers in the English fashion by means of a bicameral legislature with the power of taxation and legislation. Even the American Bill of Rights of 1789 is modeled upon the Petition of Right and the English Bill of Rights, largely elaborating the rights of Englishmen that had been described by Coke and Selden and their followers. Notably, these later documents breathe not a word about universal reason or universal rights.[4]

The conservative aspect of the Constitution of 1787 has been emphasized many times. But it was also a nationalist document, uniting what had been thirteen independent states—each of them, like a

Greek polis, pursuing policies of its own—under a single American national state. Indeed, members of the Federalist Party of George Washington, John Adams, John Jay, Alexander Hamilton, Robert Morris, Gouverneur Morris, James Wilson, Oliver Ellsworth, Rufus King, John Marshall, and Noah Webster were not only conservatives, but American nationalists. They regarded Americans as one nation, and they saw the establishment of the forms of the British constitution and the English common law over and above the thirteen states as the best possible instrument for ensuring that Americans would remain a single nation. Similarly, in the 1780s, the Federalists' Jeffersonian opponents were not only Enlightenment liberals who rejected the traditional English constitution. They were also anti-nationalists, who were not especially inclined to regard Americans as one nation and who were appalled by the prospect that something resembling the British government in London—which they regarded as inherently tyrannical—might be resurrected on American soil and given enough power to suppress the newly won freedom of the thirteen independent states.

As we saw in the last chapter, English conservatism was inextricably linked to nationalism, having emerged in the sixteenth century in opposition to Catholic efforts to place England under the authority of Rome; and to the Puritan inclination to subordinate English practices to the authority of Geneva. Similarly, the American conservative tradition was born in the 1780s out of a conflict between American nationalists and their opponents. The Federalist Party was from the start the party of American nationalist conservatism.

In this chapter, I will tell the story of the Federalist Party, the nationalist conservatives who initiated and secured the ratification of the Constitution of 1787 and then went on to govern a unified American nation during its first twelve years. I will then examine the principles that made the Federalists one of the most important and successful nationalist conservative movements in history—and a relevant model for nationalist conservatives in America and other countries today.

1. The Federalists, America's Nationalist Conservatives

The thirteen British colonies declared independence from Britain in 1776. But for most of the 1780s, the newly formed United States were prevented from addressing the many political challenges they faced due to the weakness of the first American constitution, the "Articles of Confederation and Perpetual Union." Adopted by the Continental Congress in November of 1777, this constitution regarded the United States as an alliance of thirteen independent republics, under which "each state retains its sovereignty, freedom and independence." Having no unified executive or judiciary, the only national institution was the Congress, which required the consent of nine out of the thirteen state delegations to take any action at all. Although nominally responsible for overseeing the war effort against Britain, Congress lacked the ability to conscript soldiers for the Continental forces fighting the British under George Washington, or even to raise the taxes needed to arm and pay them. Indeed, when the moment came to land the decisive blow at Yorktown in 1781, Congress was broke, and Robert Morris, the newly hired superintendent of finance, had to write personal checks to cover the costs of moving the army into battle.[5]

The nationalist party in American politics was born out of these experiences, with much of its leadership consisting of soldiers, businessmen, and lawyers who had witnessed firsthand the inability of the American national government to act in a decisive fashion in matters of war, diplomacy, and finance. Even before the Treaty of Paris formally ended the war, both Washington and Morris, as well their young protégé Alexander Hamilton, then a member of Congress, had gone on record calling for a revision of the first American constitution, which they blamed for having needlessly prolonged the war and almost lost it. They were joined by John Jay, the celebrated architect of the peace with Britain, who had discovered that in the absence of a national government with appropriate coercive powers, the terms of the treaty could not be enforced on the American states. These nationalists urged a unification of the American nation under a government with the authority to conduct national finances and diplomatic and military affairs. But they found themselves opposed by a large anti-nationalist or confederationist camp, which regarded proposals to establish a national government possessing significant coercive powers, a standing national army, national taxes, and a national bank as a betrayal of the ideals of the revolution and a return to the "monarchical" government of Great Britain.

Although the divide between nationalists and confederationists seemed, at first, to be a disagreement over practical proposals for how best to govern postrevolutionary America, it quickly became clear that the argument was far deeper than that. In fact, the sides in this argument were inspired by competing visions of American identity and citizenship, which drove the formation of two clearly opposed political parties. The first of these, which came to be called the Federalist Party, wished to see America become a unified nation and an industrial, commercial, and military power—in effect a republican version of Britain. Nationalist and conservative, the Federalists admired British constitutional structures, including the British political tradition of a strong executive and judiciary alongside the elected legislature; the common law heritage that had governed Americans in the 150 years preceding independence, upholding property and liberty as inherited rights; and the Protestantism that was still the established religion in most states. They were, in other words,

Anglo-American traditionalists, who regarded national identity as rooted in the particular traditions of a people and expected newcomers to adopt these traditions as a prerequisite to becoming citizens. For the most part, they looked forward to the decline of slavery and its eventual abolition.

Against this nationalist vision of America, there emerged a confederalist vision that was eventually called "democratic republicanism"—and finally gave its name to the Democratic Republican Party. This view, whose greatest spokesmen were Thomas Jefferson and Tom Paine, regarded the American Revolution as having been fought not only against British monarchy and aristocracy, but more generally against Britain's centralized government, established religion, and financial system. On this view, political society was founded on the virtue and natural rights of the consenting individual, who owed little or nothing to national and religious tradition. Such a society needed little government besides local government, an arrangement as close as possible to the small republics of the ancient world, with no armed forces beyond the local militia except in times of emergency. For Democratic Republicans, the ideal citizen was the independent farmer, to a great degree self-sufficient, even if this sometimes involved owning slaves to work his fields; whereas large-scale commerce, manufacturing, and public debt were regarded as threats to the independence and virtues of the individual. In a country as large as America, the only way to maintain such a regime was by creating a loose confederative arrangement of individuals, cooperating within a larger confederation of states.

The first American constitution, the Articles of Confederation, had been cast in precisely this democratic-republican mold, and for nearly a decade the political viewpoint that had created it remained ascendant. But by 1786, with the states embarking on an increasingly bitter tariff war against one another, Hamilton seized the opportunity at a failed conference on interstate trade, to announce a national convention to discuss revising the Articles of the Confederation. This initiative bore no relation to the decision-making processes described in the constitution of the confederation. But the need for it was dramatically demonstrated in the fall and winter of 1786, when the states found themselves unable to raise an army to meet "Shays' Rebellion," an organized insurrection in western Massachusetts that had to be put down by privately funded troops. Against the backdrop of these events, Jay and Hamilton sought and won Washington's agreement to serve as chairman of their proposed constitutional convention. In this effort, they were joined by other nationalists such as Robert Morris, Gouverneur Morris, and James Wilson, as well as by James Madison, until recently a protégé of Jefferson, who had swung into the nationalist camp after his mentor left to serve as ambassador to France. The Constitutional Convention met from May 25 until September 17, 1787.

Some accounts downplay the fact that the Constitutional Convention was orchestrated by what would soon become the Federalist Party. Of the initiators and the most consequential participants, most were longtime nationalists and later Federalists—the principal exceptions being Madison and his fellow Virginian Edmund Randolph. Only four years into civilian life, Washington was intent on avoiding the suggestion of a military intervention in political affairs. But it appears that Washington agreed to participate as the highly visible chairman of the convention only on condition that its agenda would be the establishment of a nationalist government.[6] These prior guarantees to Washington largely assured the outcome of the convention, but it also helped that thirty-five of the fifty-five participants of the convention were former officers who had served under Washington in the Continental Army.[7] Thus while the nationalists were forced to compromise on some points, the convention did indeed open by passing a resolution outlining a new national government along lines agreeable to Washington. Thereafter, the text of America's second constitution was drafted by a committee controlled by nationalists John Rutledge, Oliver Ellsworth, and James Wilson. And the final draft was written by a leading nationalist, Gouverneur Morris.

It was at the Constitutional Convention, as well, that the term "Federalist" came into use to refer to the nationalist party and its program. Up until this point, Americans had used the terms *federal* and *confederal* interchangeably to describe the cooperation of the thirteen independent states under the Articles of Confederation and Perpetual Union.[8] However, as the Constitutional Convention opened in 1787, nationalists discovered that the word "national" was troubling to some of the participants, precisely because it implied a single, unified nation rather than a coalition of independent states.[9] The nationalists decided to concede the term, while preserving the substantive achievement of a national government. On June 20, the prominent Connecticut nationalist Oliver Ellsworth moved to simply strike the word "national" from the proposed constitution. Thereafter, all of the descriptions of the American government as "national" were removed and replaced by the terms "United States," "general," and "federal." In this way, the term *federal* became a synonym for *national* (and the opposite of "confederal"). It was soon widely popularized after Hamilton initiated a defense of the new national constitution in a series of newspaper essays in which he was joined by Jay and Madison, which were known collectively as *The Federalist: A Collection of Essays in Favor of the New Constitution*. From this point on, the term "Federalist" denoted a political view and then a party devoted to a nationalist government. American nationalists were called "federalists."[10]

The nationalists' success at the convention and in the subsequent ratifying conventions of the states amounted to what has rightly been called the Second American Revolution.[11] A series of unconstitutional but democratic and peaceful political maneuvers led to the retirement of the decentralized and anti-nationalist American constitution of 1777 and to its replacement by the new nationalist Constitution of 1787, modeled on the British constitution.[12] The first administration under this nationalist Constitution was inaugurated when Washington took office as president on April 30, 1789. In addition to nationalists such as himself, John Adams (vice president), Hamilton (secretary of the treasury), Henry Knox (secretary of war), and Jay (chief justice of the Supreme Court), Washington sought to give his administration the appearance of a unity government by appointing the leading Democratic Republican, Jefferson, as secretary of state and the moderate Randolph as attorney general.

But Washington also made sure that both foreign policy and judicial matters remained firmly under nationalist control, and a frustrated Jefferson began orchestrating public pressure against the administration in which he was serving by means of a proxy war in the press. In 1791, Jefferson and Madison founded a newspaper to counter Federalist policies. Jefferson resigned from office two years later, and in 1795 launched a campaign against a treaty of friendship and commerce with Britain initiated by Hamilton and concluded by Jay, still serving as chief justice. The famous "Jay Treaty" in effect ended America's alignment with France, blocking the Jeffersonians' desired alliance with the revolutionaries who had overthrown and executed the French king. Jefferson, Madison, and others, including many former opponents of the nationalist Constitution, assembled what became the Democratic Republican Party, which supported states' rights over the power of the national government, state courts over national jurisdiction, the disestablishment of religion, the expansion of slavery, and a foreign policy favorable to France, while opposing the Federalist Party's nationalist economic and immigration policies.

Democratic Republican enthusiasm for the French Revolution increased support for the Federalist Party among some southern conservatives, despite the nationalists' generally northern and commercial orientation. But it wasn't enough. Too many Americans resented the Federalists' affinity for Britain and their opposition to essentially unregulated immigration. In 1800, Jefferson's Democratic Republicans took office, and the political fortunes of the Federalist Party swiftly declined. At this critical moment, the Federalist Party lost its three most prominent leaders in quick succession. During the latter part of the Adams presidency, a quarrel between the president and Hamilton degenerated into an ugly pamphlet war that destroyed the reputations of both men, as well as the chances of the party uniting behind one of them. Meanwhile, Washington, the man who might have imposed a truce or thrown his weight behind one of them, died suddenly in 1799. Adams retired from political life when his presidency ended in 1801, and Hamilton's death in a duel with the Democratic Republican Aaron Burr in 1804 deprived the Federalists of the remaining leader of sufficient stature to reenergize them. Lacking clear leadership and split between feuding factions, the Federalists quickly disintegrated as a political force outside of New England. Their political fortunes were dealt a death blow by their perceived disloyalty to the Democratic Republican government during its war with Britain beginning in 1812. Rufus King, the last Federalist senator, was also the last, informal Federalist Party candidate for president when he ran unsuccessfully in 1816.[13]

However, the political decline of the Federalist Party did not mean the end of the American nationalists' political ideals. Washington and Adams appointed only committed Federalists to the Supreme Court, which was dominated by justices such as Jay, Ellsworth, Rutledge, Wilson, William Cushing, Bushrod Washington, and John Marshall through the 1830s. Wielding the doctrine that the Supreme Court was responsible for interpreting the Constitution, and later the resulting power of "judicial review," these Federalist judges continued to protect the nationalist Constitution of 1787 until many of their ideas had been adopted, whether completely or partially, even by their Jeffersonian opponents.[14]

It is true that nationalism did not come easily to Americans. Hostility to British rule brought many to regard the "Spirit of '76" as being opposed to strong government in general, and to a distant national government in particular. But the Second American Revolution—and the "Spirit of '87"—was by no means conducted along these lines. The new nationalist Constitution was a restoration of the Anglo-American political inheritance that Washington and many of his officers and supporters had fought to preserve in the War of Independence. The Constitutional Convention of 1787 brought America's nationalists, the Federalist Party, into a position of decisive influence, permitting them to unite the American nation and establish nearly all of the institutions and traditions that came to characterize it. The Federalists' principles went on to serve as the model for subsequent American nationalism.

What principles defined the American Federalist Party? As in any political alliance, there were many differences of opinion and temperament among the Federalists. Moreover, the views of the leading Federalists clearly evolved over time. Nevertheless, we can point to eight broad political principles that may be said to have characterized the Federalists in their struggle against the anti-nationalists and the Democratic Republican Party. All of these principles derived from their belief in a unique American nation with a unique cultural inheritance derived from Britain, and the desire to unite the various parts of this American nation under a strong central government. These principles include regarding Americans as a distinct nation of British heritage, American constitutional continuity with the British constitution, the Supreme Court as the body responsible for interpreting the Constitution, economic nationalism, a nationalist immigration policy, alliance with Britain, an alliance between religion and state, and opposition to slavery.

Let us look more closely at each of these.

2. *A Distinct American Nation of British Heritage*

As America gained its independence, nationalist and anti-nationalist visions were advanced for what should replace British rule. The argument ultimately came down to whether there really was such a thing as an American nation, with the weak constitution of 1777 reflecting the frailty of the fellow feeling tying the states to one another. For example, the Virginian Patrick Henry, a great proponent of independence from Britain, was also a great opponent of American nationalism. Henry rejected the concept of an "American people," arguing that the Constitution of 1787 would amount to taxation without representation, much as British rule had. As he put it:

> Suppose every delegate from Virginia in the new [national] government opposed a law levying a new tax, but it passes. So you are taxed not by your own consent, but by the people who have no connection to you.[15]

The idea that there was "no connection" between the peoples of the various states obviously spoke to the feelings of a large public. Yet it was opposed by nationalists who felt that a genuine mutual loyalty already did exist among many Americans, and could be kindled in the hearts of many more.

In *The Federalist* 2, for example, John Jay supplied the nationalist framework for the entire series by describing the bond of mutual loyalty that he could see animating the American nation. As he wrote:

> I have as often taken notice that Providence has been pleased to give this one connected country to one united people—a people descended from the same ancestors, speaking the same language, professing the same religion, attached to the same principles of government, very similar in their manners and customs, and who, by their joint counsels, arms, and efforts, fighting side by side throughout a long and bloody war, have nobly established general liberty and independence.... It appears as if it was the design of Providence that an inheritance so proper and convenient for a band of brethren, united to each other by the strongest ties, should never be split into a number of unsocial, jealous, and alien sovereignties.[16]

This is as compelling a nationalist view as one finds anywhere, arguing that a shared ancestry, language, religion, laws, and customs, as well as a common history of war against shared enemies, has made the American nation "a band of brethren united to each other by the strongest ties." At the outset, then, *The Federalist* rejects the concept of a "creedal nation" bound by nothing other than reason and consent, of which Jefferson and Paine were the precursors. Instead, Jay describes a thick matrix of inherited language, values, and history, which those of foreign descent—such as Jay himself, descended from French Huguenot and Dutch immigrants—could nevertheless choose to adopt.[17]

A similar nationalist view is evident in Hamilton's writings as early as his *Continentalist* essays of 1781, and certainly in *The Federalist*, where Hamilton too refers to "the affinity of language and manners; the familiar habits of intercourse" that characterize Americans.[18] Hamilton's nationalism was likewise rooted in a culture one chooses to adopt, for he was himself a relative newcomer to America, having been born to a Scottish father and a half-French mother on the Caribbean island of Nevis, and having arrived in the country only in 1772. Thus the "affinity" and the "familiar habits" to which he was referring were, for him, not native and local, but acquired and Anglo-American ones.[19]

The same outlook informed George Washington's "Farewell Address" of 1796, in which he argued:

> The name of American, which belongs to you in your national capacity, must always exalt the just pride of patriotism more than any appellation derived from local discriminations. With slight shades of difference, you have the same religion, manners, habits, and political principles.[20]

3. *Continuity with the British Constitution*

The Federalists of the 1780s and 1790s were not radicals who considered America a clean slate on which they could try out new schemes devised by the philosophers of the "Age of Reason." They came to abhor Jefferson and others who favored such schemes, especially after 1789, when these were increasingly identified with the murderous policies of the French Revolution.[21] The Federalists understood that the freedom of Americans was a gift of the British constitutional tradition and the English common law, which had been incorporated into American colonial law, often formally so in the constitutions of the colonies. Indeed, it is telling that in the four years prior to independence, no fewer than twenty-one editions of Blackstone's *Commentaries on the Laws of England* had been published in America.[22] And when the thirteen newly independent states turned to writing their own constitutions after 1776, these were to a significant extent designed on the pattern of the English system of dispersed power, with a strong executive balanced by a bicameral legislature and an independent court system.

Today, it is difficult to imagine how bizarre this adherence to the English constitution seemed to the enthusiasts of Enlightenment at the time. French philosophers such as Anne Robert Turgot and the Abbé de Mably, as well as the English Lockean Richard Price (the "Dr. Price" who is the target of Edmund Burke's *Reflections on the Revolution in France*), argued that by the light of reason, the best and most effective government would be one in which all powers—legislative, executive, and judicial—were combined in a single popular assembly. This view was influential in radical circles in America, where it informed the Pennsylvania Constitution of 1776, which placed dictatorial powers in the hands of a single assembly, unchecked by an executive or an upper house. The mob violence and attacks on property that followed foreshadowed, in many respects, the revolutionary regime in France a few years later. Similar radical experiments were undertaken in Georgia and Vermont.[23] But the most glaring deviation from the English constitutional tradition had been the first American constitution itself, the Articles of Confederation, which likewise mandated a government consisting of a single assembly in which all powers were vested.

Against these revolutionary proposals, the Federalists sought to restore continuity with the English constitution and common law. It has often been pointed out that much of the Constitution of 1787 and the subsequent Bill of Rights is borrowed from English constitutional documents or conventions. This English inheritance includes a long list of constitutional procedures and legal concepts, including the unitary executive power resting with the king; the bicameral legislature; the taxation initiative vested in the lower house of the legislature; the executive veto and the pardoning power; the procedure of impeachment; due process of law; the jury trial; the right to free speech, to bear arms, and to be immune from unreasonable search and the quartering of soldiers; and so forth. At least sixteen of the twenty-one sections making up the first four articles of the Constitution, as well as much of the first eight amendments to the Constitution, implicitly refer to English sources.[24]

But it is rarely acknowledged that this conformity of the Constitution of 1787 to the English constitution was a matter of theoretical significance for the American nationalists. Earlier that year, John Adams, writing in London during Shays' Rebellion, published the first volume of his *Defence of the Constitutions of the United States of America*, which sought to vindicate the Anglo-American constitutional tradition in the face of attacks by rationalist philosophers. Adams's argument is two-pronged: He argues that even if English constitutional traditions were neither good nor evil in themselves, and "the people, by their birth, education, and habits, were familiarly attached to them," this would provide "motive particular enough for their preservation," which would be better than to "endanger the public tranquility... by renouncing them."[25] But Adams does not believe that English laws are neither good nor evil. Rather, he takes up a survey of constitutions throughout history in order to demonstrate that the greatest insights into the nature of free government have been implemented only in the English constitution, which is therefore closer to perfection than any other known to mankind. As he writes:

> The English constitution is, in theory, the most stupendous fabric of human invention, both for the adjustment of the balance, and the prevention of its vibrations; and the Americans ought to be applauded instead of censured for imitating it as far as they have. Not the formation of

> languages, nor the whole art of navigation and ship building, does the human understanding more honor than this system of government.[26]

Indeed, although Adams recommends reforms in the British House of Commons so that it may better carry out its democratic function, he nonetheless foresees the possibility that the Americans will, with time, "make transitions to a nearer resemblance of the British constitution."[27]

Adams's book arrived in the United States in mid-April of 1787. A few weeks later, Washington, Madison, and other members of the Virginia and Pennsylvania delegations agreed upon the so-called "Virginia Plan," which outlined a national government based on three branches of government and a bicameral legislature. At the convention itself, Oliver Ellsworth, John Dickinson, and others defended the British constitution. But the most prominent Federalist figure in this respect was Hamilton, who told the delegates explicitly that the closer the Constitution could be brought to the British one the better, explaining that "the British government was the best in the world, and that he doubted much whether anything short of it would do in America." Like Adams, Hamilton praised the English constitution for balancing a strong democratic element in a representative, elected lower house against an executive and upper house that served for life, and so were shielded from wild swings in public opinion. In this way, the British constitution "unites public strength with individual security."[28]

These views concerning the English constitution made both Adams and Hamilton early opponents of French revolutionary ideas. Adams was especially proud to have published his book before the outbreak of the French Revolution, and sometimes suggested it had influenced Burke's *Reflections on the Revolution in France*, which appeared in 1790. Adams's later *Discourses on Davila* (1790) was written in the same anti-revolutionary spirit. Meanwhile, Hamilton encouraged and even funded several anti-revolutionary publications in the 1790s, himself composing a series of Burkean *Letters of Pacificus* in 1793.[29] At the same time, the Federalist judges on the newly appointed national Supreme Court determined, in a series of rulings during the 1790s, that the entire body of English common law was the inherited law of the federal government at its creation.[30]

The chief opponent of the nationalist conservatives in these debates was Jefferson. Long venerated for his role in securing American independence, Jefferson is now a hero to a large section of conservatives who admire him for his opposition to a strong national government. It is therefore sometimes hard to understand the ferocity with which the nationalist conservatives loathed their opponent, whom they saw as representing everything they abhorred: rationalism as opposed to traditionalism, states' rights and the philosophy of the individual as opposed to the building up of the American nation, agrarianism as opposed to an urban and commercial future, and, of course, the twin evils of atheism and slavery.[31] Nor was Jefferson a friend to the Federalists' Constitution of 1787. As a devotee of Enlightenment rationalist philosophy, he held tradition to be unimportant at best, and considered constitutions to be merely transitory and technical devices, to be rewritten from scratch every twenty years. For him, the only real constitution was the universal rights of man, which could be known by reason and had no need for constraints inherited from the past.

The historian Gertrude Himmelfarb once said, only half-jokingly, that the absence of Jefferson from the American Constitutional Convention was the clearest sign of Providence intervening in American history.[32] There is much to be said for this view. Jefferson was in

Paris from 1784 to 1789, where he and Tom Paine were active in assisting the efforts of the French revolutionaries. But France's loss was America's gain. For the fact that the two most outspoken and radical figures among the American philosophical rationalists were abroad in the crucial period when the restorationist Constitution of 1787 was composed and ratified meant not only that they were not around to oppose it. Their absence also meant that moderate Virginians such as Madison and Randolph were released from Jefferson's orbit and able to render crucial assistance to the nationalist effort. Indeed, by 1786, Madison had become one of Washington and Hamilton's closest nationalist allies, and he remained allied with the Federalists until shortly after Jefferson returned to America.

In 1791, Jefferson's hostility to the Federalists was made public when a laudatory note from his pen was published (apparently without his permission) as a preface to the American edition of Tom Paine's *Rights of Man*, which had been written as a refutation of Burke's *Reflections on the Revolution in France*. In the preface, Jefferson, the sitting secretary of state, endorsed Paine and praised his support for the French Revolution, attributing to it the same ideals that had animated the American Revolution. The same preface went on to condemn the "political heresies" of the new American "monarchists"—a reference to Adams and Hamilton. In a follow-up letter to Washington, Jefferson laid out the battle lines for the coming struggle, explaining that the American press was now divided into two camps, with the camp of Hamilton and Adams ("since his apostasy to hereditary monarchy and nobility") taking the side of Burke, and the other side supporting Paine.[33]

With regard to Burke's *Reflections on the Revolution in France*, Jefferson wrote to an English correspondent that it demonstrated "the rottenness of his mind." He continues:

> We have some names of note here who have apostatized from the true faith.... Mr. Paine's answer to Burke will be a refreshing shower to their minds. It would bring England itself to reason and revolution if it was permitted to be read there.[34]

In this letter, Jefferson refers to his own Enlightenment liberalism as "the true faith" and his Federalist opponents as "apostates" from it. Moreover, he does not hesitate to hope that Paine's book will bring "reason and revolution" to Britain. In 1795, with Revolutionary France at war with Britain, and the Netherlands recently conquered by the French armies under General Pichegru, we find Jefferson writing to a member of Congress that he hopes soon to visit occupied London and to dine there with the general: "For I believe I should be tempted to ... go and hail the dawn of liberty and republicanism in that island."[35]

This division between Jeffersonian imperialist liberals, eager to spread "the true faith" by force of arms, and nationalist conservatives, who wish to have no part in their forever wars—remains very much with us to this day.

4. Executive Power Vested in One Man

Uniting the American nation and bringing it under an effective national government was the most prominent Federalist goal, which early American nationalists pursued by a variety of means. The best-known part of this program was the Federalists' support for a powerful chief executive modeled on the British one. It is difficult today to fully appreciate how offensive the unitary chief executive was to enthusiasts of Enlightenment rationalism, who insisted on a plural executive—in effect, government by a committee—as a crucial impediment to tyranny. This model of a plural executive appeared repeatedly in constitutions written under the sway of rationalist political theories: in the radical Constitution of Pennsylvania (1776), in which the executive consisted of twelve members appointed by the popular assembly; in the first constitution of the United States, the Articles of Confederation (1777), which made decisions by a vote of nine of the thirteen state delegations; and in plural executives such as the nine-man Committee of Public Safety (1793) that ruled during the French Revolution.

Conservative arguments against the plural executive were drawn from experience: Although it may seem "rational" to restrain the executive by multiplying its members, the actual experience of government shows that such committees are generally unable to make rapid, firm, and coherent decisions. And when a committee is able to wield executive power effectively, it is only because it is dominated by a single individual, albeit one whose responsibility for its actions is obscured from view by the multiplicity of its members. These arguments stood behind the "Virginia Plan," prepared under Washington's supervision and presented to the Constitutional Convention at the outset of its deliberations, which proposed to vest powers in the president that would be comparable to those of the British king.[36] This decision was explained by Hamilton in *Federalist* 70, which argues that a necessary characteristic of good government is energy:

> Energy in the executive is a leading character in the definition of good government. It is essential to the protection of the community against foreign attacks; it is not less essential to the steady administration of the laws; to the protection of property against those irregular and high-handed combinations which sometimes interrupt the ordinary course of justice; [and] to the security of

> liberty against the enterprises and assaults of ambition, of faction, and of anarchy.[37]

Notice that Hamilton goes well beyond the common supposition that a strong executive is needed only to fight wars and prosecute criminals. He doesn't believe that the "ordinary course of justice" will always be sufficient to ensure the safety of property, and regards the energetic executive as a force necessary to break up "irregular and high-handed combinations" by powerful interests that manipulate the laws to their advantage. He sees clearly that without an energetic executive, the country is constantly threatened by individuals and factions that seek to advance themselves at the expense of the integrity of the nation as a whole. This constant threat of anarchy goes hand in hand with a "feeble executive"—precisely what Americans had experienced under the Articles of Confederation.

But the requisite energy, Hamilton argues, is generally possible only where the executive power is "in a single hand." As he writes:

> Unity is conducive to energy.... Decision, activity, secrecy, and dispatch will generally characterize the proceedings of one man in a much more eminent degree than the proceedings of any greater number.... This unity may be destroyed in two ways: Either by vesting the power in two or more magistrates of equal dignity and authority, or by vesting it ostensibly in one man, subject in whole or in part to the control and cooperation of others....
>
> No favorable circumstances palliate or atone for the disadvantages of dissention in the executive department. They serve to embarrass and weaken the plan or measure to which they relate, from the first step to the final conclusion of it. They constantly counteract those qualities in the

> executive which are most necessary ingredients in its composition—vigor and expedition, and this without any counterbalancing good.[38]

This view of the unitary executive appears time and again in the arguments of the Federalist Party. James Wilson, for example, presented much the same arguments in the ratifying convention in Pennsylvania:

> The *executive authority is one.* We may discover from history, from reason, and from experience, the security which this furnishes. The executive power is better to be trusted when it has no screen. Sir, we have a responsibility in the person of our President; he cannot act improperly, and hide either his negligence or inattention; he cannot roll upon any other person the weight of his criminality; no appointment can take place without his nomination; and he is responsible for every nomination he makes. We secure vigor. We well know what numerous executives are. We know there is neither vigor, decision, nor responsibility, in them.[39]

These descriptions of a powerful executive—one characterized by vigor and expedition, decision, activity, secrecy, and dispatch—are, as we know, unappealing to many Americans today, who hear in them premonitions of authoritarianism. This is because the powers of the American president in the Constitution of 1787 were modeled on those of the British king, and Jefferson and his allies never tired of accusing the Federalist Party of being monarchists. ("Their sight must be perfectly dazzled by the glittering of crowns and coronets," Jefferson wrote to Madison concerning Washington's administration in

1794.)[40] But setting aside these slanders, we see that Washington's nationalist conservatives really did advance a very different theory of government from that to which Jefferson and his party subscribed. Consider these famous lines from Jefferson's inaugural address in 1801:

> What more is necessary to make us a happy and a prosperous people? Still one thing more, fellow-citizens—a wise and frugal government, which shall restrain men from injuring one another, shall leave them otherwise free to regulate their own pursuits of industry and improvement, and shall not take from the mouth of labor the bread it has earned. This is the sum of good government, and this is necessary to close the circle of our felicities.[41]

Here, Jefferson claims that "the sum of good government" is that it "restrains men from injuring one another" and otherwise leaves them alone. According to this view, there is no need for the Federalists' energetic executive, which acts with "vigor and expedition" to break up "irregular and high-handed combinations" or to counter the "enterprises and assaults of ambition, of faction, and of anarchy"—because no grave injustices are likely to arise from the free activities of private individuals, organizations, or corporations, and no threat of anarchy is foreseen from the actions of ambitious persons or factions. For Jeffersonians, the only genuine threat is from the energetic, unitary executive itself.

To be sure, the Jeffersonian suspicion of government, and the accompanying desire to limit the powers of the executive, has its roots in Anglo-American tradition, going all the way back to the Bible. Nevertheless, the Anglo-American political tradition had sought to balance a powerful executive by granting competing powers to the legislature and by recognizing certain rights of individuals under law. It had never supposed that a powerful and active executive is unnecessary for the well-being of the nation, nor had it sought to enfeeble executive power by placing it in the hands of a committee as the Americans had done under the Articles of Confederation. On this point, the Federalists saw things clearly: The preceding decade under a feeble executive—like the anarchic decades of the Wars of the Roses that preceded the rise of the Tudors in England—had revealed that a human society always stands at the edge of a precipice. And while a disciplined people may benefit from the lifting of certain constraints that have been imposed upon them, at the time of the next great threat they will invariably cry out for the energies of the executive to be unleashed in order to restore their safety, justice, and freedom. In providing their president with powers comparable to that of a British king, the Federalists made it possible for the United States to prepare for such threats and to meet them successfully, in this way proceeding as a strong, stable, and cohesive nation.

5. *The Supreme Court and the Constitution*

Less familiar, but no less significant, is the Federalists' protracted struggle to forge a national judiciary with the authority to interpret the Constitution of 1787. Such authority would enable it to impose the Constitution on the states and individual citizens, and to fend off anti-nationalist challenges to the powers of the national government, both in its executive and judicial branches. However, Article III of the Constitution did not explicitly grant such authority to the national judiciary, and attaining it required the Federalists to carry out a concerted campaign to establish a judicial branch of the national government more powerful than in any other country, including even Britain, from which this effort drew much of its inspiration.

Although much remains unknown about the origins and execution of this Federalist effort, its main outlines are clear. As mentioned above, three nationalist jurists—Ellsworth, Wilson, and Rutledge—dominated the five-man committee that wrote the first draft of the Constitution of 1787. As far as the official record is concerned, none of them raised the issue of the Supreme Court's authority to interpret the Constitution during the convention itself. But at their respective state ratifying conventions, both Ellsworth and Wilson, as well as Hamilton, Marshall, and others, went on record arguing explicitly for the vital importance of a national judiciary with the authority to interpret the Constitution—a united effort that may already have been agreed upon in Philadelphia. As Hamilton laid out the argument in *Federalist* 78, the lifetime tenure of judges was necessary so that the courts, freed from public pressure, would be able to execute their duty of defending the Constitution against the whims of the legislature:

> Limitations [on legislative power] can be preserved in practice no other way than through the medium of courts of justice, whose duty it must be to declare all acts contrary to the manifest tenor of the Constitution void.... The courts were designed... to keep [the legislature] within the limits assigned to their authority. The interpretation of the laws is the proper and peculiar province of the courts.

Hamilton thus argues that the courts, exercising "judicial discretion" and strengthened by the institution of lifetime appointments, will be able to act as "the faithful guardians of the Constitution" against legislative encroachments. He concludes by commenting: "The experience of Great Britain affords an illustrious comment on the excellence of this institution."[42]

During the first session of the national Congress in the fall of 1789, Ellsworth, now a senator from Connecticut, took the next step by drafting the Judiciary Act, which gave form to the federal judiciary and explicitly granted it appellate jurisdiction over decisions of state courts that touched on the interpretation of the national Constitution or on treaties and laws enacted by the national government. This meant that all state and local laws, having been upheld by state supreme courts, could be appealed to the national Supreme Court, which if it chose could reject them as being unconstitutional or incompatible with nationally enacted treaties or laws. This remarkable piece of nationalist legislation was passed that year in a package deal together with the Bill of Rights.[43]

Soon afterwards, Washington appointed a panel of Federalist judges to the first United States Supreme Court. During the Court's first decade of existence, Jay, Rutledge, and Ellsworth served consecutively as the first three chief justices. Together with Wilson and the prominent Massachusetts jurist William Cushing, they constituted a permanent nationalist majority on the court that was preserved as additional Federalists were appointed to fill vacancies.[44] The role of these first Supreme Court justices is today obscured by the subsequent long dominance of the court by another Washington ally and nationalist, John Marshall. Nevertheless, it was these early Federalist justices who laid the foundations that permitted Marshall to carry out the nationalist program. I have already mentioned the early Court's determination that the English common law was the law of the United States—a determination that Jefferson realized would subordinate the laws of the states to the national courts. As Jefferson put it in a letter to Randolph: "Of all the doctrines which have ever been broached by the federal government, the novel one, of the common law being in force and cognizable as an existing law in their courts, is to me the most formidable," as it would give the national government general jurisdiction over "all cases and persons."[45]

The Federalists' aim of establishing a united American nation under a single constitution was given dramatic expression when the Supreme Court heard *Chisholm v. Georgia* (1793), in which the state of Georgia was sued by a private individual seeking payment for goods supplied during the Revolution. The state of Georgia refused to appear, claiming that it was a sovereign state and that a sovereign, by definition, could not be summoned without its consent. In a 4–1 ruling, the Supreme Court determined that the property rights of a private citizen were protected by the national government even against the states. As Wilson put it:

> This is a case of uncommon magnitude. One of the parties to it is a State, certainly respectable, claiming to be sovereign. The question to be determined is whether this State, so respectable, and whose claim soars so high, is amenable to the jurisdiction of the Supreme Court of the United States? This question, important in itself, will depend on others, more important still, and may, perhaps, be ultimately resolved into one, no less radical than this: Do the people of the United States form a Nation?

Wilson's question was, in other words, whether there exists an overarching American nation on behalf of whom the Supreme Court is responsible to impose its law. His answer to this question was unequivocal:

> Whoever considers, in a combined and comprehensive view, the general texture of the Constitution, will be satisfied that the people of the United States intended to form

> themselves into a nation for national purposes. They instituted, for such purposes, a national government, complete in all its parts, with powers legislative, executive and judiciary; and, in all those powers, extending over the whole nation.[46]

The decision caused an immediate uproar, bringing about a congressional resolution to amend the Constitution under Article V. The Eleventh Amendment, which grants the states immunity from suits by individuals, was adopted by twelve state legislatures by 1795. President Washington declined to certify its ratification, and it was only recognized as a part of the Constitution by Adams three years later.

Although the Supreme Court's ruling in *Chisholm* was overturned by Congress and the states, the very fact that a constitutional amendment was needed to do so firmly established the authority of the national court to interpret the Constitution and to rule against the states. The nationalist ruling in the case of *Ware v. Hylton* (1796), which held that treaties made under the Constitution supersede state law, cemented this authority. And in *Calder v. Bull* (1798), Justice James Iredell, the most prominent Federalist in North Carolina, affirmed that laws of Congress and of the states could not be voided for violating abstract "principles of natural justice," but that they could be overturned and declared void by the Supreme Court if they violated an explicit textual provision of the Constitution. As he wrote:

> The principles of natural justice are regulated by no fixed standard; the ablest and the purest men have differed upon the subject.... If any act of Congress, or of the legislature of a state, violates those constitutional provisions, it is unquestionably void.... If, on the other hand, the legislature of the Union, or the legislature of any member of the

> Union, shall pass a law within the general scope of their constitutional power, the Court cannot pronounce it to be void merely because it is, in their judgment, contrary to the principles of natural justice.[47]

Thus by the time Adams appointed the Federalist John Marshall as the fourth chief justice in January 1801, he had in his hands the tools necessary to assert the national judiciary's role as the principal interpreter of the Constitution, including voiding acts of Congress and of the states regarded as unconstitutional. This authority was exercised in the famous decision of *Marbury vs. Madison* (1803), which overturned a portion of an act of Congress as unconstitutional. Echoing Hamilton, Marshall emphasized in his opinion that "it is emphatically the province and duty of the judicial department to say what the law is." Marshall's long tenure of thirty-five years gave nationalists effective leadership of the Court up until the 1830s.

Although the anti-nationalist theory of "nullification"—the putative ability of a state to nullify a federal law, which was proposed by Jefferson and Madison as early as 1798—never succeeded in gaining the support of the national Supreme Court, another contentious issue involving national authority did indicate the eventual abandonment of the Federalist constitutional tradition. In 1857, the Supreme Court decided in the *Dred Scott* case, by a majority of 7–2, that blacks had no standing to sue a state in a federal court because they "are not included, and were not intended to be included, under the word 'citizens' in the Constitution, and can therefore claim none of the rights and privileges which that instrument provides for and secures to citizens of the United States." In other words, the ruling declared that blacks might be citizens of particular states, such as New York or Connecticut, but not of the United States—thus effectively overthrowing the idea of a single American nation.

This ruling unified nationalist opinion against what was seen as a corruption of the Constitution, and became a major step on the path to the Civil War. Not incidentally, the two dissenters from the majority were nationalists: Benjamin Robbins Curtis, the only Supreme Court justice appointed by a Whig president; and John McLean, who, while originally appointed by Andrew Jackson, had moved gradually towards nationalist positions, and in 1860 even contended for the Republican Party nomination for president, which Abraham Lincoln won.[48]

6. Economic Nationalism

Although led by George Washington, a Virginian, the Federalists were from the outset a party dominated by businessmen, lawyers, and soldiers from northern cities such as New York (Jay, Hamilton, G. Morris), Philadelphia (R. Morris, Wilson), and Boston (Adams, Knox).[49] Whereas the Democratic Republicans followed Virginians Jefferson and Madison in envisioning America as a vast confederacy of plantations and farms, American nationalists recognized that the might of the new nation would be determined by its capabilities in manufacturing and commerce. The Federalists took inspiration from the most developed economy of that time, that of Great Britain, which had built its advantage over other nations through a nationalist economic policy focused on developing its own manufactures while suppressing, as far as possible, the manufacturing capacity of its rivals.

As early as 1781, Robert Morris's *Report on Public Credit* proposed to found a solid national credit by establishing a national bank, a system of compulsory national taxes and a tariff on imports, as well as the assumption of state debts by the national government. The plan failed due to lack of support from the states, including state legislation that prevented Morris's Bank of North America from functioning as a de facto central bank. But the Federalist economic program was put into action in 1789 when Washington chose Hamilton, upon Morris's suggestion, as the first secretary of the treasury of the United States. In 1791, Hamilton proposed establishing a federal mint and a new central bank. These measures were opposed by Jefferson, Randolph, and Madison, who feared the growth of the national government and opposed the bank, especially, as an instrument that would encourage merchants and investors at the expense of the majority of Americans who were farmers. Jefferson and Randolph appealed to Washington, arguing that a national bank was unconstitutional since provision had not been explicitly made for it. To this, Hamilton replied that the Constitution authorized any activity that was needed to attain the purposes for which government was established, so long as they were not explicitly unconstitutional or immoral. As he wrote:

> This general principle is inherent in the very definition of government, and essential to every step of progress to be made by that of the United States, namely: That every power vested in a government is in its nature sovereign, and includes, by force of the term, a right to employ all the means requisite and fairly applicable to the attainment of the ends of such power, and which are not precluded by restrictions and exceptions specified in the Constitution, or not immoral, or not contrary to the essential ends of political society.[50]

Hamilton's First Bank of the United States was established by act of Congress in February 1791. Later that year, Hamilton submitted his famous *Report on Manufactures*, in which he argued for a policy of government-subsidized industrial development, whose aim was to actively promote economic activity in key sectors and to assist those importing manufacturing technologies. Hamilton favored national subsidies for industry and tariffs on imports to keep out goods from rival nations while American manufacturing was developing to competitive levels. He even supported industrial espionage and technological piracy—including issuing American patents for inventions manifestly stolen from Britain—where such policies could be used to challenge British economic supremacy.[51] Hamilton also advocated an immigration policy focused on skilled workers in specific industries that the United States wished to develop, including targeted recruiting abroad, travel expenses for immigrant artisans, and customs exemptions for their tools and machinery.[52]

Thus Hamilton's desire to build an American manufacturing economy in Britain's image found expression in a dual policy: On the one hand, he sought close trade ties with Britain and chose to acquiesce in some British restrictions on American commerce—such as limitations on American cotton exports under the Jay Treaty of 1795—when these were needed to reach a mutually beneficial agreement. On the other, Hamilton encouraged aggressive competition with the British where collaboration was plainly impossible.

After the Jeffersonians took control of government in 1801, they gradually dismantled many of these nationalist economic policies, and even let the charter of the First Bank expire in 1811. But in the wake of war with Britain from 1812 to 1815, a new generation of nationalists emerged calling for a renewal of Hamiltonian economic policies. These nationalists included die-hard Federalists led by Daniel Webster, as well as former Federalists such as John Quincy Adams and William Plumer, who combined with disaffected Jeffersonians such as Henry Clay to found what eventually became a new, aptly named, National Republican Party. This nationalist economic coalition supported what Clay called the "American System," which sought to end economic dependence on foreign imports by protecting "infant industries" and those facing unfair competition from abroad, establishing a new central bank tasked with regulating credit and issuing currency, and developing national infrastructure such as roads and railroads. These policies were elaborated by the Baltimore lawyer Daniel Raymond, whose *Elements of Political Economy* (1820) criticized classical liberal economic theories for ignoring the possibility of divergence between national interest and individual interest. Clay's coalition succeeded in establishing a Second Bank of the United States, which operated from 1816 to 1836, as well as in reinstating protective tariffs.

Although this resurgence was cut short by the rise of the Jacksonian Democrats, the nationalist economic ideas of Hamilton and Clay were taken up by the American Whig Party and then put fully into effect by Abraham Lincoln in a series of laws designed by his economic advisor Henry Carey. This revived economic nationalism included tripling the average defensive tariff, subsidizing construction of a transcontinental railroad, and signing the Legal Tender Act of 1862, which empowered the secretary of the treasury to issue paper money not immediately redeemable in gold or silver.[53] Economic nationalism guided the policy of Lincoln's Republican Party during its long period of ascendancy from the Civil War into the twentieth century.

7. Nationalist Immigration Policy

During the 1790s, immigration policy emerged as an important point of contention between American nationalists and their Jeffersonian opponents. Because nationalists regarded membership in the nation as arising from shared traditions and values, they tended to prefer regulated immigration policies and a long process of naturalization, during which new citizens could become acclimated to American values and traditions. It was Jay, for example, who suggested in a letter to Washington that the American president should be "natural born," an idea that was adopted by the Constitutional Convention and included in the Constitution of 1787.[54] A typical Federalist view expressing concern for the assimilation of immigrants into American "customs, measures, and laws" was expressed by President Washington in a letter to Adams in 1794:

> The policy or advantage of [immigration] taking place in a body (I mean the settling of them in a body) may be much questioned; for, by so doing, they retain the language, habits, and principles (good or bad) which they bring with them. Whereas by an intermixture with our people, they, or their descendants, get assimilated to our customs, measures, and laws—in a word, soon become *one people*.[55]

Jefferson was not initially keen on immigration either, and in his *Notes on the State of Virginia* (1782), he worried that European immigrants would bring a belief in monarchy with them—or that, having thrown their customary support for monarchy away, would exchange it for "an unbounded licentiousness, passing, as is usual, from one extreme to another."[56] But by the 1790s, it had become clear that new immigrants arriving in America usually wanted to own and work their own land, and so were inclined to support the Democratic Republican vision of America as a nation of farmers. This led Jefferson to reconsider, and in his first message to Congress as president in 1801, he expressed strong support for immigration and for a rapid grant of citizenship to newcomers. As he wrote:

> I cannot omit recommending a revisal of the laws on the subject of naturalization.... Shall we refuse to the unhappy fugitives from distress that hospitality which the savages of the wilderness extended to our fathers arriving in this land? Shall oppressed humanity find no asylum on this globe?... Might not the general character and capabilities of a citizen be safely communicated to everyone manifesting a bona fide purpose of embarking his life and fortunes permanently with us? With restrictions, perhaps, to guard against the fraudulent usurpation of our flag?[57]

Here, Jefferson proposes that citizenship may be safely granted to "everyone manifesting a bona fide purpose of embarking his life and fortunes permanently with us." Other than cases of outright fraud, he sees no purpose in restrictions on immigration or a lengthy process of naturalization, in effect proposing a policy of open borders.

The Federalists responded to this reversal with astonishment. In three essays on immigration, Hamilton replied by quoting Jefferson's own earlier views at length, arguing that this change of heart was the result of electoral considerations. The truth, Hamilton urged, is that unrestricted immigration endangers the "common national sentiment" of the country, and should be undertaken with a due concern to maintain, as much as possible, a "uniformity of principles and habits":

> The safety of a republic depends essentially on the energy of a common national sentiment; on a uniformity of principles and habits; on the exemption of the citizens from foreign bias and prejudice; and on that love of country which will almost invariably be found to be closely connected with birth, education and family.... In the recommendation to admit indiscriminately foreign emigrants

> of every description to the privileges of American citizens on their first entrance into our country, there is an attempt to break down every pale which has been erected for the preservation of a national spirit and a national character; and to let in the most powerful means of perverting and corrupting both the one and the other.... To admit foreigners indiscriminately to the rights of citizens the moment they put foot in our country would be nothing less than to admit the Grecian horse into the citadel of our liberty and sovereignty.[58]

Concerns of this kind led to Federalist efforts to make the path to citizenship more restrictive and gradual. In 1790, naturalization required only two years of residency in the United States. But in 1795, Congress created a five-year process. Finally, in 1798, the Federalists passed the Alien and Sedition Acts requiring a nineteen-year path to citizenship: fourteen years of residency, and then, after filing a declaration of intent, another five years before naturalization. The Federalists' embrace of such a prolonged procedure reflected a rising fear that new immigrants would help shift the country's politics in a more radical direction. But on a deeper level, it reflected the Federalist view that the American nation was characterized by distinctive values and traditions that one had to adopt in order to join it. In short, the Federalists wanted newcomers to become Americans before they became American citizens.

The Jeffersonians vehemently contested this approach to immigration and citizenship. Ultimately, theirs became a Lockean, voluntarist view of citizenship, in which everyone has a natural right to leave one country and become the citizen of another at will. By simply choosing to come to the United States, one was made fit to be a citizen. The growing strength of such views effectively neutralized

Federalist efforts to control immigration, with Democratic Republican officials at the state level resisting the implementation of the national government's restrictive naturalization policies. It appears that the immigrant vote did play an important role in Jefferson's victory of 1800, which led to the 1802 Naturalization Act and the formal return to the naturalization requirements of 1795.[59]

8. Alliance with Britain

In the early 1790s, the ideas of the French Revolution were still openly advocated in Britain, challenging the legitimacy of the English constitution and threatening to overthrow it. But by 1793, the situation had changed considerably. Revolutionary France was now at war with Britain, and public opinion in that country had rallied around the traditionalist views of Burke and the government of William Pitt. In America, however, a ferocious debate broke out over how to respond to the conflict. Democratic Republicans such as Jefferson, Paine, and Madison, combining a deep hostility to Britain with an attraction to French revolutionary notions, wished to see the United States openly side with France. They argued that America was still bound by the defensive Treaty of Alliance it had concluded with the Kingdom of France in 1778—a rather remarkable proposition given that the revolutionaries in Paris had abolished the monarchy and executed the king who had signed the treaty. But more than this, the Jeffersonians proposed that the interests of the United States and France coincided because of their ideological affinity as sister republics. In effect, they proposed an international alliance of revolutionaries that would work to establish a new world order.

The Federalists' view was precisely the opposite, supporting a formal neutrality that would, in practice, lean towards Britain. The American nationalists recognized that the United States shared not only a language, but a political, legal, and religious tradition with Britain, and believed that America would benefit materially from good commercial and political relations with London. But they also thought that Americans had little in common with revolutionary France, and no interest in aiding the French project of bringing revolution to every corner of Europe. Indeed, the American nationalists tended to endorse Washington's view, declared shortly after he became president in 1789, that America's interest was for God to "protect and guide all sovereigns and nations (especially such as have shewn kindness unto us)."[60]

In April 1793, President Washington issued a Neutrality Proclamation, declaring that the United States would maintain impartial and friendly relations with each of the belligerent powers. This policy, whose immediate consequence was the termination of the Treaty of Alliance with France, was immediately lauded by Federalists and attacked by Jeffersonians. Hamilton joined the debate in June and July, publishing seven public letters under the pseudonym Pacificus (and two more the following year under the pseudonym Americanus) taking Washington's side, and defending the president's constitutional authority to conduct foreign affairs against Jeffersonian claims that Congress must be involved in making such decisions. The heart of Hamilton's argument was that the interests of the nation, rather than any internationalist revolutionary brotherhood, had to be the primary consideration guiding foreign relations. As he wrote:

> [Americans ought] not to over-rate *foreign friendships*—[we ought] to be upon our guard against *foreign attachments*. The former will generally be found hollow and delusive; the latter will have a natural tendency to lead us aside from our own true interest, and to make us the dupes of foreign influence. They introduce a principle of action,

> which in its effects, if the expression may be allowed, *is anti-national.*[61]

In this passage, Hamilton follows Vattel in arguing against permanent alliances, instead proposing that "self-preservation is the first duty of a nation."[62] But in addition to offering this nationalist framework for thinking about foreign affairs, Hamilton also observed that revolutionary France presented the United States with a peculiar situation, in which a foreign state was waging a war that was not only offensive, but also had the explicit ideological purpose of exporting revolution everywhere possible:

> It is not warrantable for any nation beforehand to hold out a general invitation to insurrection and revolution, by promising to assist every people who may wish to recover their liberty, and to defend those citizens of every country who may have been or who may be vexed for the cause of liberty; still less to commit to the generals of its armies the discretionary power of judging when the citizens of a foreign country have been vexed for the cause of liberty by their own government.[63]

Hamilton understood that a blanket invitation to "insurrection and revolution" in all countries in the name of liberty would not advance the cause of freedom, whether in France or anywhere else. Rather, in raising armies whose aim was to overthrow the constitutional order throughout Europe, France might "find herself at length the slave of some victorious Scylla or Marius or Caesar"—a prediction that soon proved correct.[64]

When Jefferson, still serving as secretary of state, read the *Pacificus* essays in July 1793, he wrote a furious letter to Madison demanding that he write a rebuttal: "For God's sake, my dear sir, take up your pen, select the most striking heresies and cut him to pieces in the face of the public."[65] Madison, now firmly back in Jefferson's orbit and leading the opposition to Washington's administration in Congress, acquiesced and penned a series of five essays in which he accused Hamilton and the Federalists of being "degenerates" and of "hat[ing] our republican government":

> Several pieces with the signature of *Pacificus* were lately published, which have been read with singular pleasure and applause by the foreigners and degenerate citizens among us, who hate our republican government and the French Revolution.[66]

Madison goes on to deplore Montesquieu for his "warped" admiration, "bordering on idolatry," for the British constitution, and ridicules Hamilton for arguing that foreign policy is chiefly the prerogative of the American president: "The power of making treaties and the power of declaring war, are royal prerogatives in the *British* government, and are accordingly treated as executive prerogatives by *British* commentators," he wrote.[67]

The Federalists were not content with neutrality in the war between Britain and revolutionary France. While maintaining military neutrality, Washington and Hamilton sought to establish a more supportive relationship with Britain, designing a treaty that would put the United States on friendly terms with London and resolve issues remaining from the 1783 accords. The Treaty of Amity, Commerce, and Navigation, commonly known as the Jay Treaty, was signed in November 1794. It allowed the two former enemies to trade on a reciprocal "most favored nation" status—quite an achievement for the young American government. In return, the United States acquiesced in British maritime policies designed to damage France. Several contentious border issues were also resolved by the treaty, paving the way for a decade of peaceful and mutually profitable trade between the United States and Britain in the midst of the French Revolutionary Wars.

The Jeffersonians bitterly opposed the Jay Treaty for effectively aligning America with Britain. Randolph, who had replaced Jefferson as secretary of state, resigned as well. Opposition to the treaty became the signature issue for the Democratic Republicans in the 1796 presidential elections, in which Jefferson carried all the southern states as well as Pennsylvania. Adams, winning by a mere three electoral votes (71–68), was able to extend America's pro-British orientation for another four years. But after Jefferson's victory of 1800, relations with Britain began a downward spiral that eventually resulted in an unnecessary war against Britain during Madison's presidency.

9. Alliance between Religion and State

In 1776, the Continental Congress called upon the thirteen states to write their own constitutions as part of the drive for independence from Britain. This meant the relationship between religion and the governments of the various states was reexamined in the midst of a revolutionary backlash against all symbols of British rule. Nine of the thirteen colonies—New York, Maryland, Virginia, North Carolina, South Carolina, Georgia, New Hampshire, Massachusetts, and Connecticut—had established churches at the time, of which all but the last three were Anglican. Subordinated to English bishops who were in fact a branch of the British government, these Anglican churches in America were quickly disestablished almost everywhere: in Maryland and North Carolina in 1776, in Georgia and New York in 1777, and in South Carolina in 1778. Only in Virginia did the Anglican church hang on for another decade, finally succumbing, after concerted efforts by Jefferson and Madison to eradicate it, in 1786. This was in sharp contrast to the established churches in New England, which were Congregationalist and continued to receive state support for two more generations: until 1818 in Connecticut, 1819 in New Hampshire, and 1833 in Massachusetts.[68]

The Federalists who came to the Constitutional Convention in Philadelphia tended to favor some kind of an alliance between Christianity and the state. But the form this alliance would take was uncertain: Although only a few northern states still had established churches, most of the other states still required a religious test or oath for officeholders, and continued to assist Protestant churches in various ways. Under these circumstances, the Constitution of 1787 conceded that these matters were to be left in the hands of the states. Similarly, the First Amendment to the Constitution (1791) prohibited the national Congress from making any "law respecting an establishment of religion or prohibiting the free exercise thereof"—again leaving the matter in the hands of the states.

But the Federalists were not supporters of a Jeffersonian policy of building a "wall of separation between church and state."[69] On the contrary, they hoped to cultivate a tolerant Protestant nationalism, which they believed would strengthen the constitutional republic they had created by teaching its citizens morality, self-discipline, and deference. In addition to defending the existing state provisions for the encouragement of Christianity, Federalists at the national, state, and local levels were prominent in honoring and promoting traditional expressions of Christian public religion, including government-sponsored prayer services, days of thanksgiving, and fasts. Washington was particularly concerned with public religion. As early as 1777, as head of the Continental Army, he proclaimed a day of prayer and thanksgiving after the great victory at Saratoga. As president of the new national government in 1789, he issued a proclamation designating November 26 as a national day devoted to thanksgiving, emphasizing that all nations have a duty to honor God:

> It is the duty of all nations to acknowledge the providence of Almighty God, to obey his will, to be grateful for his benefits, and humbly to implore his protection and favor....
>
> Now therefore I do recommend and assign Thursday the 26th day of November next to be devoted by the People of these States to the service of that great and glorious Being, who is the beneficent Author of all the good that was, that is, or that will be—That we may then all unite in rendering unto him our sincere and humble thanks—for his kind care and protection of the people of this country previous to their becoming a nation—for the signal and manifold mercies, and the favorable interpositions of his Providence which we experienced in the course and conclusion of the late war—for the great degree of tranquility, union, and plenty, which we have since enjoyed—for the peaceable and rational manner in which we have been enabled to establish constitutions of government for our safety and happiness, and particularly the national one now lately instituted....
>
> We may then unite in most humbly offering our prayers and supplications to the great Lord and Ruler of Nations and beseech him to pardon our national and other transgressions.[70]

During the 1790s, in the wake of the atheistic French Revolution and the perceived adherence of the Jeffersonians to its ideals, the Federalists became more active in their attempts to find a role for religion, even if non-established, in the public life of the nation. An evangelical Christian, John Jay repeatedly defended his and America's religious beliefs in debates with European enthusiasts of the French Revolution and Paine's *Rights of Man*. Later, he joined another prominent American nationalist, Elias Boudinot, in founding the American Bible Society.[71] Similarly, John Adams, as president in 1798 during the French Revolutionary Wars, condemned the "principles and manners which are now producing desolation in so many parts of the world," and emphasized that America's political order must be a religious one:

> We have no government armed with power capable of contending with human passions unbridled by morality and religion. Avarice, ambition, revenge or galantry would break the strongest cords of our Constitution as a whale goes through a net. Our Constitution was made only for a moral and religious people. It is wholly inadequate to the government of any other.[72]

Although "a zealous believer in the fundamental doctrines of Christianity" as a young man, Hamilton did not initially show much interest in matters of religion and state.[73] However, during the 1790s, he too came to regard religious faith as the indispensable antidote to the spread of radical views. By 1802, while discussing the decline in support for the Federalist Party, he explained that the struggle for nationalist conservative principles could not be won only with reasoned arguments, because the Jeffersonians, while "eulogizing the reason of men and professing to appeal only to that faculty," were constantly "courting the strongest and most active passion[s] of the human heart." Unless the Federalists could enlist "some strong feelings of the mind," all their political plans and efforts would eventually be in vain. He therefore proposed the formation of a "Christian

Constitutional Society," whose objective would be to "support the Christian religion" and the Constitution—in effect a Christian nationalist organization, with clubs meeting across the country. But Hamilton's death less than two years later prevented him from attempting to implement this plan.[74]

10. Opposition to Slavery

As a party, the Federalists regarded the goal of unifying the thirteen states under a national government as precluding an attempt to abolish slavery in their generation. At the Constitutional Convention in 1787, for example, the debate over slavery was largely suppressed to allow the southern states to join the Union. Nevertheless, the Federalist Party was from the outset distinguished from its Democratic Republican opponents by the fact that many of the leading Federalists, including Jay, Hamilton, Adams, Gouverneur Morris, Oliver Ellsworth, and William Cushing, were prominent in the effort to end slavery in America (although Jay owned slaves and released them only upon his death). Washington, too, upon his death, became the only southern plantation owner among the American leadership to free all of his slaves. Thus while the founding generation of Federalists did not elevate anti-slavery into a central political principle, it remains the case that the opponents of slavery found a home in the Federalist Party. This pronounced anti-slavery tendency grew directly from other Federalist principles already discussed: from the vision of America as an industrial and commercial republic, in which men would be free to sell their labor as they chose; from an affinity for Britain, whose courts had decreed slavery to be odious and without support in the common law; and from a Christian commitment to all men as having been created in the image of God. And the Federalist Party laid the foundations for the anti-slavery views of the next generation of American nationalists, including Federalists such as Daniel Webster and Rufus King, Whigs such as John Quincy Adams and Henry Clay, and, ultimately, the Republican Party of Abraham Lincoln.

During the Revolutionary War, an Act for the Gradual Abolition of Slavery (1780) was part of the radical democratic program of the anti-nationalist regime in Pennsylvania. But with independence won, the effort to end slavery was taken up by leading Federalists. In 1783, William Cushing, chief justice of the Massachusetts Supreme Court (later a Federalist appointment to the U.S. Supreme Court), followed the example set in Britain eleven years earlier by Lord Mansfield, who had ruled that slavery has no basis in the laws of England.[75] Regarding the law in Massachusetts, Cushing wrote:

> As to the doctrine of slavery and the right of Christians to hold Africans in perpetual servitude, and sell and treat them as we do our horses and cattle...nowhere is it expressly enacted or established.... This being the case, I think the idea of slavery is inconsistent with our own conduct and Constitution; and there can be no such thing as perpetual servitude of a rational creature unless his liberty is forfeited by some criminal conduct or given up by personal consent or contract.[76]

Arguing that as slavery had never been enacted as law in Massachusetts, Cushing found this institution incompatible with the state constitution drafted by Adams and adopted in 1780. In this way, legal protection for the institution of slavery was brought to an end, eliminating slavery in the state almost immediately and beginning a process that brought about the gradual freeing of slaves throughout New England.

But the largest emancipation of black slaves in North America before the Civil War took place in the state of New York, where this effort was led by prominent nationalists. Jay had proposed a state law abolishing slavery in 1777, but it had been defeated. Then, in 1785, Jay and Hamilton were founding members of the "New York Society for Promoting the Manumission of Slaves and Protecting Such of Them as Have Been or May be Liberated," which succeeded that year in passing a state law prohibiting the sale of slaves brought into the state. Jay was the society's first president, with Hamilton briefly serving after him. In 1799, as governor of New York, Jay finally signed into law the Act for the Gradual Abolition of Slavery, which decreed that from July 4 of that year, all children born to slave parents would be free, and that more than thirty thousand adult slaves would gradually be freed thereafter. In 1821, the Federalists Rufus King and Augustus Jay (son of John) successfully blocked an attempt to introduce a clause to the New York State Constitution that would have disenfranchised black voters.[77]

While the Federalists and their allies were able to make steady progress in dismantling slavery in some of the states, they had much more limited success at the national level. At the Constitutional Convention in 1787, another Federalist member of the New York Manumission Society, Gouverneur Morris, who authored the final text of the Constitution, gave an impassioned speech condemning slavery, calling it "the curse of heaven." According to Madison's notes, written in the third person, Morris said of slavery that:

> It was a nefarious institution. It was the curse of heaven on the states where it prevailed. Compare the free regions of the Middle States, where a rich and noble cultivation marks the prosperity and happiness of the people, with the misery and poverty which overspread

> the barren wastes of Virginia and Maryland, and the other states having slaves.... The moment you leave the [north-]eastern states and enter New York, the effects of the institution become visible.... Proceed southwardly, and every step you take through the regions of slaves presents a desert increasing with the increasing proportion of these wretched beings.
>
> Upon what principle is it that the slaves shall be computed in the representation? Are they men? Then make them citizens and let them vote.... He would sooner submit himself to a tax for paying for all the Negroes in the United States, than saddle posterity with such a Constitution.[78]

In the end, the Federalists yielded to the notorious three-fifths formula for calculating the representation of southern slave populations in Congress, in exchange for a provision in the Constitution ending the importation of slaves by 1808. Similarly, in 1789, Federalists supported the Northwestern Ordinance, which banned slavery beyond the Ohio River, while having to capitulate to the southern states in allowing slavery in the Mississippi and Southwest territories, as well as in the nascent District of Columbia. This would remain the pattern at the national level until the Civil War, with nationalists generally opposing the extension of slavery, while repeatedly proposing federally funded manumission schemes that failed to gain sufficient support. As late as the 1820s, the last Federalist senator, Rufus King, proposed a plan for the Federal government to encourage manumission of slaves, but it was once more rejected.[79] Only with the founding of the Republican Party in 1854 did the nationalist campaign for a united American nation free from the curse of slavery finally attain critical mass.

11. The Federalists and Modern American Nationalism

American nationalist conservatives took the lead in writing and ratifying the Constitution of 1787, and in establishing the national government of the United States. Indeed, the decline of the Federalists as a political party occurred, in no small part, because of the grudging acceptance by the first Democratic Republican presidents, Jefferson and Madison, of key aspects of the Federalist platform. Most Americans soon came to regard themselves as members of a single nation and to accept the Federalists' national government with its strong executive and judiciary. Moreover, their American national identity remained attached to a powerful Anglo-American tradition in language, law, and religion that was still plainly visible to Tocqueville when he traveled in the United States during the 1830s.

Even as the Federalist Party waned, nationalist conservatism continued to be a force in American politics. Younger Federalists in Congress organized around Daniel Webster and combined with a group of renegade Democratic Republicans led by Henry Clay, who became the standard-bearer for a return to Hamiltonian ideas. They succeeded in securing the election of former Federalist John Quincy Adams as president in 1824, and created the National Republican Party and later the American Whig party—a name strikingly intended to invoke the Anglo-American conservative tradition and the ideas of Edmund Burke.[80] These American nationalists came together around Federalist causes such as economic nationalism and opposition to the expansion of slavery, even as they supported Congress against Andrew Jackson's strengthening of the executive.

In the 1850s, Whigs such as William Seward and the almost unknown Abraham Lincoln coalesced into a new nationalist political grouping, the Republican Party. This nationalist revival succeeded, at the cost of a terrible civil war, in saving the Federalists' national government and implementing Hamiltonian economic policies, while at the same time burning to the ground the most monstrous legacy of Jefferson's America—the institution of slavery. Although Lincoln comfortably mixed Jeffersonian rhetoric with his imposing biblical imagery, his policies as president were in a tradition the Federalists would have easily recognized. After the Civil War, even Lincoln's assassination could not derail this decisive nationalist victory, which forged an American political consensus that lasted into the twentieth century.[81]

To this day, we encounter Jeffersonians who insist that nationalism is "un-American." But the nationalist conservatism of the American Federalist Party is, to a great extent, the force that made America. Certainly, the United States has changed immensely since the days of Washington, Jay, Adams, Morris, and Hamilton, the leaders of the original American nationalist conservative party. Nevertheless, it is difficult to miss the way in which, at a time in which the indications of national dissolution grow ever more insistent, the issues that animated the Federalist Party have returned to the fore in our own day. For decades, American political life has been dominated by a Jeffersonian discourse focused on universal theories of individual rights, at the expense of a careful cultivation of America's strength and cohesion as a nation. This Jeffersonian intellectual hegemony encouraged regime-change adventures in distant lands, recklessly indiscriminate immigration and trade policies, the elimination of even the slightest echo of religious observance from public life, and a growing hatred toward the country's Anglo-American constitutional and cultural inheritance.

Today, national conservatives are rediscovering the worth of Federalist ideas: Of a foreign policy based primarily on national interest, and on an alliance with English-speaking countries and like-minded national states sharing America's commitment to national independence and individual liberties. Of an economic policy directed toward a renewal of American industry and technological leadership in the face of dangerous rivals abroad. And of immigration policies emphasizing the need for newcomers to integrate into a culture that cherishes inherited American traditions and the values they bear. It may be that as Americans regain an appreciation of the Federalist Party's principles, their wisdom will be retrieved in other areas as well, leading to a recognition, for example, that the American nation will not endure without a return to religion to public life and without ensuring that the descendants of slaves are an integral and honored part of the American nation.

On one issue, however, today's nationalists may well wonder at the views of their Federalist predecessors. The Federalists' national Supreme Court, with the power to void legislation, played a crucial role in establishing a unified American national state—just as they intended. But the Federalists assumed that the justices would be traditionalists, wishing to serve as "faithful guardians of the Constitution," as Hamilton wrote. None of them imagined the circumstances that most Western nations face today, in which jurists use the national Supreme Court to impose what is in effect a new constitution—one that is post-national and hostile to Christianity—by judicial fiat. Under these conditions, contemporary nationalists have no choice but to seek ways of limiting the power of the judiciary to subvert the Constitution, just as their forefathers sought ways to limit the power of the executive and the legislature to do so.

In these areas and others, a nationalist politics must be built upon a fundamental understanding that was embraced by the Federalists—and that can be embraced again in our day as well: the insight that

Americans are not merely a collection of individuals, an essentially arbitrary subset within some universal brotherhood of individuals. They are a distinct nation, with a proud and important Anglo-American heritage that is unique in the world, and that still has much to achieve and much to contribute, both to America and to others.

Part Two

Philosophy

Chapter III

The Conservative Paradigm

1. Paradigm Blindness

A *paradigm* consists of fundamental concepts and the principles by which these concepts are related to one another. We use it to describe a certain domain in which we seek understanding. A well-framed paradigm will capture the most consequential features of the domain being studied, whereas a poorly framed one will let crucial elements slip away unnoticed. But whether well-framed or not, a paradigm always involves a reduction or simplification of the material. There is always something that has been left out. This is important because the principal function of the paradigm is cognitive. The basic concepts and relations are what permit us to identify the events taking place within the domain and to understand their significance. When an important concept or idea has been left out of a given paradigm, those relying on it will be blind to objects of the kind this concept is meant to identify. They will neither see them nor understand their role in the domain.

This is true in the political domain as well. A *political paradigm* provides us with the basic concepts and relations needed to recognize events taking place in the political arena and to understand their significance. When an important concept or idea has been left out of a political paradigm, those who rely on this paradigm will be blind to political objects of the kind this concept is meant to identify. They will neither see them nor understand their role in the political domain.

The concept of the *nation* offers one of the most fateful examples of our age. In Chapters 1–2, we saw that national independence has played a central role in the Anglo-American conservative tradition. More generally, we may say that a conservative political theory begins with the understanding that individuals are born into families, tribes, and nations to which they are bound by mutual loyalty. This means that a conservative recognizes the nation is an ineliminable reality. Political reality, as the conservative sees it, is full of competing nations, each of which consists of a number of tribes tied to one another by bonds of mutual loyalty. Each nation and tribe is engaged in a constant competition with its neighbors, allying or warring with them as circumstances dictate. Each nation and tribe possesses a unique cultural inheritance carrying forward certain traditional institutions, which can include its language, religion, laws, and the forms of its government and economic life.[1]

From this we understand that the nation is not the same thing as the government or the state that rules over it. A nation can and often does exist without any fixed government established over it, as was the case in the Greek city-states, whose citizens were well aware of the existence of a Greek *ethnos* or nation that had never been united under a single government. And there are also many governments or states that rule over multiple nations, as was the case in the Austro-Hungarian Empire, which set out to war with fourteen officially recognized nations at its command.

By a *nation*, then, we mean a number of tribes with a shared heritage, usually including a common language, law, or religious tradition, and a past history of joining together against common enemies and to pursue common endeavors—characteristics that permit tribes united in this way to recognize themselves as a nation distinct from the other nations that are their neighbors. By a *national state*, we mean a nation whose disparate tribes have come together under a single standing government, independent of all other governments.[2]

The liberal paradigm is blind to the nation. Nothing like the nation is to be found in the premises of Enlightenment liberal political theory. In the rationalist political tracts of the Enlightenment, the term "nation" (or "people") is merely a collective name for the individuals who live under the state. On this view, the nation comes into existence with the establishment of the state and is dissolved when the state is dissolved. This is another way of saying that the nation has no real existence of its own. There are only individuals and the state that rules over them.

Thus we find that instructors in political theory (whether in high school civics classes or at the university level) avoid discussing the nation, as well as those characteristics of the nation that explain its behavior in the political world. Instead, they discuss the political world using only concepts such as *the individual*, *freedom*, *equality*, *government*, and *consent*, which appear in the premises of Enlightenment liberal political theory, and additional terms such as *rights* that permit liberal premises to be elaborated in greater detail. But such instruction is powerless to explain many of the most basic phenomena of political life. It has no resources to describe the rivalry among nations and their ceaseless quest for honor, their pursuit of internal unity and cohesion, their struggle to maintain their own language, religion, and political traditions, or their insistence on the inviolability of their laws and borders. And indeed, entire generations of political and intellectual figures have been educated in such a way as to leave them blind to the importance of these things—or else to see them as "primitive" phenomena that will disappear from the world as reason and liberalism take hold.

This blindness to the real existence of the nation as something distinct from the individual or the state stands behind almost all of the great policy disasters of the last generation.

Consider the policy of "free trade." For an entire generation, democratic nations have sought a regime of free business transactions with China as a way of securing an unlimited supply of inexpensive labor for their industries—a policy that reached its climax in 2001 with the entry of China into the World Trade Organization. These policies were supported not only by the desire of private individuals (and, by extension, corporations owned by private individuals) to exercise their freedom in order to earn higher profits. They were also promoted by governments, media, and academics committed to the liberal theory that there should be no state-imposed barriers preventing individuals and corporations from freely buying whatever they want at the lowest price and selling whatever they want to the highest bidder.

This is a policy couched entirely in terms of the individual, the state, and the individual's presumptive freedom to do whatever he and his trading partners consent to do without state interference. It is blind to the nation, and to the bonds of mutual loyalty that bind nations and tribes together. Indeed, to the extent that bonds of national loyalty are even mentioned in discussions of free trade, they are described as irrational "market distortions" that may cause inefficiencies and make life more expensive—and therefore presumably less free. An "ideal world" is said to be one in which such distortions are eliminated in order to maximize the freedom of the individual. In other words, an ideal world is imagined to be one in which the effects of national and tribal loyalties are suppressed.

In light of this ideal, national loyalty was suppressed as a significant factor in policymaking. American and European industrialists were encouraged to move manufacturing to China and other Asian countries, even as millions of Chinese were invited to attend Western universities to study engineering and the sciences. These expressions of individual and corporate freedom had two crucial consequences: First, the Chinese economy grew rapidly, both in absolute size and in its technical capacities in numerous fields, until it began to challenge American and European dominance of the world economy. Second, more expensive American and European workers lost their livelihood. For years, liberals in America and Europe cheered these developments, emphasizing that free trade was lifting hundreds of millions of individuals in China out of poverty, that Enlightenment ideas were striking root in China and transforming it into a liberal democracy, and that Western workers who had lost their jobs would have new and better employment as private corporations reinvested their enlarged profits.

But these claims were made by political and academic figures who had been blinded by the liberal paradigm, and so were unable to understand the political world in terms of nations, their rivalries, their cohesion, and their dissolution. Incredible, but true: They were unable to see that massive, sustained industrial growth and gains in scientific expertise would transform a hostile, authoritarian China into a fearsome new enemy. Nor did they recognize that abandoning America's manufacturing capabilities would lead workers to regard themselves as betrayed by the business leaders who had transferred their jobs to China, and by the liberal governments that had encouraged this, bursting the bonds of mutual loyalty that had made America a cohesive and internally powerful nation. Yet this is what happened. Western liberals, who see the political world in terms of the freedom of the individual and cannot see the nation as having a real existence in the political sphere, inadvertently succeeded in immensely strengthening the Chinese nation at the expense of the American nation.

This inability to see tribe and nation as central in political affairs is reflected in debates on immigration as well. Viewed through the lens of Enlightenment liberalism, immigrants and prospective immigrants are indistinguishable from the native individuals of a given country. They are perfectly free and equal, just as the natives are. Nothing in the liberal paradigm justifies depriving them of their freedom of movement into a given country, or their freedom to compete with native individuals for employment and other resources. From a strict, free-trade perspective, preventing immigrants from arriving in the country and selling their labor is just another market distortion introduced by the national and tribal loyalties of the natives, which, again, leads to reduced freedom and to economic inefficiency.

But national and tribal loyalties are powerful and real, and tribes and nations compete with their neighbors when they feel strong enough to do so. As soon as national and tribal competition is seen as having a real existence, it is obvious that the adoption of immigrant communities into a new nation can only be successful if the immigrants are sufficiently weak, and therefore willing to assimilate themselves into the language, laws, and traditions of their adopted nation. Where immigrant communities are too large and internally cohesive, they resist such dissolution and begin to compete with the native population. This can result in open hatred, domestic tension, and violence.

Borders are a spatial expression of the bonds of mutual loyalty that hold nations together. An internally cohesive nation will establish borders to protect its people, its assets, its laws, and its traditions from being exploited and weakened by outsiders who are not bound to it by ties of mutual loyalty. Among other things, the purpose of a border is to resist the immigration of cohesive tribes that are strong enough to mount a challenge to the nation. Of course, there may be circumstances in which a well-defended border is not necessary. But Enlightenment liberal political theory, which does not recognize strong national and tribal loyalties as an important factor in political affairs, cannot generate any real justification for maintaining what seem, from a liberal perspective, to be arbitrary curtailments of individual liberties. Thus with the advance of Enlightenment liberalism, borders have come to seem as though they have no purpose: Liberalism has brought about the elimination of borders between European nations and the opening of the borders in both America and Europe to large-scale immigration from all over the world.

The 2015 decision by the German government to admit more than a million immigrants from the Middle East into Europe was plainly a destructive measure. The willingness of liberal European leaders to constantly strengthen domestic Muslim communities, without any recognition that such measures have the potential to contribute to internal dissension, dissolution, and violence, has been astonishing to behold. Similarly, America's rapid strengthening of immigrant communities has fueled the rise of aggressive anti-American ideologies on the political left, as well as a militant racialist politics on the political right. Here, too, liberal blindness to the nation has led to the fragmentation and weakening of the nation.

Blindness to the existence of competing nations, each with unique laws and traditions that are its own, has likewise found expression in the aspiration to establish a "liberal world order." In their campaign to establish a universal political community, liberals have assumed that the various rights and liberties associated with the traditional Anglo-American constitution, developed and inculcated over centuries, are in fact dictates of universal human reason and will be recognized as desirable by all human beings. Since the 1990s, this belief has led to American military intervention, with European assistance, in countries such as Bosnia, Serbia, Somalia, Iraq, Afghanistan, Libya, and Syria. These operations have sometimes involved protracted military occupations, whose aim has been to impose liberal democracy upon peoples that have no such traditions. At other times, they have involved aerial bombardment aimed at destroying an existing political regime, on the assumption that this would bring the people to rise up and establish a liberal-democratic regime in its place. In all these cases, intervention was shaped by the belief that because liberalism is a dictate of universal human reason, foreign peoples would shrug off their own national and tribal traditions to embrace reason and a liberal form of government.

These policies have had an almost unblemished record of failure. In no case have the intensive military operations of recent decades led to the establishment of something resembling liberal democracy—this despite the deaths of perhaps a million foreign nationals, the loss of thousands of American and European lives, and the expenditure of trillions of dollars on these futile foreign adventures. Indeed, far from understanding Enlightenment liberalism as a universal truth, these peoples have tended to retain their national and tribal loyalties and to regard liberalism as the false inheritance of a foreign nation. The more Americans and Europeans seek to instill these ideas in the nations they have conquered, the more certain these peoples become that the ideas in question are nothing more than tools for the extension of American empire and the subjugation of foreigners. Meanwhile, liberals say that such failures are due to "poor implementation," and continue viewing liberal democracy as a universal truth, which is therefore impervious to alteration in the face of experience.

Finally, consider the almost complete incapacity of liberals to think competently about the ongoing destruction of family life in America and Europe. The phenomenon is well known. A dogmatic belief in the individual's freedom has moved liberals to destigmatize—and, eventually, to actively legitimize—sexual license, narcotics, and pornography, as well as abortion, easy divorce, and out-of-marriage births, until finally the family has been broken and fertility ruined in nearly every Western country. At this point, most Western nations have achieved an average fertility rate well below two children per woman, a trend that is incompatible with the continued existence of any nation.

A shrinking population is, of course, one of the reasons that liberal elites hunger for foreign immigration. But immigration is no solution to the problem of population decline, for it does nothing to address its causes. Paradigm blindness doesn't only affect policymakers and political elites. At every level of society, people no longer feel a sense of responsibility to marry and raise up a new generation of the family, tribe, and nation. Marriage and children are regarded as nothing more than one possible choice within the sphere of individual freedom. Many public figures refuse even to discuss the need for marriage and children, out of fear that they will be regarded as insufficiently solicitous of the perfect freedom with which every individual is supposedly endowed.

In this way, the greatest calamity of all is permitted to proceed without anyone speaking of it: the downfall of the nation through infertility, because too few are left who see their nation as a valuable thing, and even fewer feel called to do their part to sustain it.

I have mentioned one fundamental political concept, that of the nation, which is absent from Enlightenment liberalism, and some of the consequences of this defect in the liberal paradigm. There are other basic political concepts whose absence from liberal discourse is no less debilitating. I will examine some of the others presently.

2. *The Premises of Conservatism*

Enlightenment liberalism has one great strength: Its early proponents reduced it to a small number of clearly articulated premises, which are easy to summarize and teach, even to children. Conservatives have rarely attempted to reduce their worldview to a small number of explicit premises, much less to teach conservatism in this way. There are good reasons for this hesitation. The reduction of any worldview to a number of explicit premises invites rigidity and dogmatism, even as important matters go unmentioned.

But let us admit that the liberal technique, while philosophically problematic, has been pedagogically effective. If conservatives want to convey their teaching in a way that can be understood by a broad public, there is no choice but to present their premises clearly and to make sure that students who wish to understand conservative thought are familiar with them. I will therefore present both liberalism and conservatism as systems of premises and compare these systems to each other.

Because of its overwhelming dominance in recent decades, the premises of Enlightenment liberalism are familiar to almost everyone. This political paradigm is based on four assumptions:

1. **All men are perfectly free and equal by nature.**
2. **Political obligation arises from the consent of the free individual.**
3. **Government exists due to the consent of a large number of individuals, and its only legitimate purpose is to enable these individuals to make use of the freedom that is theirs by nature.**
4. **These premises are universally valid truths, which every individual can derive on his own, if he only chooses to do so, by reasoning about these matters.**[3]

Notice, first, that these assumptions describe the political order as having a certain shape. This shape consists of two levels, one above the other: There are individuals and there is a government established over them. On the lower level, there are individuals who are understood to be free and equal to one another. This means that, by nature, there is no authority or power to which they owe obedience (or anything else). The only authority or power to which they owe anything is the government established above them.

This structure is held in place by the *consent* of the individual. The government exists only because the individuals below it have consented to it, and they owe it obedience only because they have consented to it. And since these individuals are free by nature, it is obvious that if their consent is withdrawn, then they cease to owe the government obedience (or anything else).

This paradigm also offers a view of government's responsibilities. Free individuals consent to establishing a government because they have exercised their reason and have determined that government is needed to protect them against criminals or conquerors who would deprive them of their lives and their freedom. In other words, government is established by free individuals to better secure the freedom they already have. Since this is the reason that government was instituted, it has no other legitimate purpose. And if it should cease to fulfill this purpose, then the individuals who constituted it can withdraw their consent and transfer it to another government that will do so.

This picture is undergirded by a certain view of the human person. According to this view, people are first and foremost individuals possessing *reason*, which is the ability to determine the course of action that will protect their lives and their freedom. This capacity to reason is considered to be *universal*, in that all individuals, when they exercise their reason, will come to the same conclusions. The pronouncements of reason are therefore assumed to be *necessary*—meaning that no individual, if he is exercising his reason properly, can come to any other conclusion. There is, in other words, only one framework for political order that can be considered correct, which is Enlightenment liberalism. All other views are mistaken.

The premises of Enlightenment liberalism are taught at every level of our educational system. I studied them in high school, in college, and again in my graduate program in political theory. They are so pervasive that my students often ask me whether they are not just "obviously true" (or "self-evident"). Many find it difficult to imagine that there might be a different way of thinking about political life.

But Enlightenment liberalism is not self-evidently true. Alternative paradigms are possible, and these can have significant advantages over the liberal view. One such alternative is the conservative paradigm, which underpins most of the nationalist and realist critiques of Enlightenment liberalism that have been articulated in America and Europe in recent years. Its premises can be described as follows:

1. **Men are born into families, tribes, and nations to which they are bound by ties of mutual loyalty.**
2. **Individuals, families, tribes, and nations compete for honor, importance, and influence, until a threat or a common endeavor recalls them to the mutual loyalties that bind them to one another.**
3. **Families, tribes, and nations are hierarchically structured, their members having importance and influence to the degree they are honored within the hierarchy.**
4. **Language, religion, law, and the forms of government and economic activity are traditional institutions, developed by families, tribes, and nations as they seek**

to strengthen their material prosperity, internal integrity, and cultural inheritance and to propagate themselves through future generations.

5. **Political obligation is a consequence of membership in families, tribes, and nations.**
6. **These premises are derived from experience, and may be challenged and improved upon in light of experience.**

These conservative premises are by now less familiar than those of Enlightenment liberalism. But they are not entirely unfamiliar. Many of us learned something like this view of the political world from our parents and grandparents, or from the Bible and the religious community to which we belong. Others encountered similar views while taking part in electoral politics or government, where our mentors were often more realistic about political life than our teachers in school and university. And there are certainly academic disciplines that discuss elements within this framework as well.

Yet this conservative political framework is rarely recognized for what it plainly is: an alternative way of thinking about political life.

The conservative paradigm regards political order as hierarchical in nature, consisting of multiple levels: An *individual* is born into a *family*, which combines with other families to form a *clan* (today often called a *community* or *congregation*). Clans combine to form a *tribe* within the alliance of tribes that together constitute a *nation*. This natural hierarchical ordering means that the individual is not perfectly free and equal, but is born into a structure that involves certain constraints and unequal relations from the start. As far as we know, human beings have been born into such political hierarchies for as long as we have lived upon the earth.

This political hierarchy is held in place by bonds of mutual loyalty. The human individual is by nature concerned to protect the well-being and integrity of his own self. But this "self" is not limited to the individual's body, his reputation, and his possessions. The human individual regards family members such as his parents, husband or wife, and children as an integral part of himself, and strives to protect them accordingly. This attachment to others whom I experience as a part of myself is called *loyalty.* When two or more individuals are loyal to one another in this way, a bond of *mutual loyalty* emerges. Bonds of mutual loyalty are what make collections of individuals into families, tribes, and nations—strong political structures capable of sustaining great duress and propagating themselves over generations. Political obligation, whether to one's family, tribe, or nation, does not arise from consent but from the bonds of mutual loyalty and gratitude that bind us to the other members of such *loyalty groups*, including especially the past generations that built up what we have and handed it down to us.[4]

This conservative view does not eliminate consent from the foundations of politics. Individuals can become members of a new family, tribe, or nation in adulthood, and such membership is often by way of mutual consent. Marriage is usually by consent, and families, tribes, and nations adopt members that were not born into their circle, also generally by consent. But the fact that some relations are established by consent does not alter the fundamental character of political life. It remains the case that mutual loyalty—which is largely inherited, rather than chosen—is the primary force that establishes political order and holds its constituent parts in place.

The conservative sees this hierarchical ordering of human individuals as characterized by constant competition and rivalry. Each individual competes with his neighbors so as to rise in strength and status; and in the same way, families, tribes, and nations compete with their neighbors so as to rise in strength and status. Even within the most peaceful families, husbands and wives bicker and children fight to improve their standing in relation to one another. Yet this competition is set aside when a challenge or threat from the outside, or some common endeavor, recalls them to a posture of mutual loyalty and obligation. This is true at the higher levels of the political hierarchy as well: The infighting among competing families and clans is set aside when unity is needed to cope with a danger to the tribe as a whole, or to engage in a pressing common enterprise involving the tribe as a whole, just as infighting among rival tribes is set aside to meet a threat to the nation or to pursue some great national endeavor.

The profusion of competing families, tribes, and nations generates diversity in political societies. Each family, tribe, and nation inherits a unique worldview and unique ways of doing things, including its own language, religion, law, economic arrangements, and forms of government. And it innovates upon these received traditions so as to better compete with its neighbors and advance the welfare of its members. But the loyalty of the individual is never given to institutions simply because they are admired in the abstract. We are loyal to a given institution because it is part of the traditional inheritance of the family, tribe, or nation to which we are attached by bonds of mutual loyalty. For example, a nation may put an end to the destruction caused by warfare among its competing tribes by uniting under a national government, a development that may take place by conquest or voluntarily, or by some combination of the two. Then the loyalty that binds the individual to his tribe and nation will also bind him to the national government, so that he obeys its laws, pays taxes to it, and serves in its military when summoned. But the individual's obligation to the government is not a consequence of his deliberation and consent, which often does not take place at all. It is a consequence of his loyalties, which are largely inherited.

While national government is instituted to put an end to the hardships caused by the rivalry of its member tribes, government is a traditional institution whose particular characteristics vary according to the distinctive traditions of each nation. These varieties of government may be regarded as so many experiments, which, by trial and error, permit mankind to discover the principles most conducive to strengthening the nation against its rivals and securing the welfare of its members.

Perhaps the most significant difference between the conservative political paradigm and that of Enlightenment liberalism is that conservatives are not rationalists. This does not mean they disdain the competent exercise of reason. On the contrary, a conservative takes pleasure in the achievements of reason as much as anyone else. But a conservative recognizes that human reasoning is far less reliable than rationalists suppose. He sees that the way people think and the things they believe are largely the product of the particular culture in which they were raised and that, for the most part, human beings believe that the way their own tribe or nation thinks about things is best. Conservatives do believe there are truths that hold good in all times and places, but given the extraordinary variety of human opinions on any given subject, they are skeptical about the capacity of the individual to attain universal political or moral truths simply by reasoning about them. Indeed, the only realistic prospect for advancement in politics and morals is by means of an empirical method, which requires a course of trial and error over centuries.

Conservatives are especially unimpressed by the claims that Enlightenment liberalism is itself a universal truth at which all mankind will soon arrive, given that Enlightenment liberalism has gained dominance in most countries only briefly and its record of success has been limited.

Having sketched the premises of the conservative paradigm in brief, I will devote the rest of this chapter to a more careful investigation of this way of understanding the political world. I will begin with the last premise, that of an empirical politics, before proceeding to consider the others in order.

3. *Rationalism and Empiricism*

Enlightenment liberalism is a political paradigm based on a *rationalist* theory of knowledge, whereas conservatism is based on an *empiricist* theory of knowledge. This is perhaps the most important difference between Enlightenment liberalism and conservative political theories. For this reason, it makes sense to begin a more careful examination of the conservative paradigm with what I have described as its last premise: *These premises are derived from experience, and may be challenged and improved upon in light of experience.*

Enlightenment liberalism is a poorly constructed framework for understanding political affairs, and the poor quality of this theory stems, first and foremost, from the fact that it is a sub-species of the failed philosophical enterprise of Cartesian rationalism. Descartes believed he had discovered the proper method for unfailingly ascertaining universal truth. This method begins with "clear and distinct ideas," proceeds by means of infallible deductions, and attains unassailable conclusions.[5] His magnum opus, *The Principles of Philosophy* (1644), claimed to have used this method to reach a final determination of the nature of all things in the physical universe. In its day, it was considered a masterpiece, and it was for decades the principal textbook of the school of Cartesian science. Kant followed this example with his *Metaphysical Foundations of Natural Science* (1786), in which he claimed to have deduced Newton's laws of motion using pure reason, without empirical evidence. He insisted that his a priori derivation of the laws of motion was infallible and therefore qualified as science, whereas Newton's empirical derivation did not.[6]

But it was all folly. There is no way to reach a final determination of the nature of the physical universe by moving from self-evident premises through infallible deductions to unassailable conclusions. Descartes's *Principles of Philosophy* is today regarded as such an embarrassment that it is not studied anywhere. The same is true of Kant's a priori physics. In the physical sciences, the Cartesian method was swept away, after a prolonged struggle, by the empiricist method of Newton's *Principia* (1687). Newton taught that in natural science, the premises of each system must be gathered from phenomena by induction. Such induction from experience does not produce universal truths and is not infallible.[7] As Newton wrote in his *Opticks*, "Although the arguing from experiments and observations by induction be no demonstration of general conclusions, yet it is the best way of arguing which the nature of things admits of."[8]

While physical science concluded that the method of Cartesian rationalism is worthless, political theorists embraced it and it remains the dominant view. Descartes's method was adopted by Thomas Hobbes and John Locke in England, and later imported back into France by Jean-Jacques Rousseau's *The Social Contract* and into Germany in the form of Kant's political essays such as *Perpetual Peace*.[9] A long line of empiricist political philosophers, including John Selden, Montesquieu, David Hume, Adam Smith, Adam Ferguson, Edmund Burke, and John Stuart Mill, has sought to dislodge this discredited method from political theory, at times appealing explicitly to Newton's empiricism for support.[10] But so far, these efforts have not succeeded in dampening the enthusiasm for Cartesian rationalism in political theory. In our day, this rationalism is the accepted basis for most public discussions of political and moral matters, which tend to be conducted as though empiricist political theory had never existed.

Nevertheless, rationalist political theory has failed. And it has failed for the same reason that Descartes's rationalist physics failed: Its premises are constructed without reference to experience. For example, experience suggests that *Men are born into families, tribes, and nations to which they are bound by ties of mutual loyalty.* Wherever we look, throughout history and in every corner of the globe, we see that mutual loyalty or group identification is the strongest force operative in politics, pulling individuals tightly together, forming them into families, clans, tribes, and nations. Indeed, because individuals experience what happens to the collectives to which they are loyal as things that are happening to themselves, they are ceaselessly engaged in strengthening the material prosperity, internal integrity, and cultural inheritance of the loyalty groups of which they are members. No universal ideology has succeeded in eliminating this intense desire to protect and strengthen the collective, or even in diminishing it much. It is the cause that establishes tribes and nations, states and empires, making them the stable and enduring entities that are the subjects of competent political theory.

Yet Enlightenment liberals have failed for centuries to recognize this fact. Time and again, they have predicted that the loyalty of human beings to their respective nations and tribes would disappear. Yet each time, reality has embarrassed them anew, and the intense desire to secure the honor and freedom of nations and tribes has reasserted itself. They have been embarrassed in this way because their commitment to the Cartesian method means that they are preoccupied with elaborating a political theory that they suppose is a construct of "reason," when in fact their deductions proceed from a series of fictions. These include the assertion that

All men are perfectly free and equal by nature; the claim that *Political obligation arises from the consent of the free individual*, so that human individuals have no political obligations unless they agree to them; the claim that *Government exists due to the consent of a large number of individuals, and its only legitimate purpose is to enable these individuals to make use of the freedom that is theirs by nature*; and the supposition that *These premises are universally valid truths, which every individual can derive on his own, if he only chooses to do so, by reasoning about these matters.*

None of these premises is empirically true. In saying this, I do not mean only to dispute a certain account of the origins of government. Rather, my observation concerns empirical human nature in general. There is no historical context in which these premises can be said to have been true. Nowhere in history do we find conditions in which all human beings, or even most, are capable of attaining universal political insight by means of reason alone; are blessed with perfect freedom and equality; are without membership in, and obligation to, any political collectives except those they have consented to join; and live under a government whose sole purpose is to enable them to enjoy their freedom. And if these things are not empirically true in even a single case, they cannot serve as the foundations for a political theory whose purpose is to understand the political world.

Liberals sometimes reply that the empirical falsity of their premises can be ignored because what they propose is not meant to be a descriptive political theory, but a normative one. That is, their aim is not to discover what political institutions are like in reality, but what they ought to be like (or what makes them legitimate). But words such as "normative," or "what ought to be," are not a magic wand that can, simply by being waved, turn an argument that is entirely detached from reality into one that is competent and true. For instance, if it is empirically untrue that human beings can sprout wings and fly about if they choose to do so, then it is nonsensical to say that, as a normative matter, human beings "ought to" sprout wings and fly about (or that they are "legitimate" only if they do so).

In the same way, an argument does not become a competent exercise in "normative political theory" by detaching itself from everything we know about human nature and political order from experience. In the example before us, one may claim that all human beings *ought* to be capable of attaining universal political insight by means of reason alone; that they *ought* to live in perfect freedom and equality; and that they *ought* to be without membership in, and obligation to, any political collectives except those that they have consented to join. But this is all just playing at make-believe. These things are so far removed from anything human beings are actually capable of, and from the way they actually live, that one might as well say that they all ought to sprout wings and fly to the moon and back at least once each year.

There is no way to save Enlightenment liberalism by claiming its aims are normative and not descriptive. To be successful, even normative political theory must be constructed on the basis of an understanding of the constraints imposed by empirical human nature, and of the possibilities for political order that this nature allows.

Considering how detached from reality Enlightenment liberalism's premises are, it is frightening that many today believe these premises should be used to judge the legitimacy of all existing governments. It is just this kind of rationalism that brought America and other Western countries into the last generation of costly and unsuccessful wars seeking to bring Enlightenment liberalism to the Balkans, the Middle East, South Asia, and Africa. At its root, these recurring failures reflect the inability of Western statesmen, steeped in Enlightenment rationalist political theory, to imagine that there may be societies that will resist, with all their might, the effort to overthrow their traditions and their way of life and replace them with an American understanding of what constitutes a legitimate regime. By the same token, it is just this kind of rationalism that has led American jurists, steeped in Enlightenment political theory, to imagine they can repeatedly overthrow the centuries-old religious and national traditions of their countrymen without ill consequences—and this on the basis of nothing but a deduction from a supposedly universal "right to define one's own concept of existence, of meaning, of the universe."[11]

The compulsion to judge all existing institutions wanting on the basis of an Enlightenment liberal political theory has drawn America and the Western nations into a perpetual cultural revolution. I say it is a perpetual revolution, because no human society can ever, in reality, live up to the ideal image of Enlightenment liberals' state of nature, no matter how much force is applied in the attempt to reshape it. This means that the revolution must continue its work of uprooting and overthrowing, both at home and abroad, for as long as the Enlightenment rationalist political theory continues to guide the public life of nations.

For political theory to become a discipline capable of doing more than inspiring reckless political activity, it will have to undergo the same difficult transition that visited the physical sciences more than three centuries ago in response to Newton's *Principia*. On the way there, we will have to become accustomed to regarding Enlightenment rationalist political tracts in the same way that we see Descartes's *Principles of Philosophy*—as a wholly misguided attempt to build up human knowledge on the basis of a priori, rather than empirical, reasoning. Once this happens, the discipline of political theory will be able to take up the methods of the great thinkers of antiquity and modernity, who sought to derive the general causes of things, including the principles of human nature, political society, and government, from experience by induction.

4. Mutual Loyalty

The first premise of a conservative political theory is that *Men are born into families, tribes, and nations to which they are bound by ties of mutual loyalty*. Let us examine it more carefully.[12]

The human individual acts constantly to secure his own well-being. That is, he acts to pursue the well-being of what can be called his *self*. But as he does so, he understands his self to be something more extensive than is commonly supposed. His body and mind, achievements and reputation, are all part of his self, of course. But he also conceives of his physical possessions, livestock, or land as though they are a part of himself, and he will defend these things as though he were defending a part of himself. In the same way, the love he feels for his wife and children, and for his parents and siblings, which moves him to care for them and protect them, is nothing but this same urge to protect the well-being and integrity of his own self, because these family members are encompassed within his conception of his self, so that he experiences what happens to them as if as if they were happening to him.

Nor is his desire to protect others as if they were a part of himself limited to family members. It can appear as a fierce desire to defend friends or townsmen, or the members of a military unit. Many other examples could be mentioned. We see, across the range of human activities and institutions, that the conception of the individual's self is flexible and expandable, and is constantly being enlarged so that persons and things we might have regarded as being outside of him are nevertheless of concern to him as if they were an integral part of him.[13]

When I include another human being within the perimeter of myself in this way, this attachment is called *loyalty*. When it is reciprocated, so that another individual has taken me under the protection of his or her own extended self, the resulting bond is one of *mutual loyalty*. Of course, the existence of such bonds of mutual loyalty do not mean that we cease entirely to be independent persons. The bond of mutual loyalty does not eliminate the competition, insult, and quarrels that are always present between individuals who are loyal to one another. A husband and wife may quarrel, and brothers or sisters may bicker and fight, and while these conflicts are taking place, they are experienced as a struggle between independent persons. But when one of them faces hardship, the other experiences it as if it were his own. Then the disputes that troubled them are suspended or forgotten. And once the hardship before them has been overcome, they experience a sense of relief and pleasure, of walking together in joy, each recognizing the happiness of the other as his own. These experiences, in which another individual is recognized as a part of one's self in hardship and in triumph, establish a strong distinction between what is *inside* and what is *outside*: an inside, comprising the two individuals, each of whom regards the other as part of a single unity; and an outside, from which a challenge arises against them, and in the face of which they experience a joint suffering and a joint success.

Human beings know of ways to inspire something resembling this group solidarity on a temporary basis. An individual may be coerced for a time, or his services may be bought. But enduring and resilient institutions are those that are constructed principally out of bonds of mutual loyalty. The family is the strongest and most resilient of all small institutions known to human politics, precisely due to the existence of such ties of mutual loyalty between each member of the family and all of the others. And it is out of such small units that larger-scale political institutions of every kind are built. It is possible, for example, to establish an association of mutual loyalty among the heads of a number of families, in this way tying together the members of these families in a collective called a clan, community, or congregation. And indeed, all over the world, and in all ages, clans have been established to provide for the collective defense, to establish procedures for justice between them, and to pursue common service to their gods. A child growing up in one of these families will experience the suffering and triumphs of his parents as if they were happening to him. And since his parents are bound by ties of mutual loyalty to the other heads of families, and feel the suffering and triumphs of these others as their own, the child will feel the suffering and the triumphs of the clan as his own as well. In this way, the child's self is extended to embrace the entire clan, and he will set aside even the most bitter disputes with other members of his clan when a threat from the outside is experienced as a challenge to all.

When we speak of the *cohesion* of human collectives, we have in mind the bonds of mutual loyalty that hold an alliance of large numbers of individuals firmly in place, each of them sharing in the suffering and triumphs of the others.[14]

Cohesion of this kind is not limited to the family and clan. Heads of clans can unite to form a tribe that has tens of thousands of members. And the heads of a number of tribes can come together to form nations whose members number in the millions. As in the clan, the bonds of loyalty that tie a child to his tribe or nation grow out of the loyalty he feels to his parents: The child experiences the suffering and triumphs of his tribe or nation as his own because he experiences the suffering and triumphs of his father and mother as his own, and they feel and give expression to the suffering and triumphs of the tribe or nation as these unfold. And again, this attachment means that the individual will set aside disputes with other members of his tribe or nation in times of danger or when great public projects are underway.

Can such bonds of mutual loyalty go even further, beyond the nation? We know that nations can develop attachments to other nations, and that there is such a thing as a "family of nations," as the English-speaking nations often regard themselves. But what brings these families of nations together is, again, a mutual loyalty that is strengthened by joint adversity and achievement. The solidarity of English-speaking peoples, for instance, becomes most prominent during their common struggle against the Axis powers or against the Communist nations. And the same can be said of other families of nations. But what is never seen is a mutual loyalty binding all human beings to one another.

Mutual loyalty is the most powerful force operative in the political realm. Feelings of mutual loyalty pull individuals together, forming them into families, clans, tribes, and nations, just as the force of gravity pulls molecules together, forming them into planets, star systems, galaxies, and systems of galaxies. Modern writers tend to look for ways of explaining this as a process driven by biological kinship. But politics cannot be reduced to biology. An isolated human individual, if he is cut off from his family and his clan, will attach himself to a new family and a new clan, adding his strength to theirs and receiving their protection in return. In so doing, he establishes new bonds of mutual loyalty to replace those that had been lost, and this without any necessary tie of biological kinship. This constant regeneration of bonds of mutual loyalty means that families can adopt individual members that were not born among them, and that clans adopt entire families that were not born among them. In the same way, nations adopt not only foreign individuals and families, but entire tribes that were foreigners once, but are not considered foreigners any longer. Thus while all nations use the metaphor of brotherhood to invoke a family-like relationship of mutual loyalty among their members, actual biological kinship is never more than a raw material upon which a nation is built, if it is even that. Indeed, nations such as the English and the French preserve strong traditions of their mixed origins.

The constant regeneration of bonds of mutual loyalty, which we find in every human being, means that there can be no human society in which individuals are loyal only to themselves. This is true even in modern society, in which the order of tribes and clans has been weakened by the national state and liberal philosophy has taught individuals to see themselves as free of unchosen obligations to others. Even here, collectives built from bonds of mutual loyalty are visible everywhere, and not only within the family: Local political chapters, churches and synagogues, schools and other community organizations are still strongly reminiscent of the old clans. And on a national scale, powerful religious, ethnic, sectoral, and professional associations play a role in the life of the nation that is still very much that of the tribe, with its fierce mutual loyalties, striving against other tribes to turn the course of the nation in their favor. Their ongoing presence in the modern state points to an undying tendency of individuals to form collectives at the level of the family, clan, tribe, or nation—a tendency that becomes dramatically more pronounced when the "clan" or "tribe" comes to believe that the national state is no longer able to protect it as before.[15]

The bonds of mutual loyalty that make families, clans, tribes, and nations stable and enduring also ensure that human beings work constantly to advance the health and prosperity of the family, clan, tribe, or nation to which they are loyal, even in ways that put their own life and property at risk.

But what is the health and prosperity of the family, clan, tribe, or nation? Consider first the family. The health and prosperity of the family, we can say, consists in three things. First, it requires *material flourishing*. This means that children are born and grow strong, that the family gains in terms of the property at its disposal, and that its physical capabilities and productivity advance from year to year. Second, a healthy family possesses a strong *internal integrity*: Its members are loyal to one another, celebrate one another's achievements, and defend one another in adversity, even at risk to themselves; its members readily honor the differences in age or status among them, so that the family can take effective, unified action without coercion; and the competition and tensions that inevitably arise among them are conducted in relative peace, so that they do not lastingly damage the family as a whole. Third, the health of the family is recognized in the extent and quality of the *cultural inheritance* that parents and grandparents transmit to the children. Both the physical capabilites and the internal integrity of the human family depend to a great degree on the cultural inheritance that the older generations bequeath to the younger generation, and on the degree to which this inheritance is successfully handed down.

These are the measures of the health and prosperity of the family, and every member of a family has an intuitive understanding of these things, just as he has an intuitive understanding of what contributes to his personal life and property. Moreover, the individual experiences the strengthening or weakening of his family as something that is happening to himself. Because this is the case, he is moved to take action to defend and build up his family in its material prosperity, in its internal integrity, and in its capacity to transmit an appropriate cultural inheritance to the children. Indeed, parents ceaselessly act out of such motives. They take employment that is not to their liking so as to be able to feed their family. They humble themselves to mend relations with an unhappy husband or wife so that there will be peace in the home. They devote long hours to the tutelage of the recalcitrant young, whose ability to recognize the value of what they are taught is often limited. And they do so not out of an altruistic impulse to help a stranger, but because strengthening the family is experienced as strengthening themselves.

The health and prosperity of other human collectives is measured in much the same way. We can measure the health of the tribe or nation by taking stock of its material prosperity, its internal integrity, and the strength and quality of the cultural inheritance that is being transmitted in it from one generation to the next. Moreover, the individual who is loyal to his tribe or nation cannot avoid sensing that the nation is growing stronger or weaker, and feeling that this strengthening or weakening is something that is happening to him, just as he feels this with respect to his family. And for this reason, when the tribe or nation are felt to be weakened, we will see individuals rise up to take this matter into their own hands, acting to strengthen the tribe or the nation, just as they act to strengthen their family.

Human beings constantly desire and actively pursue the health and prosperity of the family, clan, tribe, or nation to which they are tied by bonds of mutual loyalty. Nor should we wish to see this desire eliminated or diminished, any more than we want to see the desire of the individual to defend his own life and improve his material circumstances diminished. Certainly, this fierce concern to protect and strengthen the collective makes every family, clan, tribe, and nation into a kind of fortress surrounded by high, invisible walls. But these walls are a necessary condition for all human diversity, innovation, and advancement, enabling each of these little fortresses to shelter its own special inheritance, its own treasured culture, in a garden in which it can flourish unmolested. Inside, what is original and different is given a space of its own where it can be tried and tested over the course of generations. Inside, the things that are said and done only in this family, clan, or tribe, and nowhere else, are given time to grow and mature, becoming solid and strong as they strike roots in the character of the collective's various members—until they are ready to make their way outward from the family to the clan, from the clan to the tribe and the nation, and thence to all the families of the earth.

5. Honor

The second premise of the conservative paradigm is that *Individuals, families, tribes, and nations compete for honor, importance, and influence until a threat or a common endeavor recalls them to the mutual loyalties that bind them to one another.*

This premise introduces one of the central concepts in conservative political theory, the concept of *honor*. I will not here discuss a particular code of honor, such as that which was accepted among English gentlemen two hundred years ago. Rather, I wish to discuss honor as a general phenomenon appearing across all human societies. In examining it, we will find that there can be no conservative society—by which I mean a society capable of conserving any teaching or text, institution or form of behavior, so that it persists from one generation to the next—unless it is permeated throughout by a concern and regard for honor.

Enlightenment liberalism supposes that children owe obedience to their parents until they are twenty years old, or some similar age. At that point, they are assumed to have reached the age of reason, and therefore to have acquired the right be free and equal to their parents, and, in particular, to be free of the obligation to obey them. By contrast, one of the primary precepts of a conservative society is the commandment to *Honor your father and your mother*—a precept that is emphasized time and again in Hebrew Scripture.[16] Notice that "honoring" one's parents is not the same as obeying them, and that there is no expiration date on this commandment. The precept of honoring one's parents continues to be in force throughout one's entire life, even after one's parents are no longer living. One is never free from this obligation.

But what does it mean to honor one's parents? The original Hebrew instructs us to give *kavod* (honor) to our parents. This is a cognate of the word *kaved*, which means "heavy" or "weighty." In fact, Scripture instructs us to give weight to our father and mother. In English, we may say that we "give weight" to someone's words when we take them to be important. But the Hebrew *kavod* is not a weightiness that is given only to words, advice, or opinions. It is given to the person himself.[17]

We need to think carefully about what this means. Human beings understand reality in terms of relations of cause and effect. An object is understood to be important or significant to the extent that it acts as a cause affecting other things, and unimportant or insignificant to the extent that it fails to have an effect on other things. The same is true of the way we understand people. We regard them as important to the extent that they have an effect on others, and unimportant if they fail to have an effect on others. For example, a king or president is considered an important person because what he says and does has an effect on millions of people. However, notice that the king's importance or significance does not depend on the effect he is having at a given moment. He may be thinking silently or sleeping, and yet he is still important. His importance or significance is determined by the things he has already done and the things he may yet do. Indeed, he may continue being important even after he has died, so long as the effects of his actions continue to be felt in life.

The importance of an individual—his *kavod* or weightiness—is not just something we think about in the abstract. We sense the *kavod* or weightiness of every person we meet, judging him to be more important or less so, and we act in accordance with this judgment. When I am in the presence of an important person, I experience his or her weightiness as a pressure in my chest, which can make my breathing more difficult, introduce a tremor into my voice, and cause me to avert my eyes. These and other effects should not be dismissed as merely physical. They are the outward signs of a more profound accommodation to the presence of persons possessing great *kavod* or weightiness: We tend to believe the things that individuals we consider important tell us, to act in accordance with their preferences, and to imitate them in their style of speech and behavior, and in countless other ways. And because every human individual immediately senses the *kavod* or weightiness of others whom he meets, judging them to be more or less important, the reactions of each individual act as a mirror in which I can sense my own *kavod* or weightiness as well. That is, I can sense the degree to which I am important in the eyes of other individuals when I am in their presence.

This is the basis for all competition among individuals. Human beings take pleasure in being regarded as important in the eyes of others and find it painful when they are considered insignificant or disregarded. And because being regarded as weighty or important is pleasurable, individuals compete to be considered weighty or important. In its most basic form, this involves contests of strength, in which one individual proves his physical superiority over another, thereby gaining in importance and weightiness in the eyes of his adversary and of anyone else who witnessed the fight or heard tell of it. But in civilized society, this competition tends to take other forms, and the individual may strive to be regarded as a great military commander, or a man of influence in political affairs, or a wealthy businessman, or a great scholar or physician or artist. Indeed, while we say that politicians compete to attain the greatest power, and businessmen to exceed their rivals in wealth, and scholars to achieve the utmost in knowledge, the truth is that all of them compete for only one thing, which is *kavod*, or honor. That is, they compete to be recognized as important in the eyes of others.

Recall that the importance of an individual is the extent to which he is recognized as a cause of effects. This suggests that I can purposely increase the importance of another person by speaking or acting in such a way as to emphasize that he is the cause of various effects. And indeed, in every field of endeavor, one can "give honor" to another individual by praising his abilities, by referring to his accomplishments, and by deferring to his judgment, acting in accordance with his preferences, or adopting his manner of speech and behavior. On the other hand, I can decrease the *kavod* or weightiness of another by speaking or acting in such a way as to emphasize his insignificance, "showing contempt" for him, or humbling or humiliating him. This can be done by defeating him in some confrontation or competition, or by ridiculing or severely criticizing him, his ideas, or his deeds, or by slighting or ignoring him where I might have taken him into account.

With these things in mind, we can now return to the matter of honoring one's parents. I have said that we tend to believe the things that important individuals tell us, to act in accordance with their preferences, and to imitate their speech and behavior. This is what we do by nature. Indeed, we tend to do these things automatically, without even being aware we are doing them. But the Mosaic law does not instruct us to do what we would have done in any case. The law is intended to repair our nature and to improve upon it in keeping with the understanding that "the nature of man's mind is evil from his youth." And if a principle is included among the Ten Precepts, it is to instruct us concerning things that are not according to our nature and that may, in fact, be very difficult for us to do.[18]

What is required, then, is behavior beyond the usual tendency to exhibit deference in the presence of someone who is more powerful and accomplished than we are. The precept itself instructs us: *Honor your father and your mother*, or *Give honor to your father and your mother.* It makes use of an active verb, enjoining us to act with intention, purposely seeking to give *kavod* or weightiness to our parents by inquiring regarding their preferences and their counsel; by acting in accordance with their preferences wherever possible, and by avoiding contradicting or embarrassing them when it is not; and in general, by praising their achievements and their virtues, their speech and their behavior, both in words and by imitating them ourselves. All of this takes place in their presence, but it also takes place when we are not in their presence: In conversation and interaction with others, we continue to recall and to imitate whatever is strong, just, and praiseworthy about our parents, often explicitly telling others that this is what we are doing, while scrupulously avoiding disparaging or diminishing them in any way.

As we do these things, we inevitably increase the weight and significance of our parents in our own eyes—something that, when it happens, is plainly visible to them, just as it is plainly visible to our friends and associates. And because we are always a mirror set before our parents' eyes, their increasing importance in our estimation imparts to them a greater weight and significance in their own self-estimation as well. This is true even when a small child gives honor to his parents, and in a conservative society, the education of children, whether at home or in school, is focused above all on teaching the child to constantly find ways to honor his father and his mother. But honoring one's parents is even more important in adulthood, when the increasing strength of the child relative to his parents, and his increasing capacity to recognize his parents' flaws and failures, naturally diminish them in his eyes. As parents age, they long to see that their life has been worthy despite the mistakes they have inevitably made. And nothing gives them happiness, strength, and consolation as much as being honored by their adult children, their grandchildren, and their great-grandchildren.

Of course, for such happiness, strength, and consolation to take place, adult children must live in proximity to their parents, must see them frequently, and must have children of their own in a timely fashion. And in a conservative society, living in proximity to one's father and mother, seeing them frequently, and bringing grandchildren and great-grandchildren into the world are central aspects of honoring one's parents. Everyone understands that not every child will be able to do these things. Nevertheless, they are things that children who are concerned to honor their parents strive to do, in consideration of those who gave them life and remained loyal to them during long years and under difficult conditions.

There is no more obvious difference between a liberal political order and a conservative political order than this. In a liberal order, the things that a child must do to honor his parents and remain loyal to them are found to be, for one reason or another, distasteful or wrong. The liberal emphasis on the freedom and autonomy of the individual makes every act of honoring one's parents seem to be servile, or mere flattery, or "living for others." Children, who are supposed to be "free to choose," are thought to be stifled, their individuality and creativity repressed, by the constraints imposed on their lives by the imperative of honoring their parents. Indeed, receiving one's education near home and living in proximity to one's parents as an adult are viewed as an aberration and a failure to "attain one's potential." Moreover, the liberal belief that a child becomes the equal of his father and mother once he is twenty years old, and that thereafter the relationship is one of consent, suggests that those twenty years of tutelage, hardship, and sacrifice on the part of the parents are to be regarded as a free gift, which creates no enduring obligation on the part of the child.

No wonder, then, that honoring one's parents is taught almost nowhere today. The implications of this one principle, if taken seriously, would undermine much of the public philosophy of liberalism.

In this context, I must say a few words about the care of elderly parents. In a conservative society, one is not relieved of the responsibility to honor one's parents at the age of eighteen or twenty. On the contrary, this obligation remains throughout life, and it only grows more difficult as one's father and mother become infirm with age. In affluent societies, this hardship is suppressed by means of institutions such as "retirement communities" and "old-age homes," which permit individuals to deny their responsibilities to their parents on the grounds that they have paid someone else to discharge them. In this way, the individual damaged by Enlightenment philosophy demonstrates that he is incapable of even the most rudimentary gratitude to those who gave him life, fed him and nursed him in times of illness, taught him a language and a manner of speaking to others, gave him the knowledge and skills needed to survive and to flourish in the world, and established him within a network of relations and acquaintances who would be able to help him as he grows. Everything that the individual has is, in the end, because of his parents. But under a liberal regime, these parents are not regarded as important enough to be cared for by their children in their last years. Liberal societies ceaselessly manufacture new "rights" so that the young and healthy may do whatever they please—but know nothing of the right of the aged to live among their children, grandchildren, and great-grandchildren, to be honored by them, and to receive care at their hands.

True, a child in a conservative society must shoulder these burdens, whereas a liberal society makes no comparable demands. But in time, this same child grows old himself, and then the circumstances are reversed: Then the young man and woman, who once carried the burden of honoring their parents and grandparents, are themselves the family patriarch and matriarch. Now it is they who live among their grandchildren and great-grandchildren. Now it is they who are honored by two or three new generations of young people who inquire after their words and deeds, learn from them and imitate them, and care for them in gratitude. Meanwhile, in a liberal society, the aging individual, who was spared the burden of honoring his parents and grandparents in his youth, finds that he is disregarded and neglected—which is to say that he his abused—in the same way by his own children and grandchildren (if he has any children and grandchildren). Having dishonored his own parents by leaving them to age without him, he now finds that he is dishonored by his own children in turn, who find it convenient to let him age without them.

I consider with unspeakable sadness the millions of old men and women who lived their lives in freedom, as if there are no unchosen obligations in life, and in the end find themselves discarded by their own children, who owe them everything, and yet are convinced that they owe them nothing.

6. Hierarchy

The third premise of the conservative paradigm is that *Families, tribes, and nations are hierarchically structured, their members having importance and influence to the degree they are honored within the hierarchy.*

We experience the political world as consisting of hierarchies, by which I mean pyramidal structures whose members are ranked according to their importance or weightiness. This structuring of the political world is natural and inevitable. Take any number of human individuals and set them to work at a given task, or at multiple tasks, or at merely amusing themselves without any particular goal, and their relations will immediately take the form of a hierarchy, or of two or more competing hierarchies, in which individuals are ranked in accordance with their importance in comparison to one another. Established loyalty groups of different kinds and on different scales are always hierarchically structured as well: A clan, community, or congregation is a hierarchically structured group of families, with each member family having greater or lesser importance in comparison to the others. Similarly, competing tribes or political parties are ranked in accordance with their importance within the nation, and competing nations are ranked in accordance with their importance within families or alliances of nations.

These hierarchies often appear to be stable and solid. At first glance, a given hierarchical ordering will frequently seem to be unchanged when compared to the same hierarchy five years earlier. But in fact, every hierarchy is constantly in motion. Every individual constantly strives to strengthen himself and to improve his standing within a hierarchy of which he is a member, and in doing so, he is always rising or falling in importance in comparison with other members of the same hierarchy, who are themselves striving to strengthen themselves and improve their standing. This competition occurs at all levels in the pyramidal structure, as those individuals who are in a position to contend for the highest degree of importance pursue the competition at that level; while those who are not positioned to contend for the highest degree of importance offer assistance to those who can, in this way gaining in importance themselves. And all of this is true, as well, of hierarchies consisting of loyalty groups such as families, tribes, or nations.

Institutions such as government, the military, business enterprises, and religious orders often have an inherited and publicly acknowledged structure of offices, ranks, and honors, as well as inherited procedures for conferring these offices and honors on individuals whose significance and weightiness is increasing. In the same way, they often have inherited procedures for honorably retiring individuals, and for dishonorably demoting or expelling others, as their significance declines. But we must be careful not to take formal ranks and honors at face value, for these are never more than an indication of the true status and importance of the members within a given hierarchy. Individuals may, for various reasons, prefer to avoid publicly acknowledged offices and honors, and yet their actual stature within the hierarchy may be rapidly rising behind the scenes and away from the prying eyes of onlookers. Similarly, institutions at times prefer to express a public commitment to the equality of all their members, as in a commune or kibbutz. And yet the members of these egalitarian institutions never fail to be aware of the true structure that exists behind these formal declarations. They know precisely who the leading figures are; who is of secondary importance, perhaps having his high position due to some special competence; who is well-regarded, but not especially important; and who is disdained.

One of the consequences of this hierarchical ordering of human societies is the particular way in which beliefs and behaviors propagate through them. Because we tend to believe the things that important individuals tell us and to imitate their style of speech and behavior, we can often recognize the supporters, adherents, or students of a certain individual by taking note of the thoughts they express and the mannerisms that characterize their speech and behavior. It amuses us to see adolescents painstakingly outfitting themselves to look like a prominent actor or musician they take to be important. But adults are no different, following the leaders of their particular tribe, party, or profession, often in excruciating detail. No less than the most ardent defenders of tradition, liberals and Marxists tend to move with the herd, painstakingly embracing every new opinion, gesture, and turn of phrase that is adopted by the leading figures of their tribe, party, or profession, even as they proclaim themselves to be reasoning freely and deciding things for themselves. Much of the time, the claim to be "thinking for myself" is no better than a vain conceit, itself adopted in imitation of the more important members of the hierarchy to which they are loyal.

None of this is said with the intention of insulting or demeaning anyone. It is simply a description of human beings as they are, rather than as we wish them to be.

When we speak of a certain person having *influence*, we refer to his ability to affect a change in the beliefs and behaviors of others who regard him as having weight and significance. The influential individual, for his part, takes pleasure in noticing his own influence over others and feels discomfort or even pain when such influence is not in evidence. And so the competition for honor and status is always, in a large measure, a competition over the influence that comes with honor and status—which is to say, it is a competition over whose words are to be believed, and whose preferences are to be acted upon.

With these things in mind, we can better understand the functioning of the family hierarchy. Like all loyalty groups, the family is a hierarchical structure reflecting the importance or weightiness of its members, which shifts as they rise and decline in stature over time. And as in other loyalty groups, the true hierarchy within a family is not to be learned by examining formal titles. A father may be recognized as the head of the household, and yet his wife or one of his children may have a greater weight and influence, especially as he grows older and his strength wanes. But of course, children are born into a family in which their parents have, at first, a vastly greater weight and significance than they do. In the beginning, the child is utterly dependent on his parents to feed and protect him, as well as to teach him. These things, in addition to their greater physical strength, make the relationship between parents and children radically unequal, and parents have little trouble seeing their own importance reflected in the mirror of their children's eyes. And since his mother and father are so much more important than anyone else, the child spends his first years believing what they tell him, imitating their speech and behavior, and, for the most part, acting in accordance with their preferences, even if he tests his strength on occasion by misbehaving.

But as the child approaches adolescence, he becomes increasingly capable, both physically and mentally. And as he does, he comes to see weaknesses in his parents. Of course, this is inevitable as well as necessary, so that the child may learn to stand by his own strength. But it is also dangerous for the child and for the family. This is because the child, in coming to have regard for his own abilities, may come to despise his parents, thinking them unimportant. And if he comes to think that his parents are unimportant, he will also cease to believe the things they say, to imitate them, and to act in accord with their preferences. In this way, an adolescent may cut himself off entirely from what his parents have to teach him, and may remain cut off in this way for the rest of his life. Perhaps this would not be a great calamity if children were able, as is sometimes said, to absorb most of what their parents have to teach them in their first ten or twelve years of life. But there is no reason to think this is true. On the contrary, the intellectual and moral capacities of the child only begin to solidify in late adolescence. If he is still capable of learning from his parents at this stage, the child will frequently gain as much from his parents in early adulthood as he did during childhood. This will perhaps include a deeper and more sophisticated awareness of the significance of the tribe and nation to which he belongs, and of the laws and customs and sacred texts of his people. It is in this context that it becomes possible for parents to teach the child a mature and fitting love of God, an adult understanding of moral boundaries and moral obligations, and traditional skills and practices that have been developed over thousands of years, including the ability to establish personal relationships, to marry and raise children, to manage a household or a business, and much else.

Of course, the child's relationships with his parents is only the first and most basic unchosen hierarchical relationship into which he will enter. After these, there will be further hierarchical relationship with his grandparents, uncles and aunts, with his teachers, with the leading members of his community or congregation, with the clergyman and the constable and others. And in a conservative society, the child is expected give honor to these figures, all of them superior to him within the broader hierarchy in which he is raised. In the same way, when he serves in the military, he must give honor to his officers and commanders; when he is hired by a businessman or tradesman, he must honor the accomplished practitioners from whom he will learn his trade. And when he marries, he is adopted into the hierarchy of a second family, where he will owe honor to his wife's parents and the other relations he has acquired.

In each and every one of these relationships, a young individual will need to consistently give honor to those whose stature is greater than his. And this is not merely for the sake of being liked by his superiors and fitting in. Rather, it is because his capacity to learn from these important persons—to learn how to speak and how to behave, what to do and how to do it—depends on his ability to give them a weight and significance that they will not naturally have in his eyes.

Attend to this well. In all these relationships and others, this young person will have to give honor to elders and superiors that he has not chosen. Even under a liberal regime, in which it is claimed that consent is the basis for political and moral obligation, the truth is that a young person rarely has any meaningful influence over who will be his elders and superiors in any of the hierarchical relationships into which he enters. The individual may be free to move from one place to another, and yet when he arrives in a new locale, he encounters a new hierarchy and is again faced with having to give honor to elders and superiors that he has not chosen.

This is the reason that the precept of honoring one's parents is at the center of moral teaching and practice in every conservative society. The ability to give honor to a superior in an unchosen hierarchical relationship is the one capacity on which all other gains in knowledge, wisdom, skills, and capacities depends. And this ability is most easily acquired in the process of learning to give honor to one's parents and other close relations during childhood, in adolescence, and in early adulthood. The family is therefore the training ground for one's participation in all other hierarchies, whether one has joined them by consent or not. In a well-functioning family, the child learns the skills needed to maintain a hierarchical order, how to benefit from such a structure, and how to rise in it over time.

As long as children are able to honor their parents into adolescence and adulthood, all of this remains possible. But not all children emerge from childhood having acquired this ability. Where children are not able to honor their parents, the line of transmission from the older generations to the younger is severed. Then the adolescent, regarding himself and a few friends his age as the most significant individuals in his universe, comes to attribute a greater weight and importance to their beliefs and behaviors than to those of anyone else. Having in this way armored himself against all tradition, experience, and wisdom, he goes astray after that paltry and haphazard collection of supposed insights that are shared within his set. In all this, he receives shocking encouragement from Enlightenment liberalism, with its baseless doctrine that children become the equals of their parents—and indeed, of all adults—once they are capable of reasoning well enough to pass exams in high school math. This fraudulent pretense has combined with the natural rebelliousness of adolescence to turn each new generation into an assembly of know-nothings, without a real capacity to gain from previous generations' experience of the past, whether in political, moral, and religious affairs, or in trades and professions, or in arts and crafts.

This problem of young men and women having contempt or disregard for the parents, teachers, and elders is not unique to the age of Enlightenment liberalism. We find many examples of it in Hebrew Scripture, and Plato already describes it as a disease of democratic regimes in particular. What is unusual about the age of liberalism is that the reigning public philosophy, which is studied and taught everywhere, justifies this disregard of parents, teachers, and elders by inculcating the liberty and equality of the individual as the ultimate political and moral principle. In this way, what was until recently considered to be a vice and a tragedy is now almost universally held to be a positive good, if not a natural right.

No doubt, some will object that the relationship between parents and children cannot remain hierarchical forever, and that a grave injustice will have been introduced into the fabric of the world if children are not, early in life, told that they are the equals of their parents and teachers. I reply as follows:

The human individual is not born free and equal. On the contrary, he is born weak, dependent, and ignorant—in the lowest position within a family hierarchy in which everyone he meets is stronger, wiser, and more capable than he is. However, there is a natural progression in every human hierarchy, whereby the young begin at the bottom, in positions having the least importance. In these lower positions, they give honor to their superiors and elders, treating their words and actions as having great weight. It is this, and only this, which permits the young to learn and attain competence and wisdom in any kind of endeavor. With time, these youths gain in knowledge, experience, and skill, and they rise in status until they take the place of their elders, who have died or stepped aside. What "equality" exists in this progress of human society results from the fact that the young may advance in knowledge and status, until one day they will acquire the importance and weightiness that now belongs to their elders and superiors. Then they will be parents and teachers, rulers and commanders, proprietors and accomplished scholars. And when this day comes, they themselves will be honored by the young, who will in this way repay them for having honored their own parents and teachers.

In a conservative society, then, young men and women have no wish ever to be the equals of their parents and their teachers. Their wish is rather to preserve intact and advance within the hierarchy into which they were born, while introducing improvements that will bring honor to their forefathers and benefit to their children and grandchildren. To this end, their childhood and young adulthood is spent learning everything they possibly can from their parents and elders, seeing that their time with them is limited and precious. They know that, while they will never be their parents' equals, all too soon they will have to part from them forever. Then they will have no choice but to be their parents' heirs and successors. And they hope and pray to be worthy when that day comes.

7. Cohesion and Dissolution

An important characteristic of human hierarchies is the quality that empiricist philosophers have called *cohesion* or *fellow feeling*, which is sometimes also called *solidarity*. Cohesion is that quality of hierarchies which describes the degree to which they maintain their shape under conditions of stress or adversity. A cohesive nation, tribe, or family is one that retains its integrity, remaining unified and whole, under conditions of material poverty, internal dissention, and war. This means that the respective tribes of the nation, or the individuals within the family, remain loyal to one another under duress. It means that decisions are made in accordance with a tolerable procedure and implemented without generating great internal strife and resistance. This is true even where these decisions are painful, where hardship and suffering is not distributed evenly, and where terrible mistakes are made, because all involved recognize that they must hold firm if they are to see the whole emerge intact and, if possible, strengthened. On the other hand, a hierarchy is said to be lacking in cohesion, or to be moving toward *dissolution* or *disintegration*, where the tribes within the nation, or the individuals within the family, are unable to remain loyal to one another under duress. This means that rather than pulling together in the face of adversity, they fall apart. It means that decisions cease to be accepted, and that they cease to be carried out. Instead, there is internal strife and resistance, and little ability to accept hardship and suffering, even where it is distributed evenly. And where mistakes are made, there is no forgiveness, because each part has lost the capacity to think of the whole and thinks only of itself.

A family undergoing dissolution ends in divorce. A nation undergoing dissolution moves toward secession, civil war, and foreign occupation.

Liberals, who wish to avoid thinking of society as characterized by mutual loyalty and hierarchy, are often appalled by talk of its cohesiveness and dissolution. The very idea of a cohesive society, they believe, is the product of an authoritarian cast of mind, which regards a people not as a collection of individuals but as a single organic substance. But every society is more or less cohesive, even if we pretend it is not so. And the relationship between cohesion and tyranny is actually the reverse of what is commonly supposed. Where a nation, tribe, or family is cohesive, it may be ruled with a light hand, and a greater degree of freedom can be entrusted to its constituent members. This is because the people are loyal to one another, and the leadership, even when it is not loved, is nevertheless honored. And so times of crisis bring about a revived unity and a capacity for joint action. Whereas when a nation, tribe, or family has become dissolute, its rulers respond with a heavy hand and suppress the freedom of the constituent members. This is because the people are not loyal to one another, and when they are given freedom, they use it only to express their anger, jealousy, hatred, and fear of one another in acts of abuse, cruelty, violence, and destruction, and in words of recrimination and defamation. Once this has gone far enough, the rule of a despot who will restrain the torrent of villainy comes to seem preferable, and talk of a savior eats away whatever traditions of distributed powers and individual rights there may have once been in the land, until no one can recall why they ever praised them.

In other words, it is precisely those who wish for mild government and generous liberties who should make it their business to speak of the cohesiveness of their society and to find ways of heightening this cohesion and resilience, rather than ceaselessly breaking it down.

Let us see how this may be done.

Consider, first, the cohesion of the family. As many already know, the dissolution of the family has been the great plague of our time. Since the hegemony of liberalism was established after the Second World War, men and women have found it progressively more difficult to marry, to remain married, to bring children into the world, and to raise them to maturity and adulthood. Although the dissolute character of today's families owes much to the fact that children see themselves as their parents' equals and find it demeaning to honor them, the ultimate source of this plague is the incapacity of adults to keep a marriage from failing. The constant shattering of families by divorce has unleashed a terrible fear of committing to marriage and having children among the young, who prefer to invest their time and resources in projects that seem more likely to end well. The result has been a dramatic decline both in marriage and in childbearing, as well as a generation of children who have grown up with little or no experience of cohesive families governed by a father and a mother.

It is a commonplace in our culture that the marriage of a man and a woman is largely the result of a sexual attraction on both sides. But a marriage that is based on sexual attraction alone will quickly disintegrate, because this kind of attraction weakens with time. The principal force that preserves a marriage in the face of inevitable hardship is mutual loyalty, which is maintained and strengthened through the constant giving of honor. To see why this is so, remember that we are always a mirror to others, reflecting the degree to which we recognize them as possessing weightiness or importance. A wife can increase the *kavod* or weightiness of her husband, and a husband can increase the *kavod* of his wife, in much the same way that they each give honor to their parents: by inquiring regarding their preferences and their counsel; by acting in accordance with their preferences wherever possible, and by avoiding contradicting or embarrassing them when it is not; and in general by praising their achievements and their virtues, their speech and their behavior, both in their presence and when not in their presence. Of necessity, husbands and wives must criticize and correct one another, but traditional societies teach the young how to do this in a manner that contains the least insult—for example, by making sure that criticism is delivered in private, in quiet tones, and in a context that emphasizes that one's spouse is still honored in spite of the criticism or correction.

Such a constant concern of a husband and wife to honor each other and to avoid, at all costs, insulting, embarrassing, disregarding, and dishonoring each other, has a decisive effect on the mutual loyalty that binds them together. This loyalty is experienced by each as a feeling that the other is "mine" and "a part of me." Where a husband is constantly honored by his wife, he easily sees that he is important in her eyes, and this has the effect of increasing her importance in his own. And the same is true where a wife is constantly honored by her husband. These acts of honoring, whereby a husband intentionally and consistently elevates his wife to greater significance, and where a wife elevates her husband to greater significance, cause the feelings of loyalty that are experienced by each to intensify. For the force of every emotion varies with the significance of the individual to whom it is directed. So a mutual loyalty, constantly strengthened by acts of honoring, has sweeping effects in marriage, intensifying the desire that each feels for the other—just as insult and dishonor breed feelings of disgust and anger, which are the seeds of disloyalty and dissolution.

Constant acts of honoring, of giving *kavod*, are thus the source of a cohesive marital bond, which retains its integrity, remaining unified and whole, under conditions of material hardship, internal disagreement, and external predation. On the other hand, a marriage becomes dissolute where a husband and wife do not constantly give honor to each other. Then every disagreement becomes an excuse for insult and anger, accusations and slanders proliferate, and where mistakes are made, there is no forgiveness, because each has lost the capacity to think of the other as a part of himself. When contempt and humiliation have in this way dissolved what loyalty there once was, strangers lie in wait, ready to invade the home and take what they can for themselves.

Moreover, children growing up in a home in which both father and mother consistently honor each other find it relatively easy to follow their lead and to give honor to their parents. But the opposite is true as well. Where a wife fails to honor her husband, demonstrating his insignificance to her and her disloyalty to him, or when a husband mistreats his wife in this way, the parents' weightiness in the eyes of the children is damaged. Children growing up in a home in which their parents frequently express contempt for each other find it easy to have feelings of contempt for their parents. In this way, the dissolution of the marital bond works as an acid on the loyalties that bind the children to their parents. The children become confused as to where their loyalties lie and confused regarding their obligations. We find, therefore, that expressions of contempt between a husband and wife are not merely indications of a dissolute marriage, but of the dissolution of the family as a whole.

The same thing is true when parents express contempt for other figures who are superior to them in the workplace or in the political life of the nation, or if they express disregard for persons who are superior to their children in hierarchies outside the home. An example is a father who shows by his speech or actions that he considers his child's teacher to be of little significance. This brings the child to see his teacher as a person who may be disregarded, and he will quickly cease to learn from his teachers as a result.

As a young father, I made this mistake once in a scene that will remain in my mind forever. My son, then twelve, was excitedly recounting something he had learned from a torah instructor in school, and at a certain point I foolishly intervened to correct him. Upon hearing my words, my son's smile disappeared from his face and his spirit gave out within him. He bowed his head in shame. I knew at that moment that I had dishonored my son's teacher and humiliated my son for having accepted instruction from him. I had been eager to make sure that my son should immediately know the truth of the matter, when I should have been more concerned to preserve his ability to honor his teacher. This is because honoring one's teachers is difficult, just as honoring one's parents is difficult, and a child who has mastered this discipline has gained one of the most important skills he will need in life. But it is also because the cause of truth is not served by embarrassing or making light of a teacher from whom a child is able to learn. Upon reaching adolescence, a young man will in any case begin working out the truth for himself in various matters, and in these efforts, there is never any fear that he will give insufficient weight and thought to his parents' views, so long as he has learned to honor his parents and his teachers. Whereas if an adolescent is quick to express contempt for his teachers because of his father's pronouncements against them, he will soon discover that he can easily dismiss his father's views in just the same way. And then learning any truth from his parents will become a difficult matter indeed.

The cohesiveness of a strong family is born out of the honor that a husband and wife give each other, and of the honor that children learn to give their parents as a result. Where a husband and wife do not constantly give honor and weight to each other, the children will likewise cease to give honor and weight to their parents. Then the bonds of mutual loyalty that are the substance of the family will tend toward dissolution, and the family's ability to retain its integrity, unity, and wholeness under conditions of duress will dissipate.

All these things are true, as well, of larger loyalty groups such as the nation. While the ties that are established through consent may seem strong in a given moment, they are variable and unreliable in the longer term. The kind of bond that endures, one of mutual loyalty, is established and grows ever stronger where the heads of the tribes or factions that make up the nation give honor and weight to one another in words and deeds. This is the source of a cohesive national bond, which retains its integrity, remaining unified and whole, under conditions of material hardship, internal disagreement, and external predation. On the other hand, a nation becomes dissolute where the heads of the various tribes or factions do not give honor and weight to one another. Then every disagreement becomes an excuse for insult and anger, accusations and slanders proliferate, and when mistakes are made there is no forgiveness, because each has lost the capacity to think of the other as a part of himself. When contempt and humiliation have dissolved what loyalty there once was, the nation moves toward violence between these brutalized tribes, and strangers appear at the perimeter, waiting for the right moment to invade the country and take what they can for themselves.

For many in America, Britain, and other countries today, wracked as they are by an internal strife that never sleeps, these observations may seem difficult to credit. After all, when a nation is governed as a democracy, the respective factions compete with one another for the votes of the public. Does this not inevitably involve insult and anger, accusations and slanders? Why would any political party give honor to its rivals?

To be sure, democracy involves the public airing of disputes. But we need only recall the political culture of a generation ago to recognize that the expressions of loathing, wild accusations, conspiracy theories, and boycotts that have lately come to characterize American and British public life are not an inevitable accoutrement of a democratic regime. Watch the old videotapes of John F. Kennedy debating Richard Nixon in 1960, or of Ronald Reagan debating Jimmy Carter in 1980. Whatever the true feelings of these men may have been, their public demeanor was one of restrained, and even good-natured, competition. In these debates, their comportment is mild, relentlessly focused on proposed policies and their effects, and avoids the direct expressions of personal disregard and disdain that constantly emerge from the mouths of our public figures today. While a great deal is at stake in these contests, the champions of the rival parties display a degree of respect for one another, and at times even of trust in one another, which is meant to leave the possibility of future cooperation intact and to guarantee that the voting public's respect for its elected government will not be severely impaired if the rival party should hold office until the next election. Moreover, both parties are careful to invoke those interests of the nation concerning which they believe there can be genuine agreement, and to focus attention on the external threats that are commonly understood to face the nation as a whole. In this way, they frame the disagreements between them as having less than paramount importance, especially when compared to the challenges the people must meet together.

There is no need to be naïve about this. Rival political parties, even in those better days, were not above fearmongering and hurling mud at one another. And yet the fact remains: This was a democratic culture in which the major parties found ways to compete effectively while giving honor to one another and granting legitimacy to one another, thereby strengthening the cohesiveness of the nation. Today, politics has declined to the point that fearmongering and hurling mud is what is constantly put before the public. No signs of respect, no shred of legitimation for the other side, is permitted to enter discourse between rivals, but only vile expressions of contempt, disgust, distrust, and hatred. This is a dissolute politics, in which concern for the cohesion of the nation is subordinated to personal and party ambition, and the mutual loyalty of the people is burned away on the bleak altar of momentary advantage.

Like children whose parents incessantly quarrel before them, and who, for this reason, find they cannot honor their parents or remain loyal to them, but instead think only of saving themselves, the competing parties in such a riven country eventually cease to regard the continued unity of the nation as worth defending. And then the most extreme proposals for how to escape a now forsaken union come to be entertained.

8. Traditional Institutions

The fourth premise of the conservative paradigm is that *Language, religion, law, and the forms of government and economic activity are traditional institutions, developed by families, tribes, and nations as they seek to strengthen their material prosperity, internal integrity, and cultural inheritance and to propagate themselves through future generations.*

This premise regards families, tribes, and nations as collectives that propagate themselves through time, raising up new generations of men and women and teaching them to participate in, and to pass on, a diverse array of traditional institutions. By a *traditional institution*, I mean any social structure or form of speech or behavior that is passed down from one generation to the next. The language of a people is in this sense a traditional institution. So are the skills used to hunt and to farm the land, to keep order and fend off intruders, to celebrate victories and mourn tragedies, to recall great persons and great deeds, to permit competition and recognize status, to increase knowledge and preserve it, to educate the young and bring them into a capable adulthood, to care for the sick and part from the dead. Similarly, the way in which God (or the gods) is perceived and understood, the proper rituals for honoring him, and the venerated literature and laws of a people, are traditional institutions. Places and place names that are handed down from one generation to the next are traditional institutions, which transform a natural landscape into one that is endowed with a particular meaning for a certain family, tribe, or nation. So are the names and symbols we associate with the various families, tribes, and nations of mankind.

We have seen that a family, tribe, or nation is always ordered as a hierarchy, and that this hierarchy results from the awarding of honor, which gives the various members greater or lesser weight and significance in comparison to one another. What I wish to understand now is how the transmission of traditional institutions—which is the heart of any conservative politics—is related to honor and hierarchy.

We can think of the hierarchical structure of the nation, tribe, or family, as the medium through which traditional institutions propagate. Much as a wave propagates in a liquid, maintaining its form as it moves through the medium, a belief or behavior can be seen to propagate in a given hierarchy, descending vertically from the older generation to its children, from the generation of the children to the grandchildren, and so on. Since new generations are always being added to the hierarchy from below, even as the older generations die away, a traditional institution can continue to propagate through the medium of the hierarchy indefinitely. Indeed, it will continue to propagate so long as new generations are inducted into the hierarchy and so long as these new generations honor their parents and teachers, thereby gaining the ability to learn from them. At the same time, each traditional institution is a constitutive element within the unique character of the nation, tribe, or family in which it propagates, serving as a sign of its particular identity and worth.

What is the mechanism by means of which such propagation takes place?

The persistence of a traditional institution depends on the honor that is awarded to individuals for upholding it. This is because people persist in any effort when they are honored for it, or when they believe they will be honored for it in the future; and they become dispirited and desist when their effort is met with disregard and contempt. Of course, we have all witnessed instances in which individuals persist in saying and doing things that they know will bring disdain and abuse upon them at the hands of the surrounding society. But if we investigate such cases, we find that much of the time, the persons in question choose to endure abuse from outside of their own family, community, tribe, or nation, because they know they will be honored for their fortitude within their own loyalty group. Alternatively, they may be willing to accept the disdain of their family, community, tribe, or nation, because they believe they will be honored for it by a dissident or breakaway faction that has emerged within their own loyalty group. It is rare, however, to find an individual who is willing to endure contempt and abuse for words and deeds that he believes will be honored nowhere and by no one.

In this context, it is worth noticing that an individual will at times be honored from outside of a hierarchy to which he is loyal. There is no one who is not pleased to be honored by a rival, or by the members of a different tribe or a foreign nation. At times, honor is all the more precious because it comes from an unexpected place, and we entertain a special fondness for those rivals or strangers who have troubled themselves to honor us. And such alien honors may have lasting consequences. When a husband leaves his wife for another woman, or, more generally, when an individual abandons his community, tribe, or nation and becomes loyal to another, he is usually motivated by the sense that he will be better honored elsewhere. Similarly, much of the erratic behavior of adolescents arises from just this source: the craving to be highly regarded, which, when it cannot be sated in the circle of their own family, drives them to seek and find honor in other, often quite dubious, circles.

We may therefore take this to be a principle of human nature: We wish to be honored by the hierarchy to which we are loyal. But wherever we are honored, our loyalty tends to take root and grow.

With this in mind, let us ask: How do certain things come to be honored within a given hierarchy, and not others?

When we consider the endless variety of tribes and clans, families and nations into which human beings are divided, we find that every one of them is characterized by a certain *consensus*, by which we mean an inclination or judgment that is felt generally throughout a particular public. This general inclination determines which opinions and behaviors are deemed praiseworthy and honorable and which are held to be despicable and dishonorable. It may also determine that certain opinions or behaviors are a matter of indifference, to be tolerated without being honored or dishonored. And in many cases, we find that two competing opinions are both honored, or perhaps several. In all these cases, we may say that the various honored options, as well as those that are tolerated, are considered *legitimate*, whereas those that are dishonored are taken to be *illegitimate*. For instance, it may be honorable in a democratic society to support any of a number of competing political parties that are held to be legitimate, and yet dishonorable to support fanatical or fringe parties whose aim is to overthrow the traditional regime of the country.

The consensus as to what is honored and dishonored, legitimate and illegitimate, varies from one family to the next, from one community to the next, and from one nation to the next. But it is often stable within a given family, community, tribe, or nation for generations. And wherever we see that a traditional institution or norm propagates from one generation to the next, we find that this is because there exists a stable consensus that awards honor to those who uphold this traditional institution or norm, and that has disregard, and sometimes outright contempt, for those who undermine it. We can also see that when the consensus that gives honor to a certain institution falters, the institution itself begins to fail; and when the consensus to honor an institution is restored, the institution itself is restored. For example, when marriage and child-rearing ceased to be honored above other ways of conducting one's life in the 1960s, the familiar forms of marriage quickly began to disintegrate. Within a few years, age-old stigmas against divorce, adultery, cohabitation, abortion, single motherhood, homosexual unions, pornography, prostitution, and many other formerly disreputable behaviors were disarmed, and the ability of much of the public to maintain marriages and raise children collapsed.

Of course, not everything that is honored within a given loyalty group is a traditional institution. In every society, many things that are widely honored are passing fads or fashions. But in a conservative society, many of the most honored forms of speech and behavior are handed down from one generation to the next. Whereas in a revolutionary society, what is honored and dishonored shifts constantly, so that even the passage of a few years leaves the previous forms of speech and behavior in ruins, while new ones are enthusiastically embraced. Nevertheless, the propagation of an institution or norm from one generation to the next depends entirely on the existence, within a given loyalty group, of a consensus honoring those who uphold the institution in question. And so, if we want anything at all to be conserved across generations, we must understand where such consensus comes from.

Enlightenment rationalism supposes that individuals, if they reason freely about political and moral subjects without reference to tradition, will quickly discover the truth concerning these matters and move toward a consensus. But experience suggests just the opposite: When people reason freely about political and moral questions, they produce a profusion of varying and contradictory opinions, reaching no consensus at all. Indeed, the only thing that reasoning without reference to some traditional framework can do with great competence is identify an unlimited number of flaws and failings, both imagined and real, in whatever institutions and norms have been inherited from the past. Where individuals are encouraged to engage in this activity, the process of finding flaws in inherited institutions proceeds with ever greater speed and enthusiasm, until in the end whatever has been inherited becomes a thing of lightness and folly in their eyes. In this way, they come to reject all the old ideas and behaviors, uprooting and discarding everything that was once a matter of consensus. This means that Enlightenment rationalism, to the extent that its program is taken seriously, is an engine of perpetual revolution, which brings about the progressive destruction of every inherited institution, yet without ever being able to consolidate a stable consensus around any new ones.

In reality, consensus does not arise from free debate without reference to any particular tradition of ideas. Instead, consensus is a characteristic of human hierarchies, and it is only within a given hierarchy that this characteristic appears. We tend to believe the things that we hear from important individuals within a hierarchy to which we are loyal, to act in accordance with their preferences, and to imitate them in their style of speech and behavior.[19] This natural influence, which the most important members of every hierarchy exert over its less prominent members, is the mechanism by which consensus is produced in human societies. Hierarchies tend to reach consensus regarding a given belief or behavior after a few prominent individuals—at times, only one or two are enough—have expressed their views on a subject. Once these prominent individuals have taken more or less the same position, persons of lesser status within the hierarchy will seek praise by endorsing what these important individuals say and do in order to gain in status or weightiness both in the eyes of their superiors, who are pleased with this reinforcement of their views; and in the eyes of their inferiors, who will usually admire them for defending the views and behaviors of the leading figures in the hierarchy to which they are loyal. At the same time, those who disagree with the leading figures in their hierarchy will soften their own views, go silent on the subject, or reverse themselves entirely. Indeed, I have found that in every social hierarchy, many individuals are entirely unaware of the fact that they accept whatever the important individuals at the top of their own hierarchy say or do.

I remember this every time someone urges some supposedly "self-evident" principle on me, informing me that the error is entirely mine when I reply that it does not appear to be self-evident at all. Usually, the person in question is unaware that he has adopted the ideas and thoughts of important persons within a particular hierarchy to which he is loyal; and that he now goes about applying these ideas and invoking these thoughts with disturbing frequency, in all sorts of circumstances that seem relevant. Yet the more often he applies these ideas and invokes these thoughts, the more "clear and distinct" and "self-evident" they become to him. And so the self-evidence he keeps talking about is quite real. But it means something very different from what he thinks it means. For "self-evidence" is an indication that something has been said a great many times within a certain social hierarchy, so that it has become a matter of consensus in that closed circle. It tells us nothing about whether the thought in question is true or not.

These things are true of all human hierarchies. We see the same things repeating themselves in every profession and discipline, congregation, tribe, nation, and family of nations. We see them in conservative hierarchies, in which ancient institutions that have been handed down for centuries continue to be honored and upheld. And we see precisely the same phenomenon among Marxists and liberals, academics and journalists—social groups in which it is often said that a person should "think critically" and "think for himself," yet no one seems to notice how rare it is for anyone to mount a dissent once the leading figures within these respective hierarchies have made their views known. Indeed, even if the consensus on a given subject was born only recently, and even if it will change again tomorrow, the great majority of these "critical thinkers" can be counted on to accept the new thinking when it comes.

Of course, a human hierarchy is not a machine, and there will always be a small number of individuals who disagree with certain views held by the important persons within the hierarchy to which they are loyal. And on rare occasion, their determined opposition may even alter the consensus, especially when circumstances change or new facts come to light, paving the way for some prominent individuals to revisit the matter. Nevertheless, it is important to recognize that these occasions are so much discussed and admired because they are exceptions. In almost every case, the great majority fall into line, embracing the consensus that arises once the most important individuals have endorsed a particular view or behavior.

From these considerations, we understand as follows. Human hierarchies tend to move rapidly toward consensus regarding what is honored and dishonored once a number of their most prominent members have expressed similar views on a given subject. This means that where the leading figures in a given hierarchy treat the views of the generations that preceded them as a matter of no great weight or importance, the entire hierarchy will be cut loose from its inherited institutions and will cease to transmit them to new generations. But where the leading figures in a given hierarchy regard the views of their predecessors as things of great weight and significance, and speak and behave in such a way as to emphasize this weight and significance, the hierarchy will tend toward a consensus that honors those who uphold the traditional institutions and disregards or dishonors those who fail to uphold them. This is what makes the hierarchy a medium capable of propagating traditional institutions through the generations. And wherever such a propagation of traditional institutions occurs, we find that the leading figures within the hierarchy in question are diligent in cultivating and defending a consensus that honors those who uphold inherited institutions, and disregards or dishonors those who do not.

Marxists and liberals have often deplored this kind of conservative leadership, arguing that where honor is awarded to those who uphold the traditional institutions, this must come at the expense of reason, justice, and truth, which are thereby suppressed. But in my experience, conservative figures of consequence are at least as concerned with reason, justice, and truth as their Marxist or liberal counterparts—and frequently more so. However, conservatives understand what is required by these principles in a different way from their revolutionary critics.

Consider, for example, the famous question of how one goes about repairing and improving inherited institutions. Actual conservatives—as opposed to the ones who live in the imagination of their detractors—know very well that repairs must periodically be introduced into traditional institutions to ensure their preservation and transmission, and in consideration of the requirements of justice and truth. However, a conservative also recognizes that any repair tends to discredit those who uphold tradition and shifts honor to those who advocate change. This is dangerous because it means that society may be cut loose from the entire edifice of its beneficial traditions in the wake of a necessary repair. Thus conservatives seek to undertake repairs in such a way as to increase the weightiness and importance of the edifice of traditional institutions in the eyes of the public, thereby strengthening it even as alterations are introduced. The techniques for doing this are well known. Conservative leadership tends to introduce repairs, wherever possible, by means of limited shifts in the extent to which the respective elements of the tradition are honored. This involves placing a renewed emphasis on neglected provisions of the traditional law, or on historical figures or revered texts that have been forgotten but are now seen as relevant once more. When the necessity of a more dramatic change is recognized, conservative leadership will seek a *restoration*, which is a public effort to reinstate institutions that are known from the past but have been weakened or eliminated over time. Honoring past institutions in this way permits the inherited edifice as a whole to be strengthened, even as alterations are introduced.

There are also cases in which conservative leadership, recognizing that certain innovations are needed, relies upon precedents from neighboring nations whose traditional institutions have demonstrated their beneficial character. A useful example is the introduction of the mercantile law into the common law courts as Britain's commercial activities increased in the eighteenth century. On the one hand, the mercantile law allowed the common law courts to oversee an immense strengthening of the country's economy by introducing legal forms in areas such as contracts and insurance, which had been developed in Italy and the Netherlands to support commercial activity. On the other hand, it was the mercantile law that permitted merchants to bring slaves purchased overseas to England, forcing the courts to fight this repugnant innovation through a restoration of the traditional view that the common law does not support the institution of slavery. In this example, we see both the promise and the danger of introducing foreign institutions, which can do great harm as well as good. The success of such a reliance on foreign precedents depends on the presence of a self-consciously conservative leadership, which recognizes that innovations introduced in the past have been carried too far, and is willing to impose a partial restoration of previous conditions when this proves necessary.

With these things in mind, let us turn to the claim that conservative political and moral discourse places a commitment to existing institutions above the exercise of reason.

Anyone who takes part in the life of a conservative nation or tribe, community or family, profession or discipline, knows that reasoned discourse and argument take place constantly in such societies. But the reasoning is of a different kind from that of Enlightenment rationalists, who begin by saying something about all human individuals or all governments and then try to deduce what is right and wrong for all mankind from these assertions. In conservative societies, arguments proceed differently, beginning with the existence of a given nation, tribe, congregation, or family, or some other loyalty group, and proceeding to ask what steps must be taken to strengthen the loyalty group and improve conditions for its members. Such *constructive reasoning* reaches conclusions by balancing the demands of material prosperity, security, internal cohesion, and the preservation and transmission of traditional institutions—demands that often conflict with one another, and whose relative weight and significance change with the actual circumstances. In this context, arguments over what is just and true arise constantly, but they are made with reference to practical issues and framed in terms of inherited principles. As this discussion proceeds, proposals are made for applying the inherited framework to new subjects, for introducing concepts that simplify the framework and render it more compelling, and for repairing those aspects of the tradition that have become dated or harmful—but generally in a manner that increases the honor that is given to the tradition and those who uphold it. In this way, a greater justice and truth can be sought, yet without bringing the existing society to dissolution and overthrowing everything that is productive and valuable in it; and while leaving open the option of restoring earlier conditions if the repairs introduced turn out to do more harm than good.

Constructive reasoning is rightly regarded as a conservative form of reasoning, since its purpose is to build upon the earlier achievements of a given nation or tribe, or of some other loyalty group. Through it, we adapt a political or legal system to new contingencies and concerns. But this is possible only where the statesmen, jurists, philosophers, and theologians involved in this work are loyal to the nation, seeking to honor inherited institutions and their great predecessors who established them, to maintain the cohesion of the people by avoiding unnecessary internal divisions and hatreds, and to refrain from introducing repairs that are more general than the present adjustment requires. Where such loyalties are weak, statesmen, jurists, philosophers, and theologians are given to praising their own powers of reason rather than the achievements of their forefathers. Then the humility and empiricism of the conservative is encountered less frequently, the desire to ponder old books grows slack, and the method of constructive reasoning comes to seem too burdensome to be borne.

This is in contrast to what is called *critical reasoning*, which positions itself outside the framework of a given nation and its inherited institutions, without a prior commitment to their preservation. Such reasoning identifies an unlimited number of flaws and failings, both imagined and real, in the traditional institutions of any nation or tribe it examines. And since its purpose is not the preservation of the nation and its institutions, it is satisfied with multiplying and amplifying the grounds for criticism until all the old ideas and behaviors are dishonored and discarded. Critical reasoning is properly regarded as a revolutionary form of reasoning.

9. Political Obligation

The fifth premise of a conservative political theory is that *Political obligation is a consequence of membership in loyalty groups such as the family, tribe, and nation.*

Enlightenment liberalism supposes that political obligation has its source in the consent of the individual. Although this is regarded as a theory of political obligation, it is more accurately described as a theory of the individual's freedom from political obligation. Because if the source of political obligation is consent, political obligation ceases when consent is withdrawn. This theory was originally intended to establish a right of revolution, by which a people, not consenting to be ruled in the present manner, might depose their government; or a right of secession, whereby a colony, such as the British colonies in America, might withdraw from any obligation to the mother country. It also suggested that slaves who were unwilling to continue in their servitude were to be freed—perhaps the most beneficial consequence of the theory. Yet by this same argument, a husband who no longer consents to remain with his wife is thereby freed of the obligations of marriage; and a child, reaching the age of maturity, is likewise liberated from having any obligations to his parents; and a citizen, if he does not consent, is for this reason free of the obligation to render military service in wartime; and so on. In the hands of liberal political theory, all of these relationships and others, which were once considered to bear obligations, were transformed into things one might choose to do or not do with one's freedom.

The results of this happy form of reasoning, according to which no one is ever under any obligation he does not want, are plain to see. Liberal society is one in which everyone is free to pursue happiness, but the most obvious things that must be done to ensure that a family, community, or nation remains functional and whole have become optional. Thus men are free to abandon their wives, leaving them to raise their children alone. Children are free to abandon their parents in old age. Business enterprises are free to abandon their employees and relocate their jobs to foreign lands. Communities are free to teach a condescending disdain for their forefathers in the schools. The mentally ill are free to roam the streets, abusing alcohol and narcotics without appropriate care. And no one is under any obligation to rise in the defense of his country or to acknowledge God, creator of heaven and earth. And the same is true for most of the other obligations that were known to earlier generations.[20]

Such conditions cannot endure—because, in reality, there are many things that we must do if our families and communities are to prosper and grow strong in the face of duress, and if the nation that is our home is to escape descending into civil war or being overrun. And we must do these things even if we do not wish to do them. This is to say that we are under certain obligations, whether we consent to them or not.

But if obligation does not arise from the consent or agreement of the individual, where does it come from?

We can take a first step toward answering this question by observing that while consent is required to establish certain kinds of obligations, as a general matter, political obligation has little or nothing to do with consent. A child does not, after all, consent to being born to his parents. Nevertheless, the child bears an obligation to honor his parents and care for them in old age, even if he should loudly protest that he never consented to these things and wants nothing to do with them. Indeed, we would regard such protests as a deformity in his character, or perhaps simply as wickedness, rather than as an indication that he has no obligations to his parents. Similarly, a child does not consent to being born into a given tribe or nation. Yet he is obliged to obey its laws, to pay its taxes, and to take up arms to defend it in time of war. And where an individual refuses to obey the laws, pay taxes, or serve in wartime on the grounds that he never consented, he is treated as a criminal and subjected to fines, imprisonment, or death. His lack of consent does not mean he is free of any obligation to his country.

These things are well known to anyone with experience of how human beings actually live. And once we admit them, it is evident that political and moral obligation arises not from the consent of the individual, but from the existence of a certain *relation* between the individual and another person or collective. It is the existence of a relation of parent and child, and not anyone's consent to it, that is the source of the obligations of children toward their parents and of parents toward their children. Similarly, it is the existence of a certain relation between the individual and the family or nation to which he belongs, and not anyone's consent, that is the source of his obligations to his family or nation, as well as of the obligations of his family and nation toward him. And the same can be said of most other political or moral obligations that arise.

We must better understand such relations, then, and see how their existence establishes political and moral obligation.

What binds the respective members of a family, tribe, or nation to one another is mutual loyalty, and the basis for a relation of loyalty is the recognition and feeling that another individual or a collective is a part of my self.[21] Because individual human beings instinctively seek to protect, strengthen, and advance themselves, this recognition and feeling means, in practice, that human individuals seek to protect, strengthen, and advance other individuals and collectives as if they were a part of themselves. And the relation is mutual if the individual to whom I am loyal likewise seeks to protect and strengthen me out of a recognition and feeling that I am a part of his self; or, in the case of a collective, if its leading figures seek to protect and strengthen me out of a recognition and feeling that I am a part of themselves.

Of course, not everyone lives up to the demands of these relations at all times. A husband may betray his wife by carrying on with another woman, and a citizen may betray his nation by passing information to a hostile government. Nevertheless, the existence of a relation of mutual loyalty establishes a standard or norm that the individual may attain or fail to attain, and against which his behavior can be judged.[22] When I act to protect, strengthen, and advance another person to whom I am bound in a relation of mutual loyalty, I am doing what I must to uphold this standard or norm. Whereas if I act to harm and humiliate someone to whom I am bound in this way, I am failing to uphold this standard or norm. And the same can be said of my relations with my family, tribe, or nation.

From these things, we understand that when we speak of an obligation or a duty, we are usually referring to an action or inaction that is needed to uphold a particular relation of mutual loyalty.[23] When I am doing what I must to uphold the relation in question, I am fulfilling my obligation under this relation; and when I fail to uphold it, I am violating my obligation under this relation and failing or betraying those to whom I am bound by this relation.

We now have an initial view of the source of political and moral obligation in relations of mutual loyalty. But my description, being very general, obscures the variety that exists in relations of different kinds, and in the specific ways in which the obligation to protect, strengthen, and advance another manifests itself in these different kinds of relations. For example, the relation between a parent and child is one of mutual loyalty. However, it is also steeply hierarchical, with no hint of equality in it. Indeed, in a traditional relation of parent and child, the substance of what each side gives the other is not similar at all. The parents' obligation is to protect and educate their child, whereas the child's obligation is to honor his parents. This distinction is important because in educating children, a parent must reinforce certain behaviors by honoring them, while deterring misbehavior by administering measured doses of disapproval and dishonor. In fact, the skill of raising children is, in no small part, that of administering honor and dishonor in appropriate measure, and in ways that are fitting to the changing needs of the child as he grows. The parent's obligation to educate the child is therefore incompatible with a general obligation of giving honor—that is, with an obligation of the kind that characterizes the relation of the child to the parent.

As is evident from this example, the particular form of a given relation is not something that can be known by reasoning deductively from abstract propositions concerning the essential nature of human beings. For instance, we cannot know anything about a child's obligation to honor his father and his mother, or about their obligation to educate their son or daughter, from an abstract proposition that human beings are "free" and "equal" by nature. Nor does it help much to say that human beings are "rational" and "social" by nature, or that it is their nature to procreate. These statements are so broad, and can be understood in so many different ways, that they tell us almost nothing about the real relations between parents and children. A true understanding of the obligations on either side of these relations is learned only with difficulty. It is the result of long experience, including the observation of many instances of such relations, both those that have been successful and those that have failed. It is such experience that stands behind each of the traditional forms of human relations with which we are familiar. And each society will have its own scheme of such forms, which will vary in light of the divergent experiences of different tribes and nations.

Are there circumstances in which the obligations arising from a certain relation may be abrogated? This is obviously so. In a case of grave abuse, in which a child is severely damaged by a parent, or in which a tribe or nation does extreme and unjustified harm to some of its members, an obligation that was otherwise firm will be weakened or rendered void. For this reason, we may say that Moses was right to flee the decree of death at the hands of Pharaoh, although his flight involved severing the bonds that must have existed between an adopted son of Pharaoh's daughter and the royal court in which he was raised. For similar reasons, we should say that Socrates would have been justified in fleeing Athens, rather than drinking the hemlock as the laws of the city called upon him to do. But as the extremity of these examples suggests, no mere absence of consent is sufficient to void the obligations that arise from bonds of mutual loyalty within a family or a nation. One is not released from a political or moral bond simply because one chooses not to be obligated by it any longer. And this applies, as well, to the famous case of American independence, which was not justified by the colonials having withdrawn their consent to be governed by Britain, but by their claim, elaborated in the Declaration of Independence, that they had been gravely abused by their king. The institution of slavery in the American South should also have been recognized as a matter of grave abuse, just as the bondage of Israel in Egypt is so recognized in Scripture.[24]

Having recognized these characteristics of political obligation, we can better understand the character of those obligations that are established by an act of consent. It is true that a marriage comes into being through the consent of a man and a woman. But the obligations of a husband toward his wife—to honor her, to be faithful to her, to provide and care for her, to be a good father to her children, and more—do not arise from consent, and her obligations to him do not arise from consent. Rather, these obligations arise from the existence of a relation of husband and wife, just as various obligations arise from the existence of a relation of parent and child and from the existence of a relation between an individual and the nation into which he was born. This is why, even if a husband should awake one morning and announce that he no longer consents to the marital relation between himself and his wife, and thereafter takes up living with another woman he has met, still the original relation of husband and wife persists, and the obligations that arise from this relation persist. Of course, there exists the possibility of divorce or annulment, and the respective political and religious traditions describe the precise conditions under which the obligations imposed by a marital relation can be considered to have been lifted. Nevertheless, the withdrawal of consent is never sufficient to lift these obligations by itself.

The same is true when a family adopts a child, or when an immigrant chooses to become a member of a new nation. In these cases, too, a relationship is established by choice and consent. Yet once the relationship has been established, the relation is itself the source of obligation, and withdrawal of consent cannot, in and of itself, lift the obligations established by this relation.

Until now, I have been discussing obligations that arise from relations of mutual loyalty within the family, tribe, and nation. But more generally, we can see that obligation arises wherever a relation of mutual loyalty exists. Thus there is an obligation to honor one's mentor or teacher, which cannot be discharged simply by paying the teacher the wages that are owed to him according to his contract. Similarly, there are obligations that exist between individuals who have been business partners of long standing, or between an employer and an employee of long standing, and here, too, the obligations that derive from these relations of mutual loyalty cannot be exhausted simply by fulfilling the terms of a written contract. There are relations of mutual loyalty, as well, among soldiers who have served together in combat, whose obligations to one another cannot be said simply to have ended because the term of their military service is done. And other such relations could be named, in which an obligation to protect, strengthen, and advance another individual is recognized and felt to exist, though the nature and extent of these obligations is not so well-defined as those between a parent and child or those between a husband and wife.

Although relations based on mutual loyalty are the principal source of political and moral obligation, biblical tradition establishes obligations that arise from relations of other kinds, such as the relation between judge and litigant, between warrior and captive, between seller and buyer, and between the stronger individuals in society and the widow, the orphan, and the poor. In all of these relations, a bond of mutual loyalty seems to be absent, or at least weak. Yet the Mosaic law strengthens these relations by invoking more general bonds of mutual loyalty: For instance, a principle of loyalty to each individual member of one's nation is proposed in the famous exhortation to "love your neighbor as yourself."[25] We are also told to love the stranger who is living among us as we love ourselves, "for you were strangers in the land of Egypt."[26] Here, a principle of mutual loyalty is proposed between ourselves, as the descendants of foreigners who once suffered abuse, and others who now suffer as we once did. From these two principles—love of one's nation and love of the stranger—it might be possible to derive most of the interpersonal obligations of the Mosaic law that do not arise directly from relations of mutual loyalty. But the biblical tradition does not seek to place such a burden on these principles. Instead, all of our obligations are understood to derive from the terms of the covenant, which has established a relation of mutual loyalty between man and God.[27]

The political and moral arena is filled with obligations. However, since attention and resources are limited, the various obligations can and do compete with one another: Our obligations to our parents cannot be so great that we neglect our children, and our obligations to our children cannot be so great that we do not defend our country in time of need. And the same will be true of the obligations that arise from our other relations. Each one limits the resources available for carrying out the others, so that in practice, each obligation is limited by the others. The precise manner in which the respective obligations are balanced against one another is known only by common sense, which is to say, by means of traditions honored and elaborated within particular families, tribes, and nations.

When a person acts in a balanced and proportionate manner, so that he upholds his obligations to every individual and every loyalty group, this quality is called *justice* and the person himself is said to be *just*. But what is balanced and proportionate can never be established by deduction from abstract principles. Justice itself must be discovered in the life of actual nations, tribes, and families, as they seek to establish a righteous and sustainable understanding of the obligations that are due in complex and difficult circumstances.

10. Freedom and Constraint

A competent political theory is concerned not only with *freedom*, but also with its opposite, which is *constraint*. When we consider it, we see that human individuals need constraint as much as they need freedom. Constraint, in other words, is no less essential to our nature than freedom. We must therefore ask what constraint is for, where it comes from, and how it can be built up to create a political order that is stable and resilient, and capable of maintaining itself from one generation to the next.

Every skill I possess, every behavior that permits me to create something of value, is a consequence of my capacity for constraint. If I wish to be able to read from the torah in the traditional manner, or to prepare cooked meals, or to disarm an armed assailant bare-handed, or to play a musical instrument, I gain these skills not by insisting on my freedom to do as I please, but through a deliberate exercise of constraint: I imitate others who are proficient in the relevant techniques, forcing myself to repeat the precise forms that must be acquired time and again, even when I am weary and do not wish to continue. In the same way, my marriage, remaining faithful to my wife and bringing children into the world and raising them, involves a disciplined, ongoing curtailment of my freedom. To make it work, I am constrained to refrain from relations with other women. I am constrained to care each day for young people who are often angry, troubled, or sick. I may be constrained to take work that I do not wish to do in order to earn a living. Yet all these constraints are the price of building up a family that can endure and flourish. This, too, is a skill that must be learned by observing and imitating others. And the same can be said of serving in the military and paying taxes, observing holy days and sabbaths, honoring one's parents and teachers, giving honor to one's rivals in games and competitions, and everything else that is of worth. Constraint is, in fact, the key to everything productive or good that can be accomplished in life.

Moreover, there can be no freedom of any kind without constraint. In fact, what we call freedoms or rights always turn out, on inspection, to be forms of disciplined constraint to which others conform so that I can possess a certain measure of freedom. For instance, my freedom to drive my car whenever I want depends entirely on the fact that countless other individuals refrain from stealing or vandalizing it or letting the air out of the tires. In the same way, my freedom to say what I want depends on others tolerating what I have to say, which means that they refrain from suppressing my words and punishing me for them afterward. In our day, we are increasingly aware of how much all of us depend on such toleration of our views, how quickly it can be revoked, and how frightening it is to find oneself publicly disgraced where such toleration is no longer extended.

We are also aware that there is nothing natural about tolerating the speech of others. On the contrary, human beings are by nature intolerant. We find it annoying and difficult to hear the opinions of others. Anyone who has taught children to wait their turn to speak, and to listen respectfully while others have their say, knows how very unnatural this discipline is, and how difficult it is to learn. Indeed, it is only tradition and training that establish a right to speak freely. But when others tolerate what I have to say, this requires constraint on their part, not freedom. And the same is true of every other freedom that I might wish to exercise.

Everything that we call a freedom of the individual, or one of the individual's liberties, is a traditional institution whose particular form is learned by imitation, maintained through honor and self-discipline, and handed down, in a given society, from one generation to the next. Every freedom emerges through a well-structured constraint, and so it is worse than merely misleading to say that our political freedoms come to us by nature, or that reason leads easily to them, or that nothing is needed to maintain them but for government to let us be. All of this mythology diverts our eyes from the difficult road that must be traveled in order for the necessary constraints to be instilled in society, so that even the most rudimentary freedom or right can become a reality.

Where do these constraints come from?

They can come from the laws of the state and the commands of its officials, of course. And indeed, this is the most common Enlightenment-rationalist depiction of constraint. In Hobbes's *Leviathan*, for example, fear of the government provides the constraint needed to bring peace and order to a society that would otherwise tear itself apart.

But constraint can also come from another source. In a free society, the principal constraining force comes not from fear of the government, but from the self-discipline of the people, who provide the necessary constraint themselves by upholding inherited relations and the obligations that attend them. This point was emphasized by the English political theorist John Fortescue in the fifteenth century, and taken up by Montesquieu, Burke, and the American founding fathers centuries later. Where nations can impose the needed constraints themselves, the government can be mild or moderate, offering them greater freedom to conduct their affairs without interference. But where a people is incapable of self-discipline, a mild government will only encourage licentiousness and division, hatred and violence, eventually forcing a choice between civil war and tyranny.

For centuries, foreign observers have admired the British and Americans for their political freedom, which was made possible by their great capacity for self-discipline or self-constraint. But in recent generations, this famous capacity for self-constraint has disappeared. Why? Because the British and American capacity for self-constraint was an inherited tradition, a tradition of how to think and live in accord with what was, until recently, called *common sense.* An individual who was guided by common sense enjoyed a broad range to think things through for himself. But his originality and divergences from the way others spoke and behaved were always constrained by a thick fabric of inherited relations and norms, which included the obligation to maintain and defend the place of God and religion, nation and government, family, property, and so on.

These inherited norms provided the framework (or "guardrails," as we now say) within which reason was able to operate, yet without overthrowing every inherited institution as today's adulation of perfectly free reasoning does. In our day, these inherited norms have been discarded in the name of the freely reasoning individual and his right to be rid of any constraint he has not himself chosen. God and religion, nation and government, marriage and children and caring for the aged—all these traditional ideas and institutions that once constrained the individual are now regarded as burdensome and difficult things, to be avoided because of the limits they impose on our freedom.

What would be required to build up this voluntary self-constraint rather than ceaselessly working to destroy it?

The propagation of such self-constraint depends on the honor that a given society is willing to award those who practice it.[28] Indeed, the only known means of causing individuals to shoulder hardship and constraint without coercion or financial compensation is by rewarding them with honor. Thus, for example, under the old Christian and Jewish order, individuals were honored for marrying and raising children; for military service; for national and religious leadership; for teaching the young; for knowledge of Scripture, law and custom; for performing religious duties; and for personally caring for the aged. This is to say that the status of the individual, his weightiness and stature in the eyes of others, was tied to his upholding inherited obligations and norms rather than choosing to be free of them.

Such honor has largely disappeared because it violates the Enlightenment conceit (supposedly a dictate of universal reason) that all must be regarded as equals. Think about this point: If those who serve in the military are honored for doing so, it means their decision to serve is better than that of their friends who choose not to serve. Similarly, if those who remain married are honored, it means that their choice is regarded as better than that of those who choose divorce. And the same is true for all other cases. In a society in which all are supposed to be equal, how is it possible to justify public recognition of some and not others? In a society in which all are supposed to be free to live according to their own reasoning, how is it possible to justify publicly praising certain choices and not others—a custom that, if adopted consistently, will impose a strong constraint in a certain direction?

The answer to these questions is obvious to anyone familiar with the liberal societies that have come into being in recent decades. In these societies, any public pronouncement to the effect that a married life is more praiseworthy than the life of a bachelor, or of a divorcée, or of a single mother, is vigorously condemned as an expression of intolerance. Indeed, it is said that such praise is itself a form of oppression directed against those who have chosen a different path or who have been forced by circumstances onto a different path. What is honored in liberal society is only the insistence that all choices are equal.

The reality, then, is that postwar liberalism replaced traditional institutions and common sense with an insatiable egalitarianism of choices, in light of which all choices that the individual might make were to be regarded as equal—first by the state, which was declared to be neutral among the different ways of life that one could adopt; then by the public schools, since they were operated by the state; and finally, by private institutions of all kinds, as the equality of all choices seeped into every crevice. Within a generation or two, the declared neutrality of the government had been transformed into a neutrality of society itself, so that today one may choose to be a Christian, a Jew, or a pagan, and none of these choices will be honored above the others by the government, schools, or anyone else. Similarly, one may choose to be gainfully employed or to live on a stipend from the government, and again, neither alternative will be honored more than the other. In the same way, one may choose to serve in the military or to evade such service; to be married with children, divorced, or never married; to keep the sabbath, go to the beach, or continue working straight through as though nothing on this blessed earth is sacred—and none will utter a syllable of praise or disparagement in any direction. And the same is true for everything else that was once a matter of tradition and common sense.

As the cultural revolution has progressed, everything that was once honored has become a matter of public indifference. And as this has happened, every traditional constraint has been lost. At first, it was thought that the result would be only license and abandon. And indeed, this is a fine description of what Enlightenment liberalism looked like one generation after its triumph. At that time, one could win praise and honor for daring acts of transgression—for evading military service, for sexual profligacy and adventurism, for drug use, for blasphemy and obscenity, for desecration of the sabbath, and so on. But by the second generation, this too has dissipated, and little is to be gained by violating the old norms with acts that are by now commonplace. No one is left who will be impressed by them. Now an entirely different kind of decay is ascendant: a growing lassitude and despair, a true decadence in which no praise is to be gained from moving in any direction. And so meaningful movement ceases, and all that is left is the monotonous parade of sensations induced by alcohol, drugs, and flickering screens.

No human society can remain in such a condition indefinitely. A shattered society will eventually regenerate itself. The human ruins will cohere into households and clans, and then tribes. Their leading figures will teach self-discipline and constraint, and individuals will be honored and advanced for upholding certain beliefs and behavioral norms. All of this is inevitable. What is not inevitable is the character of these revived loyalty groups: Will they be Christian or Jewish, seeking to restore and build upon the traditional inheritance of the Western nations? Or will they be variants of religious traditions from other lands? Or will they be entirely new cults, devised of late and unknown to our forefathers?

For now, the new Marxism is everywhere ascendant, and the roads to restoration and recovery are shrouded in uncertainty.

Nevertheless, some things are certain. It is certain that if a conservative society is to be built, one that will have the strength to displace the Marxist dystopia that stands at the threshold, it will have to offer a regenerated political life that is characterized not only by freedom, but also by constraint. And it is certain that such a regeneration of the capacity for constraint requires a return, at all levels, to a public life in which honor and loyalty are at the very center. This means that, where possible, honor and praise for a renewed constraint should come from the most prominent political figures—kings, presidents, and prime ministers. Where it cannot, it should come from the leadership of political and religious factions, and from anyone else who is regarded as a significant public figure. And where this is impossible, the initiative will belong entirely to congregations and families. Let all who can emphasize honor and loyalty in speaking to adults and in teaching children. Let them be zealous in giving weight to parents and grandparents, elders and teachers. Let them honor our forefathers, their political and intellectual achievements, their military service and their acts of righteousness, their God and their Scripture.

Where honor and praise are given to those who came before us, restoration and renewed health become possible again.

11. Tradition and Truth

The rationalist political theories of the Enlightenment were meant to be independent of tradition. They were said to be derived from "reason alone," meaning that they could be understood and agreed upon by anyone, regardless of the religious or national traditions with which they were raised. The difficulty with this claim is that it is not actually true. In fact, individuals exercising "reason alone" do not tend to reach a stable consensus about anything. As John Selden argued against Grotius and the other pioneers of Enlightenment rationalism, reason alone is capable of reaching virtually any conclusion:

> This brings us to the uncertainty and inconsistency with which the free and unadorned application of reason has always been burdened.... No one of any education can be unaware that in ancient times even the masters and practitioners of right reason, i.e., the philosophers, took part in endless discussions about good and evil, and the boundaries that separated them, in which they were completely at odds with one another. There was no one to put an end to these disputes. The number of sectarian groups multiplied....

Hence both Zeno and Chrysippus, as well as the Persian Magi, considered relations with one's mother and even with one's daughter to be permitted, just as were relations with other men; and the philosopher Theodorus said the same about theft, sacrilege, and adultery. And yet the jurist Ulpian (who was not even a Christian) and others of the pagans said explicitly that these are crimes against nature; while Theodotus, Diagoras of Melos, and some other well-known writers completely undermined all the fear and respect that rein in humanity by claiming that the gods did not exist. Add to these Plato, the most divinely inspired of all philosophers, who believed that women should be held in common and people should be able to have sex with almost anyone they want; and the others who thought that all possessions should be shared as though the law required it. Then there are the teachings of Archelaus, Aristippus and Carneades, according to which nothing at all that is just depends upon nature; rather, what we call "just" is based on written law and on the preferences or interests of human beings.... And yet we hear everywhere that law (especially natural law) is right reason; and everyone agrees with this sentiment, even those who disagree fiercely about what "right reason" is....

We should therefore use with caution, and not be too quick to depend upon, the unfettered and simple application of analytical reason alone, which is often so unpredictable and unstable that what one person sees...as a very evident principle, or a conclusion which follows from a principle, will often seem to another person of equal intelligence to be obviously false and worthless, or at least inadmissible as truth. This is just what happened all the time

> among those heroes of the discipline who used free and untrammeled reason to argue about the nature of good and evil, the shameful and the honorable, as everyone knows who is even slightly familiar with their writings. This is why Tertullian says as follows about the philosophy of the gentiles, i.e., about using the kind of reason which they generally called "right": *It reserves nothing for divine authority; it makes its own opinions into laws of nature*. Considering the variety of philosophical schools and sects, you are not likely to find anything as unclear and contradictory as these "laws of nature."[29]

Selden published these words in 1640, but they could easily have been written today. Even now, many liberals continue to insist that when "reason alone" is exercised freely in public debate, it leads inexorably to their preferred conclusions about politics and morals. Yet we see every day how free human reasoning, when conducted without reference to tradition, leads to Marxism or to a quasi-Darwinian racial politics as easily as it does to liberalism. And tomorrow it will lead somewhere else entirely, abandoning the conclusions of today's reasoning as relics of a bygone and benighted past.

The only way to resist this outcome is by means of a tradition carried forward through the medium of human hierarchies, which propagates to the extent that those who uphold it are honored for doing so. Even the liberal hegemony in America and Europe after the Second World War was maintained, however briefly, by a tradition that upheld it. But since liberalism constantly inculcates an aversion to tradition, it is unstable and unsustainable. For this reason, it is easily overthrown by Marxists and others claiming that their own reasoning is superior to that of any liberal.[30]

One might think that with the collapse of liberal hegemony in America and Britain, advocates of Enlightenment rationalism might reconsider their hostility toward national and religious tradition. Yet instead, many continue to expend precious resources attempting to prevent the resurgence of a conservative political theory that could perhaps save something from the conflagration. This hostility to the conservative paradigm takes many forms. But there is one argument advanced against conservative political theory that seems worthy of careful attention. This is the claim that a conservative theory must be relativist and nihilist, leaving no room for truth in politics and morals. This isn't true, but I have found that individuals who have immersed themselves in the rationalist political theories of the Enlightenment are often incapable of escaping this conclusion. Here, I will present their argument and explain why it is mistaken.

The Enlightenment argument against conservatism is usually presented in the following way. Political traditions vary from one country to another. Even within a single country, the tradition does not remain entirely fixed, but undergoes change over time. Yet conservatives are to be found defending tradition in every time and place. This proves that conservatives—so it is said—do not care whether the ideas, behaviors, and institutions that are carried forward by the tradition are in fact true. They are positivists, convinced that whatever exists is right. And they are relativists and nihilists, whose thinking has no place for general truths that transcend the notions of right and wrong prevailing in a given time and place.

This argument sounds plausible from the perspective of Enlightenment rationalism, which supposes that certain principles are self-evident to all men and that infallible deductions can be drawn from them by all men, thereby revealing political and moral truths that are accessible to all. These truths are held to be universal—and so it seems fitting to consider them to be "external" to the various local traditions in which one may have been raised. It is the aim of rationalist political and moral philosophy to attain this external point of view, and to use it as a standard against which the various local traditions may be judged. For the Enlightenment rationalist, then, it seems obvious that one is either a rationalist or a relativist. That is, one is either (i) accessing a universal standard of right that is known to all men by means of reason alone, or one is (ii) a relativist, believing that whatever is handed down by tradition is right and good. A conservative, who approaches political and moral questions from a standpoint established by his own tradition, is therefore regarded as a relativist.

Conservatives do not find this line of reasoning compelling because the crucial dichotomy—one must either be a rationalist or a relativist—is plainly false. The Cartesian supposition that truth is discovered by proceeding from self-evident principles to unassailable conclusions by way of infallible deductions has never been accepted by empiricists. Newton's mechanics made a mockery of it, and his discussion of induction and deduction (what he called the "method of analysis and synthesis") showed that our approach to the truth begins without self-evident principles and reaches no unassailable conclusions. Newton's science showed, in other words, that the empiricist tradition, which was neither relativist nor dogmatist (for Enlightenment rationalism is a form of dogmatism), offers the best method of approaching the truth.

The empiricist account represents a third alternative that the rationalists' dichotomy fails to take into account. From this perspective, no human being ever attains a point of view that is "external" to tradition. Instead, we approach the truth from within a tradition in which we were raised, elaborating and repairing it so that it comprehends the truth more fully. Of course, there are individuals who are embarrassed by their inheritance and immerse themselves in foreign ideas, believing them to be universal. But this is an illusion. The individual escapes the traditions of his own tribe only by joining a new one. The feeling that one has escaped the competition of local traditions and entered into a way of thinking that is universal is simply a part of the illusion. Certain tribes—Marxists, for example, or Enlightenment liberals—insist on the universality of their ideas, not because they have discovered a point of view that is in fact external to the world of competing traditions, but because this myth of universality strengthens their hand in their competition with other tribes.

In reality, no one ever escapes the competition among local traditions. But this way of understanding things is not relativistic because these traditions are themselves the only instrument by means of which human beings are able to approach the truth.

How does this work? Answering this question requires a view of human psychology that is different from that of Enlightenment rationalism. I have presented such an alternative view in detail in my book on human nature. Here, I will touch only on those points that are necessary for the present discussion.

To begin with, we must recognize that human beings approach reality by means of inherited schemes of ideas and relations among these ideas.[31] Earlier, I called these schemes of ideas and relations paradigms, and I devoted most of this chapter to comparing two competing paradigms that are used to understand the political domain. But if we consider human cognition more generally, we find that we rely on such inherited schemes of ideas and relations to understand every domain that is of interest to us. We rely on them, especially, to distinguish what is beneficial from what is harmful, both to us as individuals and to the families, tribes, and nations to which we are loyal.

Every inherited scheme of ideas grasps reality in one way or another. This means it can be relied upon to some degree and with respect to certain matters, and for this reason we may say that there is some truth to it. But each inherited scheme of ideas is also limited. In some things, it will be reliable only up to a point. And in other matters, an inherited scheme of ideas will be entirely blind, overlooking crucial phenomena that we must understand if we are to avoid harm and advance ourselves and others.

Because we can only approach reality through such paradigms, we are never in possession of a completed truth on any subject. However, we can improve our ideas, so that they are better framed; and we can improve the principles by which our ideas are related to one another. And in fact, human individuals and social hierarchies experience minor adjustments of the schemes of ideas with which they approach reality on an ongoing basis. Much of the time, we are not even aware that such adjustments are taking place.

A large-scale alteration in a scheme of ideas is a different matter. Human individuals are resistant to any great alteration in the ideas with which they understand reality. A proposal to introduce a major adjustment to an important scheme of ideas—whether by reframing old ideas and principles, or by introducing new ideas and principles that limit the relevance of the old ones—tends to provoke anger, hostility, and abuse. And if the individuals responding in this way are leading figures within a given social hierarchy, their anger will incite the indignation of many of its less prominent members as well. Usually, these displays of hostility are successful at suppressing the proposed adjustment. The new ideas are regarded as absurd, and those who have proposed them are stigmatized so that others fear to be associated with them.

Nevertheless, there are times when a major reframing of a scheme of ideas and the relations among them—a change in paradigm—becomes possible. In general, a scheme of ideas is blind to whatever it was not framed to describe. This means that every paradigm overlooks certain causes that are operative in the domain it is supposed to explain, so that their effects go largely unnoticed or are considered unimportant. But there comes a time when the distress caused by these hidden factors becomes so great that their existence can no longer be denied. Then we begin seeking the causes of our distress in earnest, and this search becomes the lever that pries the old paradigm loose. A period of open-mindedness is initiated, and proposed repairs that were once ridiculed are reconsidered. At this time, dissenting individuals who were once spurned and disreputable may grow quickly in importance, even as those who jealously protected the old consensus are diminished in stature and significance. By means of such changes, nations, tribes, and communities arrive at a revised consensus, which can save them from ruin if it reveals the real causes that have been affecting them.

Attend carefully to the following point: I have not said that such a crisis always leads to the adoption of an improved scheme of ideas and principles. A new scheme of ideas that comes to the fore in a time of crisis may prove worthless, and the consensus that seems to form around it can collapse within a short time. Frequently, a crisis will lead to the adoption of a series of different frameworks, which are tried and fail in rapid succession.

Nevertheless, because the crisis focuses our attention on effects that the old consensus ignored, and presses us to seek their causes, it carries within it the seeds of a great improvement in the scheme of ideas with which we approach reality. In other words, the crisis holds out the prospect of a great movement toward the truth.

We can say that a scheme of ideas is *true*, and that it describes *reality*, if it permits us to recognize the most significant causes operative in a given domain and to take reliable action with respect to them. But since different schemes of ideas are reliable in different ways and to different degrees, it is most accurate to say that one scheme is *truer* than another, and *improved* over another, if it better permits us to recognize these causes and to take reliable action with respect to them.

How does an improved scheme of ideas appear and establish itself? A realistic view must take the following considerations into account.

First, the human mind has the capacity to detect movement toward a truer or improved scheme of ideas and principles. When comparing one scheme of ideas to another, I am able to judge which brings me closer to the truth; and when considering a proposed repair to an existing scheme, I can judge whether this repair will constitute an improvement or not. This judgment is expressed by sensations of attraction and exhilaration when I have a truer scheme before me, and by sensations of aversion and anger when I consider a scheme that is further from the truth. Of course, some are more able in this than others, and even those who excel at such judgments are mistaken at times. Nevertheless, the general human capacity to detect movement toward a truer scheme of ideas is the basis for any discussion of truth.

Although a judgment of truth is experienced as a primitive action of the human mind, we can understand what is involved in such judgment by examining schemes of ideas that are accepted as true. When we do this, we find that a truer scheme of ideas (i) reveals the causes of a much broader range of effects, (ii) can be relied upon to explain these effects more precisely, and (iii) does so using fewer and simpler concepts. This empiricist account of truth suggests that our understanding of a given domain develops as the range of our experience grows: We will be more certain that a given scheme of ideas is true once it has proved itself reliable in a wide range of circumstances, and we will grow doubtful as its failures increasingly demand our attention.

This account of truth is applicable to all fields in which human beings seek knowledge. It is no less true in political theory, law, and morals—those disciplines in which we strive to identify *norms*, or *principles of behavior*, that will permit the effective operation of the causes of human health and prosperity within a nation, tribe, or family. When this search for political and moral knowledge is approached in light of an empiricist understanding of truth, it leads to an appreciation of ideas and principles that have withstood the challenges of time. This is because we become more certain that a scheme of political or moral ideas is true once it has proved itself reliable through a broad range of trials under diverse circumstances. But at the same time, such empiricism also encourages a skeptical view of abstract political principles, which are understood to hold good only up to certain limits—limits that cannot be known in advance and must be established by trial and error.

We see, therefore, that an empiricist theory of truth provides the grounds for a conservative standpoint in politics and morals.

The empiricist account of truth I have proposed helps explain the great appeal of Enlightenment liberalism. According to this view, the unsurpassed simplicity of Enlightenment liberalism allows its adherents to feel they have grasped an immensely powerful truth—one that explains a vast range of effects while employing only a handful of concepts such as *individual liberty*, *equality*, *consent*, and *reason*. But this simplicity is also Enlightenment liberalism's great weakness. Because in reality, the causes of human health and prosperity, and the norms that permit these causes to be effective within a given nation, cannot be understood through the application of these concepts alone. To understand politics, we must think in terms of causes such as *nation* and *tribe*, *mutual loyalty*, *honor*, *hierarchy*, *cohesion* and *dissolution*, *influence*, *tradition*, and *constraint*. In recognizing these fundamental causes, the conservative paradigm allows us to understand a far greater range of political phenomena and to explain how the welfare and decline of nations has come about with much greater precision. The conservative paradigm is thus rightly judged to be the truer paradigm, which is to say that it more closely approaches the truth in political affairs than anything that liberal political theory has been able to offer. If we approach political reality in terms of the concepts it provides, we are more likely to understand, for instance, why free trade with China and large-scale immigration have done so much damage to the internal cohesion of the United States; or why America and its allies have been unable to subdue Iraq and Afghanistan; or how the rise of neo-Marxist theories in American and British universities have destroyed the political traditions that had previously held these nations together.

We see something similar in the sphere of law and morals. The best summary of the moral law that has ever been proposed is the Mosaic Ten Precepts, which suggest that in a healthy society, God, parents, and the sabbath will be honored, whereas idolatry, murder, adultery, theft, and false witness will be proscribed. No one supposes that the Ten Precepts describe the legal or moral realm in its every detail. Rather, this scheme deploys a limited number of simple causes to explain what distinguishes a healthy and prosperous society from one that is in the process of dissolution and whose days are numbered.[32] These precepts can be compared to other attempts to reduce the moral realm to a small number of principles, such as the natural law system of the Aristotelians, which is derived from a certain description of human nature; or Locke's account of the individual's rights to "life, liberty, and property." Here, too, the simplicity of a scheme of concepts can induce a sense that one has grasped an immensely powerful truth. After all, "life, liberty, and property" are important causes productive of a healthy and prosperous society. But this scheme becomes false when it is mistaken for a summary of the significant causes operative in the legal or moral domain, because it blinds us to the existence of other major causes that must be held in view. Indeed, one of the chief reasons for the dissolution that is visible everywhere in the Western nations today is the fact that principles such as the public acknowledgment of God, the honor given to parents by their adult children, loyalty within marriage, and observance of the sabbath have been banished from public life and relegated to "the private sphere." This suggests that government officials and public figures can safely ignore these principles as causes of the nation's health and prosperity.

But these things cannot be safely ignored, for there is no firewall that protects the public sphere from what is done in private. It is true that the dissolute acts of a small number of persons will not bring down a society if its laws and morals, when considered in general, allow the causes of human health and prosperity to be effective. Yet when the recklessness of private individuals has become frequent enough, and has gone far enough, it does degrade—and ultimately destroys—the health and prosperity of the family, congregation, tribe, and nation that must bear it. We thus pay a heavy price for conceiving of the legal and moral sphere in terms of a simplistic system of rights, which fails to describe the principal causes of a healthy and prosperous society.

I have proposed a theory of truth that is based on a real capacity of the individual human mind—the capacity to discern an improvement in the scheme of ideas that is applied in explaining and permitting reliable action in a given domain. A political theory based on such an empiricist account of truth recognizes that truth in the political and moral realm is real. It is found in those norms, or principles of behavior, that permit the causes of human health and prosperity to be effective within a nation, tribe, or family, thereby allowing its members to grow strong and the community itself to propagate through the generations. Moreover, such empiricism recognizes that these political and moral norms can be approached by broadening our experience and improving the ideas and relations among ideas with which we grasp it.

There is no relativism, nihilism, positivism, or historicism here. Conservatives whose political theory is grounded in this kind of empiricism are not less concerned with truth than their rationalist detractors. Indeed, they are better equipped to go about finding it.

However, as this theory presently stands, it is incomplete. In particular, it does not take into account the way in which an individual's efforts to arrive at true principles in politics and morals depend upon his belonging to a family, congregation, tribe, or nation—that is, to a hierarchically structured loyalty group that transmits schemes of ideas from one generation to the next. Given that traditional schemes of ideas and principles propagate through the medium of human hierarchies, this factor must appear in any realistic account of how an improved scheme of ideas appears and establishes itself.

I have already discussed the mechanisms by which schemes of ideas and principles are transmitted from one generation to the next in social hierarchies. We tend to believe the things we hear from important individuals within a social group to which we are loyal, and to accept significant alterations in an inherited scheme of ideas only when these are broached by important figures within a hierarchy to which we are loyal. This means that our approach to the truth is governed by two factors that stand in tension with each other: On the one hand, the human mind can detect improvements that may be made to a given scheme of ideas. Yet on the other, individuals tend to see and understand things as the society to which they are loyal sees and understands them.

Our search for truth is characterized by such a tension. However, a great deal depends on how this tension is interpreted. For Enlightenment rationalists, the search for truth is an activity that takes place in the confines of the individual's mind. Meanwhile, the tradition being handed down in the society around him is regarded as little more than a collation of falsehoods.[33] Seen in this light, the tension between the individual's capacity for judgment and the propagation of ideas by society is seen as a war of independence—a war in which the individual, oppressed by a tradition and hierarchy that are external and extraneous to him, fights for the freedom to seek the truth on his own and to live according to whatever conclusions he reaches.

But the tension between the individual's capacity for judgment and the propagation of ideas in society takes on an entirely different aspect if we consider the search for truth as a collective enterprise. Seen in this light, an individual begins life as an heir to schemes of ideas that allow him, from an early age, to recognize many of the causes operative in his experience, and to take action with respect to them that is reliably productive and beneficial. From this perspective, the tradition is not external or extraneous to the individual at all. It is an integral part of who he is, without which he could neither think nor speak, much less distinguish what is productive and beneficial from what is not. He therefore embraces his place within a hierarchy that acts constantly to hand down the tradition out of loyalty and gratitude. This does not mean that the individual simply accepts everything that has been handed down. But neither does he wish to discard and overthrow what he has received to his benefit. Instead, the tension between his capacity for judgment and the tradition transmitted by society manifests itself as a desire and ambition to contribute out of his own abilities to the same search for truth that his forefathers initiated in earlier times.

In a conservative society, there is, to be sure, greater circumspection. We do not see the same kind of public disparagement of one's forefathers and abuse of important persons by the young, which is so familiar to us from a society in which everyone is told that he is the "equal" of all his predecessors from an early age. Rather, the desire to give honor to earlier generations and to important persons who are still living finds expression in the ambition to strengthen and improve the society that these earlier generations built and to which they were loyal. Because such ambitions are present, the political and moral life of conservative societies is invariably characterized by proposals for the restoration and repair of inherited schemes of ideas and principles—proposals that give rise to contention among competing factions or tribes, each with its own view of the kinds of improvements that may be made to the tradition, and of what would constitute a mistake that will impair it.

Since conservatives are not rationalists, they do not believe everyone will arrive at the same view of what would constitute an improvement in an inherited scheme of ideas. Indeed, it is assumed that even the most able and honorable men will disagree among themselves. For this reason, it is understood that the tradition will always be internally diverse, and that the best answers to the questions that arise will be settled upon in due course, in a process informed by the experiences of the various streams within the tradition as they are confronted by events. That such a process may take place over a period of centuries is not regarded as a disadvantage, but as reflecting the humility with which we rightly approach the task of maintaining and repairing our inheritance. The possibility of undertaking more drastic alterations in extreme circumstances is well known and held in reserve.

All of this is an integral part of a living tradition, in which the search for truth is conducted by means of adjustments to a scheme of inherited ideas that is handed down from one generation to the next. This means that even the most hardened and dogmatic tradition is never quite so beholden to the past as its detractors suppose. Indeed, the conservative leadership that stand at the head of an enduring hierarchy often have a more accurate understanding of what the pursuit of truth requires than the liberals and Marxists who disparage them. Recognizing that the reasoning individual is far more likely to be carried away by some worthless passing fashion than he is to discover a new and valuable truth, they prefer to uphold ideas and behaviors that have been tested for generations and have stood their ground. And where they introduce alterations, they do so according to the method of constructive reasoning.[34] That is, they avoid sweeping alterations whose consequences cannot be known in advance, instead introducing repairs that are framed to remedy a particular difficulty or hardship, and whose scale is such that they can, if necessary, be undone at a later stage. Moreover, they look to precedents that can teach what has worked well in the history of their own people, or, failing that, to the institutions of neighboring nations that have been tried and found beneficial. In this way, they advance by trial and error, adjusting the tradition so that it has a truer grasp of the causes operative in our experience, and more effectively upholds principles of behavior that permit these causes to bring health and prosperity to the nation, tribe, or community for which they are responsible.

This, then, is the conservative's reply to the claim that individuals are oppressed by tradition and prevented from seeking the truth by it. Rather than conducting his own search for truth in a manner that is largely independent of what others believe and do, the conservative finds that human beings conduct their search for truth as members of a tradition—whether the tradition in which they were raised, or another adopted in adulthood. The tradition equips the individual with a point of departure and a discourse moderated by persons who have the standing to reframe ideas and principles, and to introduce larger repairs when these are needed. Less prominent figures also introduce improvements into the tradition, but these carry far less weight and tend to be ignored unless they attract the endorsement of important persons within the hierarchy. Nevertheless, the insights of these lesser figures may attract a few adherents who are willing to risk disapproval in pursuit of a truer understanding of things. In this way, a truer scheme of ideas may establish itself in the side streets of the tradition, developing a certain standing as it awaits the crisis that will bring it to the attention of a broader audience.

The statesmen and scholars who lead traditional societies are not less interested in establishing the truth than their liberal and Marxist critics, and they are constantly concerned to move their family and congregation, tribe and nation, toward it. But they do so in a manner that escapes the understanding of persons whose education has deprived them of any meaningful contact with conservative thinkers and texts, and who have never taken part in a conservative community of any kind. When one has knowledge and understanding of these matters, it is evident that in a conservative society, tradition is the instrument that is used to advance toward a better grasp of the truth. Where conservative statesmen and scholars react with hostility to the crosswinds of some passing fashion to which parts of their community may have succumbed, it is precisely concern for the truth that motivates them. What worries them is the loss and ruin that a weak and unreliable scheme of ideas, the product of imagination and inexperience, will bring in its wake before it finally fails and collapses.

An empiricist account of truth describes how the human mind approaches a true scheme of ideas and principles, thereby revealing the causes of events and permitting reliable action in a given domain. In political theory, law, and morals, true ideas and principles are those that permit the causes of human health and prosperity to be effective within a nation or tribe, congregation or family, allowing its members to become strong and the community as a whole to sustain itself and grow through the generations. But we also know that individuals vary greatly in their capacity to judge what is true in these matters, and that, when reasoning without reference to long-standing tradition, they often come to conclusions that are wildly mistaken and destructive. Tradition equips the individual with a "common sense" that constrains and guides his thinking, anchoring it in what has held good and proved beneficial in the past. But at the same time, tradition relies on the originality of the individual to open avenues for possible renewal—avenues that may remain peripheral for years or even for generations, and yet may prove, in a time of crisis, to be precisely what the community needs in order to attain a great movement toward truth.

When considered in this way, we see that the enterprise of seeking truth is not one that the individual pursues by his own powers alone. Tradition is the instrument by means of which human societies pursue truth over time. The individual takes part in this larger enterprise, from which he has benefited from childhood, and to which he may contribute much if he continues to cultivate and develop this inheritance.

Chapter IV

God, Scripture, Family, and Congregation

Political theory begins with a *philosophy of political order*, which investigates human nature and the nature of human societies in general. It identifies those causes that are operative in political life wherever our experience reaches. This was my purpose in the last chapter.

But after a certain point, we must leave off investigating what is true of human societies in general and turn to the investigation of ideas and institutions that are the inheritance of certain nations and tribes. Philosophers often make the mistake of supposing that a subject is worthy of study only if it is found always and everywhere. But many of the most profound and important things are not found everywhere. This is because artifice, which is the alteration of untamed nature, is itself a part of man's nature. Some institutions that have been devised by man lead to human flourishing, whereas others do not. Specialized disciplines, whose subject matter is ideas and institutions that are not found everywhere, are built on top of the theory of political order like the higher floors of a building. Among them, we must include the *philosophy of government*, *philosophy of religion*, *philosophy of family and congregation*, *philosophy of law and morals*, and others without which political theory is incomplete.

In Chapter 3, I proposed an account of political order in general. In Chapters 4–5, I turn my attention to some of the ideas and institutions that have given Jewish and Christian societies their particular form. I will consider *God*, *Scripture*, *family*, and *congregation* as these relate to the political order in the present chapter, and the *government of the nation* in the next.

1. God and Scripture

Public religion has been a central pillar of Anglo-American conservatism throughout its entire history. Only after the Second World War do we see the emergence of a chameleon form of "conservatism," which accepts liberalism as the official framework within which the state operates, while insisting that conservative religion and morals should nonetheless be kept alive in the heart of every individual. This fusion of public liberalism with private conservatism has not lasted even two generations.[1] Today, a conservative Christianity or Judaism is not even the private faith of most individuals, because what is not honored in public also tends not to be honored in private.

Under these conditions, it is important to recall why, until very recently, God and Scripture—and especially the Hebrew Bible (or "Old Testament")—figured so prominently in the Anglo-American political tradition.

As is well known, the insight that turned ancient Israelite thought into a force in the history of ideas was the discovery of the one God. But though this fact is well known, its significance is no longer well understood. In the ancient world, debates about the gods were not primarily concerned with the question of whether this or that god "exists." Instead, they were focused on what can be called the *normative aspect* of divinity: the question of whether there was something the god commands, some demand to which one must respond in order to gain benefits or avoid ill consequences. There were gods for each nation, gods of weather and agriculture and fertility and war, and gods responsible for medicine, commerce, orchards, herds, vineyards, and so on. Each of these gods was understood as making normative demands upon human beings, so that, in practice, paganism amounted to the acceptance of numerous different standards for determining what is right and wrong. Although one tried to placate the relevant gods, one of them could always become agitated over something that was done or left undone and intervene to make trouble as a consequence. Thus there could be no general theory of what would bring benefit and harm, reward and punishment, to mankind.

This brings us to that famous Mosaic proposition, which Jews say twice every day: "The Lord is our God, the Lord is one."[2] What does this Mosaic declaration mean? The discovery that the world was governed by one God is the discovery that there is only one normative order, only one standard for judging what is true and right—and therefore for judging which acts will be beneficial and which harmful. In Hebrew Scripture, the distinction between what is true in general and what is only held to be true by individuals or societies is expressed by the contrast between what is true or right "in God's eyes" (*be'einei elohim*) and what is true or right "in the eyes of men" (*be'enei adam*). What is true or right in God's eyes is a standard independent of all local standards, and consequently of the claims made in the name of the gods of a given place.[3] If dishonoring one's parents, murder, theft, sexual license, desecrating the sabbath, and lying to damage others are harmful and wrong in one place, then they are harmful and wrong everywhere, for everyone.[4]

But getting anyone, whether Jew or foreigner, to accept the fact that there is ultimately only one standard of right turns out to be exceedingly difficult. Of men in general, the books of Moses tell us that "the nature of man's mind is evil from his youth."[5] Even among the Jews, Scripture teaches that "each did what is right in his own eyes."[6] And in those days as today, there were plenty of individuals who believed "there is no God," and so recognized no general standard by which mankind's deeds can be judged right and wrong.[7] Moreover, even those who accept that there is one standard of right are faced with the daunting task of discerning just what that standard requires.

The prophets and scholars who composed the Hebrew Bible developed a general approach to this subject that remains familiar in orthodox Jewish and Christian communities to this day. According to this view, *wisdom* (Hebrew, *hochma*) is knowledge of how the world actually works, and it is generally associated with age and experience, whereas *foolishness* or *folly* (Hebrew, *nevala, ivelet*) describes the way a person reasons when he is inexperienced and understands little about the way the world works. The beginning of wisdom—that is, of an understanding of how the world actually works—is to be found in a state of mind called *fear of God* (Hebrew, *yirat hashem*).[8]

What is "fear of God"? In studying the Bible, we discover that fear of God is not what we normally mean when we say that someone is afraid of another person, for example, or a wild animal. Rather, fear of God is an awareness that one cannot do an evil deed without endangering oneself and others in the process. It is experienced as a line or a boundary that one feels a strong aversion to crossing. In Scripture, this awareness is considered the most rudimentary experience of God's presence, as well as the minimum moral foundation that is required for the persistence of society. Whenever anyone, Jew or gentile, is aware of such boundaries, we are told that he or she "fears God."[9] On the other hand, when someone wanders into a city where there are no moral limits, he is said to understand that "there is no fear of God in this place"[10]—an expression that is filled with foreboding, both because there is no personal safety in such places, and because one senses that such a city is on the verge of downfall and ruin.

This is not all there is to say about man's relationship with God of course. The righteous are also said to *love God* and to *walk in all his ways.*[11] The Bible also refers to higher levels of knowledge of God, which are represented in the books of Moses by the arduous ascent up the slope of Mount Sinai.[12] Yet before we can approach these higher levels, there is the indispensable minimum of moral knowledge represented by the people standing at the foot of Mount Sinai, just close enough to the mountain so they can hear God's voice and gain an awareness of the Ten Precepts. You come to the foot of the mountain, Moses tells the people, so that you may attain this minimal level of having God's fear before you.[13]

Notice that, from this biblical perspective, there is no real difference between atheism and polytheism. A pagan is anyone who "does not fear God"—and this can be someone who believes in many gods or in no god at all. In either case, the decisive point is that he is unaware of the minimal boundaries that a God-fearing person would not cross. Thus a pagan may sacrifice his child to the Ba'al, believing that this murder is desired by the Canaanite fertility god. Or he may decide to commit a murder, saying to himself that there is no God and that, for this reason, no harm or punishment will come to him over it. In terms of their consequences, these two cases are the same: The individual in question has done this thing because he "does not fear God," and is therefore willing to cross a line that no man should be willing to cross.

But when we examine this matter more carefully, we discover that even in terms of its metaphysics, atheism is no different from polytheism. What is it that an atheist does wrong when he decides for himself that his act of murder or adultery or theft is justified? He is denying the Mosaic teaching that there is only one normative order, only one standard for judging what is true and right—and therefore for judging which acts will be beneficial and which harmful. Instead, he establishes a local standard of what is true and right that justifies his deeds, and this standard coexists with countless other local standards of what is true and right. The atheist deciding what is true and right for himself becomes, in effect, one god among many others. This case is the same as that of the Egyptian Pharaoh, who was also considered one god among many others. From a biblical point of view, every atheist is just another small-time Pharaoh—a man who denies the existence of the one normative order and sees the world as composed of countless local standards of what is true and right.

According to this biblical understanding, every atheist is a polytheist, and every polytheist is also an atheist. Atheism and polytheism are metaphysically indistinguishable, just as the moral relativism that follows from each of them is the same. The only alternative to the pagan metaphysics, and to the moral relativism that follows from it, is the recognition of the one God, creator of heaven and earth, who rules his creation in accordance with a single moral standard.

However, the existence of this single moral standard for all mankind stands in tension with the biblical anthropology, which regards mankind as divided into families, tribes, and nations. The same God who gives Moses a teaching intended for all mankind also gives the nation of Israel borders and commands that they not trouble the neighboring peoples beyond these borders. Certainly, these other nations live in the same reality and are bound by the one moral order. But it is not for Israel to try to impose an understanding of the moral order upon them. Israel is to be an example for the nations, "a light unto the nations," not the world's policeman.[14]

The biblical view of mankind as being made up of families, tribes, and nations has far-reaching consequences in the sphere of politics and morals. The prophets believed, for example, that one cannot fully separate what happens to the individual from what happens to the people among whom he or she lives. If there is no fear of God in a certain place, this general recklessness and depravity will tend to bring downfall and ruin upon everyone who lives there. Indeed, the Mosaic Ten Precepts are explicit in recognizing that sin is a family affair: Where parents do not fear God, the repercussions of their ill deeds are felt by their children and grandchildren. We may feel that this is unjust. But anyone who has seen firsthand what happens to the children of an alcoholic or a drug abuser, or to children who are victims of sexual abuse, or to the children of divorced parents, cannot doubt that in this matter, the Ten Precepts correctly describe reality. Our sins are visited upon our children, and even on our grandchildren and great-grandchildren. And later on, when the Israelites establish their kingdom, much the same is said with respect to the government: The sins of the rulers are inevitably visited upon the people.[15]

None of this is meant to downplay the importance of the individual in the Bible. Hebrew Scripture—alone among the texts of antiquity—describes the human individual, male and female, as being created "in the image of God," and takes this as the foundation of all political and moral thought.[16] Similarly, it is through the deeds of a single individual, Abraham, that "all the families of the earth will be blessed."[17] And the Mosaic Ten Precepts, too, are deeply concerned with the individual person, establishing the right of the individual to life, property, marital fidelity, protection from slander, and so on.[18] Indeed, we can say this same thing more generally: The biblical narratives are constructed entirely around the stories of individual persons—great and humble, men and women, each of them flawed, each heroic in his own way.

Yet despite the great sensitivity of Scripture to the uniqueness of the individual person, the story of the God-fearing individual is always told in the context of his or her effort to establish a God-fearing family, tribe, and nation. Just as the fear of God is presented to us as the most basic moral challenge for the individual, so too is the fear of God presented as the most basic political challenge for the family, tribe, and nation.

The proposal that unites the biblical authors is the idea of an alliance or "covenant" (Hebrew, *brit*) between a nation and God—an alliance in which God preserves the nation and gives it strength, and the people promise to uphold God's law as individuals, as families and tribes, and as a nation. This alliance is one between God and the people of Israel. But Hebrew Scripture also promises that in later days, other nations will join themselves to Israel's God as well. Through Christianity, the idea of an alliance of God-fearing nations—I am adopting a phrase used by Franklin Roosevelt on the eve of the Second World War[19]—enters into the cultural inheritance of the Western nations and of other peoples around the world.

God and Scripture thus provide the political and moral framework that directs individuals and families, tribes and nations, toward what is true and right, while providing an overarching vision of a world of independent nations, all of them God-fearing. To be sure, the nations each have their own unique understanding of both God and the Bible. Orthodox, Catholic, and Protestant Christian nations do not have the same inheritance, and all of them are quite different from the torah of the Jews. Yet all are in possession of the same broad framework. The interpretations are exceedingly diverse, yet the overarching frame in which each finds its place is one.

2. *Why There Is No Alternative to God and Scripture*

How do we determine what is good and true in politics and morals? Three principal answers contend for our attention.

First, there is the answer given in biblical tradition, the best-known modern version of which is Anglo-American conservatism. According to this view, there are general truths regarding what is good for us that derive from human nature and the nature of human societies. But we are limited in our ability to know these general truths because human reason is weak and fallible: Human beings are capable of exercising reason and yet arriving at almost any foolish, destructive, evil, poisonous thing. Given this reality, conservatives give primacy to inherited traditions, beginning with those descended from Moses. Having been tried and adapted to the needs of many nations over thousands of years, these traditions offer us examples of political and moral order that have proved both beneficial and sustainable. We can maintain and strengthen these traditions as our forefathers did, introducing repairs when necessary by a process of trial and error. When we see that a repair has failed, we must restore the sound traditions of generations past.

Second, there is the answer of Enlightenment rationalism, which builds upon foundations laid by the Stoic philosophers of antiquity. According to this view, there is a universal nature that is the same in all times and places. Mankind has been gifted with reason, which is, likewise, everywhere the same. We need only exercise reason to come to those political and moral truths that permit us to live according to nature in all times and places. Both liberalism and Marxism are descended from this Enlightenment-rationalist view.

Third, there is the answer of Nietzsche, romanticism and neo-paganism. This view is also based on an ancient philosophy, namely that of Thrasymachus and the Sophists. According to this view, there is no universal standard of right and wrong. Every society and every individual have their own answers to these questions. What is called right and wrong is nothing other than the standard of value imposed by whoever is strongest at a given moment. This view is most loudly articulated by quasi-Darwinian racialist sects on the far reaches of the political right. However, the influence of this view is today evident far outside these circles.[20]

I want to consider how God fits into each of these three approaches to the question.

In a Nietzschean world, there is no place for God. This is a pagan standpoint that recognizes no ultimate standard of what is true and good. Instead, every society and every individual has its own standard of what is true and good that is unique to it. And if every society has its own standard of what is true and good, this is the same as denying the existence of the one God, who establishes one normative standard for all. Such a view of the world can be called atheist or polytheist, for these amount to the same thing. It is a viewpoint that claims to be "beyond good and evil," and we cannot help seeing the consequences of this claim reflected in subsequent political events. No one who has understood these consequences can embrace this renewed paganism.

But what of those old rivals, Anglo-American conservatism and Enlightenment liberalism? These conflicting political theories agree that there is ultimately one standard of what is good and true. Does this mean they can both pursue a politics that is compatible with the God of Scripture?

I do not believe so. To see why, recall that one of the central issues dividing Enlightenment liberals from conservatives is the question of mankind's capacity for attaining truth through unconstrained reason. Enlightenment liberalism asserts that universal political and moral truth is readily accessible to all human beings if they only exercise reason. Conservatives regard the idea that human beings are equipped to attain universal political and moral truths by means of their own independent reasoning as nothing but a fantasy. As Selden puts it, every human mind is endowed with the same basic operations, but education and experience vary so radically that the way others think is never the way we think. Thus the conclusions of reason vary from nation to nation and from tribe to tribe, and so the political and moral truths we have inherited can only be improved upon through trial and error over long centuries. This historical empiricism makes conservatives mildly skeptical about knowledge claims, including their own. However, this does not prevent us from exercising constructive reason to improve conditions according to our present judgment, so long as we are prepared to abandon our course if it proves to be destructive.[21]

Such an empiricist view of human reason is obviously compatible with the God of Hebrew Scripture. The biblical tradition combines a recognition that there are general standards of what is good and true, which are known to God, with the view that human beliefs concerning what is good and true are limited and fallible. The result is the theory of knowledge reflected in the Exodus account of the revelation at Sinai, in which the majority of the people have difficulty even in standing at the foot of the mountain where the Ten Precepts are accessible. A handful of priests and elders can ascend partway up the mountain and gain a more extensive understanding. Only Moses, the greatest of the prophets, can attain the summit. And even with respect to Moses, the account in Exodus emphasizes that God's nature and his ways were obscured from his view, so that he was able to see them only partially.[22]

This insistence on the partial character of human knowledge, especially knowledge of God, pervades the writings of the prophets and subsequent rabbinic literature. Throughout, we see the need to embrace a plurality of viewpoints, at times in conflict with one another, since what the individual can know is limited and truth emerges only in time. Selden elaborates this theory of knowledge, providing support for the broad toleration of diverse national customs that had already appeared in the writings of Fortescue and Hooker. Later conservative writers such as Hale and Burke reiterated the belief that God has established universal moral standards, and that the various nations strive to attain these standards, each through its own unique understanding, customs, and laws. In this way, a recognition of the limited and fallible character of human reason imparts to conservative political thought its mild skepticism concerning what is known, and its consequent tolerance for a diversity of political and moral viewpoints. The God of Scripture, who is known only partially and with difficulty, and yet rewards good and punishes evil, thus provides a suitable metaphysical foundation for Anglo-American conservatism. Indeed, the God of Scripture appears to be the only appropriate foundation for this kind of conservatism.

What about Enlightenment rationalist political theories? Can such systems of thought be reconciled with the God of Scripture? This question has haunted rationalist political thought for centuries. Indeed, when Grotius published the first edition of his *On the Law of War and Peace* in 1625, he made the mistake of admitting in print that his system would hold true "even if there is no God." In view of the subsequent uproar, this remark was deleted from later editions.[23] But it was too late. The fundamental incompatibility of Enlightenment rationalism with the God of Scripture had been made plain, and it has remained visible to anyone with a sound grasp of what is at stake. Here, I can only recapitulate what has been obvious to many before me.

In many respects, Enlightenment rationalist political theories resemble the Stoic philosophical systems of antiquity from which they draw inspiration. Stoicism is a pagan philosophical tradition in which nature is often confused with reason, and both are confused with God. This confusion cannot be maintained while retaining the biblical basis for our thought. In the biblical metaphysics, the natures of things are neither perfect nor eternal, being part of a created universe that is subject to alteration and change. Similarly, reason is known to be flawed and unreliable. Like other aspects of man's nature, it can be attributed to God only metaphorically and in a limited sense. As to the claim that the individual, by reasoning from principles that are evident in nature, can deduce the political and moral rules that are "according to nature" and by which mankind should live in all times and places—this procedure is unworkable because in the biblical account, it is as much a part of man's nature to do evil as it is to do good. In fact, virtually any evil can be justified as being according to man's nature, if we confuse what is natural for what is right. In biblical thought, it is therefore crucial to maintain a clear distinction between what is natural and what is right, because what is right in God's eyes will often involve the repair and improvement of untamed nature.

Let me say a few more words about this, so that my meaning is clear. By *nature*, I mean those qualities of things that can be relied upon in experience; whatever is in the nature of a thing is *natural* to it. Thus it is natural for an apple to fall to the ground if we drop it, and it is natural for a horse to eat grass, since these are things that the apple and the horse can be relied upon to do. In the same way, it is natural for many kinds of animals to kill neighbors of their own species, conquer their territory, steal their females, and so on. And something similar can be said about human beings, who have throughout history demonstrated their inclination to murder, theft, sexual depravity, and many other evils. All of these things appear in every human society, from which it is evident that they are natural to human beings, who tend toward the basest evils as much as they do toward good.

But it is also in man's nature to devise stratagems for altering the course of nature as he finds it. Man makes bread from wheat. And so it is useful to distinguish the wild wheat, as it grows in nature, from the bread that is a product of human artifice. Originally, the use of fermentation to make bread rise must have been discovered by accident. Now, however, breadmaking is a traditional institution, by means of which mankind have improved upon untamed nature to our benefit. The same is true of institutions such as wearing clothing or living under the state. These, too, are traditional institutions by which mankind have improved upon what was originally given by nature. And when we say that God accepts the introduction of clothing so that men and women need not be ashamed of their nakedness, or when we say that God acquiesces in the state because it improves the prospects of attaining peace and justice within our borders—we are saying that God endorses human artifice when it improves upon nature in a way that benefits mankind and God's creation more generally.

Thus, while natural law is a recurring theme in the Bible, its content, insofar as politics and morals are concerned, is what will reliably bring strength, growth, and long life to individuals, families, tribes, and nations. What is right in God's eyes is what will bring about this good. But what will bring about the good cannot be known entirely in advance. Man is a partner in God's creation, and his own initiatives and innovations may improve matters in a way that will affect our understanding of what will reliably bring strength, growth, and long life to individuals, families, tribes, and nations.[24]

Enlightenment rationalism takes its cues from the Stoics in these matters, rather than from the Bible. And so we find its advocates asserting, for example, that "the law of nature is reason"—a claim that is either incoherent or false. It is true that we can discover laws of nature by skillfully reasoning from experience by induction. But nothing in this process makes it possible for the laws of nature to "be" reason itself, which is nothing more than a limited and fallible capacity of the human mind.

However, Enlightenment rationalism doesn't see reason realistically in this way. The confusion of nature with reason results from the belief that reason is a power that permits every human being directly to access eternal and unchanging "nature." And since unchanging "nature" is assumed to dictate the political and moral principles that hold good for all mankind and for all time, the belief that reason gives every human being direct access to nature means that every human being also has direct access to the political and moral principles that hold good for all mankind and for all time. In this way, Enlightenment rationalism removes us from the biblical framework, in which there is a chasm separating what is right in God's eyes from what is right in men's eyes—a chasm that forces us to acknowledge that we are not God, and to treat the deliverances of our own reasoning minds with great caution, humility, and skepticism. In the new world announced by Enlightenment rationalism, there is no such chasm between the reasoning individual and knowledge of the true character of reality. Each reasoning individual suddenly discovers that he is himself the source of reliable knowledge of what nature commands, and therefore of the political and moral principles that hold good for all mankind and for all time.

This is why there is no place for the God of Scripture in the philosophy of Enlightenment rationalism. Having placed human reason in the position of directly accessing universal political and moral truth, Enlightenment rationalism places the human mind where, in biblical philosophy, the mind of God alone is said to be. The rationalist philosophers of the Enlightenment have no need for God to make their system work because they have asserted—without evidence or proof—that whatever their own power of reason is able to produce will hold good for all mankind and for all time.

This new world announced by Enlightenment rationalism is a fraud. It is a fantasy world that does not exist. In reality, an individual who believes that the political or moral principles delivered by his own mind hold good for all mankind and for all time is a confused person. He has confused his own local, limited perspective for that of God. He has forgotten that he approaches truth by means of a scheme of ideas that blinds him to whatever it was not framed to grasp, and that there are, inevitably, hidden factors that his principles are not taking into account. These hidden factors will eventually emerge and demand their due, often bringing on a calamity that a less arrogant theory of knowledge might have avoided. For this reason, a man who has confused his own local, limited perspective for that of God is potentially a very dangerous person indeed.

The belief that one's local, limited perspective is that of a god is paganism. But Enlightenment rationalism is not the early paganism of city-states, each with its own god. Rather, it is the later paganism that we find in empires grown powerful enough to declare their own perspective to be true for all mankind. It was, for example, the paganism of the Roman emperors. But the Romans declaring their own perspective to be universal did not make it so. They mistook the local, limited perspective of a single pagan people and declared it to be universal truth for the entire world.

This is the crux of the struggle between the biblical tradition and that of the pagans. From the perspective of Scripture, a human being is not God, and the mind of man can never attain God's view of creation. Human beings are limited creatures, and because of this we are always missing something. The gap between our reasoning and God's thoughts is too great to be bridged by some philosophical system, no matter how clever it appears to us at a given moment.

We should think of this the next time we find ourselves in a room with some professor touting his universal political theory about human rights or whatever it may be. When he gets to the point in the discussion in which he says *Actually, you don't need God to make this work*, take note of this and remember: This is the same mistake that Grotius made. When one believes he has no need of God to make his system of universal political and moral thought work, the system he is proposing has confused his own local perspective for the universal, and the pronouncements of human reason for God's thoughts.

By contrast, a political theory in the conservative tradition cannot be made to work without the God of Scripture. Conservatives understand that all human perspectives are limited and local. But at the same time, conservatives recognize that some perspectives are truer than others, and that we can advance toward ideas and principles that better grasp reality in the political and moral domain.[25] This is the difference between a relativist theory and a conservative one: The relativist sees in politics and morals a realm in which an endless variety of perspectives compete with one another for power—without striving to attain what is true, and without anything being right in God's eyes. The conservative, on the other hand, sees in politics and morals a realm in which an endless variety of perspectives compete with one another for power, each of them striving to reach the one truth, which is what is right in God's eyes. Each of these perspectives emphasizes certain causes and principles at the expense of others, which it slights or ignores. When one of them strays too far, it shatters against a reality that no worldly power can in the end avoid. God has perhaps been silent for a very long time. But at this moment, he emerges into plain view. God judges and he speaks.

A ruler or a statesman, having begun to approach an understanding of the biblical God, will thereby begin to recognize that his own view is necessarily limited. From this source comes humility, and tolerance for the views of others, who are often aware of something crucial that we ourselves missed.

Notice that such epistemic humility is much like the fear of God that Scripture describes as the beginning of wisdom. Earlier, I said that the fear of God is an awareness of moral boundaries that must not be crossed. Here we see more clearly where this fear of God comes from. A God-fearing person feels that for each scheme of ideas that he applies in a certain domain, there are boundaries beyond which it can no longer be applied. The ideas and principles in question may be true enough up to this point. But when pushed beyond this boundary, they cease to be reliable and become false and dangerous.

This is precisely what the conservative feels when he follows the thinking of these Enlightenment rationalists: that there is no fear of God in the way they apply their various schemes of ideas—because these ideas and principles are said to apply to all times and to all places, when in fact nothing that is the product of human reason is true to such an extent.

No, a conservative approach to politics and morals cannot be made to work without the God of Scripture. We experience his presence as that countervailing force which stops every scheme of ideas, and every principle, from expanding infinitely outward until it has subjected all things to its rule. The God of Scripture circumscribes all human things, reducing them to their true proportions. Remove him from your thoughts, and your own scheme of ideas, which is local and incomplete, will begin to expand, overrunning its true boundaries. Indeed, it will continue to expand until you mistake it for something universal and complete, and the pronouncements of your own reason come to appear as if they were those of unchanging nature.

At this moment, you mistake your own mind for that of God.

Here all humility ends, and tolerance of alternative views evaporates. Then these foundations of a just politics are no longer visible—for the human mind, mistaking itself for God's mind, is blind to them.

3. *The Traditional Family*

Having touched on the place of God and Scripture in our tradition, I turn now to another institution that has been handed down among Jews and Christians, which I will call the *traditional family.*

Everywhere our experience reaches, human societies are hierarchically ordered into families, clans, tribes, and nations.[26] But while "the family," in a broad sense, is found in every society with which we are familiar, it is a mistake to suppose that the traditional family as it has been known in Judaism and Christianity is natural to human beings. On the contrary, the kinds of sexual relations and family relations that are found throughout the world and natural to mankind are diverse and often depart from what is required by the laws of Moses. But this is to be expected. The Mosaic law does not instruct us to do what we would have done in any case. The law is intended to repair our nature and to improve upon it.[27]

What is natural to man in the sphere of sexual and family relations? In the first place, we have the powerful impulses of man's sexual nature, which, especially in adult males, are sufficient to establish passing sexual relations with women and men, adults and children, strangers and close family members, beasts and physical objects. If permitted to engage in sexual contact according to the impulses of their untamed sexual nature, human males (and some females) would pour their energies into a variety of ephemeral sexual relations, with pregnancy, childbirth, and the raising of children as an incidental byproduct arising from some of them. Second, we have a powerful and countervailing desire to protect, nurture, educate, and advance our own children. This is especially pronounced in women, who, having carried children in the womb, continue to care for them and long for them during the years of their dependency and deep into adulthood, even where their children respond to this care and longing with contempt. Although we do see something similar to this maternal desire in some men as well, its prevalence among women is sufficient to ensure that families of some kind are present in all human societies. Third, both men and women are capable of fierce loyalties to hierarchies in which they are honored.[28]

These aspects of human nature are found everywhere. In reviewing them, we understand that the traditional family, as it is known in Judaism and Christianity, is certainly not determined by human nature. The inflammatory sexuality of men, the deep well of maternal desire, and the fierce loyalties of which both men and woman are capable—these natural impulses are combined, by artifice, with traditional laws or morals to establish the diverse forms of human sexual life and family life.

Let us now consider five principles by which the Mosaic law and the traditions descended from it channel these natural capacities of human beings to establish the traditional family—the family in which Jews and Christians lived in most times and places before the two World Wars:

1. The lifelong bond of a man and a woman. The traditional family is built upon the lifelong bond of a man and a woman. This is certainly not the dictate of untamed nature. Indeed, there is nothing that is more contrary to human nature, and, in particular, to male nature, than a man marrying a woman with the intention of foregoing all other sexual interests for the rest of his life. Here, the mutual loyalty of men facing battle with a rival tribe or clan has been bent to serve a new purpose. Now it is a man and a woman who are bound by mutual loyalty as they face a very different battle—the battle to establish a strong household and to give it permanence and life. By this artifice, the forces of loyalty and honor are turned against the urge to seek sexual gratification outside of marriage. In this way, marriage brings peace to the broader society, which no longer tolerates barbaric scenes of men shedding blood over women and of loose children who know nothing of their father. Instead, these competitive energies are turned to the building up of the household and all its members. This institution of lifelong marriage is the first pillar of what we consider a civilized life.

2. The lifelong bond between a father and mother and their children. Similarly, the traditional family is built upon the lifelong bond between a father and mother and their children. Many suppose that this bond is natural as well, but this is not the case. Children are by nature in awe of their parents in early childhood, but as their body and spirit grow to adult proportions, they tend to be filled with self-regard and to treat their parents with defiance and contempt. In this way, nature prepares children to leave their parents and lead an independent life.[29] Yet in the traditional family, the principle of honoring one's father and mother, which Jews and Christians teach as one of the Ten Precepts of Moses, establishes a lifelong relationship between parents and children that is much like marriage. By this artifice, the forces of honor and loyalty are turned against the natural tendency of adolescents to grow contemptuous and abandon their parents. This permits children to continue learning from their parents throughout life, forming a permanent community of interlocking generations. In this way, barbaric scenes of the elderly cast aside with none to care for them, and of children preying on their parents to advance themselves, are banished. The permanent bond of loyalty between parents and children is the second pillar of a civilized life.

3. The traditional family is a business enterprise. Because liberal society considers one's "career" to be the defining characteristic of the individual, we have largely forgotten that the traditional family was usually a business enterprise. The average family was engaged in farming, commerce, light manufacture, or a profession, and the family business was usually conducted close to the home, if not within the home itself. Often both parents were deeply involved with the family business, a custom that is vividly described in the Bible.[30] Parents taught their children their business, and children gained self-esteem as well as practical skills by contributing actively to the family livelihood. Where children went to school, this was balanced against responsibilities to the family business. And the family itself was often extended by the informal adoption of unmarried relations, or of young men and women who were hired to help with the business and had no other home.

4. The traditional family consists of multiple generations in daily contact. The traditional family often consisted of three generations (or even four) in daily contact with one another. The bond between parents and children was not yet imagined as something that undergoes a rupture when a child turns eighteen or twenty years old, and so the relationship of parents to children continued throughout life. And where there is no rupture between adult children and their parents, and they continue to live near their parents in the same community or even in the same household, grandchildren grow up with grandparents and perhaps great-grandparents. Thus young children were able to learn the skill of honoring their father and mother by watching their parents do it—that is, by seeing their father and mother learning from their own parents and engaging in enterprises with them even as adults, and caring for them when they become infirm. It also meant that in raising children, grandparents were often a crucial presence, providing stores of wisdom and attention to children who learned to honor earlier generations as an integral part of growing up.

5. The traditional family is part of a broader congregation with which it is in daily contact. The traditional family was part of a broader loyalty group—the clan, which in later versions became the community or congregation—with which it was concerned on a daily basis. Such communities or congregations often included adult siblings and cousins who had chosen to live in proximity to one another, assisting one another and being aunts and uncles to one another's children, thus continuing and deepening a childhood affection into adulthood and throughout their lives. But many members of the clan, community, or congregation were not kin relations in this sense. Rather, they were members of an alliance of families, who together formed a kind of adopted and extended family, which came together to celebrate sabbaths and festivals, to teach and train the community's children, to provide relief to those in distress, to improve their communal economic assets, and, where needed, to establish security and justice as well.

Of course, not every family was successful along all five of these dimensions—lifelong marriage, permanent relations between parents and children, family business operations, the embrace of multiple generations within the family, and active participation in a broader community or congregation. Nevertheless, once these principles are examined together, it becomes clear that the traditional Jewish or Christian family was a far more active, extensive, and powerful organization than the family as it exists in contemporary imagination and practice.

On the basis of these five principles, the traditional household or family developed into a remarkably resilient and versatile structure, capable of pursuing numerous purposes at once. Thus while the traditional family has as its distinctive purpose (i) bringing children into the world and protecting them until they can provide for themselves, it has other purposes as well: The traditional family has (ii) economic aims, by means of which its members are kept sheltered, fed, and in good health. It has (iii) an educational purpose, which is to equip the children with the knowledge, traditions, and skills they will need for life. The traditional family also (iv) aims at the security of the household, arming and protecting itself against threats from the outside. It aims at (v) domestic peace, establishing rules, rewards, and punishments in order to attain it. It aims at (vi) cohesion, which is best attained through a just distribution of honor and influence among its members. It aims at (vii) contributing to honorable and mutually beneficial relations with other households in the community or congregation and with the broader tribe or nation. It aims at (viii) maintaining proper relations with God and with one's ancestors, observing sabbaths and holy days and other festive occasions, with the parents and grandparents undertaking various priestly functions within the family to this end. It provides (ix) honor and care for the elderly. And it serves as (x) a home and a support for relations, friends, and strangers who do not have families of their own, or who are distant from them at a given time, or who are otherwise in distress.

I have named ten distinct purposes of the traditional family. It seems astonishing that so many different aims can be borne in mind, much less implemented. Yet where a number of individuals form a strong and cohesive whole, having inherited traditional ideas and ways of doing things, it is possible to manage all of these purposes in a manner that is magnificent to behold. Indeed, for thousands of years, Jewish and Christian households have balanced these purposes, attaining many or all of them even under conditions of great peril and oppression. And this way of life continues to exist, with certain adjustments, in many orthodox religious communities even in our day.

But most individuals who have grown up in liberal societies, have, by this point, never lived as part of a traditional family. In fact, most have not even visited a community in which the traditional family is still the norm. As a consequence, even those who regard themselves as political conservatives often have something very different from the traditional Christian or Jewish family in mind when they speak of the importance of "the family" as a cultural matter or in regard to government policy. In such contexts, what is meant by "the family" is usually the modern "nuclear family," which consists, on most tellings, of a father and mother, with perhaps two or three children in their care for the first eighteen years of these children's lives—that is, up until they leave the house, move somewhere far away, and make nuclear families of their own.

As anyone who has lived among traditional families can immediately see, the nuclear family is a weakened and much diminished version of the traditional family, one that is lacking most of the resources needed effectively to pursue the purposes of the traditional family. When this conception of the family became normative in America after the Second World War, it gave birth to a world of detached suburban homes, connected to distant places of employment and schools by trains, automobiles, and buses. In other words, the physical design of large portions of the country reflected a newly rationalized conception of what a family is, which had been reconstructed in light of the economic principle of the division of labor. In this new reality, there were no longer any business enterprises in the home for the family to pursue together. Instead, fathers would "go to work," seceding from their families during their productive hours each day.[31] Similarly, children were required to "go to school," seceding from the family during their own productive hours. Young adults would then "go away to college," cutting themselves off from family influence during the critical years in which they were supposed to reach maturity. Similarly, grandparents were excised from this vision of the home, being "retired" to "retirement communities" or "nursing homes," which cut the older generation off from the life of their family in much the same way that going away to college cut the younger generation off from it.

Under this new division of labor, mothers were assigned the task of remaining by themselves in the house each day, attempting to "make a home" using the minimalist ingredients that the structure of the nuclear family had left them. Much of this involved increasingly desperate efforts to keep adolescents somehow attached to the family—even though they now shared virtually no productive purposes with their parents, grandparents, and broader community or congregation, and instead spent their days seeking honor among other adolescents. The resulting rupture between parents and their children was poignantly described in numerous books and films beginning in the 1950s. But these works rarely touched upon the reconstruction of the family, which had done so much to inflame the natural tendency of adolescents toward agonized rebellion, while depriving parents of the tools necessary to emerge from these years with the family hierarchy strengthened.

But mothers had the worst of this new family life. Some did succeed in maintaining the cohesion of their families in a world in which grandparents and other family relations had grown impossibly distant, in which the family business had disappeared from the home, and in which the congregation or community, with its sabbaths and festivals, had likewise been reduced to something accessed by automobile once each week like a drive-in movie. However, many other "housewives" despaired and fell into the arms of the feminist movement, which, not without reason, declared the nuclear family to be a tomb for women. Feminist writers were mistaken in supposing that the reconstructed household of the postwar era was itself the traditional family. But they were right that the life of a woman spending most of her productive hours in an empty house, which had been stripped of most of the human relationships, activities, and purposes that had filled the life of the traditional family, was one that many women found too painful and difficult to bear. Many of these mothers quickly joined their husbands and children in leaving the home during the daytime—thus completing the final transformation of the post-traditional "nuclear family" into a hollowed-out shell, a failed imitation of the traditional institution of the family.

Much has been said about the dissolution of the family in liberal societies. Both scholarship and polemical treatments tend to focus on a number of important symptoms of this dissolution: Marriage now happens later in life or not at all. Divorce has become common. Childbirth outside of marriage has become common. Fatherless households have become common. The birth rate has declined dramatically, with no end in sight.

These and many other indicators reflect a widespread failure to hand down the traditional institution of the family to future generations. But discussion tends to focus on these symptoms and how to fight them. Very little is said about the disease itself, which is the removal from the physical household—I am tempted to say the "off-shoring"—of much of what the family was a little more than a century ago. Now that the household is no longer the location of a common business enterprise, of devotion to God and the study of Scripture, of a direct responsibility for the education of the young, of a direct responsibility for honoring and caring for the old, and of significant responsibilities for the establishment and growth of the community and congregation, why should anyone be surprised that what remains is neither terribly sturdy nor especially attractive to the young?

If I had been writing this book two or three years ago, I would have assumed that most of my readers had had few experiences that could even hint at the argument I am making. But the experience of conditions of worldwide epidemic have changed the circumstances somewhat. The extended closings of businesses and schools, churches and synagogues, have offered many people some insight into the potential power of the traditional family. Suddenly, they have found themselves conducting their business at home, their schooling at home, and their religious life at home. Suddenly, many young adults have found themselves returning, over great distances, to live with older and younger family members or to be in close proximity to them. Suddenly, many families have discovered the healing joys of preparing and eating meals together according to a regular routine, and the unparalleled riches that conversations in such contexts can bring into our lives.

I know that in many cases, these experiences were not always pleasant. Not everyone lives in a home that is suitable for such an experiment, and having to make a living and educate one's children under such conditions has been, in many cases, a genuine hardship. Yet in spite of these challenges, or rather because of them, many have had their first glimpse of what a family, thrown together and having to rely on its own resources, is capable of achieving when it takes on a more extensive array of common purposes. In particular, many have experienced the kind of heightened cohesion that can come of meeting such challenges together. In other words, many have had their first glimpse of what the family was like when it was a strong political institution, in which generations worked together to create a permanent community, very much resembling a little tribe or nation.

Perhaps this difficult event has paved the way for us to think more carefully about what has been lost, and about what each of us can do to revive the institution of the family in our own lives.

4. The Community or Congregation

In earlier days, an alliance of families formed a clan, which was on the verge of war with its neighbors much of the time. But with the domestication of the clans under a national or tribal state, an alliance of families came to be called a *community* or a *congregation.* To this day, if one steps into an orthodox church or synagogue that has retained its vitality, one enters into a public commons maintained by such an alliance of families. In the church or synagogue and its adjoining facilities, these families gather for a variety of purposes. Acknowledgment of God in regular prayer services, public readings of Scripture, and the observance of holidays and festivals are first among these purposes. But they are hardly the only ones. The congregation also maintains schools and educational programs directed at both adults and children, regular social functions designed to advance the common economic and political interests of the community, charitable and relief efforts, hospitality for travelers and other guests, measures to strengthen the health and security of the community, and much else.

These purposes make it clear that although the congregation is today often understood as a religious organization, it is a version of the old clans—a hierarchical structure consisting of families bound to one another by ties of mutual loyalty. This structure rightly reminds us of a large family, and in fact the congregation can be seen as serving many of the same broad purposes as the household. But because its scale is larger, the congregation can take up functions that are difficult or impossible for households to perform by themselves, such as supporting resident clergy responsible for conducting religious services, weddings, funerals, and conversions. In a traditional congregation, clergy will tend to be individuals whose personal weight and significance permit them to play a central role in the lives of its members, including providing instruction in religious subjects, counseling families undergoing hardship or distress, undertaking mediation in disputes within the congregation, and organizing relief and welfare efforts in the community. Moreover, the standing of clergy within the traditional congregation often means that they are well-placed to establish mentoring relations with the young that supplement those of parents and family relations, especially when parents are deceased, absent, or otherwise unable to mentor their child for one reason or another.

The congregation is hierarchically ordered like a family. But though we often speak of individuals as being "members" of a congregation, it is more accurate to say that its members are families. Among member families, the most weighty and significant are those who support the congregation through disproportionate financial contributions or through intensive organizational efforts provided on a volunteer basis. In traditional congregations, the appointed clergyman often exceeds the heads of the most powerful families in significance, and will generally be among its most important figures. In times of exceptional threat and adversity, other members of the congregation may rise in importance—for instance, if they are able to offer specialized leadership in defending the congregation in times of tension with neighboring congregations and communities; or in medical affairs during a time of widespread illness; and so forth.

In traditional societies, the congregation plays a decisive role in handing down inherited ideas and institutions. As a general matter, the views of the clergy and the leading families will often be adopted by the congregation across a broad range of subjects. This makes the common sense of the congregation an important asset upon which young families and unmarried individuals can rely to assist in shaping the framework for their own lives. When a young family or an unmarried individual finds that the cultural inheritance from their own parents has been weak in certain respects, they will naturally establish mentoring relations with older and more established families in the congregation, relying on them to transmit ideas and behaviors that reflect the common sense of the community. In this way, the young reconnect themselves to the tradition, taking their place within it and building up the inheritance they are able to pass to their own growing families.

The custom according to which established families invite younger families and unmarried individuals for meals on sabbaths and holidays is one of the best and loveliest means by which young families learn the ways of the congregation and increase their store of insight and understanding more generally.

All this is the case in a traditional society. In a liberal society, in which all traditions are being overturned and the capacity of individuals to uphold inherited norms of any kind has been severely damaged, the traditional congregation becomes an island and a place of refuge. In many places today, participation in an orthodox congregation is the only real alternative to drowning in an ocean of lawlessness, suffering ever greater hardship as the surrounding society becomes more arbitrary and deranged in its judgments. It is here, in the still-vital congregation, that the unmarried individual and the unaffiliated family can take their place within a healthy hierarchy of allied families. It is here that they can begin to participate in the daily transmission and elaboration of the things that have been inherited from our forefathers, which are often being conserved nowhere else. It is here that they can learn how to marry and establish traditional families, and approach God and Scripture, although they had mistakenly believed these things to be forever beyond their reach.

There has been some confusion of late concerning the role of the congregation as opposed to the broader public life of the nation. Individuals who have been raised in liberal societies find it difficult to imagine that any society is worthy of one's attention if it is larger than the individual and the family, yet on a smaller scale than the nation. It is now frequently asked whether investing one's resources in the congregation does not amount to a retreat or withdrawal from the life of the nation. Is it not irresponsible or defeatist? Does it not involve the abandonment of one's countrymen in these troubled times?

No doubt these questions are well-intentioned. But they betray not a little confusion about the nature of human societies. The nation has no existence except as an alliance of tribes or factions tied to one another by bonds of mutual loyalty. It is only from these constituent tribes or factions that the nation can draw leaders who are loyal to it and to its traditional institutions, and capable of judgment and action in accord with the common sense of the people. Likewise, these tribes or factions must draw their leadership from loyal congregations and families that have raised up men and women who are committed to them. In the end, every idea, behavior, and institution that is of value in a nation persists and is elaborated only through this medium of its constituent tribes, congregations, and families. When the congregations and families of the nation cease to perform the function of transmitting national and religious tradition to new generations—as is happening in every liberal society—men and women suitable to the task of conserving and strengthening the nation become scarce. What remains is persons whose motivations are questionable, whose grasp of the common sense of the people is unsound, and whose judgment in matters large and small is arbitrary, if not perverse.

So there is no retreat or withdrawal from the life of the nation when we involve ourselves in the upbuilding of loyal congregations and families. In part, this is because each of us needs to be a part of a congregation in which the traditions still live, and in which they are being handed down, not occasionally, but at all times and under all conditions. But it is also because constructing a traditional congregation and family—especially at a time when every aspect of our inheritance is being uprooted and sound judgment is disappearing from the land—is what all of us need to do if there is to be hope of a restoration for the nation itself.

I have been writing about the traditional Christian or Jewish congregation in a general way. But perhaps I should say something about why I, as a Jew, counsel young men and women from Christian families to find their place in a Christian congregation. This is not because I believe that the differences between Christianity and Judaism are negligible. On the contrary, I believe that the differences between these sister religions are profound. And in my view, the torah of Moses, as handed down and elaborated in Jewish tradition for the last thirty-five centuries or more, is the best of the old paths and the one that carries us most directly to a true understanding of God and Scripture.

But when we speak of the lives of particular individuals, there are other considerations that must be taken into account. From the perspective of my tradition, not every righteous person must become a Jew. There is more than one way to serve God. And it is obvious that an individual who wishes to embark on a conservative life can do so most easily by taking up the tradition handed down for many generations within his own family, tribe, and nation. This is the way of the human soul, which seeks repentance by returning to the God of his own family. As the torah of Moses teaches: "Ask your father and he will declare it to you, your elders, and they will tell you."[32] One finds God by inquiring with the elders of one's own tradition.

Thus I advise the sons and daughters of traditionally Christian families to return to a conservative life by way of a Christian congregation, just as I call upon Jews to return to a conservative life by way of a Jewish congregation.

Having said this, I know that for some the path that is familiar from their own family is, for one reason or another, impassable. And where every effort has been expended, and the way is found to be blocked, one must return to God by another path.

CHAPTER V

The Purposes of Government

1. The National Interest or Common Good

The paradigm blindness that has overtaken liberal society is manifested in many ways. But it is perhaps most obvious in the inability of educated men and women to think of the nation as something different from an arbitrary collection of individuals. This incapacity to recognize the nation as having a real existence leads some to recoil whenever there is talk of the *national interest*, or of the *general welfare* of the nation, or of the *common good* of the nation, or of the good of the *commonwealth*—as if these phrases, by their very use, endanger the freedom of the individual.

Why should such phrases, which were used until recently by nearly all statesmen and philosophers in discussing the purposes of government, be troubling to anyone? The answer is straightforward. It is a premise of Enlightenment liberalism that the only legitimate purpose of government is to enable individuals to make use of the freedom that is theirs by nature.[1] In the liberal paradigm, this is taken to be axiomatic. But terms such as the "national interest" and the "good of the nation" imply that there are legitimate purposes of government that can be identified only by considering the nation as a whole; and that cannot be reduced to ensuring the freedom of the individual alone. In this way, they directly challenge the liberal paradigm's grip on our political understanding, and the paradigm blindness it imposes.

Are there legitimate purposes of government that cannot be reduced to the freedom of the individual? In this chapter, I examine the purposes of government as these are understood in the Anglo-American conservative tradition. This tradition recognizes government as having a number of different purposes that cannot be reduced to one another, and that must be balanced against one another in pursuit of the national interest or the common good of the nation.

2. *The Government of the Family*

Every loyalty group is governed in some way. So we should be able to speak of *government* in a broad sense, comparing the various ways in which human loyalty groups are led, how they make decisions, and how their decisions are enforced. In such a broad discussion, the form of government familiar to us from modern states should be recognized as one kind of government among others, and the national state, in particular, should be recognized as one form of state. But recent political theory has been so preoccupied with the state that when the term "government" is invoked, it is almost exclusively with reference to the kind of government that we find in states.

In this section, I will depart from the current convention by considering how a family is governed. This is the right place to begin a discussion of the purposes of government because it investigates things with which most readers have had some experience. Of course, the government of a national state is unlike the government of a family in many ways, and I will touch on some of these differences below. Nevertheless, we can gain certain insights into the nature of government in general by considering how decisions are made in the government of a household.

In the previous chapter, I described the purposes of the traditional family as bringing children into the world and protecting them until they can provide for themselves; keeping its members sheltered, fed, and in good health; equipping the children with the knowledge, traditions, and skills that they will need for life; securing the household against threats from the outside; establishing rules, rewards, and punishments in order to maintain domestic peace; cohesion, which is best attained through a just distribution of honor and influence among its members; contributing to honorable and mutually beneficial relations with other households in the community or congregation and with the broader tribe or nation; maintaining proper relations with God and with one's ancestors, observing sabbaths and holy days and other festive occasions; providing honor and care for the elderly; and providing a home and a support for relations, friends, and strangers who do not have families of their own, or who are distant from them at a given time, or who are otherwise in distress.[2]

These purposes, when taken together and in the right proportions, provide an ideal against which a real instance of a family can be measured.[3] A father and mother responsible for governing a family of the traditional kind have something like this ideal before their minds; and they work each day to build up their own family in light of it, improving and repairing it so that it moves toward this ideal of what a family ought to be.

But what is it that I am comparing to this ideal as I go about making repairs and improvements to my family? Is it the family as a collective entity, or the members of my family as individuals? The answer to this question comes from the sphere of psychology, from a consideration of the operations of the human mind. Yet it shapes political theory in crucial ways.

No human being can think about ten distinct individuals at once, much less about millions. The best I can do is four or five. And even when I attempt to think about four or five distinct persons at once, I discover that I cannot do so while maintaining my awareness of their respective personalities, histories, and circumstances. Instead, when I attempt to hold a number of individual persons before my mind at once, I inevitably reduce them all to tokens or placeholders standing in a certain relation to one another. In other words, the attempt to hold a number of persons before my mind at one time reduces them all to a single shape or structure. And I cannot, under any circumstances, think about the individuals represented by this shape or structure so long as it remains before my mind.

For this reason, I find that much of them time, when I am engaged each day in building up my family, improving and repairing it, what I have before my mind—and what I compare to the ideal of what a family ought to be—is my family as a unity or a collective entity. This reliance on the idea of *my family* as a single collective entity is not culturally conditioned but determined by the nature of the human mind. I have no capacity to hold a number of persons before my mind and to think clearly about their individual wants and needs all at once, and so I have frequent recourse to the idea of *my family* as a unity or collective. And in practice, I find that the idea of *my family* as a unity or collecive permits me to recognize many of the most significant causes operative in the domain of family governance and to take reliable action with respect to them. The great worth of this idea in permitting me to understand and take reliable action in the domain of family governance is the basis for my recognition that my family has a real existence.[4]

Unfortunately, there is much mediocre philosophy in circulation, and so one sometimes hears it said that *There is no such thing as a family, only the individuals who make up the family*. This is analogous to the claim that *There is no such thing as a table, only the atoms that make up the table*—which we also hear on occasion. But in reality, there are not only atoms and molecules. There are also tables. And a real table is an object whose properties cannot by any means be derived from what we know about the atoms that make up the table. For instance, suppose that the table in my dining room is wobbly and unstable because the screws holding it together have become loose. It is only by having the dining room table before my mind and considering what can be done for the improvement of the table—which is to say, what can be done for the good of the table—that I am able to reach the conclusion that I must find a screwdriver and tighten the screws. It is precisely because I regard the table as a whole as having a real existence, and a discernible good toward which it can be moved, that I am able to engage in practical efforts to repair it. No amount of tinkering with the thought that the table consists of atoms or molecules will help me in this context. And if I try to stop the table from wobbling while thinking about the microstructures in the wood, I will find that these thoughts are worse than worthless, and in fact distract me from the purpose that is before me.

Something similar must be said regarding a human collective such as the family. It is true that a family consists of unique individuals. But in reality, there are also families. And a real family is a thing whose properties cannot be derived from what we know about the individuals comprising it. For instance, our family tradition is to join with other families in our neighborhood for public prayer and torah reading on the sabbath. We were recently forced to suspend this custom for a time because of an outbreak of disease, and so Yael and I instituted a family prayer service and a torah reading on the sabbath in our home as a substitute. Since there was no school, we had to organize lessons and activities for our younger children and our grandson. But at the same time, the family had to abide by new rules that would keep the house quiet enough for me to work during the day. All of this involves consideration of the family as a real collective entity having properties of its own: Is the family protected from disease? Is the family able to participate in a prayer service and torah reading on the sabbath? Is structured education continuing for the children? Is the house quiet during the daytime so that older family members can work? It is because Yael and I regard the family as having a real existence that we were able to engage in practical efforts to protect our family, repair damage that had been done to it, and move it toward a good that includes the family's physical well-being, its internal cohesion, and the ongoing transmission of our cultural inheritance to our family as a whole.

However, we know that the head of every household, if he is competent in performing his duties, also devotes much consideration to each member of the family in his or her particularity. Yael and I discuss the good of particular children on a daily basis, and when we do so, it is the individual child that is before our minds, not the family as a collective. Then I focus my attention on my son or daughter as an individual person, recalling his particular character and life story, as well as his circumstances right now. And in discussing these things, we become aware of actions, both small and large, that we may undertake for his sake—by which I mean, for his good or benefit or welfare or interests, or for his improvement as an individual person. Something like this may be said of each of my children, my parents and other family relations, friends and colleagues. There are moments when I bring each of them before my mind as a unique individual, considering what words I might say or things I might do for their good, by which I mean, for their improvement as individual persons.

In an extreme case, when a child is injured or otherwise in severe distress, the good of one child can determine a large part of our actions for days or even weeks at a time. However, such consideration of the good of a particular child does not mean that we have ceased to think about the good of the family as a whole. On the contrary, even as we focus attention and resources on the good of one child, we continue to alternate between our concerns for the good of that child and consideration of the welfare of our family as a whole. Such an emergency means that things the other children want or need must be set aside, which may cause strains as the other children feel pain over this diversion of resources. But in most such cases, we can see how this adversity strengthens the family as a collective entity, as the other children learn to restrain their own wants and needs and focus their attention on helping their parents and their damaged brother or sister; and how it strengthens each of the other family members, as they see that they are a part of a larger whole, which can respond with great strength when one of its members requires exceptional attention.

Yet this, too, has its limits. Parents facing chronic distress on the part of one child may eventually conclude that too much has been expended on attempting to address this distress. This is a painful conclusion, which is well-known, for example, to families battling the effects of an ongoing case of mental illness, alcoholism, or drug addiction. Eventually, steps must be taken to protect the family as a whole from an exhaustion and bitterness that can also do irreparable harm.

These experiences teach us that the just government of a family requires that we move back and forth between two operations of mind that cannot be performed at the same time: It requires (i) concern for the family as a real entity, whose welfare can be protected and improved only by attending to the family as a collective. And it requires (ii) an alternating concern for the good of each member of the family as a unique individual. This is because a father and mother have responsibilities toward each individual member of their family. But it is also because a current understanding of the needs of each individual family member changes one's view of what is needed to protect and improve the family as a collective. This change in our view of the family as a whole may be dramatic, as when a family member is badly injured. But most of the time, these periodic considerations of the wants and needs of each individual have an incremental effect, slowly altering the parents' conception of their family and their understanding of what must be done to protect, strengthen, and improve it.

But notice how far the good of a particular family member is from being something that can be determined by considering him as an isolated individual, without obligations to his family. One may suppose, for instance, that for the good of a certain child, he should be allowed to play the piano when he wishes. However, the good of the family as a whole may require that he refrain from playing the piano during daytime hours when his father is working in the house. A household rule that permits the children to play musical instruments only in the evening or when their father is not working in the home may be for the good of the family for several reasons: First, the father's work produces income that sustains the family, and so the good of the family requires an environment that is conducive to it. Second, the good of the family requires the constant cultivation of its hierarchical structure, which is what provides an environment of peace, comity, learning, and growth. The children contribute to this hierarchical structure when they honor their parents, and refraining from playing musical instruments during hours when it may be distracting is an instance of honoring one's parents. Third, such a rule strengthens the children's capacity for self-constraint, as well as their ability to give honor where it is due. This contributes directly to the well-being of the individual child, who will be a more able adult if he has gained the capacity for self-constraint and for giving honor where it is due during childhood.

Notice, too, that in this discussion of the good of the family and the good of the child, concepts such as "individual liberty" and "the rights of the individual" are not very helpful. It is true that there are elements of individual liberty in my example. We can say that the father freely chose a certain profession, and that his son freely chose to take up a musical instrument. But it would entirely misconstrue the situation—and in fact blind us to its central features—if we were to begin our analysis by saying that the father has a natural right to do as he pleases and that the son also has a natural right to do as he pleases, and that what is needed is a way to adjudicate between these conflicting natural rights. This is because the decisive features of this situation are not freedoms or rights, but responsibilities and constraints: The father is responsible for supporting his family, and this places considerable constraints on what he may do in life. He is also responsible for the education of his son, and this imposes additional, quite considerable constraints. In the same way, the son is responsible for honoring his father, which he can do by lightening his father's burdens and contributing to the peace and productivity of the household to the extent that he is able. This, too, is a significant and often difficult constraint.

When taken together, these constraints reduce the freedom available to both father and son to a narrow path. The question before both father and son is whether they will traverse it successfully, carrying out their responsibilities in a manner that is admirable and beautiful, with results that will bring pride, benefit, health, and pleasure to them and to their family; or whether they will fail, bringing hardship, dissolution, and the misery of wasted possibilities to all involved.

The government of the family thus requires that we understand the interests or the good of the family as a real entity, and this understanding, if it is just, must take into account the interests or the good of each family member as a unique individual. But this understanding cannot be attained by calculating the good of each family member taken in isolation and then finding the sum of what is good for these isolated individuals. No such means of calculating exists, because the good or interests of the individual family member cannot be determined without reference to the family to which he is tied by bonds of mutual loyalty.

Instead, the father and mother governing a household locate the good or interests of the family by moving back and forth between having the family, as such, before their minds, and attending to the particular circumstances of each family member in turn. It is the view of the family as a whole that we have in mind when we speak of the good or interests of the family, for it is only by means of this broader view that the good or interests of the family can be assessed in light of an ideal of what the family ought to be. Yet the attention given to the needs and wants of each family member means that the father and mother will have to reconsider, at certain points and to some degree, their view of the family as a whole; and that the good or interests of the family, assessed in light of the ideal, will also undergo periodic reconsideration and adjustment.

3. The State as a Traditional Institution

Let us turn our attention to the manner in which nations are governed. For the rest of this discussion, I will use the word *government*, as it is frequently used today, to refer to the governments of states.

Enlightenment-liberal political theory assumes that government serves the same purposes in all times and places. However, if government is a traditional institution, then its purposes must vary from one nation to the next, as nations strive to discover the principles most conducive to strengthening themselves against their rivals and securing the welfare of their members. This is the view of Montesquieu and of empiricist political theory more generally, and it is this view that I will discuss here.[5]

Before the invention of the state, people lived for long ages in an order of tribes and clans, and our ancestors living in this way did have institutions for governing themselves. They possessed customary law and traditional institutions such as councils and assemblies, which met intermittently to make political decisions and resolve rival claims and conflicts. But they had no standing government in command of professional armies with the ability to impose a consistent peace by force. Every household, clan, and tribe maintained a large measure of independence in matters of war, peace, crime, and punishment, and as a consequence they lived amid constant warfare and violence.

What we call the *state* is a traditional institution under which a permanent alliance has been established among rival loyalty groups, which then compete with one another by non-violent means for influence over the direction of the standing government that rules over all of them. This form of government commands a professional army and police capable of suppressing violence over a large territory, and a professional bureaucracy capable of systematic taxation. It was the wealth produced by the invention of large-scale agricultural works in the great river valleys a few thousand years ago that made a standing government commanding professional armies possible, and it was the need to protect this wealth and the people who produced it from the jealousy of local brigands and foreign invaders that made it necessary.

The state has existed on various scales. Originally, it was established over a single city and its environs (the "city-state"), in which case it ruled over a permanent alliance of rival clans. But the state as we know it today is usually the state of a certain nation—either a national state, established over a single nation and ruling over a permanent alliance of its tribes, or an imperial state, which is established as the instrument of one nation ruling over many others.

However, regardless of its scale, the introduction of the state alters the order of tribes and clans in one decisive way. The ability of families, clans, and tribes to conduct independent policies in matters of war, peace, and the punishment of major crimes is brought to an end. The competition among families, clans, and tribes, which constantly led to bloodshed in the pre-state order, becomes, in the state, a competition in which violence is proscribed, thereby establishing a sphere of domestic peace over a certain territory. While rivalry among loyalty groups continues unabated within this domestic sphere, it is now conducted in accordance with norms of speech and behavior that have been adopted to assure a certain measure of honor and influence to all sides. So long as this balance of honor and influence is maintained, the peaceful coexistence and alliance among the families, clans, and tribes living under the state can be maintained.

The state thus introduces a profound transformation in human life. But the fundamentals of human nature are not changed by it. Human beings continue to form families, clans, and tribes. And while these loyalty groups are to various degrees domesticated—meaning that they become more peaceable among themselves—they nonetheless retain their hierarchical structure, their tendency to adopt a common judgment based on the views of leading figures within the hierarchy, and their intense competition for honor and influence. All this continues, along with the insult and anger that occur when one's family or tribe has been disregarded or dishonored and its influence slighted. And if the norms of domestic speech and behavior, which have been established to guarantee a measure of honor and influence to all sides, are not upheld, then the peaceful coexistence and alliance among the tribes will quickly disintegrate. At such times, the old order of tribes and clans inevitably reasserts itself. Then the competition among the tribes becomes violent again, and their assertions of independence from one another grow more strident, until finally the state exists in name only or not at all.

Let us now consider how the national or tribal state appears in the mind of the ruler or statesman who is responsible for governing it. In a small loyalty group whose members are individuals—I have in mind a small business, a small military formation, a small boat or aircraft, and so on—the manager, commander, or captain will approach his responsibilities in a manner that is similar to that of a father and mother governing a household. That is, he will move back and forth between having the good of the collective, as such, before his mind; and attending to the good of member individuals, whose particular circumstances may necessitate an adjustment of his understanding of what the good of the collective requires.

However, this technique cannot be applied without modification to large loyalty groups consisting of thousands or millions of people. The king, president, or prime minister at the head of a nation can have the good of the collective as a whole before his mind. But he cannot move back and forth between considering the good of the nation as a whole and thinking about each individual under his rule—as the head of a household or the commander of a small military unit does—because it is impossible for him to be familiar with all of the individuals in his charge. In other words, the methods by which we govern a small loyalty group are not scalable, and the history and philosophy of government is replete with institutional innovations whose purpose is to contend with this difficulty—including the appoinment of deputies, assistants, ministers, and ministries; the holding of assemblies, councils, congresses, courts, and committees; the receiving of representatives, delegations, pleas, and suits; the collection of legal precedents and the formulation of legal codes; the assembling of bureaucracies wielding delegated authority; and many others. Ultimately, all of these innovations can be understood as attempts to improve the ability of the ruler or statesman to govern a large loyalty group, the great majority of whose member individuals he will never meet.

There is much to be said about this subject, but here I wish to focus on one crucial point. Whatever the governing institutions may be in a given nation or tribe, the mind of the ruler or statesman remains limited in the ways I have discussed. The king, president, or prime minister has no ability to consider directly the circumstances of each of the thousands or millions of persons for whom he is responsible. He has no choice, in fact, but to alternate between concerning himself with the nation as a real entity, which can be protected and advanced only by attending to it as such; and considering the good of each of the respective tribes or parties that constitute the nation.[6] This means that the member tribes or parties of the nation are, in the mind of the ruler or statesman, in a position roughly analogous to that of the member individuals within the family. Of course, each of these tribes or parties is itself a large loyalty group, which is hierarchically structured and possesses its own leadership. A competent and just ruler will devote attention to each of the various tribes and parties that constitute the nation, in a manner that is similar to the way in which a father and mother attend to each of the individuals in their family in turn. But in place of attending to the good or interests of particular individuals, he meets with the leadership of these tribes or parties to establish their views concerning the good or interests of their own particular tribe or party.

This observation is worthy of some careful consideration. The hierarchical structure of human loyalty groups dictates that congregations consist of families, that nations consist of tribes, and that, in general, every large loyalty group will consist of member loyalty groups. And it is these member groups—not individuals—that are primarily meant when we speak of the cohesion and dissolution of the collective. Thus when a nation is internally cohesive, it is because the respective tribes or parties that constitute it are loyal to one another; and though they compete with one another, at times bitterly, for honor and influence, they nonetheless assemble themselves into a united front, so as to project a unified power, when faced with a common adversity. Whereas when a nation is undergoing dissolution, it is because the bonds of loyalty between the tribes or parties of the nation have weakened or have ceased to exist entirely, so that when they are faced with a common hardship, adversity, or enemy, they waste their energies blaming one another and fighting one another. Then no unified front can be established, and no unified power projected.

To put this matter as simply as possible: The state and government are traditional institutions of certain societies. Their continued existence therefore depends entirely on the cultivation of bonds of mutual loyalty among the rival tribes that constitute the nation; and these bonds, in turn, depend on the conservation and transmission of particular traditions of speech and behavior that allow rival tribes and parties to compete, while at the same time honoring one another. There is, in other words, a causal relation between the cultivation and transmission of certain traditions within society and the existence of the state and state government. If appropriate traditions are not intensively and successfully cultivated, then the alliance among these rival tribes will end, and both the state and its government will cease to be.

These are elementary facts of human life, and they are well known to anyone who regards political matters from within a traditional or conservative framework. However, those who have been educated in the Enlightenment-rationalist political theories that are today predominant tend to be blind to these realities. Instead of understanding the causal relation between society and state—the fact that the state is brought into being and maintained by the particular characteristics of a certain society—they imagine that the state is brought into being by force of universal reason, which is independent of any given society. Indeed, they conceive of the state as a kind of wedding of power to universal reason, and for this reason recognize the causal relations between government and the society it governs as operating in one direction only: The state is imagined as imposing law and order on society by force, while society itself is passive. This philosophy is therefore blind to the causal relationship proceeding in the opposite direction—namely, from society to the state. In particular, Enlightenment rationalist political theories are blind to the fact that state government is, like the state itself, a traditional institution, and thus entirely dependent for its existence on the character and condition of the society it governs.

A particularly devastating form of paradigm blindess afflicts those liberals who believe that the alliance of tribes or factions on which the national state is based can be maintained by declaring and upholding certain general principles about the universal rights of the individual. From this point of view, the ruler or statesman is not legitimately occupied if he is not legislating into law and enforcing the rights of an abstract "individual" that he has constantly before his mind. But this activity—of fixating on a fictional abstract individual, declaring his rights and upholding them—is for the most part a distraction from the actual business of national politics. This is because the nation is composed of real loyalty groups, whose actual good and interests cannot normally be known by deduction from general formulas, because each of them has its own unique history, troubles, and aspirations.

What is needed above all else is to do the practical political work of cultivating ties of mutual loyalty among the various tribes and parties. This involves constantly balancing their interests and needs against one another, and ensuring that this balance leads to a renewed exchange of honors among them. Where the national political leadership has cultivated such mutual loyalties among the differents tribes and factions that constitute the nation, then the state can be firm and its government effective.

4. Eight Purposes of National Government

What are the purposes of government as these are understood in the Anglo-American conservative tradition? It is helpful to consult the American Constitution of 1787, which describes, with admirable clarity, the purposes of the national government as the great Federalist statesmen understood them. These purposes appear in seven clauses in the preamble, which was drafted by Gouverneur Morris:

> We the people of the United States, in order to [i] form a more perfect union, [ii] establish justice, [iii] insure domestic tranquility, [iv] provide for the common defence, [v] promote the general welfare, and [vi] secure the blessings of liberty [vii] to ourselves and our posterity, do ordain and establish this Constitution for the United States of America.

A few years later, Edmund Burke suggested another set of seven aims in describing the British constitution. As he put it:

> None, except those who are profoundly studied, can comprehend the elaborate contrivance of a fabric fitted to

> unite [i–ii] private and public liberty [iii] with public force, [iv] with order, [v] with peace, [vi] with justice, and above all, [vii] with the institutions formed for bestowing permanence and stability through the ages, upon this invaluable whole.[7]

In terms of the purposes being described, the two formulations are quite similar. Both speak of justice as a purpose of government. Both speak of peace, although Burke's "peace" is broader than Morris's "domestic tranquility," encompassing the absence of foreign war as well. Morris lists "the common defense," whereas Burke speaks more broadly of a "public force" that can provide both a common defense and the enforcement of the laws at home. Both name liberty as a purpose of government, although Burke distinguishes the "private liberty" of the individual from the "public liberty" of the nation, which is to say, national independence. The Americans speak of handing down their achievements to their posterity, and Burke, similarly, speaks of maintaining "permanence and stability through the ages." Moreover, Morris's concern "to form a more perfect union" appears to be seeking what Burke, in contemplating the British constitution, calls "order"—that is, a political settlement that allows the various factions in the nation to be loyal to one another, rendering the fundamental structure of the state cohesive and immune to fracture. Finally, Morris includes a clause concerned with the "general welfare."

None of these differences suggests a substantive disagreement between Morris and Burke as to the purposes of government. I will therefore treat the two lists as proposing a total of eight purposes of government between them. Arranged in the order that Gouverneur Morris has them, they are: (i) a more perfect union, (ii) justice, (iii) domestic peace, (iv) the common defense against foreign enemies,

(v) the general welfare, (vi) individual liberty, (vii) national liberty, and (viii) permanence and stability through the ages.

Some of these purposes are uncontroversial. Every account of the state with which I am familiar, beginning with the Hebrew Bible, names *domestic peace* and the *common defense* against external enemies among the purposes of the state.[8] Government seeks to establish domestic peace by means of a system of laws, which is enforced by a professional policing force and standing courts. It mounts a common defense against external enemies by means of a professional military, which brings to bear a much greater, more disciplined, and better armed force than was possible in the era of tribal militias.

But other purposes of government mentioned here are less familiar and require some discussion. For example, the first purpose of the American national government, as described by Morris, is *to form a more perfect union*. In other words, the American Federalists sought the kind of domestic order that Britain already possessed: a political settlement that would allow the various parts of the nation to be loyal to one another, in this way establishing a structure that is cohesive and immune to fracture. We know exactly why the American nationalists sought such an order in 1787. For eleven years, they had lived with the nightmare of waging war against Great Britain and trying to establish a durable peace thereafter, while the thirteen states considered themselves independent countries under no real obligation to back a united national effort. During these years, the Americans lacked sufficient national cohesion to raise the armed forces they needed and the funds to pay their soldiers' salaries, relying time and again on donations from private individuals that were themselves barely sufficient. Nor were the thirteen states cohesive enough to keep the terms of treaties with foreign governments or to suppress internal violence and strife when it came.

These experiences brought the American nationalists, with General Washington first among them, to suppose that a new political settlement was needed—one that would permit the necessary mutual loyalties to form and to find expression under conditions of duress. If they could establish a strong national government that would be, in many respects, like that of Britain, the Americans would have an institution of sufficient weight and significance to influence the respective states, and to make them into a unified whole capable of fighting external wars and maintaining domestic peace. And in fact, time proved this assessment correct. Americans did attribute a great weight and significance to the new national government led by Washington and his party, and the cohesion among the various states was greatly strengthened by it.

But if American national cohesion was only a possibility that men such as Washington, Jay, Hamilton, and Madison believed to be latent in the miserable conditions established by the constitution of 1777, how did the Federalists' Constitution of 1787 change this? How did the new constitution summon strong bonds of mutual loyalty and a cohesive national character into being when these things had been so lacking before? I want to consider this lesson more carefully.

Bonds of mutual loyalty grow strong where each side of a given relation is honored.[9] This is true, as well, of the bonds of mutual loyalty that tie the constituent tribes or parties of a nation to one another as well. These bonds grow strong when each tribe or party is honored by the others, and when the things that are important to each are honored—including the leading men and women among them, their traditional institutions, and their achievements, interests, and aspirations. However, because the constituent tribes or parties of the nation compete with one another for status and influence, often insulting and harming one another in the process, it may be difficult for them to give honor to one another without the direct intervention of a national leadership, and ultimately, of a national government. Frequently, it is only the leading figures of the nation who have the standing to bring the respective factions together and to induce them to honor one another, despite the differences among them.

The compromises that were required to arrive at the Constitution of 1787 are instructive in this regard. The distrust among the states was rendered tractable through a mutual exchange of honors embodied in the composition of the national Congress, and in the mechanism for electing the president. On the one hand, large states such Virginia, Pennsylvania, and New York honored the smaller states by granting them equal representation in the Senate; on the other hand, the large states were honored by having a great advantage, commensurate with their populations, in the House of Representatives. This exchange of honors was repeated in the formula for the selection of the Electoral College that would elect the president—the number of electoral votes for each state being the sum of its representatives in the Senate and in the House. A similar settlement was reached regarding slavery, which was recognized as legal, although concessions such as a moratorium on the importation of slaves beginning in 1808 granted the anti-slavery views of many of the Federalists a certain standing.

Of course, none of these arrangements—concerning the composition of the legislature, the election of the president, and the acceptance of slavery—were in any way derived from the equality of natural rights required by Enlightenment rationalist political theory. Indeed, all three compromises ignored the demands of Enlightenment rationalism in favor of a political settlement based on a dramatic exchange of honors among the rival states of America—an exchange of honors whose purpose was to allow bonds of mutual loyalty to be established among the states. This exchange of honors was possible because it was sponsored by the most significant and revered political figure in the nation, George Washington, without whose intervention it would almost certainly have been impossible.

This exchange of honors established a political order that lasted for seventy years before it finally broke down over the issue of slavery in the years before the Civil War. But the other decisive compromises of 1787 (over the composition of the Congress and the Electoral College) never did break down. They remain the basis for American union to this day.

With this American settlement in mind, let us return to the relationship between the establishment of a political order—that is, of a political form consisting of various fixed relations—and the growth of bonds of mutual loyalty among the tribes or factions of the nation. We can understand this in the following way. In every society there exists an *economy of honors*, whereby men and women are applauded for their efforts to strengthen their nation, tribe, congregation, or family; and dishonored when their actions and words are directed toward dissolution. The most important figures in every society exert a great influence on this economy of honors by way of the things they choose to honor and dishonor. This was the case with Washington's successful intervention in national politics in 1787. Although all the men present certainly wished to be honored in their home states, they were also strongly influenced by Washington's insistence on a strong national government in accordance with Anglo-American tradition—and by the threat of dishonor if their intransigence should be responsible for embarrassing the great man by producing a hung convention.[10]

Even though Washington was not yet president of the United States, his intervention in the politics of his nation teaches us much about the purposes of government, and about the national figures who are responsible for it. In a national state, the national government inevitably lays a heavy, shaping hand on the economy of honors within the nation, which in turn influences the things people say and do throughout the land. When the king, president, or prime minister shows, in his words and deeds, that he honors someone or esteems something, this person or thing will be more greatly honored and esteemed throughout the nation. When the king, president, or prime minister displays disdain for someone, or disregard for something, this person or thing will be honored less, and displays of contempt for this person or thing will proliferate. This means that the king, president, or prime minister frequently has the ability to sponsor agreements between rival factions or parties, and to bring their seemingly intractable disputes to an end with a previously unimaginable mutual exchange of honors. In such an intervention, the great esteem that the leading figures of the nation enjoy among the rival parties gives them a lever that can be used to dramatic effect: the threat of dishonor in the eyes of the king, president, or prime minister, if their intransigence should prevent a settlement from being reached and an exchange of honors from taking place. Because government does, in fact, wield this great influence over what is honored by the respective parties under its rule, and because the very existence of the government and the state itself depends on the degree to which the factions or parties under its rule give honor to one another, it is obvious that government must aim to shape the society it governs in such a way as to encourage mutual loyalty and the mutual exchange of honors that leads to it.

Of course, rival factions or parties disagree on many things, and often with good reason. It is therefore impossible that every faction should be accorded honor and influence at all times. In the end, the government has to take sides on many issues, and must often choose a course that causes division for a time. Even so, the unity of the nation must be the constant concern of government. Where it decides against a given faction or party, a competent government takes steps to diminish the insult, including compensating the stricken faction with other things it wants or needs. The ability of the nation to remain an integral whole, and not to slide into unbridgeable hatreds whose only outlet is in civil violence, depends on this work of government to maintain the delicate balance of honors and influence.

This brings us to two additional purposes of government, establishing *justice* and promoting the *general welfare*. Although not all governments concern themselves with these aims, we may say that they are found wherever a nation is blessed with rulers who are righteous and wise. For the establishment of justice involves an appropriate distribution of honors and influence—as reflected in laws, policies, and pronouncements—such that the respective factions and parties see themselves as an integral part of the nation, and none consider the government to be beyond their influence and therefore wholly inimical to their own interests and aspirations.[11] Whereas the general welfare involves the pursuit by government of the material well-being of the nation in all its parts, and of the necessary cultural inheritance to attain this and other ends. And in fact, these two purposes of government are closely related to the aim of establishing a more perfect union—because a statesman who knows how to deal justly with the respective factions and parties of the nation and to promote their welfare, will in this way strengthen the mutual loyalty that binds the various factions and parties of the nation to one another as well.

Righteous and wise rulers will also concern themselves with protecting *individual liberty*. Much has been said about individual freedom, and yet this subject remains poorly understood. Too many believe that the freedom of the individual is a gift that is ours by nature. But there is little truth to this. Every form of liberty that the individual enjoys is due to a tradition of constraint that is inculcated at every level of certain societies from childhood. For example, to be able to freely dispose of one's labor and property, there must be a carefully cultivated tradition establishing property rights and the freedom to engage in enterprises that may harm or eliminate the profits of others. Similarly, to have freedom of religion, there must be a carefully cultivated tradition of tolerating religions that in some matters seem misguided and troubling to us. Likewise, for there to be freedom of speech, there must be a tradition of allowing the other man to have his say, even though his words seem to lack truth and common sense.[12]

Moreover, these traditions do not amount to a *right*, which is something that is guaranteed and defended by consensus within a certain society, if they are only cultivated in one corner of that society and not another. In fact, when any powerful tribe or party is unconstrained in its hostility to a certain kind of religious practice or political point of view or business enterprise, and its members punish those who embrace the stigmatized ideas and practices by abusing and shaming them, depriving them of their livelihood and excluding them from public life—then one cannot say that such a freedom in fact exists. We understand from this that for a given liberty to exist, it will have to be supported by the government and protected by it in word and deed.

But notice that when the government guarantees a certain right in this way, it inevitably means defending one freedom, which is desired by some, by suppressing a different freedom that is desired by others. Which freedoms should be defended by the government cannot be determined without taking into account considerations of justice and peace, the general welfare and the cohesiveness of society, and the ability of the nation to mount a common defense. In a case of shameful and ongoing injustice, as with the racial segregation laws in the American South, there may be no choice but for the peace and unity of the country to be damaged for a time, so that injustice may be corrected. But nothing of the kind can be said concerning the American government's recognition of a freedom to unleash obscenity and pornography into the public sphere, or its elimination of God and Scripture from the schools. These new "liberties" were recognized and established despite the fact that there was no shameful and ongoing injustice to be repaired by them, and despite the evident damage done to the general welfare and the cohesion of the nation.

From these and other similar examples, we learn that even in a country that is zealous for individual liberties, a balance must always be maintained among the various liberties of the individual and between these liberties and the other aims of government.

Maintaining the *independence of the nation* is a purpose of government that is distinct from guaranteeing the liberty of the individual. Moreover, it is not the same as providing for the common defense, because the freedom of the nation may be reduced or eliminated without warfare. This happens when the leading figures of the nation agree to cede the authority of government to a foreign empire, or to international bodies, or to large business enterprises, or to any other power, whether out of fear or folly, ideology or greed. Both Britain and America have long sought to limit the powers of government with respect to other domestic actors. But they have also been diligent in building up the power and freedom of the national government with respect to foreign empires and other international powers—a tradition that was restored by Britain's recent departure from the European Union. I have written at length about this purpose of government in my book on nationalism. Here, I will only say that no greater gift can be given to a nation than the strength necessary to chart its own course in accordance with traditions that are its own.[13]

We come now to the last aim of government that is mentioned by Morris and Burke, which is *permanence and stability through the ages*. This is a purpose of government that should be constantly emphasized today, given the enthusiasm with which political leaders now uproot and overthrow whatever has been inherited, jettisoning their people's religion, its history, and its national independence as if these were things of no consequence. A wise ruler is active in introducing repairs so that the nation and its institutions may regain their fading splendor and move forward through the coming generations with renewed strength. He consistently honors religion and virtue, the history of the nation's achievements and its laws, and the respective tribes and parties in the land—so that this esteem may be taken up by the people as well, and that the mutual loyalty and cohesiveness of the constituent tribes of the nation may grow stronger. He pursues this aim because he wishes to honor his forefathers, safeguarding their names and accomplishments by securing their inheritance for several generations more. But foolish rulers are moved by ideology and arrogance, or by an eagerness to make a name for themselves that will be remembered in place of those who came before them, to create everything they touch anew.

5. *Religion as a Purpose of Government*

Perhaps the most striking innovation in the American nationalists' Constitution of 1787 is the absence of any explicit mention of religion. True, it was not the intention of the Federalists to do without Christianity. They saw the cultivation of specific religious establishments as a matter to be left to the thirteen states. Nevertheless, with hindsight I think we can say that the failure to acknowledge God and religion was a mistake with lasting consequences, both for the United States and for the many nations that have taken their political cues from the American government.

Whatever government does not honor is weakened by this neglect. Of course, the cultural currents that have undermined

Christianity and Judaism in the last centuries may be so strong that no government could have affected their course. The survival of the established church in England, for example, has not meant that the fate of Christianity in Britain has been much different from the fate of Christianity in America. Nevertheless, we are all obliged to do what we can to strengthen those aspects of our cultural inheritance that have been beneficial, and this is certainly true of the leading figures in every nation, whose words and deeds have such a great effect on the common sense of the public. They must ask whether the traditional religion of their nation is beneficial to it—for if so, then the government and the other leading figures in public life must do what they can to ensure that it is upheld and handed down to future generations.

A typical conservative view of public religion is articulated by Burke, who wrote that the established Church of England is "the first of our prejudices... involving in it profound and extensive wisdom." He explained as follows:

> We continue to act on the early received and uniformly continued sense of mankind. That sense not only, like a wise architect, has built up the august fabric of states, but, like a provident proprietor, [in order] to preserve the structure from profanation and ruin, as a sacred temple purged from all the impurities of fraud and violence and injustice and tyranny, has solemnly and forever consecrated the commonwealth and all that officiate in it [by means of the established church]. This consecration is made that all who administer the government of men... should have high and worthy notions of their function and destination, that their hope should be full of immortality, that they should not look to the paltry pelf of the moment, nor to the

> temporary and transient praise of the vulgar, but to a solid, permanent existence in the permanent part of their nature, and to a permanent fame and glory in the example they leave as a rich inheritance to the world. Such sublime principles ought to be infused into persons of exalted situations, and religious establishments provided that may continually revive and enforce them. . . .
>
> The consecration of the state by a state religious establishment is necessary, also, to operate with a wholesome awe upon free citizens, because, in order to secure their freedom, they must enjoy some determinate portion of power. To them, therefore, a religious connection with the state, and with their duty toward it, becomes even more necessary than in such societies where people, by the terms of their subjection, are confined to private sentiments and the management of their own family concerns. All persons possessing any portion of power ought to be strongly and awfully impressed with an idea that they act in trust, and that they are to account for their conduct in that trust to the one great Master, Author, and Founder of society.[14]

According to this view, cultivation of the national religion is an indispensable purpose of government, since both state officials and free citizens must exercise power, and in doing so they must be encouraged to think of this exercise of power in light of a certain understanding of their place in the world and of the weight and significance of their duties. The role of the established religion, then, is to offer an overarching frame of reference—today we might call it a "public philosophy"—so that both the government and the public may decline the temptations of the moment and seek to the higher things that are of this world and beyond it, "so that their efforts might be in the service of beneficial ends." Without such a framework, Burke believes that both government officials and the public more generally will be moved only by the desire for immediate gain and the applause of the crowd—motivations that cannot, in the end, redound to the good of the nation.

The possibility that government can avoid having such a religious framework to guide it is, of course, an experiment that has been embarked upon in recent times. Both the Jacobins and the Communists sought to uproot Christianity from the state. But they were not under the illusion that the post-Christian state could be "neutral" on the question of the overarching framework within which officials and the public were to understand human life. Instead, they were conscious of the need to substitute what was, in practice, an atheistic religion of Enlightenment so that the state might continue to provide a philosophical framework directed toward supposedly beneficial ends.

By contrast, the Enlightenment liberalism that became dominant in America and Europe after the Second World War did claim to have made the state neutral with respect to all such grand philosophical frameworks. But there is no such thing as a neutral state, and within a generation, leading public figures had openly embraced a messianic vision of the "end of history" and of the worldwide redemption that Enlightenment liberals would bring.[15] Like their Jacobin and Marxist predecessors, Enlightenment liberals ended up promoting an atheistic religion to take the place of Christianity.

This substitution of Enlightenment rationalism for Christianity has not been kind to America and other nations that attempted it. No doubt, there were some good intentions behind this effort. But the destruction of the public's willingness to honor the God, Scripture, and religion of their ancestors has opened the door to the overthrow of every significant concept and principle that once permitted these nations to make their way as strong and cohesive peoples. Having seen this with our own eyes, a reasonable conclusion is that government cannot deny its purpose as a support for the traditional religion (or religions) of the nation—there being no known substitute that can be adopted without the devastating effects that we have before us.[16]

Burke himself seems to have considered the established church as one of those "institutions formed for bestowing permanence and stability through the ages," which I have counted here as the eighth purpose of national government. However, we now know beyond any reasonable doubt that a national government cannot, in fact, be neutral regarding the overarching framework that upholds the political life of the people. We know, too, that every government will uphold traditional religions such as Christianity and Judaism, or else it will substitute for them an atheistic framework such as Marxism or Enlightenment liberalism.[17] And since we do know these things, I believe the time has come to regard the encouragement of the traditional religion (or religions) of the nation as having a place of especial importance among the responsibilities of national government. We should, in other words, regard the encouragement of religion as a distinct purpose of national government.

6. The Balance of Purposes in the State

I have named nine purposes of government within the Anglo-American tradition. And it often happens that the pursuit of one of these purposes brings about an improvement with respect to others. For instance, when government is concerned for the honor and influence of the respective tribes or parties that constitute the nation, and for their general welfare, this is likely to improve the cohesion and resilience of the nation. The same can be said of a government that is zealous for the protection of certain individual liberties of the people, because in freeing them from constraints they consider onerous, it may win their gratitude and loyalty as well. This suggests that if the government is attentive to the demands of justice, the general welfare, and individual liberties, the resulting cohesion of the people will better enable it to offer a common defense against foreign adversaries and to maintain peace at home. In the same way, a regime that is strong enough to fend off foreign enemies and maintain its national independence will be best able to protect the regime of justice, well-being, and liberty that has been established at home.

This having been said, we must admit that the proper balance among the various purposes of government is always difficult to find and maintain, and it is inevitable that certain purposes will come into severe conflict with others. For example, the Federalist authors of the American Constitution of 1787 were well aware that in their generation, justice for those enslaved in the South was being sacrificed in the name of establishing a stronger national union and a more effective common defense.[18] And when, after the secession of the South in Lincoln's day, the government found that the preservation of the union and justice for the slaves had finally come together in a single cause, it led to the destruction of domestic peace and great harm to the material welfare of the country.

Similarly, since the rise of mechanized industry at the end of the nineteenth century, the most evident conflict has been between the claims of the general welfare, on the one hand; and those of individual liberty, on the other. Facing widespread disruption of traditional economic forms, while at the same time witnessing a vast growth in national wealth, conservative statesmen such as Disraeli and Bismarck sought to strengthen the cohesion of the nation and to lessen the likelihood of violence through what is now called social welfare legislation. These conservative political figures did not suppose, as socialists do, that a government can plan the economic life of an entire country, directing what should be produced, at what price, and by whom out of some central office manned by supposedly rational experts. Rather, they offered a guarantee of basic subsistence and safety in exchange for working-class support for industrialization and private enterprise. In other words, they sought to award a measure of honor and influence to a large part of the population, whose labor under unprecedented conditions had left them humiliated and degraded.

But the limited social programs these statesmen envisioned did not avert the rise of socialist government, which abused the principle of the "general welfare" to justify pursuing the rationalist dream of a centrally planned economy. By the end of the Second World War, liberals and conservatives found themselves together fighting a two-front battle to maintain the sphere of individual liberty in the face of Communist governments abroad and socialist ideals of government planning at home.

The belief that the economic activities of an entire nation can be planned in advance is a sickness of government. And in their insistence on reviving the principle of individual liberty, the postwar coalition of liberals and conservatives was in the right. However, in their struggle against the indefinite expansion of government, they embraced a dogmatic rejection of government, and moved toward a fantasy of their own: the belief that the several purposes of government could ultimately be reduced to a single purpose, namely, ensuring the freedom of the individual. By now, this tendency has been carried so far that even the most necessary action of government to secure the general welfare of the nation is regarded by some as a violation of the legitimate purposes of government. Thus many express doubts about government efforts to prevent undesired immigration, or to prevent the intentional destruction of domestic industries by hostile foreign actors, or to prevent public debate on political matters from being suppressed by partisan private corporations, or to prevent the enslavement of young women and men to a burgeoning trade in narcotics and pornography. In all these cases, arguments deduced from the principle of individual freedom are thought to defeat concerns for the general welfare of the nation, or for the mutual loyalty and cohesion of the nation, or for a just economy of honors, or for the common defense.

This dogmatic insistence on individual liberties at the expense of every other purpose of national government cannot be maintained for long. The harm caused by this blindness to the other purposes of government has already been severe, and so painful that the framework upon which national life has rested for the past sixty years is plainly undergoing a profound revision. An attempt will be made to restore the balance among the respective purposes of government. It remains to be seen whether this attempt can succeed in bringing the national interest, which is the good of the nation, back into view.

Part Three

Current Affairs

Chapter VI

Liberal Hegemony and Cold War Conservatism

The two World Wars brought unprecedented changes in the political life of the English-speaking world. By the 1960s, the Protestant nationalism that still animated America in the generation of Franklin Roosevelt and Dwight Eisenhower had been set aside, and Enlightenment liberalism was adopted as the new framework within which American political life was conducted. America was given what was, in effect, a new Enlightenment-liberal constitution.[1] Academics and intellectuals even gave a new name to the regime, which they now called "liberal democracy."[2] This period of liberal hegemony was to last until the 2010s, when a revived nationalist conservatism on the political right, and the fall of many of the leading liberal institutions to an updated Marxist ideology on the left, returned open ideological competition to the American political arena.

In this chapter, I would like to ask two questions about the rise of Enlightenment liberalism in America during the Cold War.

First, I would like to understand what characterized this period of liberal hegemony, and how it differed from the more conservative America that had existed before the World Wars.

Second, I would like to understand the role played by conservative political ideas during this period. This question is important because these same years—from the founding of William Buckley's *National Review* in 1955 to the end of Margaret Thatcher's ministry in Britain in 1990—are often described as a time of resurgence for Anglo-American conservatism. No doubt, there is a measure of truth to this. But in an important sense, it is also false. What was called "conservatism" during these years was in fact a self-conscious and self-proclaimed "fusion" of liberalism and conservatism. The reasons for this fusion are well known. The need to fight Soviet Communism abroad and a rising tide of socialism at home obviously called for an alliance between liberals and conservatives. And this alliance was also remarkably successful in attaining its stated aims: By 1990, the Soviet Union was in the final stages of collapse, and the idea of the socialist planned economy was in retreat almost everywhere.

Yet this great victory was not, as it appeared at the time, a victory for Anglo-American conservatism. In retrospect, we can see that the politics which emerged from the end of the Cold War in America, Britain, and other countries was devoted almost exclusively to the advancement of liberalism. And it is fair to ask: If Cold War "conservatism" was indeed such a successful alliance of liberals and conservatives, then how did it come about that, by the time this alliance had triumphed in 1990, Anglo-American conservatism had been as soundly defeated as the Communist enemy?

I raise this vexing historical question in part because I was myself active on behalf of conservative causes during the 1980s, and I would like to understand how a moment of seeming triumph for Anglo-American conservatism could have turned out, in the end, to have been a rout for this very cause. But this question is also especially important today because there are such strong parallels between our own time and the world in which the Cold War alliance of conservatives and liberals was originally concocted. The threat posed by the Chinese Communist Party today is not the same as the Soviet threat of the 1950s, and the racialist neo-Marxism that is seizing power throughout the English-speaking world is not the same as the socialism of that era either. Yet this combination of a hostile Communist power overseas and a domestic rivalry against socialism is strongly reminiscent of the onset of the Cold War, and this structural parallel again urges us to accept another alliance between liberals and conservatives.

Before entering into another such alliance, I think we had better understand how conservatism ended up faring so badly the first time around.

1. From Christian Democracy to Liberal Democracy

For most of their history, Americans did not know or use the term *liberal democracy*. Since the eighteenth century, they had usually described their system of government as *republican government*, a term that expressed their pride in having broken away from the British monarchy and aristocracy, and their ongoing conviction that this had been the right thing to do. But it is easy to overestimate how much of a change was involved in this establishment of republican government in America. After all, in the 150 years during which the American English had built up their new nation, never once had a king visited their shores. They had known no nobility either. Indeed, the republican America that emerged from the revolution was in most respects very much like America before the revolution: Christianity, the English common law, and English language and literature still provided the basis for daily life, and the American nationalist party had even succeeded in retaining much of the British constitution in the national government inaugurated in 1789.

America was, in other words, a traditional society—and it remained a traditional society, in many respects, until the upheaval of the two World Wars. Indeed, when liberal internationalists led by President Woodrow Wilson promoted a League of Nations as an instrument for governing the world in 1919, this proposal was defeated by conservative nationalists in the Senate by a vote of 53–38, on the grounds that the scheme compromised American national independence. (The terms *liberal internationalist* and *conservative nationalist* were already in use at the time.)[3] And as late as 1931, the United States Supreme Court again upheld the view that, as a matter of constitutional law, "We are a Christian people... acknowledging with reverence the duty of obedience to the will of God."[4]

Today, many avoid the term "Christian nationalist" as if it were in some way dishonorable. But before the Second World War, that is what most Americans still were: Christian nationalists. Nor was such Christian nationalism restricted to the decades of Republican Party political dominance that ended with the Great Depression. The Democratic president Franklin Roosevelt became famous for describing himself politically as "a Christian and a democrat,"[5] and in 1942, FDR was still counting the United States among those "nations which still hold to the old ideals of Christianity and democracy."[6] That same year, Roosevelt's secretary of state, Cordell Hull, declared, "All will agree that nationalism and its spirit are essential to the healthy and normal political and economic life of a people."[7] And it was precisely this nationalism that was reflected in the pledge of allegiance to the American flag that was adopted by Congress at that time:

> I pledge allegiance to the Flag of the United States of America and to the Republic for which it stands, one Nation under God, indivisible, with liberty and justice for all.[8]

One of the most important statements of the prevailing Protestant nationalism of those years can be found in Franklin Roosevelt's State of the Union address of January 4, 1939. By this point, Roosevelt recognized that America, Britain, and their allies would soon be at war, and he was concerned to clarify what would be at stake in the coming struggle. In Roosevelt's eyes, the war would be fought for three things. As he put it:

> [Events] abroad directly challenge three institutions indispensable to Americans, now as always. The first is religion. It is the source of the other two—democracy and international good faith.

According to this view, both America's liberties and its ability to live as an independent nation among others had their source in one place—namely, in its Christian inheritance. Roosevelt supposed that the Nazis and the Marxists knew this as well as he did and were seeking to overthrow not only democracy and the order of independent nations, but their Christian source too. Their aim, he said, was to achieve a reordering of the world in which all these things would be lost. But America would stand by "its ancient faith":

> An ordering of society which relegates religion, democracy, and good faith among nations to the background can find no place within it for the ideals of the Prince of Peace. The United States rejects such an ordering and retains its ancient faith.

Roosevelt's framing of what was at stake made the impending conflict a war not only about freedom, although it was surely that. It was also fundamentally a war about religion. In fact, in the same address,

Roosevelt described the conflict as one between the "God-fearing democracies" and their enemies.[9] Roosevelt knew the Bible well, and his use of this phrase associated America's enemies with the archetypal nation that "did not fear God," the biblical Amalek.[10]

This framing of the Second World War is strikingly different from what is taught in schools and universities today. It is a rare instructor in history or politics who describes the struggle against Nazism or Marxism as one fought between "God-fearing democracy" and its enemies. Instead, the war is said to have been fought between "liberal democracy" and its enemies. But terms such as "liberal," "liberalism," and "liberal democracy" appear nowhere in the eight pages of Roosevelt's address. This is because such terms did not describe the cause for which hundreds of thousands of Americans were about to give their lives. The term that did describe that cause was *God-fearing democracy*.

However, such expressions of traditional Anglo-American nationalism and public religion would soon come to an end. In the wake of the Second World War, America, Britain, and other Western countries underwent a dramatic change in self-understanding. Somehow, a war fought to defend God-fearing democracy inadvertently ended up destroying the religious foundations of the victorious Western nations. Within a few years, the God-fearing democracies came to see themselves as liberal democracies, and liberalism replaced Christianity as the perceived source of whatever was good about America and other Western nations.

We can see the beginning of this change immediately after the Second World War in the American Supreme Court's determination, in *Everson v. Board of Education* (1947), that state governments could no longer support and encourage religion—whether a particular religion or any religion.[11] In theory, this decision is deduced from the First Amendment of the Constitution as applied through the

Fourteenth. But the Fourteenth Amendment, passed after the Civil War to protect black Americans from violations of their right to due process under the law, had by this point been on the books for seventy-nine years without anyone supposing that support for religion by the states was a violation of anyone's right to due process.

What had changed in the interim was not the letter of the law, but the narrative framework through which the justices of the Supreme Court, as representatives of elite opinion, understood the relationship between Christianity and the American nation. That there had been such a change is obvious from the fact that, in the aftermath of the Second World War, Justice Hugo Black felt he needed to provide a new story of the American founding—one broadly hostile to government encouragement of religion. Among other things, he writes:

> It is not inappropriate briefly to review the background and environment of the period in which that constitutional language was fashioned and adopted. A large proportion of the early settlers of this country came here from Europe to escape the bondage of laws which compelled them to support and attend government favored churches. The centuries immediately before and contemporaneous with the colonization of America had been filled with turmoil, civil strife, and persecutions, generated in large part by established sects determined to maintain their absolute political and religious supremacy. With the power of government supporting them, at various times and places, Catholics had persecuted Protestants, Protestants had persecuted Catholics, Protestant sects had persecuted other Protestant sects, Catholics of one shade of belief had persecuted Catholics of another shade of belief, and all of

> these had from time to time persecuted Jews. In efforts to force loyalty to whatever religious group happened to be on top and in league with the government of a particular time and place, men and women had been fined, cast in jail, cruelly tortured, and killed.[12]

In Black's retelling, religion is no longer the source of American democracy and independence, as it had been in Roosevelt's State of the Union address eight years earlier. On the contrary, religion is now portrayed as a danger and a threat to democratic freedoms. Indeed, the very form of the American Constitution is now said to have resulted from the excesses of religion that drove the first Europeans to settle in America. It is in the *Everson* decision, in other words, that we find some of the first intimations of the transition from a God-fearing democracy to a liberal democracy: one in which religion is perceived as being so great a threat that the federal government must act to safeguard every child in the country from being taught religion in a publicly supported school.

In the matter of public religion, the transition to liberal democracy was completed in the Supreme Court's decisions in *Engel v. Vitale* (1962) and *Abington School District v. Schempp* (1963), which overturned centuries of common practice by abolishing organized prayer and Bible reading in public schools across the country. Immediately thereafter, another series of Supreme Court decisions paved the way for the legalization of pornography by overturning traditional Christian standards of public decency. In *Jacobellis v. Ohio* (1964), the Court ruled that the states had no authority to impose merely local standards of what constitutes obscenity, and in *Memoirs of a Woman of Pleasure v. Massachusetts* (1966), it determined that the national standard of public decency would permit the circulation of sexually explicit material so long as it was not "utterly without redeeming social value"—a bar so low that almost anything could clear it.

These and other Supreme Court decisions signaled the end of Christianity as a decisive and legitimate influence on public life in America.

But postwar liberals had other aims as well, of which the most laudable was the elimination of racial segregation targeting black Americans. In *Brown vs. Board of Education* (1954), a unanimous Court ordered an end to state-mandated racial segregation in schools throughout the United States. This famous decision applied the "equal protection" clause of the Fourteenth Amendment to education, finding that "separate educational facilities are inherently unequal."[13] Based upon this finding, the Court ordered the integration of white and black students into a single school system throughout the country—a decision perhaps most memorably associated with President Eisenhower's decision, in 1957, to deploy 1,200 troops from the 101st Airborne Division to Little Rock, Arkansas, where they ensured the safe passage of nine black students into Little Rock Central High School.

The *Brown* decision can be regarded as parallel to the Supreme Court's earlier decision in *Everson*. Whereas *Everson* had mandated the elimination of concern for religious particularity from the American public school education, the *Brown* decision ordered the elimination of racial particularity from these same schools. I point out this parallel not because I consider the removal of racial barriers to be substantively similar to the removal of religion from the schools. In fact, I don't believe these aims are substantively similar at all. However, it is important to recognize that the U.S. Supreme Court did find them comparable. Indeed, it is fair to say that these two goals—erasing distinctions based on race and religion—were the principal engines driving the establishment of liberal-democratic government in America after the Second World War.

The year after the Supreme Court banned prayer and Bible study from public schools, Congress passed the Civil Rights Act (1964), which outlawed discrimination, whether by government or private institutions, on the basis of "race, color, religion, sex, and national origin." And a year later, Congress passed the Immigration and Naturalization Act (1965), which ended the use of immigration quotas based on national origins, thereby eliminating the preference for immigrants belonging to Western and Northern European nationalities. These sweeping pieces of legislation added sex and national origin to the list of categories that were, in principle, to be removed from consideration in the conduct of both public and private institutional life (with certain exceptions, such as women's sporting events).

Taken together, these acts of the Supreme Court and Congress amounted to a fundamental revision of the constitutional structure of the United States, a bloodless revolution in which the old assumption of a Christian nation rooted in the English legal tradition was replaced by a liberal state modeled on the social-contract theories of Enlightenment rationalist philosophers.

As we've seen, Enlightenment rationalist theories similar to those proposed during the French Revolution were not new in America. During the American Revolution, Enlightenment rationalists such as Thomas Jefferson and Tom Paine had articulated this kind of a vision, and it had gained wide influence. But a powerful stream of Anglo-American conservatism had always held Enlightenment rationalism in check—until the 1960s, when these conservative influences were finally and forcefully suppressed and the system of abstract reasoning promoted by the French revolutionaries was finally adopted by the American government as well.

What caused this bloodless revolution? What caused this radical change of heart?

Although one can see the signs of what was coming earlier in the twentieth century, the determination of America's elites to pursue the constitutional revolution of the 1960s was a consequence of the Second World War and America's bitter struggle against Hitler's racialist regime. The war had imposed long years of suffering, including the deaths of over 400,000 American servicemen. But it was the torrent of film footage and photographs from the death camps, where Nazi race theories had brought about the torture and murder of millions of Jews, gypsies, and others, that ultimately had the most enduring effect. These images scorched the minds of an entire generation, providing the unspoken fixed point around which their politics turned. Thus while the radicalism of the "Sixties Generation" has become the stuff of legend and song, the truth is that it was their parents' generation—men and women who were already in their twenties, thirties, and forties in 1945—who were most deeply affected by the Second World War and the Holocaust. It was their parents who turned their revulsion over Hitler's racial politics into a revolutionary political agenda for their own country, seeking to pull down the legal and social structures that still oppressed the black minority and excluded Jews and Asians from many aspects of national life.

The intense revulsion against the use of racial and religious categories by the Nazis and their allies was the force that brought large majorities on the U.S. Supreme Court and in Congress to embrace Enlightenment liberalism as the sole legitimate foundation for American government. And it isn't hard to see why. After all, it is only in the geometrical abstractions of Enlightenment rationalist political theory that one can find a discussion of what human beings are, need, and deserve without any reference to their race, color, religion, sex, or national origin. No conservative political theory, from the Bible to Burke, had ever dared to reach political conclusions stripped clean of all these considerations. But in Enlightenment liberalism, such theories had been advanced and such conclusions had been drawn. And now America was going to implement these conclusions: Both public and private institutions would henceforth operate as though none of these considerations could be relevant to ordering the public life of the nation.

Of all the sweeping generalizations that American liberals adopted in the 1960s, I have the most sympathy for the earnest desire to eliminate considerations of race. From the outset, the kidnapping of Africans and their importation into America to be sold into a life of forced enslavement was an act of unspeakable cruelty and barbarism, and the story of the injustices committed against these slaves and their descendants is one that cries out to heaven, much as another story of a people enslaved does in Scripture. I admire the fact that the war against Nazi Germany, as well as the military service of over one million African Americans during the Second World War, moved Americans to repent and rid themselves of this ongoing injustice.

The desire to avoid having racial laws on the books in America was, for these reasons, ample motive for resorting to legal action prohibiting "discrimination on the basis of race."

But the persecution of blacks in the American South was not identical—in substance or in degree—to the hardships endured by Americans of diverse national origins, or by religious groups such as Catholics and Jews, and these were altogether different from the challenges faced by women at that time. Yet instead of regarding each of these categories of persons as having a unique history and character of its own and facing unique difficulties requiring attention, American liberals piled all these categories of persons together and called all the various difficulties they faced by a single highly abstract term—*discrimination on the basis of X.*

This was precisely the kind of exercise in writing vast abstractions into law that conservative thinkers had warned against time and again. Consider, for example, the fact that discrimination against blacks was expressed in establishing racially segregated athletic facilities or washrooms, whereas discrimination against women involved just the opposite (that is, in *not* having special athletic facilities or washrooms for women). The same can be said about devout Catholics and Jews, or members of Native American nations, whose desire to have separate schools in which they could educate their children in their own traditions posed exactly the opposite of the problem faced by blacks, who justifiably sought to racially desegregate educational institutions. And such examples only scrape the surface of the problem. The real issue is that just policies require government to make all sorts of distinctions among different groups of people, while paying genuine attention to what these respective groups actually want and need. Whereas the Enlightenment liberal constitutional revolution of the 1960s sought, absurdly, to impose an anti-racialist legal tool, which was designed to provide relief for black Americans, on the difficulties faced by members of different religions, sexes, and national communities. And of course, once this fantastically abstract legal instrument had been written into law, it was inevitable that other categories of persons would be added, without anyone knowing where the revolution should stop.

Thus, instead of engaging in a focused effort to assist black Americans in overcoming the racial barriers that had been placed in their way, the constitutional revolution of the 1960s set out to reconstruct America in the image of the social-contract theories of Enlightenment rationalist philosophy. This grand social reconstruction has taken place in keeping with the pattern established during the French Revolution and followed thereafter in Communist countries, in which an abstract theory is imposed from the top down, seeking to abolish both public and private distinctions based on any kind of particularity, including not only race, nationality, religion, and sex, but an expanding list of other categories, including age, mental and physical condition, and sexual preference. All the while, the demands made in the name of this Enlightenment rationalist political theory continue to grow wilder and more disconnected from reality, even as the legal and social tools used to impose it become ever more aggressive.

2. *Russell Kirk and the Conservative Revival*

Until the two World Wars, "liberalism" had referred to one side of a political debate that had two sides: liberals and conservatives. But by the 1960s, liberalism had won this contest. It became the dominant ideology in America, Britain, and Western Europe, and the term "liberal democracy" was adopted to describe countries in which liberalism had displaced Christianity as the basis for political life. An elaborate rationale was developed explaining the pedigree of this new regime to those who had to live under it, with a slightly different story circulating in each country. Thus Europeans were told that the French had invented liberal democracy in 1789, the Americans were told that their founding fathers had invented liberal democracy in 1776, and the British were told that they had invented liberal democracy in the Glorious Revolution of 1688. But all of them were told that liberal democracy had been born out of "the Enlightenment"—a movement that was credited with having discovered "reason" and redeemed mankind from the absolute monarchies and religious ignorance of the Middle Ages. None of this was really true, but it worked to justify liberal political hegemony.

Even into the twentieth century, American historians still knew that the Constitution of 1787 was an adaptation of the British constitution, and that the American nation had been steered in a nationalist and conservative direction by the Federalists and subsequently by the Republican Party. But this story was already being rewritten under FDR: The American Constitution was declared to be the product of the Enlightenment rather than an adaptation of the British constitution; Jefferson displaced Washington as the father of his country; and liberalism was transformed into the state ideology (or "civil religion") of America, supposedly from its inception. After the Second World War, this reconstructed view of American history was propelled forward by the works of prominent liberal scholars, including Louis Hartz's *The Liberal Tradition in America* (1952) and Arthur Schlesinger Jr.'s "The New Conservatism in America" (1953), which argued that the United States had been a liberal nation from its birth, and had never really had a conservative political party to speak of. (This did not prevent Hartz from deploring the Federalist administrations of Washington and Adams, but he deplored them for being mediocre liberals, rather than for being genuine conservatives.) After a certain point, both the Democratic and Republican parties became proponents of this new view of America as a liberal nation from its birth, as well as of the new liberal constitutional order that this historical narrative was meant to support.[14]

What of conservatism? As is well known, the 1950s saw the rise of a political movement that rallied around the term "conservatism," and came to power a generation later with the administrations of Ronald Reagan in America and Margaret Thatcher in Britain. However, this movement was from the start an alliance of anti-Communist liberals and conservatives—and in the end, its energies were much more effectively applied to advancing anti-Communist liberalism than to any kind of conservatism. This is another way of saying that Cold War conservatism was as much a pillar supporting the hegemony of liberal ideas in America as it was any kind of opposition to them.

Much excellent work has already been done in providing a detailed account of the different currents of American conservatism after the Second World War.[15] Here, I will focus only on a handful of the most influential thinkers, and on the question of their relationship with the hegemony of liberal ideas in America.

In 1952, Dwight Eisenhower was elected president of the United States, apparently reflecting a turn toward Christian tradition and nationalism at a time when the atheist empire of Soviet Communism was devouring one country after another and expanding its influence within democratic nations as well. Proposals for a renewed conservatism at this time included works such as Robert Nisbet's *The Quest for Community* (1953) and Peter Viereck's *Conservative Thinkers* (1956). But the most important book by a postwar American conservative was Russell Kirk's remarkable bestseller, *The Conservative Mind* (1953), which sought to trace the tradition of Anglo-American conservatism from the time of Edmund Burke and the Federalists up until the publication of T. S. Eliot's *Christianity and Culture* a little more than a decade earlier. By presenting the story of dozens of great statesmen, scholars, and poets who had contributed to the Anglo-American conservative tradition in word and deed, Kirk succeeded in imparting a sense of historical depth and intellectual attractiveness to a movement that many had assumed to be disappearing.[16]

Kirk's account of the Anglo-American tradition is in many respects similar to the one I have presented in this book. Kirk emphasized that, for conservatives, (i) "custom, convention, and old prescription are checks both upon man's anarchic impulse and upon the innovator's lust for power"—although they also recognize that "prudent change is the means of social preservation." Conservatives regard (ii) religion as indispensable, including "belief in a transcendent order" and the recognition that "political problems, at bottom, are religious and moral problems." They see that (iii) "freedom and property are closely linked," and that the attempt to eliminate "orders and classes" from society could only end in tyranny. And they view human life as (iv) a "proliferating variety and mystery" that cannot readily be reduced to universal formulas.[17] Kirk regarded these principles as being given voice, most importantly, by Edmund Burke in Britain and by John Adams and the Federalist Party in America. Like them, Kirk recognized that the Constitution of 1787 was a reframing of the English Constitution.[18] Indeed, in a later book he was particularly incensed that this great achievement of Anglo-American constitutionalism should be imagined, absurdly, as a deduction from the ideas of "that great rationalist, Locke," rather than emerging from "a century and a half of civil social order in North America and more than seven centuries of British experience."[19] This liberal myth, he understood, would be used to hold Americans in thrall to a rationalist liberalism that had, in reality, little to do with the American constitutional inheritance. As he wrote:

> It is a sad error, with unpleasant consequences, to fancy that the American Revolution and the Constitution broke with the British past; [and] that the republic of the United States was a radical undertaking, a repudiation of European civilization. It is no less an intellectual folly to argue that the Constitution of the United States was written in conformity to the ideas of John Locke, subjecting the American people to perpetual obedience to what are alleged to be Locke's political principles.[20]

Kirk emphasized the influence on the Federalists of empiricist thinkers such as Hooker, Montesquieu, Hume, Blackstone, and Burke—all of them harsh critics of the deductive method employed by Enlightenment rationalism. After examining the works of these writers and tracing their influence on the American founding, Kirk concludes:

> Historical experience, practical considerations, religious convictions, established political usage: These were the foundations of the Constitution of the United States.[21]

In addition to this concern for the empiricism of the conservative tradition, Kirk also emphasized the standing of the Christian religion in Anglo-American law, beginning with Sir Matthew Hale's 1676 ruling that "the Christian religion is a part of the law itself," continuing through Blackstone, and then on to American lawyers such as Daniel Webster, James Kent, and Joseph Story. These conservative jurists did not believe that Christianity should be "enforced upon the general public," as Kirk wrote. But they did observe that "Christian moral postulates are intricately woven into the fabric of the common law, and cannot be dispensed with, there being no substitute for them from any other source. Furthermore, the Christian religion, as the generally recognized faith... of the American people, is protected against abuse by defamers, that the peace may be kept and the common good advanced."[22]

Kirk made a magnificent start to reinvigorating the Anglo-American conservative tradition in America. But his interpretation should not be accepted without question. On two issues, especially, I think his writings deserve to be challenged. The first is Kirk's emphasis on regional traditions. Conservatives of all kinds—I include myself in this—recognize that local and regional diversity is not only inevitable, but also something to be honored and celebrated. The uniqueness of local customs and ways of thinking about things is the original source of all great traditions and improvements in the nation.

A nationalism that suppresses local traditions is for these reasons both destructive and not very conservative. Yet at the same time, there can be no doubt that some local traditions are morally questionable and must be fought against, just as some nationalist calls for unity and uniformity are problematic and must be rejected.

In the perennial tension between regional and national concerns, Kirk was decidedly a regionalist, defending the customs of the Midwest and South against American national conservatives such as Hamilton. This often gives Kirk's conservatism an overly domestic cast: He often regards nationalists as expressing a merely regional sentiment (for example, of the East or the North), rather than struggling for the independence, unity, and viability of America as an independent nation.

Kirk's sympathy for the South leads to a second, more serious problem with his historiography. Kirk's incorporation of enthusiastic Southern defenders of slavery such as John Calhoun into the American conservative tradition raises the question of whether conservatives, in proposing a defense of tradition, are not ultimately defending moral relativism. In particular, Kirk's decision to "try to keep clear" of the controversy over slavery in his description of Southern political theories appears misguided at best.[23] And when he describes Calhoun's "devotion to freedom," or when he depicts Calhoun's political philosophy as a great defense of "minority rights"—the minority here being the rights of the South, not that of the men and women enslaved in the South—one wonders whether Kirk does not suffer from a debilitating moral blindness in this matter.[24] And it is fair to ask, as his critics do, whether this moral blindness is not a consequence of his conservatism.

In sum, Kirk represents a genuine and profound effort to recover the Anglo-American conservative tradition in the United States in the 1950s and thereafter. But his diligent efforts to retrieve what was supposedly worthy in Southern political thinkers who provided the intellectual framework for defending chattel slavery was a mistake from which American conservatism has not yet entirely recovered.

3. *Friedrich Hayek's Liberalism*

The most consequential philosophers of liberalism in the 1950s and 1960s were Friedrich Hayek and Leo Strauss. Both consistently presented themselves as advocates of liberalism. And both were careful to explicitly distinguish their own liberalism from the thought of political conservatives. Confusingly, many of their adherents have subsequently chosen to describe Hayek and Strauss as "conservatives." Here, I will regard these important thinkers as they regarded themselves—as liberals. I intend no disparagement or disrespect in emphasizing their liberalism. My aim is only to understand their thought and to place it in its proper relationship with Anglo-American conservatism.

Both Hayek and Strauss devoted their prodigious intellectual efforts to developing a response to the horrors of the Second World War. Both were German-speaking émigrés: Hayek left Austria in 1931, living in England for nearly twenty years before moving to America; Strauss left Germany in 1932, eventually settling in the United States. Both taught at the University of Chicago during the 1950s and early 1960s. And both feared that America and Britain were proceeding down the same path that had brought Nazism to Germany and catastrophe to the world. However, Hayek and Strauss gave diametrically opposed accounts of "what went wrong," with Hayek arguing that Nazism arose because the Germans had abandoned philosophical empiricism, while Strauss argued that Nazism arose because the Germans had abandoned philosophical rationalism. Although Hayek's immediate impact in shaping British and American political debate was greater in both Britain and America, Strauss's influence has grown steadily over the years, so that it now rivals that of Hayek.

During the 1950s and 1960s, both liberal and conservative writers devoted much of their attention to efforts to stop the rapid growth of socialism: Soviet Communism had scored impressive victories in Eastern Europe and in Asia, and was increasingly influential in democratic countries as well. But no less alarming was the increasing reliance on government planning as a substitute for the market economy in America and Britain. Government welfare programs were first introduced as conservative policies by the chancellor of the German Empire, Otto von Bismarck, in the 1880s. Referring to them as "practical Christianity," he envisioned health and disability insurance, a pension for retirees, regulated working hours and conditions, protections for women and children, and a system for reporting abuse of laborers. But these relatively modest "safety-net" programs failed to prevent the rise of socialist parties demanding deeper government control of the economy. In Germany, Socialists had become the most popular political force by 1912, and they won the presidency of the Weimar Republic in 1919. In Britain, the socialist Labour Party first came to power in 1924. In the United States, the Great Depression swept Franklin Roosevelt into office in 1932 on the strength of his promise of an "economic declaration of rights" that would provide a "more permanently safe order of things."[25]

Roosevelt's conception of a "permanently safe order" proved to require government involvement in almost every aspect of the country's economic life. In his infamous State of the Union Address of 1944, Roosevelt asserted that traditional Anglo-American political liberties had been "inadequate to assure us equality in the pursuit of happiness," and that "true individual freedom cannot exist without economic security." This, he said, was now "self-evident." And he proceeded to declare that a "Second Bill of Rights" had, in fact, already been accepted—one that would guarantee a host of new economic rights to every individual. These included the right to a "useful and remunerative job in the industries or shops or farms or mines of the nation"; "the right to earn enough to provide adequate food and clothing and recreation"; the right of every farmer "to raise and sell his products at a return which will give him and his family a decent living"; the right of every businessman "to trade in an atmosphere of freedom from unfair competition"; "the right of every family to a decent home"; "the right to a good education"; and more.[26] Unmentioned was the fact that this socialist conception of what "freedom" and "equality" require had to involve a vast expansion of the powers of the state, which would need an immense bureaucratic apparatus to impose the new reality on the nation.

Roosevelt's social-democratic vision was challenged in a series of books by liberal thinkers, including Friedrich Hayek's *The Road to Serfdom* (1944) and *The Constitution of Liberty* (1960); Ludwig von Mises's *Human Action* (English edition, 1949) and *Liberalism* (English edition, 1962); Milton Friedman's *Capitalism and Freedom* (1962); and Ayn Rand's *Atlas Shrugged* (1957) and *The Virtue of Selfishness* (1964).[27] Hayek's bestselling *The Road to Serfdom* set the tone for this genre of works, warning British and American audiences that the newfound enthusiasm for "central planning" was precisely what had brought Nazism to Germany. As Hayek wrote:

> It is necessary now to state the unpalatable truth that it is Germany whose fate we are in some danger of repeating.... Only if we recognize the danger in time can we hope to avert it.... There is more than a superficial similarity between the trend of thought in Germany during after the last war [i.e., World War I] and the present current of ideas in the democracies. There exists now in these

> countries certainly the same determination that the organization of the nation which had been achieved for the purposes of defense shall be retained for the purposes of creation. There is the same contempt for nineteenth century liberalism... and at least nine out of every ten of the lessons which our most vociferous reformers are so anxious we should learn from this war [i.e., World War II] are precisely the lessons which the Germans did learn from the last war, and which have done much to produce the Nazi system.[28]

Thus, according to Hayek's account, political elites in both Britain and the United States, having had a taste of complete control of the economy during the Second World War, were persuaded that such control should be continued in peacetime and used to bring about deep social change for the good. Yet it was precisely this socialist view among German government officials and intellectuals after the First World War that had given birth to the "National Socialism" of the Nazi state.

A large part of *The Road to Serfdom* is devoted to tracing the actual policies of German socialists and the manner in which they gave birth to Nazi socialism. Hayek points out that in 1928, the German government directly controlled the use of more than half of the national income.[29] This vast intervention of the German government in the economy involved the rise of an immense bureaucracy of experts formulating and handing down rules for the operation of national life. It also meant that instead of being governed by laws negotiated among the people's elected representatives in parliament, Germany was actually governed by the planning and rule-making of a bureaucracy under the authority of the executive branch. This destroyed the democratically elected parliament, which became the very symbol of political dissention and impotence, and gave birth to the demand for a dictator powerful enough to direct the bureaucracy:

> It is important to remember that for some time before 1933, Germany had reached a stage in which it had, in effect, to be governed dictatorially. Nobody could then doubt that for the time being, democracy had broken down.... Hitler did not have to destroy democracy; he merely took advantage of the decay of democracy and at the critical moment obtained the support of many to whom, though they detested Hitler, he yet seemed the only man strong enough to get things done.[30]

But Hayek was not satisfied to show that Nazism arose from well-meaning socialist policies of the kind endorsed by Roosevelt. His principal aim was to rebuild the theoretical framework that would permit a revival of liberalism and the defeat of socialism. In *The Constitution of Liberty*, Hayek correctly points out that in the Western nations, there are in fact "two different traditions in the theory of liberty: One empirical and unsystematic, the other speculative and rationalistic." The empiricist tradition is "based on an interpretation of traditions and institutions which had spontaneously grown up, but were imperfectly understood." Among its practitioners, Hayek names English common lawyers and political philosophers such as Coke, Hale, Burke, and Josiah Tucker; the Scottish philosophers David Hume, Adam Smith, and Adam Ferguson; and the French empiricists Montesquieu and Tocqueville. This empiricist tradition, Hayek emphasizes, is in direct and bitter opposition to philosophical rationalism, which is descended from Descartes and Hobbes, and continues with the Encyclopedists and Rousseau, the Physiocrats and Condorcet, as well as English and American rationalists such as Godwin, Price, Paine, and Jefferson. Philosophical rationalism becomes dominant in Britain with Bentham, and in Germany with Hegel and Marx.[31]

In this dispute between empiricists and rationalists, Hayek has no doubt which side is right. He says that the empiricist, anti-rationalist tradition "laid the foundations of a profound and essentially valid theory, while the rationalist school was simply and completely wrong."[32]

What is it, in Hayek's view, that permits the empiricist, anti-rationalist tradition to lay the foundations of a profound and valid political theory? According to Hayek, the central insight of the empiricist tradition is the recognition that "institutions and morals, language and law, have evolved by a cumulative process of growth" spanning centuries or even thousands of years. This means that social institutions such as the law and the forms of economic activity were not designed by anyone, but rather emerge through a process of trial and error.[33] The argument of the empiricist political philosophers "is directed throughout against the Cartesian conception of an independently and antecedently existing human reason that invented these institutions, and against the conception that civil society was formed by some wise original legislator or an original 'social contract.'"[34] Hayek emphasizes the empiricist rejection of the rationalist "social contract" theory because this ahistorical fantasy gives the impression that nations can peacefully assemble and design a successful political order from scratch by exercising reason alone—when in fact the British and American constitutional order, which is the best known to mankind, is one that evolved and was never "designed" or "planned" by any human mind.

Hayek's own contribution to the empiricist political tradition revolves around a single theoretical distinction: the dichotomy between (i) a planned order, which is given its form by the conscious human mind and implemented by command and coercion, and (ii) a spontaneous order, which arises out of the free competition of individuals and groups, unimpeded by coercion. Hayek's theory of spontaneous order derives, in the first instance, from the economic sphere, in which competition among individuals and groups has led to the emergence, over many centuries, of institutions such as money, the price mechanism, contracts, corporations, banking, the stock market, industrial manufacturing, and much else. But Hayek extends this theory of spontaneous order into the sphere of law and political organization more generally, which he likewise regards as having arisen from the competition among individuals and groups. As he writes, "The competition on which the process of selection rests must be understood in the widest sense. It involves competition between organized and unorganized groups, no less than competition between individuals.... The endeavor to achieve certain results by cooperation and organization is as much a part of the competition as individual efforts."[35]

It is under such conditions of free competition that innovations arise, as individuals and organizations struggle to succeed and devise new ways of cooperating to advance common interests. As individuals and groups prosper thanks to innovations they have adopted, these innovations spread through imitation, and eventually end up improving the entire society.

Particularly striking is Hayek's emphasis on the unconscious character of many of the innovations that arise under conditions of free competition and then go on to become part of the general inheritance of society as a whole:

> We understand one another and get along with one another, are able to act successfully on our plans, because, most of the time, members of our civilization conform to

> unconscious patterns of conduct, show a regularity in their actions that is not the result of commands or coercion, often not even of any conscious adherence to known rules, but of firmly established habits and traditions. The general observance of these conventions is a necessary condition of the orderliness of the world in which we live, of our being able to find our way in it, though we do not know their significance and may not even be consciously aware of their existence.... It is this submission to undesigned rules and conventions whose significance and importance we largely do not understand, this reverence for the traditional, that the rationalistic type of mind finds so uncongenial.[36]

This means that the greatest difference between empiricist and rationalist political theory is in their respective ideas about the role of traditions and the worth of other products of unconscious growth over long ages.[37] The rationalist sees inherited tradition, including traditional laws and institutions, as a burden that the dead past imposes on the present, preventing the free individual from expressing his own personality and attaining the things he desires. Whereas an empiricist philosophy regards inherited traditions as the most important consequence of the choices and innovations that arise when individuals and groups freely compete. As Hayek puts it:

> To the empiricist evolutionary tradition... the value of freedom consists mainly in the opportunity it provides for the growth of the undesigned, and the beneficial functioning of a free society rests largely on the existence of such freely grown institutions. There probably never has existed a genuine belief in freedom, and there has

> certainly been no successful attempt to operate a free society, without a genuine reverence for grown institutions, for customs and habits and "all those securities of liberty which arise from regulation of long prescription and ancient ways." Paradoxical as it may appear, it is probably true that a successful free society will always in a large measure be a tradition-bound society.[38]

Passages such as this one show clearly that, for Hayek, freedom is not something that is "natural" to all men, as rationalists claim. Freedom is rather something that we find only in a "tradition-bound" society. It is inherited traditions that permit individuals raised in such a society to know (whether consciously or unconsciously) what they must do to maintain their inherited liberties and hand them down to future generations.

Moreover, Hayek argues that it is not only freedom that depends on the quality of the inherited traditions in a given society. The most important inherited traditions are what he describes as "moral rules of conduct," which regulate the manner in which we behave toward other members of society. With regard to moral rules, too, Hayek insists that we remain largely ignorant about how they work or what they do for us.[39] Yet despite our ignorance about what the various rules in fact do, it is these general rules that determine whether a given society will rise or fall:

> Just as a group may owe its rise to the morals its members obey, and their values in consequence be ultimately imitated by the whole nation which the successful group has come to lead, so may a group or nation destroy itself by the moral beliefs to which it adheres. Only the eventual results

> can show whether the ideals which guide a group are beneficial or destructive.[40]

Hayek's theory of spontaneous order leaves precious little room for the state. Government, he writes, is nothing but a large organization, whose central feature is that it issues commands and ensures that they are obeyed by way of coercion. It is, according to this view, the antithesis of a spontaneous order, and the principal effect of government control in any sphere is to suppress the process of free innovation and the development of beneficial traditions in this area. Hayek's conclusion is that we must at all costs decline the expansion of government advocated by socialists, whose effect is "to turn the whole of society into a single organization built and directed according to a single plan." Such a coerced plan, no matter how well intended or how well designed, necessarily means the extinction of the spontaneous evolutionary processes that have allowed human beings to advance and improve in every sphere.[41] Instead, Hayek argues that the state should leave individuals and private organizations to their free competition, restricting itself to "formal rules," which "do not involve a choice between particular ends" that individuals and private organizations may wish to pursue.[42]

Hayek's was the most sophisticated defense of inherited tradition to appear during the twentieth century. He added significantly to the theory of tradition and custom, in the process making the Enlightenment liberal rejection of inherited tradition look amateurish and ill-considered.

Nevertheless, Hayek insisted he was not a conservative, instead identifying his views with "the liberal position."[43] This self-identification was surely correct. But Hayek's liberalism did not derive from his empiricist and traditionalist theory of knowledge, which consciously follows conservative thinkers such as Hale and Burke. Rather, Hayek was a liberal because, in addition to his empiricist theory of knowledge, his writings also contained repeated—and crucial—eruptions of the very same rationalist liberalism that he so strongly criticized.

Thus in *The Road to Serfdom*, Hayek asserts that individual liberty is "itself the highest political end."[44] Likewise, in *The Constitution of Liberty*, he says that the freedom of the individual must be treated as "the supreme principle" and the "ultimate ideal about which there must be no compromise."[45] And in his magnum opus, *Law, Legislation, and Liberty*, Hayek claims that there is a single "chief aim" of the Anglo-American constitutional tradition, and that this aim is "individual freedom."[46]

Where are these sweeping pronouncements about individual liberty being the "highest political end," "the supreme principle," and the "ultimate ideal" coming from? Both in Britain and America, the empiricist writers whom Hayek praises had considered the purposes of the traditional Anglo-American constitution as being variegated, with the liberty of the individual being only one of its aims.[47] Even according to Hayek's own theory of knowledge, the status of the principle of individual liberty would have to be that of an empirically derived moral rule—which would have to be balanced against other similarly derived moral rules such as peace, justice, stability and permanence, national independence, and national cohesion, in an ongoing process of adjustments in light of experience.[48]

But that is not how Hayek presents the freedom of the individual. In fact, the claim that individual liberty is "the supreme principle" of politics appears to be a dogma or axiom that Hayek imports from Enlightenment rationalism. Consider, for example, the following passage from *The Constitution of Liberty*, in which Hayek describes individual liberty as a "creed or presumption" that must not be limited by any considerations of expediency:

> We shall not achieve the results that we want if we do not accept [individual freedom] as a creed or presumption so strong that no considerations of expediency can be allowed to limit it.... Where no such fundamental rule is stubbornly adhered to as an ultimate ideal about which there must be no compromise... freedom is almost certain to be destroyed by piecemeal encroachments.[49]

And in a similar passage in *Law, Legislation, and Liberty*, Hayek regards the supremacy of the principle of individual liberty as being a matter of "dogma" and "requiring no justification":

> A successful defense of freedom must therefore be dogmatic and make no concessions to expediency, even where it is not possible to show that, besides the known beneficial effects, some particular harmful result would also follow from the infringement. Freedom will prevail only if it is accepted as a general principle whose application to particular instances requires no justification.[50]

From these and similar passages, it is clear that the freedom of the individual is not, for Hayek, an empirically derived moral rule which must be balanced against other such principles in seeking to steer the ship of state. What he calls "our faith in freedom" is, in fact, an axiom or dogma from which other articles of belief can be deduced as in any rationalist system.[51] And this insistence on individual freedom as a dogma, as "the supreme principle" and the "highest ideal" of politics, is not something that can be reconciled with an empiricist or conservative political outlook. It is a statement of a liberal faith that is intended to override evidence and argument.

Hayek's defense of the Anglo-American empiricist tradition—and, in particular, his appreciation of the common lawyers and Burke—can be read as providing much-needed support for Russell Kirk's efforts to revive political conservatism in America. But Hayek's dogmatic insistence on individual liberty as the "supreme principle" in political life makes it clear that his heart was, in the end, with Enlightenment liberalism. Such a profound contradiction at the center of Hayek's philosophy only makes sense in the context of the trauma of the World Wars, which drove many intelligent men and women to embrace liberalism as a new religion that would save mankind from a repetition of the horrors they had witnessed.[52]

4. Leo Strauss's Liberalism

Like Hayek, Leo Strauss believed that after the Second World War, America and Britain were making the same mistakes that the Germans had made only a few years earlier. But in Strauss's philosophy, it is philosophical rationalism—precisely the same rationalism that Hayek had so ardently warned against—that is supposed to provide the English-speaking countries with a sound political foundation, whereas the traditionalism and empiricism of philosophers such as Burke is said to have paved the way for the rise of Nazism in Germany. In other words, Strauss's account of modern political theory and of the causes of Nazism is exactly the opposite of that found in Hayek's work.

The philosophy of Strauss is also built around a single dichotomy, which he presented in *Natural Right and History* (1953) and other works. This is the dichotomy between (i) rationalist philosophy, which is said to be the quest for eternal, universal truths discovered by "unaided reason," and (ii) the devotion to the traditional and ancestral, which is said to be guided by authority. He argues that philosophy is identical with the rise and development of the concept of nature, where nature is defined as those aspects of reality that exist necessarily. According to this view, there is a sharp distinction to be drawn between things that are genuinely true in all times and places, and so are true "by nature"; and things that may be held to be true in certain times and places, but are in fact only so "by convention." Strauss's historiography posits a past in which all societies were "pre-philosophical," in that all of them associated the true and the good with those laws and teachings that had been devised by their ancestors, hallowed by age-old tradition, and handed on to each new generation by means of unquestioned authority. Such pre-philosophical societies recognize no universal natures, but rather consider all things to be governed by customs or ways that are appropriate to them.[53]

Strauss supposes that the unquestioning character of pre-philosophical society is ultimately undermined when certain individuals—whom Strauss considers the first philosophers—discover that there are things that are true by necessity, and therefore universal, whereas other things are only held to be so because revered local authorities insist upon it. As he writes:

> The right way is now no longer guaranteed by authority. It becomes a question or the object of a quest. The primeval identification of the good with the ancestral is replaced by the fundamental distinction between the good and the ancestral; the quest for the right way or for the first things is the quest for the good as distinguished from the ancestral. It will prove to be the quest for what is good by nature as distinguished from what is good merely by convention.[54]

There is thus an inevitable antagonism between those individuals and societies that associate the good with custom and the ancestral, and those for whom the good is a universal truth to be discovered by philosophy, and who must therefore, for this reason, undermine custom and the ancestral.

In *Natural Right and History*, Strauss applies the dichotomy between the rational and the ancestral to a powerful discussion of the way in which Germany had abandoned the rational basis for knowledge of the right and the good. He begins the book by quoting the famous Enlightenment rationalist formula incorporated into the American Declaration of Independence: "We hold these truths to be self-evident, that all men are created equal," and so on. Strauss proceeds to identify this credo as an inheritance of the tradition of rationalist philosophy, with its roots in Plato and Aristotle, extending through Aquinas and up to John Locke. Strauss attributes to this entire tradition a belief in "natural right"—that is, the belief that eternal, universal, necessary political truths can be discovered by reason. But he expresses doubt that this belief has been preserved in America:

> Does this nation in its maturity still cherish the faith in which it was conceived and raised? Does it still "hold those truths to be self-evident"?[55]

Strauss answers this question in the negative. He argues that Americans have abandoned their belief in universal natural right, and are instead adopting the "unqualified relativism" of the very Germans they conquered.[56] He describes this relativism as follows:

> Many people today hold the view that the standard [by which we judge political right] . . . is in the best case nothing but the ideal adopted by our society or our

> "civilization" and embodied in its way of life or its institutions. But, according to the same view, all societies have their ideals, cannibal society no less than civilized ones. If principles are sufficiently justified by the fact that they are accepted by a society, the principles of cannibalism are as defensible or sound as those of civilized life.... And, since the ideal of our society is admittedly changing, nothing except dull and stale habit could prevent us from placidly accepting a change in the direction of cannibalism.[57]

Strauss thus associates German thought of the previous generation with the discovery that every society has its own standards of political right, a view that quickly leads to the conclusion that "our ultimate principles apparently have no other support than our arbitrary and hence blind preferences." And if this is so, then everything a man is willing to dare will be permissible. "The contemporary rejection of natural right leads to nihilism—nay, it is identical with nihilism."[58] And it is "obvious that consequences that are regarded as disastrous by many men, and even by some of the most vocal opponents of natural right, do follow from the contemporary rejection of natural right."[59] In this way, Strauss sees a straight line from the abandonment of eternal, universal, and necessary natural right by German historians and anthropologists to the historicism, relativism, nihilism, and eventual Nazism of Germany.

There is much to be said in response to this argument, which denies the possibility of empiricist philosophy and tars traditionalism with the brush of nihilism and Nazism.[60] But here I want to understand the impact of Strauss's argument on the development of the Anglo-American conservative tradition after the Second World War. As I've said, Strauss regarded John Locke, and the American Declaration of Independence after him, as the modern instantiation of the

Western tradition of rationalist natural right theories. He begins a fifty-page discourse on Locke's natural rights teaching by citing Locke's infamous declaration of allegiance to the rationalist method in moral and political matters in his *Enquiry Concerning Human Understanding*. In this passage, Locke claims that moral and political principles can be deduced from self-evident propositions concerning God and man, by way of necessary deductions "as incontestable as those in mathematics." It is this rationalist epistemology upon which the deductive system of his *Second Treatise of Government* is based.[61]

Surveying the results of Locke's handiwork, Strauss concludes that "by building civil society on 'the low but solid ground' of selfishness or of certain 'private vices,' one will achieve much greater 'public benefits' than by futilely appealing to virtue."[62] And while "low but solid" is not exactly high praise, Strauss does in this way endorse the theory that Lockean rationalism is the last great avatar of natural right. And as such, it may have the capacity to stave off relativism and nihilism.

What of conservatism? We've seen that Strauss regards the philosophical rationalism he favors as standing in opposition to the traditional and the ancestral, and that he writes with contempt about the "dull and stale habit" that is left holding society together once a belief in natural right has been abandoned. But in *Natural Right and History*, Strauss goes further. He devotes several pages to making the claim that, in rejecting Enlightenment rationalism, Burke "paves the way" for the historicism and relativism that brought cataclysm to Germany. As Strauss writes:

> Burke's opposition to modern "rationalism" shifts insensibly into an opposition to "rationalism" as such.... What is needed is not "metaphysical jurisprudence" but "historical jurisprudence." Thus Burke paves the way for "the

> historical school." . . . It is only a short step from this thought of Burke to the supersession of the distinction between good and bad by this distinction between . . . what is and what is not in harmony with the historical process.[63]

In a work devoted to deploring historicism as leading inevitably to Nazism, this is damning indeed. And in fact, by the time he is done, Strauss has accused Burke of proposing that "everything good is inherited" and of seeking to discover the good in the British constitution, which he dismissed as an attempt to find political right "in the actual."[64] He even suggests that Burke's conservatism is further from ancient theories of natural right than the rationalism of "the theorists of the French Revolution."[65]

Strauss's attack on conservatism is thus thoroughgoing. In teaching that Burke "paves the way" for relativism, nihilism, and Nazism, Strauss uses the strongest rhetorical tools in his arsenal to dismiss tradition as a legitimate source of knowledge and to accuse conservatives of pressing civilization toward destruction. He regarded philosophical rationalism, of which Locke was the most important exponent in the American and British context, as the only possible way of averting the collapse of Western societies into "cannibalism"—by which he meant the justification of slavery by Calhoun, or of the destruction of European Jewry by Hitler.

In the context of the 1950s, Strauss's liberalism amounted to a rejection of Kirk's revived conservatism, and an endorsement of Enlightenment liberalism.[66] It is interesting to note, however, that although Strauss insisted that philosophical rationalism holds the key to delivering America from a repetition of German Nazism, he opens *Natural Right and History* by describing the belief in the self-evident truths of individual liberty and equality as "the faith in which [America] was conceived."[67] That is, Strauss does not trust philosophical rationalism enough to insist that Americans really can arrive at the natural liberty and equality of the individual by exercising "unassisted reason." Instead, he calls on Americans to accept these liberal axioms as a matter of "faith," just as Hayek does.[68]

Thus while Strauss and Hayek provide us with diametrically opposed accounts of the rise of Nazism—with Strauss claiming that rationalism is the only sound defense, and Hayek making the same claim for empiricism—in the end they agree on one essential point: Both suggest that the supremacy of the principle of individual liberty should be accepted on faith.

5. *William Buckley, Frank Meyer, and "Fusionism"*

Neither Hayek nor Strauss considered themselves conservatives. They were liberals whose ideas enter the story of twentieth-century conservatism primarily because, during the 1950s, the rise of the Soviet Union abroad and economic planning at home threw liberals and conservatives into a single political camp—the camp of Cold War opponents of Communism and socialism. This alignment of liberals and conservatives was assembled, first and foremost, by William F. Buckley Jr., the young founder and editor of the conservative weekly, *National Review.* But its principal theoretician was his close associate, Frank Meyer, who was credited with having devised a "fusion" of liberalism and conservatism appropriate to conditions in America during the Cold War.[69] That this "fusionism" was politically successful cannot be denied. It was the intellectual force that ultimately brought about the defeat of Soviet Communism and forced the retreat of socialism for a generation.

But Meyer's fusion was also a version of Enlightenment liberalism, and its embrace by the most outspoken opponents of Communism and socialism had the effect of ratifying the hegemony of liberalism as the sole legitimate political creed in America and Britain for the next sixty years. I want now to look more closely at the nature of this fusion and how it had this effect.

William F. Buckley Jr. began publishing *National Review* in 1955. This was two years after Russell Kirk's bestseller *The Conservative Mind* had cleared the way for a renewed use of the term "conservative" in American public life. In the mission statement Buckley wrote for the magazine, he referred to his publication as a "conservative weekly journal of opinion."[70] But in certain respects, its worldview was quite liberal. The first of the magazine's principles was that "it is the job of centralized government in peacetime to protect its citizens' lives, liberty and property," and that "all other activities of government tend to diminish freedom and hamper progress." This view of government as harmful outside of matters of defense and domestic security was the traditional liberal standpoint which had been so powerfully articulated by Mises, Hayek, and Ayn Rand in the years leading up to the founding of *National Review.* Buckley was himself a liberal in this respect, but he declined to use the term "liberal" because it had been appropriated to describe Roosevelt's vision of a planned economy. Instead he called himself a "libertarian."[71]

How, then, was Buckley a conservative? Three considerations place Buckley and his enterprise within the Anglo-American conservative tradition: First, he was a nationalist, and his magazine stood in opposition to "the fashionable concepts of world government, the United Nations, internationalism."[72] This put him squarely in opposition, for example, to Hayek's advocacy of a liberal world government, to which thirteen pages are devoted in *The Road to Serfdom.*[73] Second, Buckley saw himself as an empiricist, and his mission statement argued that truth is known by "the study of experience," a principle which he rightly identifies as conservative, and contrasts with that of "the social engineers, who seek to adjust mankind to conform with scientific utopias." Third, Buckley was a committed Catholic, and *National Review* was a palpably Christian magazine, although it is surely significant that neither God nor religion were mentioned in the magazine's mission statement.

These considerations justify Buckley's self-identification as a conservative. But Buckley was not a systematic political thinker, and there was from the start a tension between his insistence that *National Review* was a conservative magazine and his embrace of anti-Communist liberals (some of whom were at this point calling themselves "libertarians"). Buckley could have chosen to describe the magazine as what it was: an alliance of anti-Communist liberals and conservatives. But instead, he made the strategic decision to redefine "conservatism" so as to include the anti-Communist liberals that he drew into his alliance.

Among these anti-Communist liberals was his close friend and associate, Frank Meyer. A Jewish convert to Catholicism, Meyer was also a former Communist who had become a fierce advocate of liberalism after having read Hayek's *The Road to Serfdom*. The principal theoretical statement of Meyer's liberalism is provided in his book *In Defense of Freedom* (1962).[74] Reading it today can be a shocking experience.

Unlike Hayek, Meyer really was a full-blown philosophical rationalist, whose argument begins from supposedly unassailable premises and proceeds deductively to produce as rigid and dogmatic a structure as one finds anywhere in political theory.[75] Given his commitment to philosophical rationalism, I suppose it makes sense that much of Meyer's book is devoted to repeated attacks on Edmund Burke, Russell Kirk, and other defenders of the Anglo-American conservative tradition. Among other things, Meyer accuses Burke of having inspired a standpoint characterized by "an organic view of society, by a subordination of the individual person to society, and therefore, by a denial that the freedom of the person is the decisive criterion of a good polity."[76] Like Strauss, he accuses Burke of substituting tradition and prudence for "a transcendent standard of truth and good," and therefore of being unable to provide criteria by which political societies should be judged.[77] And he quotes Strauss's *Natural Right and History* as support for his argument that Burke's thought was "undoubtedly in the direct ancestry" of German historicism and nihilism.[78] Indeed, Meyer returns so frequently to his attack on Burke and his followers that anti-conservatism—and not anti-Communism—seems to be the principal focus of this book.

But if Meyer wishes to discredit political traditionalism as the basis for British and American government, what does he propose in its place? Meyer offers what he takes to be a universal political theory, applicable in all times and places, which he deduces from a single axiom whose source, he says, is in a "simple apprehension" of man's nature. This simple apprehension is that "man is of such a nature that innate freedom is of the essence of his being."[79] And because innate freedom is of the essence of man's being, Meyer concludes from this that the sole legitimate function of the state is to guarantee that individual human beings will be able to exercise the innate freedom that is of their essence.

Having supposedly deduced the sole legitimate purpose of government from a simple apprehension, Meyer returns to his conclusion time and again:

> [Rights] are obligations upon the state to respect the inherent nature of individual human beings, and to guarantee to them conditions in which they can live as human beings, that is, in which they can exercise the freedom which is their innate essence.[80]

> Freedom is the aspect of the nature of men which political institutions exist to serve.[81]

> Political theory and practice, therefore, must be judged by criteria proper to the political order; and the decisive criterion of any political order is the degree to which it establishes conditions of freedom.[82]

> The problem of political theory and political practice is to bring about such conditions of order as make possible the greatest exercise of freedom by the individual.[83]

These are just a few of the many passages in which Meyer hammers home the results of what he evidently takes to be an infallible deduction.

But is it really possible that freedom is the only quality that is essential to human nature? And by the logic of Meyer's argument, would not the discovery that there are additional qualities essential to human nature generate additional purposes of government?

Meyer does recognize one other aspect of man's nature that he considers essential: He believes that there are "good ends, and it is the duty of man to pursue them."[84] And if this is the case, one might conclude—by analogy to Meyer's argument about individual freedom—that government officials have an obligation to guarantee whatever conditions best allow the individual to identify, pursue, and attain these good ends. But Meyer firmly rejects the proposal that government might legitimately have anything to do with attaining the good ends which it is man's duty to pursue. The reason, he says, is that "good and truth cannot be enforced, because by their essential nature, they cannot be made real in men unless they are freely chosen."[85] Any form of virtue imposed or enforced by the state would therefore be "meaningless."[86] In fact, the idea that the state has a role to play in securing the good of society as a whole was, for Meyer, simply "the central tenet of totalitarianism."[87]

Meyer concedes that the state has three necessary functions, given its one legitimate purpose of protecting individual liberty: The state should protect the individual against violence, domestic and foreign, and operate courts of law.[88] But other than these, there are no duties or responsibilities that should concern the elected government. As Meyer writes:

> To give [the government] in addition any further power is fraught with danger.... Its natural functions should be its maximum functions.... Those living under the state, to which they have yielded up the monopoly of legitimate armed force, cannot afford to yield it an iota more of control over their lives.[89]

One may well wonder how this view, which has nothing in it at all besides liberalism, constitutes a "fusion" between liberalism and conservatism (or, in Meyer's terms, between libertarianism and traditionalism). The answer is: It doesn't. There is no "fusion" to be found in Meyer's political theory, which is as much an expression of rigid, dogmatic, Enlightenment liberalism as that of Ayn Rand. The fact that Meyer also insists that a private individual should choose for himself a life of Christian virtue is—as he himself writes—irrelevant to his political theory.[90]

In other words, the "fusion" that has been so much discussed is nothing other than the view that one should be a liberal in one's political commitments, and a Christian in private.

It has been argued that William Buckley's *National Review* was intentionally designed as an expression of just this kind of a view: It stood for a public philosophy of liberalism wedded to a private Christianity, and was consciously guided by the imperative of eliminating Burkean, traditionalist influences from American conservatism. I don't believe this view is fair to Buckley. The presence of Russell Kirk and other traditionalists in the pages of *National Review* meant that, in the name of the battle against Communism abroad and socialism at home, *National Review* did patch together an alliance between anti-Communist liberals and conservatives. Moreover, an important part of Buckley's genius as a coalition-builder was his exclusion of figures whose presence would have upset the nationalist or religious character of the enterprise. The magazine's savage attacks on Ayn Rand, for example, made it clear that one could not be a Cold War conservative and wage war against Christianity at the same time. Similarly, its rejection of the anarchist philosopher Murray Rothbard made it clear that one could not be a Cold War conservative while waging war against an order based on independent national states.[91] In this way, a broad coalition based on a recognizably conservative combination of individual liberty, nationalism, and Christianity was formed.

Buckley's strategy made sense in context, and it proved itself thirty years later when his Cold War conservatism came to power in America and Britain and enjoyed a crucial period of influence in foreign affairs and over economic policy. What it could not do was prevent American and British political culture from turning ever-more decisively toward Enlightenment liberalism.

6. What Cold War Conservatives Contributed to Liberal Hegemony

Debates within the camp of Cold War conservatives were many-sided, and the preceding sketch does not do justice to this complexity. What this analysis offers is a clear view of the principal fissures dividing liberals from conservatives within this broad camp—and of the dynamic that permitted Enlightenment liberalism to become predominant in a political movement that still maintained a genuine, if steadily weakening, attachment to Anglo-American conservatism.

The liberals and conservatives who joined this alliance did share some common ground. Both sides cherished the Anglo-American tradition of individual liberty, which meant, as Russel Kirk would later put it, that they shared "a detestation of collectivism. They set their faces against the totalist state and the heavy hand of bureaucracy."[92] In addition, Buckley made sure that personalities who were too hostile to nationalism or religion were placed out of bounds, in this way preserving something of the old contours of Anglo-American conservatism. It was this common ground that permitted his *National Review* to form a united front in which liberals such as Frank Meyer made common cause with conservatives like Russell Kirk—even though Meyer had devoted much of his book *In Defense of Freedom* to expressing how much he detested Kirk's conservatism, and despite the fact that Kirk believed fusing libertarians and conservatives into a single movement was "like advocating a union of ice and fire."[93] In the end, the imperative of bringing together the strongest possible alignment against Communism and socialism prevailed over philosophical coherence, and both camps followed Buckley in declaring this Cold War alliance of liberals and conservatives to be "conservatism."[94]

It is difficult to argue against Buckley's alliance-building. His version of conservatism—a full-throttle emphasis on individual liberty, combined with a judicious measure of nationalism and religious tradition—turned out be attractive to voting majorities throughout the English-speaking world and beyond it. In 1979, this formula brought Margaret Thatcher to power in Britain, and in 1980 it elected

Ronald Reagan to the presidency of the United States. By 1989, it had brought down the Berlin Wall and freed the nations of Eastern Europe. In 1991, the Soviet Union was no more. Those of us who lived through those years know very well that Reagan and Thatcher were intuitive and unyielding conservatives, who hammered on that note of individual freedom until the sound of it brought their enemies crashing to the ground. It is rare indeed to see political ideas have such a direct and desirable effect.

However, the great strength of Cold War conservatism was also its greatest weakness: In binding liberals and conservatives together in a maximally effective wartime alliance against Communism and socialism, it also suppressed American and British conservatism. Having been "fused" into a politically liberal movement, conservatives found that they were incapable of mounting an effective challenge to—or even an effective dissent against—the hegemony of liberalism that was established in America and other democratic countries in the mid-1960s. Indeed, by placing individual freedom at the center of its account of political order, Cold War conservatism itself became an important part of this liberal hegemony.

The Achilles' heel of Cold War conservatism was the fact that individual liberty has a very different place in Enlightenment liberalism than it does in the Anglo-American conservative tradition. In Enlightenment liberalism, the consent of the free and equal individual is the ultimate principle from which everything else in the system is deduced. Indeed, a dogmatic liberal finds it difficult to justify any kind of law or policy that is not derived from this principle. Conservatives, on the other hand, consider the liberty of the individual to be a precious good to be cultivated and protected, but one that finds its place within a complex of competing principles that must be balanced against one another if the life of the nation is to be sustained. Thus Gouverneur Morris's preamble to the United States Constitution of 1787 describes the purposes of the new national government in terms of seven different principles, only one of which is to "secure the blessings of liberty"; and Edmund Burke, a few years later, describes the purposes of the British constitution in terms of a slightly different palette of seven principles, only one of which is "private liberty."[95]

Although these texts do not pretend to provide a complete account of the aims of the American and British constitutions, they remind us of how government appears to statesmen in the Anglo-American conservative tradition. These men regarded individual liberty as one crucial principle, which stands in frequent tension with others that are not less important. They would have regarded the attempt to turn individual liberty into a kind of supreme political principle, from which everything in political life must be made to flow, as bespeaking a detachment from political reality, and a kind of intellectual fanaticism that could only end in reckless policies and political ruin.

But from the perspective of Enlightenment rationalism, this conservative view of politics as depending on an ever-shifting balance among competing political principles is difficult, if not impossible, to accept. Rationalist liberals such as Meyer are constantly troubled by the plurality of principles in conservative political thought, and it is common for them to accuse conservatives of a "dread of definition, of distinction, of clear rational principle."[96] Conservatives, who regard the successful political order as too complex to be deduced from the freedom of the individual, tend to be sympathetic to Russell Kirk's angry rejoinder:

> The ruinous failing of the libertarians is their fanatic attachment to a simple solitary principle—that is, to the notion of personal freedom as the whole end of the civil social order, and indeed of human existence.[97]

Kirk's exasperation stems from what—to conservatives such as Morris and Burke—seems an obvious fact: Human societies need much more than the freedom of the individual if they are to flourish and grow strong, and these other public goods must be the concern of the leadership of both government and private institutions such as the family, the congregation, and the business enterprise.

On this point, Kirk received firm support from some of the most influential intellectuals of the Reagan-Thatcher years, including George Will, who was at that time a committed and trenchant Burkean; as well as Irving Kristol and his wife, the historian Gertrude Himmelfarb, who promoted a synthesis based on the empiricism of Edmund Burke and Adam Smith.[98] Indeed, Kristol was famous for giving only "two cheers for capitalism," recognizing that the power of the market mechanism, if not balanced by due concern for the cultivation of the nation and religion, would end in ruin.[99] For him, conservatism had to be based on three pillars: "religion, nationalism, and economic growth."[100]

But on the whole, Cold War conservatism did not develop in such a Burkean direction. And the preceding discussion makes it clear why. We've seen how the fear that Nazism could arise again in Britain or America suffused the political theories of liberal writers such as Hayek, Strauss, and Meyer. Although they approached political theory from different directions, all of them came to the same extraordinary conclusion that individual liberty had to be established as an ultimate political principle ruling over all the others—because only in this way could Western nations prevent a return to the horrors of Nazi Germany, which were waiting in the wings. Thus Meyer's rationalist theory asserted that individual liberty was the sole aim of political theory, and claimed that this fact could be deduced directly from a "simple apprehension" of human nature. Whereas for Strauss, Americans had to retrieve their lost faith in America as a nation built on the "proposition" that all men have a natural right to life and liberty. Even Hayek, whose empiricist and traditionalist political theory plainly called for humility and skepticism regarding the proper balance among political principles, nevertheless insisted strenuously that individual liberty had to be regarded as the "supreme principle" and the "ultimate ideal about which there must be no compromise."

Although the Eisenhower years at first seemed to herald a return to prewar Christian Protestantism, this turned out to be an illusion. Soon enough, the entire spirit of postwar America was in rebellion against tradition. Americans no longer believed that a Christian republic had the resources to repair the injustices that persisted within it. Instead, they saw traditional political life as a bulwark supporting racial and religious prejudice—precisely the things Americans had fought and died to defeat in Nazi-controlled Europe. Americans moved quickly now to eliminate traditional political structures and norms, unleashing the principles of individual liberty and equality to do their work of uprooting and destroying the inherited evils of the past, in the process establishing Enlightenment liberalism as the new public religion in America and across the democratic world.

In the end, Hayek, Strauss, and Meyer, no less than Milton Friedman or Ayn Rand, were products of this moment. Each argued for his own version of liberalism at a time when Enlightenment liberalism was being ushered in as a replacement for the traditional political order. To be sure, theirs was a "right-wing" version of liberalism, emphasizing individual liberty rather than equality. This was in contrast to the "left-wing" liberalism of Franklin Roosevelt, with its emphasis on more extensive government programs aimed at attaining greater equality at the expense of individual liberty. But it was liberalism nonetheless.[101]

As liberal thinkers gained in weight and importance within the alliance of Cold War conservatives, their presence cemented Cold

War conservatism into the structure of hegemonic liberalism in America. This was especially true of Meyer's "fusion" of liberalism and conservatism, which was ascendant among Cold War conservatives by the early 1970s.[102] This fusionist view wedded a public liberalism to a private Christianity, in effect accepting Meyer's claim that since man's essential nature is to be free, the only legitimate purpose of government is to "make possible the greatest exercise of freedom by the individual."[103] Any public concern that could not be reduced to this formula was to be privatized, and the Federalist and Burkean tradition of balancing among competing principles of government was gradually rendered suspect or even illegitimate.

Of course, Meyer and his followers believed that they were being faithful to Christianity, nationalism, and tradition by privatizing these things, restricting them to the personal sphere in which the individual was, in Milton Friedman's words, "free to choose." But this was just wishful thinking. At a time when Enlightenment liberalism was systematically stripping religious and national tradition from public life, there was never any possibility that Cold War conservatives would somehow save religious and national traditions by insisting that they were of great importance "in the private sphere." There is, after all, no "wall of separation" dividing government from the society it governs. Government is a traditional institution that arises and is maintained by a given society. The leading personalities in government are always among the most important figures of this society, and the things they say and do have a vast influence on its character. Thus where elected official show, in words and deeds, that the traditional religion and the mutual loyalties of the nation are matters of indifference to the government, one can be sure that it is only a matter of time before traditional religion and the mutual loyalties of the nation become matters of indifference throughout society as well.

This means that "right-wing" liberalism—which by the late 1960s had declared itself the dominant force in Cold War conservatism—was never a realistic program for conserving anything. From that time onward, American conservatives lacked a clear understanding of the role that good government plays in maintaining the religious and national traditions of the people, and in cultivating the mutual loyalties that bind the nation together.

Ronald Reagan, who had voted for FDR four times, still expressed an evident concern for these things, and was able to govern within the Anglo-American conservative tradition: Reagan was moved in a profound and visceral way by the Catholic nationalist uprising in Poland, and he stood by Thatcher's Britain in its risky nationalist war to retain the Falkland Islands. He had no qualms about nationalist economic policies when he believed they were needed to protect American steel and manufacturing, and he applied anti-Soviet pressure around the globe without sending American forces to invade anything bigger than Grenada. He embraced the rise of a revived Christian nationalism, introduced a constitutional amendment to allow prayer to be restored to America's public schools, and fought passionately against the liberal enthusiasm for making narcotics, pornography, and abortions available to all. In these and many other matters, Reagan reminded us of the spirit of the old Protestant republicanism.

But by the time Reagan had left office, few of his followers understood what any of this had ever been about. By 1990, both Reagan and Margaret Thatcher were gone. And what followed in their wake was not an expression of a renewed conservatism of "religion, nationalism, and economic growth." Indeed, what followed was something else entirely: an outpouring of a dogmatic Enlightenment liberalism. In America and in Britain, a new generation of "conservatives" dropped nationalism and public religion and threw themselves into the pursuit of a borderless "liberal world order." The Cold War alliance of liberals and conservatives came to an abrupt and humiliating end. With the Communist threat gone, "right-wing" liberals joined with "left-wing" liberals in the project of refashioning the entire planet in the image of Enlightenment liberalism.

Those who were still committed to Anglo-American conservatism—that is, to Burke and the Federalists, to tradition and empiricism, to the independence of nations and public religion—were sent into political exile on the fringes of party politics. It would be another generation before Anglo-American conservatism began to find its footing again.

Chapter VII

The Challenge of Marxism

1. The Collapse of Liberal Hegemony

For a generation after the fall of the Berlin Wall in 1989, most Americans and Europeans regarded Marxism as an enemy that had been defeated once and for all. But they were wrong. A mere thirty years later, Marxism is back. By the summer of 2020, even as American cities succumbed to rioting, arson, and looting, the liberal custodians of many of the country's leading institutions adopted a policy of accommodating their Marxist employees by giving in to some of their demands: dismissing liberal employees at the *New York Times*, removing President Woodrow Wilson's name from the halls of Princeton University, and so forth.[1] But what initially looked like a temporary policy of appeasement has since become a rout. Control of many of the most important American news media, universities and schools, major corporations and philanthropic organizations, and even the government bureaucracy, the military, and some churches has passed into the hands of Marxist activists. We know that most of these institutions will never return to what they were before. Liberalism has lost its ability to command its former strongholds. The hegemony of liberal ideas, as we have known it since the 1960s, has ended.[2]

Anti-Marxist liberals now find themselves in much the same situation that has characterized conservatives, nationalists, and Christians for years: They are in the opposition. This means that a few brave liberals are now waging war on the very institutions they so recently controlled, trying to build up alternative educational and media platforms in the shadow of the prestigious, wealthy, powerful institutions they have lost. Meanwhile, others continue to work in the mainstream media, universities, tech companies, philanthropies, and government bureaucracy, learning to keep their liberalism to themselves and to let their colleagues believe that they too are Marxists—just as many conservatives learned long ago how to keep their conservatism to themselves and let their colleagues believe they are liberals.

This is the new reality that has emerged in the United States, Britain, Canada, and some European countries. Now it is being replicated throughout the democratic world. No free nation will be spared this trial. In this chapter, I offer some initial remarks about the new Marxist victories in America—about what has happened and what's likely to happen next.

2. *The Marxist Framework*

Anti-Marxist liberals have labored under numerous disadvantages in the recent struggles to maintain control of liberal organizations. One is that they are often not confident they can use the term "Marxist" in good faith to describe those seeking to overthrow them. This is because their tormentors do not follow the precedent of the Communist Party, the Nazis, and various other political movements that branded themselves using a particular party name and issued an explicit manifesto to define it. Instead, they disorient their opponents by referring to their beliefs with a shifting vocabulary of terms, including "the Left," "Progressivism," "Social Justice," "Anti-Racism," "Anti-Fascism," "Black Lives Matter," "Critical Race Theory," "Identity Politics," "Political Correctness," "Wokeness," and more. When liberals try to use these terms, they often find themselves deplored for not using them correctly, and this itself becomes a weapon in the hands of those who wish to humiliate and ultimately destroy them.

The best way to escape this trap is to recognize the movement presently seeking to overthrow liberalism for what it is: an updated version of Marxism. I do not say this to disparage anyone. I say this because it is true. And because recognizing this truth will help us understand what we are facing.

The new Marxists do not use the technical jargon that was devised by the nineteenth-century Communist Party. They don't talk about the *bourgeoisie*, *proletariat*, *class struggle*, *alienation of labor*, *commodity fetishism*, and the rest, and in fact they have developed their own jargon tailored to present circumstances in America, Britain, and elsewhere. Nevertheless, their politics are based on Marx's framework for critiquing liberalism (what Marx calls the "ideology of the bourgeoisie") and overthrowing it. We can describe Marx's political framework as follows:

1. Oppressor and Oppressed. Marx argues that, as an empirical matter, people invariably form themselves into cohesive groups (he calls them *classes*), which exploit one another to the extent they are able. A liberal political order is no different in this from any other, and it tends toward two classes, one of which owns and controls pretty much everything (the *oppressor*); while the other is exploited, and the fruit of its labor appropriated, so that it does not advance and, in fact, remains forever enslaved (the *oppressed*).[3] In addition, Marx sees the state itself, its laws and its mechanisms of enforcement, as a tool that the oppressor class uses to keep the regime of oppression in place and to assist in carrying out this work.[4]

2. False Consciousness. Marx recognizes that the liberal businessmen, politicians, lawyers, and intellectuals who keep this system in place are unaware that they are the oppressors, and that what they think of as progress has only established new conditions of oppression. Indeed, even the working class may not know that they are exploited and oppressed. This is because they all think in terms of liberal categories (for example, *the individual's right to freely sell his labor*) which obscure the systematic oppression that is taking place. This ignorance of the fact that one is an oppressor or oppressed is called the *ruling ideology* (Engels's later coined the phrase *false consciousness* to describe it), and it is only overcome when one is awakened to what is happening and learns to recognize reality using true categories.[5]

3. Revolutionary Reconstitution of Society. Marx suggests that, historically, oppressed classes have materially improved their conditions only through a *revolutionary reconstitution of society at large*—that is, through the destruction of the oppressor class and of the social norms and ideas that hold the regime of systematic oppression in place.[6] He even specifies that liberals will supply the oppressed with the tools needed to overthrow them.[7] There is a period of "more or less veiled civil war, raging within existing society, up to the point where that war breaks out into open revolution" and the "violent overthrow" of the liberal oppressors. At this point, the oppressed seize control of the state.[8]

4. Total Disappearance of Class Antagonisms. Marx promises that after the oppressed underclass takes control of the state, the exploitation of individuals by other individuals will be "put to an end" and the antagonism between classes of individuals will totally disappear. How this is to be done is not specified.[9]

Marxist political theories have undergone much development and elaboration over nearly two centuries. The story of how "neo-Marxism" emerged after the First World War in the writings of Antonio Gramsci and the Frankfurt School has been frequently told, and academics will have their hands full for many years to come arguing over how much influence was exerted on various successor movements by Herbert Marcuse, Michel Foucault, post-modernism, and more. But for present purposes, this level of detail is not necessary, and I will use the term "Marxist" in a broad sense to refer to any political or intellectual movement that is built upon Marx's general framework as I've just described it. This includes the "Progressive" or "Anti-Racism" movement that has overtaken liberal institutions in America and other countries. This movement uses racial and gender categories to describe the oppressors and the oppressed in our day. But it relies entirely on Marx's general framework for its critique of liberalism and for its plan of action against the liberal political order. It is simply an updated Marxism—one that has taken the oppressed to be *people of color* and *LGBTQ* rather than the working class.[10]

3. *The Attraction and Power of Marxism*

Although many liberals and conservatives say that Marxism is "nothing but a great lie," this isn't quite right. Liberal societies have repeatedly proved themselves vulnerable to Marxism. And now we have seen the greatest liberal institutions in the world handed over to Marxists and their allies. If Marxism is nothing but a great lie, why are liberal societies so vulnerable to it? We must understand the enduring attraction and strength of Marxism. And we will never understand it unless we recognize that Marxism captures certain aspects of the truth that are missing from Enlightenment liberalism.

Which aspects of the truth?

Marx's principal insight is the recognition that the categories liberals use to construct their theory of political reality (*liberty*, *equality*, *rights*, and *consent*) are insufficient for understanding the political domain. They are insufficient because the liberal picture of the political world leaves out two phenomena that are, according to Marx, absolutely central to human political experience: the fact that people invariably form cohesive *classes* or *groups*, and the fact that these classes or groups invariably *oppress* or *exploit* one another, with the state itself functioning as an instrument of the oppressor class.

My liberal friends tend to believe that oppression and exploitation exist only in traditional or authoritarian societies, whereas liberal society is free (or almost free) from all that. But this isn't true. Marx is right to see that every society consists of cohesive classes or groups, and that political life everywhere is primarily about the power relations among different groups. He is also right that at any given time, one group (or a coalition of groups) dominates the state, and that the laws and policies of the state tend to reflect the interests and ideals of this dominant group. Moreover, Marx is right when he says that the dominant group tends to see its own preferred laws and policies as reflecting "reason" or "nature," and works to disseminate its way of looking at things throughout society, so that various kinds of injustice and oppression tend to be obscured from view.

For example, despite decades of experimentation with vouchers and charter schools, the dominant form of American liberalism remains strongly committed to the public school system. In most places, this is a monopolistic system that requires children of all backgrounds to receive an atheistic education stripped clean of references to God or the Bible. Although liberals sincerely believe that this policy is justified by the theory of "separation of church and state," or by the argument that society needs schools that are "for everyone," the fact is that these theories justify what really is a system aimed at inculcating their own Enlightenment liberalism. Seen from a conservative perspective, this amounts to a quiet persecution of religious families. Similarly, the pornography industry is nothing but a horrific instrument for exploiting poor women, although it is justified by liberal elites on grounds of "free speech" and other freedoms reserved to "consenting adults." And in the same way, indiscriminate offshoring of manufacturing capacity is considered to be an expression of property rights by liberal elites, who benefit from cheap Chinese labor at the expense of their own working-class neighbors.

No, Marxist political theory is not simply a great lie. By analyzing society in terms of power relations among classes or groups, we can bring to light important political phenomena to which Enlightenment liberal theories—theories that tend to reduce politics to the individual and his or her private liberties—are systematically blind.

This is the principal reason that Marxist ideas are so attractive. In every society, there will always be plenty of people who have reason to feel they've been oppressed or exploited. Some of these claims will be worthy of remedy and some less so. But virtually all of them are susceptible to a Marxist interpretation, which shows how they result from systematic oppression by the dominant classes and justifies responding with outrage and violence. And those who are troubled by such apparent oppression will frequently find a home among the Marxists.

Of course, liberals have not remained unmoved in the face of criticism based on the reality of group power relations. Measures such as the U.S. Civil Rights Act of 1964 explicitly outlawed discriminatory practices against a variety of classes or groups, and subsequent "affirmative action" programs sought to strengthen underprivileged classes through quotas, hiring goals, and other methods. But these efforts have not come close to creating a society free from power relations among classes or groups. If anything, the sense that "the system is rigged" in favor of certain classes or groups at the expense of others has only grown more pronounced.

Despite having had more than 150 years to work on it, liberalism still hasn't found a way to persuasively address the challenge posed by Marx's thought.

4. The Flaws That Make Marxism Fatal

We've looked at what Marxist political theory gets right and why it's such a powerful doctrine. But there are also plenty of problems with the Marxist framework, a number of them fatal.

The first of these is that while Marxism proposes an empirical investigation of the power relations among classes or groups, it simply assumes that wherever one discovers a relationship between a more powerful group and a weaker one, that relation will be one of oppressor and oppressed. This makes it seem as if every hierarchical relationship is just another version of the horrific exploitation of black slaves by Virginia plantation owners before the American Civil War. But in most cases, hierarchical relationships are not enslavement. Thus, while it is true that kings have normally been more powerful than their subjects, employers more powerful than their employees, and parents more powerful than their children, these have not necessarily been straightforward relations of oppressor and oppressed. Much more common are mixed relationships, in which both the stronger and the weaker receive certain benefits, and in which both can also point to hardships that must be endured in order to maintain them.

The fact that the Marxist framework presupposes a relationship of oppressor and oppressed leads to the second great difficulty, which is the assumption that every society is so exploitative that it must be heading toward the overthrow of the dominant class or group. But if it is possible for weaker groups to benefit from their position, and not just to be oppressed by it, then we have arrived at the possibility of a *conservative society*. This is a society in which there is a dominant class or loyalty group (or coalition of groups) which seeks to balance the benefits and the burdens of the existing order so as to avoid oppression and repair it where it arises. In such a case, the overthrow and destruction of the dominant group may not be necessary. Indeed, when considering the likely consequences of a revolutionary reconstitution of society—often including not only civil war, but foreign invasion as the political order collapses—most groups in a conservative society may well prefer to preserve the existing order, or to largely preserve it, rather than to endure Marx's alternative.

This brings us to the third failing of the Marxist framework. This is the notorious absence of a clear view as to what the underclass, having overthrown its oppressors and seized the state, is supposed to do with its newfound power. Marx is emphatic that once they have control of the state, the oppressed classes will be able to end oppression. But these claims appear to be unfounded. After all, we've said that the strength of the Marxist framework lies in its willingness to recognize that power relations exist among classes and groups in every society, and that these can be oppressive and exploitative in every society. And if this is an empirical fact—as indeed it seems to be—then how will the Marxists who have overthrown liberalism be able use the state to obtain the total abolition of class antagonisms?

At this point, Marx's empiricist posture evaporates, and his framework becomes completely utopian.

When liberals and conservatives talk about Marxism being "nothing but a big lie," this is what they mean. The Marxist goal of seizing the state and using it to eliminate all oppression is an empty promise. Marx did not know how the state could actually bring this about, and neither have any of his followers. In fact, we now have many historical cases in which Marxists have seized the state: in Russia and Eastern Europe; China, North Korea, and Cambodia; Cuba and Venezuela. But nowhere has the Marxists' attempt at a "revolutionary reconstitution of society" by the state been anything other than a parade of horrors. In every case, the Marxists themselves form a new class or group, using the power of the state to exploit and oppress other classes in the most extreme ways—up to and including repeated recourse to murdering millions of their own people. Yet for all this, utopia never comes, and oppression never ends.

Marxist society, like all other societies, consists of classes and groups arranged in a hierarchical order. But the aim of reconstituting society and the assertion that the state is responsible for achieving this feat make the Marxist state much more aggressive, and more willing to resort to coercion and bloodshed, than the liberal regime it seeks to replace.

5. *The Dance of Liberalism and Marxism*

It is often said that liberalism and Marxism are "opposites," with liberalism committed to freeing the individual from coercion by the state and Marxism endorsing unlimited coercion in pursuit of a reconstituted society. But what if it turned out that liberalism has a tendency to give way and transfer power to Marxists within a few decades? Far from being the opposite of Marxism, liberalism would merely be a gateway to Marxism.[11]

I'd like to propose a way of understanding the core relationship that binds liberalism and Marxism to each other and makes them something other than "opposites."

Enlightenment liberalism is a rationalist system built on the premise that human beings are, by nature, free and equal. Moreover, this truth is said to be "self-evident," meaning that all of us can recognize it through the exercise of reason alone, without reference to the particular national or religious traditions of our time and place.[12]

But there are difficulties with this system. One of these is that, as it turns out, highly abstract terms such as *freedom*, *equality*, and *justice* cannot be given stable content by means of reason alone. To see this, consider the following problems:

1. *If all men are free and equal, how is it that not everyone who wishes to do so may enter the United States and take up residence there?*

By reason alone, it can be argued that since all men are free and equal, they should be equally free to take up residence in the United States. This appears straightforward, and any argument to the contrary will have to depend on traditional concepts such as *nation*, *state*, *territory*, *border*, *citizenship*, and so on—none of which are self-evident or accessible to reason alone.

2. *If all men are free and equal, how is it that not everyone who wants to may register for courses at Princeton University?*

By reason alone, it can be argued that if all are free and equal, they should be equally free to register for courses at Princeton on a first-come-first-served basis. This, too, appears straightforward. Any argument to the contrary will have to depend on traditional concepts such as *private property, corporation, freedom of association, education, course of study, merit*, and so on. And, again, none of this is self-evident.

3. *If all men are free and equal, how do we know whether a man who feels he is a woman should be able to compete in a women's track and field competition in a public school?*

By reason alone, it can be said that since all are free and equal, a man who feels he is a woman should be equally free to compete in a women's track and field competition. Any argument to the contrary will have to depend on traditional concepts such as *man, woman, women's rights, athletic competition, competition class, fairness*, and so on, none of which is accessible to reason alone.

Such examples can be multiplied without end. The truth is that reason alone gets us almost nowhere in settling arguments over what is meant by freedom and equality. So where does the meaning of these terms come from?

I've said that every society consists of classes or groups. These stand in various power relations to one another, which find expression in the political, legal, religious, and moral traditions that are handed down by the strongest classes or groups. It is only within the context of these traditions that we come to believe that words like *freedom* and *equality* mean one thing and not another, and to develop a "common sense" of how different interests and concerns are to be balanced against one another in actual cases.

But what happens if you dispense with those traditions? This, after all, is what Enlightenment liberalism seeks to do. Enlightenment liberals observe that inherited traditions are always flawed or unjust in certain ways, and for this reason they feel justified in setting inherited tradition aside and appealing directly to abstract principles of freedom and equality. The trouble is, there is no such thing as a society in which everyone is free and equal in all ways. Even in a liberal society, there will always be countless ways in which a given class or group may be unfree or unequal with respect to the others. And since this is so, Marxists will always be able to say that some or all of these instances of unfreedom and inequality are instances of oppression. Thus the endless dance of liberalism and Marxism, which goes like this:

1. Liberals declare that henceforth all will be free and equal, emphasizing that reason (not tradition) will determine the content of each individual's rights.

2. Marxists, exercising reason, point to many genuine instances of unfreedom and inequality in society, decrying them as oppression and demanding new rights.

3. Liberals, embarrassed by the presence of unfreedom and inequality after having declared that all would be free and equal, adopt some of the Marxists' demands for new rights.

4. Return to step 1 above and repeat.

Of course, not all liberals give in to the Marxists' demands—and certainly not on every occasion. Nevertheless, the dance is real. As a generalized view of what happens over time, this picture is accurate, as we've seen throughout the democratic world over the last seventy years. Liberals progressively adopt the critical theories of the Marxists over time, whether the subject is God and religion, man and woman, honor and duty, family, nation, or anything else.

A few observations, then, concerning this dance of liberalism and Marxism:

First, notice that the dance is a byproduct of liberalism. It exists because Enlightenment liberalism sets freedom and equality as the standard by which government is to be judged, and describes the individual's power of reason alone, independent of tradition, as the instrument by which this judgment is to be obtained. In so doing, liberalism creates Marxists. Like the sorcerer's apprentice, it constantly calls into being individuals who exercise reason, identify instances of unfreedom and inequality in society, and conclude from this that they (or others) are oppressed and that a revolutionary reconstitution of society is necessary to eliminate the oppression. It is telling that this dynamic is already visible during the French Revolution and in the radical regimes in Pennsylvania and other states during the American Revolution. A proto-Marxism was generated by Enlightenment liberalism even before Marx proposed a formal structure for describing it a few decades later.

Second, the dance only moves in one direction. In a liberal society, Marxist criticism brings many liberals to progressively abandon the conceptions of freedom and equality with which they set out and to adopt new conceptions proposed by Marxists. But the reverse movement—of Marxists toward liberalism—seems terribly weak in comparison. How can this be? If Enlightenment liberalism is true, and its premises are indeed "self-evident" or a "product of reason," it should be the case that under conditions of freedom, individuals will exercise reason and reach liberal conclusions. Why, then, do liberal societies produce a rapid movement toward Marxist ideas, and not an ever-greater belief in liberalism?

The key to understanding this dynamic is this: Although liberals tend to believe that their views are "self-evident" or the "product of reason," most of the time they are actually relying on inherited conceptions of what freedom and equality are and inherited norms of how to apply these concepts to real-world cases. In other words, the conflict between liberalism and its Marxist critics is one between a dominant class or group wishing to conserve its traditions (liberals) and a revolutionary group (Marxists) combining critical reasoning with a willingness to jettison all inherited constraints to overthrow these traditions. But while Marxists know very well that their aim is to destroy the intellectual and cultural traditions that are holding liberalism in place, their liberal opponents for the most part refuse to engage in the kind of conservatism that would be needed to defend their traditions and strengthen them. Indeed, liberals frequently disparage tradition, telling their children and students that all they need is to reason freely and "draw your own conclusions."

The result is a radical imbalance between Marxists, who consciously work to bring about a conceptual revolution; and liberals, whose insistence on "freedom from inherited tradition" provides little or no defense—and indeed, opens the door for precisely the kinds of arguments and tactics that Marxists use against them. This imbalance means that under the hegemony of liberal ideas, the dance moves only in one direction—and that liberal ideas tend to collapse before Marxist criticism in a matter of decades.

6. The Marxist Endgame and Democracy's End

Not very long ago, most of us living in free societies knew that Marxism was not compatible with democracy. But with liberal institutions overrun by "Progressives" and "Anti-Racists," much of what was once obvious about Marxism, and much of what was once obvious about democracy, has been forgotten. It is time to revisit some of these once obvious truths.

Under democratic government, violent warfare among competing classes and groups is brought to an end and replaced by non-violent rivalry among political parties. This doesn't mean that power relations among loyalty groups come to an end. It doesn't mean that injustice and oppression come to an end. It only means that instead of resolving their disagreements through bloodshed, the various groups that make up a given society form themselves into political parties devoted to trying to unseat one another in periodic elections. Under such a system, one party rules for a fixed term, but its rivals know they will get to rule in turn if they can win the next election. It is the possibility of being able to take power and rule the country without widespread killing and destruction that entices all sides to lay down their weapons and take up electoral politics instead.

The most basic thing one needs to know about a democratic regime, then, is this: You need to have at least two legitimate political parties for democracy to work. By a *legitimate* political party, I mean one that is recognized by its rivals as having a right to rule if it wins an election. For example, a liberal party may grant legitimacy to a conservative party (even though they don't like them much), and in return this conservative party may grant legitimacy to a liberal party (even though they don't like them much). Indeed, this is the way most modern democratic nations have been governed.

But *legitimacy* is one of those traditional political concepts that Marxist criticism is now on the verge of destroying. From the Marxist point of view, our inherited concept of legitimacy is nothing more than an instrument the ruling classes use to perpetuate injustice and oppression. The word *legitimacy* takes on its true meaning only with reference to the oppressed classes or groups that the Marxist sees as the sole legitimate rulers of the nation. In other words, Marxist political theory confers legitimacy on only one political party: the party of the oppressed, whose aim is the revolutionary reconstitution of society. And this means that the Marxist political framework cannot coexist with democratic government. Indeed, the entire purpose of democratic government, with its plurality of legitimate parties, is to avoid the violent reconstitution of society that Marxist political theory regards as the only reasonable aim of politics.

Simply put, the Marxist framework and democratic political theory are opposed to each other in principle. A Marxist cannot grant legitimacy to liberal or conservative points of view without giving up the heart of Marxist theory, which is that these points of view establish systematic injustice and must be overthrown, by violence if necessary. This is why the very idea that a dissenting opinion—one that is not "Progressive" or "Anti-Racist"—could be considered legitimate has disappeared from liberal institutions as Marxists have gained power. At first, liberals capitulated to their Marxist colleagues' demand that conservative viewpoints be considered illegitimate (because conservatives are "authoritarian" or "fascist"). This was the dynamic that brought about the elimination of conservatives from most of the leading universities and media outlets in America.

But by the summer of 2020, this arrangement had run its course. In the United States, Marxists were now strong enough to demand that liberals fall into line on virtually any issue they considered pressing. In what were recently liberal institutions, a liberal point of view had likewise ceased to be legitimate. This is the meaning of the expulsion of liberal journalists from the *New York Times* and other major media. It is the reason that Woodrow Wilson's name was removed from buildings at Princeton University, and it is the reason for similar actions at other universities and schools. These expulsions and renamings are the equivalent of raising a Marxist flag over each university, newspaper, and corporation in turn, as the legitimacy of the old liberalism is revoked.

Until 2016, America still had two legitimate political parties. But when Donald Trump was elected president, the talk of his being "authoritarian" or "fascist" was used to discredit the traditional liberal point of view, according to which a duly elected president, the candidate chosen by half the public through constitutional procedures, should be accorded legitimacy. Instead, a "resistance" was declared, whose purpose was to delegitimize the president, those who worked with him, and those who voted for him.

I know that many liberals believe that this rejection of Trump's legitimacy was directed only at him, personally. They believe, as a liberal friend wrote to me, that when this particular president is removed from political life, America will be able to return to normal.

But nothing of the sort is going to happen. The Marxists who have seized control of the means of producing and disseminating ideas in America cannot, without betraying their cause, confer legitimacy on any conservative government. And they cannot grant legitimacy to any form of liberalism that is not supine before them. This means that the "resistance" is not going to end. The revolutionaries who rallied under this banner are just getting started.

With the Marxist conquest of the great liberal institutions, we have entered a new phase in American history (and, consequently, in the history of all democratic nations). We have entered the phase in which Marxists, having conquered the universities, the media, and major corporations, will seek to apply this model to the conquest of the political arena as a whole.

How will they do this? As in the universities and the media, they will use their presence within liberal institutions to force liberals to break the bonds of mutual legitimacy that bind them to conservatives—and therefore to two-party democracy. They will demand the delegitimization of all conservatives, and of liberals who treat conservative views as legitimate. As was the case in the universities and media, many liberals will accommodate these Marxist tactics in the belief that by delegitimizing conservatives, they can appease the Marxists and turn them into strategic allies.

But the Marxists will not be appeased, because what they are after is the conquest of liberalism itself—already happening as they persuade liberals to abandon their traditional two-party conception of political legitimacy, and with it, their commitment to a democratic regime. The collapse of the bonds of mutual legitimacy that have tied liberals to conservatives in a democratic system of government will not make the liberals in question Marxists quite yet. But it will make them the supine lackeys of these Marxists, without the power to resist anything that "Progressives" and "Anti-Racists" designate as being important. And it will get them accustomed to a one-party regime, in which liberals will have a splendid role to play—if they are willing to give up their liberalism.

I know that many liberals are confused, and that they still suppose there are various alternatives before them. But it isn't true. At this point, most of the alternatives that existed a few years ago are gone. Liberals will have to choose between two alternatives: Either they will submit to the Marxists and help them bring democracy in America to an end. Or they will assemble a pro-democracy alliance with conservatives. There aren't any other choices.

Chapter VIII

Conservative Democracy

1. Conservative Democracy as an Alternative

For many years, prominent scholars and public figures campaigned to reassure the public that things were constantly "getting better" under the hegemony of liberal ideas.[1] Indeed, they continued to cheer even as the most significant institutions that had characterized America and Britain for centuries—the Bible, public religion, the independent national state, and the traditional family—went into precipitous decline.

But with the rise of the new Marxism, and the capitulation of the leading liberal institutions before it, these voices are no longer cheering. They can see that something has gone terribly wrong. But they refuse to admit that the catastrophe unfolding before us is a consequence of the Enlightenment liberalism adopted as a framework for public life in America and Europe after the Second World War, and of the regime to which this theory gave rise, which is now called *liberal democracy.*

Those who support this theory have repeatedly claimed that the only genuine alternatives to liberal democracy are Marxism and fascism. But I don't believe this is true. There are other alternatives to liberal democracy. I want to sketch an alternative viewpoint that I will call *conservative democracy.* This position is closer to the spirit of the traditional constitution in both America and Britain than the liberal political theories of our day. And it is far better equipped to avert the complete collapse of political order and to maintain the free institutions of these nations.

2. *Liberalism vs. the Bible*

I take "liberalism" to refer to a political tradition descended from the principal texts of Enlightenment rationalist political philosophers such as Hobbes, Locke, Spinoza, Rousseau, and Kant. By "rationalist," I mean that this kind of political thought is intended to imitate a mathematical system, which begins with axioms taken to be self-evident and proceeds by supposedly infallible deductions.

The axioms on which the liberal system is founded are these:

1. Availability and Sufficiency of Reason. Human individuals are capable of exercising reason, which "teaches all mankind who will but consult it." By reasoning, they are able to discover universal truths that hold good across all human societies and in every historical time frame.

2. The Free and Equal Individual. Human individuals are by nature in a state of "perfect freedom" and "perfect equality."

3. Obligation Arises from Choice. Human individuals have no obligations to political institutions until "by their own consent they make themselves members of some political society."[2]

These fundamental axioms are important not only for understanding a certain stream of early-modern political rationalism. The axioms of the liberal-rationalist system have dominated discourse wherever liberalism has advanced in Europe and America up until our own day. Attempts to alter the foundations of liberalism are well known. Indeed, since the 1990s, many liberal political theorists have sought to distance themselves from the Enlightenment rationalism of earlier liberal thought. But these trends have made little difference. It is still the free and equal individual, who takes on obligations only after reasoning about them and choosing them, that is the basis for liberal political theory and for liberal public discourse.

Of course, one does not have to accept the liberal axiom system as a closed and complete system. I don't doubt, for example, that many individuals have embraced some or all of these liberal premises while at the same time believing in God, or in the binding character of Scripture, or in the sanctity of the family and the congregation, or in the national state as the best form of political order, and so forth.

But the crucial point is that none of these things—God, the Bible, the family, the congregation, and the independent national state—can be derived from liberal premises, nor are any of them promoted by liberal premises. In other words, there is nothing in the liberal system that requires you, or even encourages you, to also adopt a commitment to God, the Bible, family, congregation, or nation. If one is committed to these things, it is for reasons that are entirely "external" to the liberal political system.

The fact that conservative political institutions such as God, Scripture, family, congregation, and the national state derive from sources external to liberalism is not, in principle, fatal. In theory, one can imagine a world in which liberalism coexists with the sources of religion and nationalism—and even that these might be complementary to liberalism, providing it with crucial resources that it itself cannot generate.

This is, implicitly, the strategy of those who say that liberalism is "only a form of government designed to permit a broad sphere of individual freedom." On this view, liberalism has no aim and no consequences other than to ensure that no one is coerced, for example, into becoming a Christian, or conducting his personal life within the framework of a traditional family. These things, it is said, can be relegated to a separate sphere of privacy and personal liberty—a sphere in which religious tradition, national cohesion, the family, and the congregation will flourish, even as liberal premises are made the official governing doctrine of the state.

This proposal has by now been empirically refuted. Both in Europe and in America, the principles of liberalism have not brought a greater honor for God and Scripture, national cohesion, and the flourishing of the family and the congregation—but the opposite. Everywhere it has gone, the liberal system has brought about the dissolution of these traditional institutions.

Nor is the reason for this hard to find. For liberalism is not "only a form of government designed to permit a broad sphere of individual freedom." In fact, liberalism is not a form of government at all. It is a system of beliefs taken to be axiomatic. In other words, it is a system of dogmas. About what? About the nature of human beings, reason, and the sources of the moral obligations that bind us.

This means that liberal dogmas concern many of the same subjects that are at the heart of biblical political thought. However, liberal dogma offers a very different view from that of, for instance, the Hebrew Bible. Whereas Hebrew Scripture depicts human reason as weak, capable only of local knowledge, and generally unreliable, liberalism depicts human reason as exceedingly powerful, capable of universal knowledge, and accessible to anyone who will but consult it. Similarly, whereas the Bible depicts moral and political obligation as deriving from God and inherited by way of family, national, and religious tradition, liberalism makes no mention of either God or inherited tradition, much less the specific institutions that permit its transmission across generations. And while the Bible teaches that all are created in the image of God, thus imparting a dignity and sanctity to each human being, it says nothing about our being by nature perfectly free and perfectly equal.

Thus there are no grounds for the claim that liberalism is merely a system of "neutral" rules, a "procedural" system. Liberalism is a substantive belief system that provides an alternative foundation for our views concerning the nature of human beings, reason, and the sources of the moral obligations that bind us. This alternative foundation has not coexisted with earlier political tradition, rooted in the Bible, as we were told it would. It has rather cut this earlier tradition to ribbons.

For example, the liberal belief that reason is powerful, universal, and reliable has meant that there is, in principle, no need to consult national and religious tradition, or even to accord such traditions honor and respect. Private individuals can toy with such things if they so choose. But public life, we have been led to suppose, can be conducted perfectly well without them.

Similarly, the belief that political obligation derives only from the consent of the reasoning individual has meant that political and religious tradition has, in principle, no weight at all, or at least no weight that can be admitted as legitimate. Any political right or freedom that appears at a given moment to be the deliverance of public reason will, within a short time, overthrow any and every traditional institution that stands in its way.

3. *Anglo-American Conservatism Revisited*

But is there an alternative? Many of our most gifted writers and intellectuals are constantly trying to convince us that we have no choice but to be liberals. It is either that or Marxism and fascism. And since these alternatives are appalling—an assertion with which I myself concur—there is, by process of elimination, no choice but to be a liberal.

Often I cannot tell whether this claim is simply the product of ignorance, or whether it is intended, by some, to be deliberately misleading. Whatever the case may be, this argument insists that there is no choice but to select one of three anti-religious, anti-traditionalist doctrines of the twentieth century, and that the only course open to us is to choose the least terrible of the three.

What is obviously suppressed by the constant repetition of this argument is the fact that there were—until quite recently—conservative alternatives to liberalism that offered a different way of thinking about public life. In this book, I have discussed a particular conservative political tradition, Anglo-American conservatism. This is a tradition whose classical period begins with John Fortescue and continues with individuals such as Richard Hooker, Sir Edward Coke, John Selden, Edward Hyde (Earl of Clarendon), Sir Matthew Hale, Sir William Blackstone, Josiah Tucker, Edmund Burke, George Washington, John Jay, John Adams, Gouverneur Morris, and Alexander Hamilton.

In Chapter I, I proposed that the Anglo-American conservative tradition can be summarized with reference to five principles:

Principle 1. ***Historical Empiricism.*** The authority of government derives from constitutional traditions known, through the long historical experience of a given nation, to offer stability, well-being, and freedom. These traditions are refined through trial and error over centuries, with repairs and improvements being introduced where necessary, while seeking to maintain the integrity of the inherited national edifice as a whole. Such historical empiricism entails a degree of skepticism regarding the divine right of the rulers, the universal rights of man, and all other abstract, universal systems. Written documents express and consolidate the constitutional tradition of the nation, but they neither capture nor define this political tradition in its entirety.

Principle 2. *Nationalism.* Human beings form national collectives characterized by bonds of mutual loyalty and unique inherited traditions. The diversity of national experiences means that different nations will have different constitutional and religious traditions. The Anglo-American tradition is rooted in the ideal of a free and just national state, pursuing the good of the nation without foreign interference, whose origin is in the Hebrew Bible. This includes a conception of the nation as arising out of diverse tribes, its unity anchored in a common traditional language, law, and religion.

Principle 3. *Religion.* The state upholds and honors God and the Bible, the congregation and the family, and the religious practices common to the nation. These are essential to the national heritage and indispensable for justice and public morals. At the same time, the state offers toleration to religious and social views that do not endanger the integrity and well-being of the nation as a whole.

Principle 4. *Limited Executive Power.* The executive powers of government are vested in a strong, unitary chief executive (that is, the king or president) by the traditional laws of the nation, which the chief executive neither determines nor adjudicates. The powers of the chief executive are limited by the representatives of the people, whose advice and consent he must obtain respecting the laws, taxation, and other crucial matters. The representatives of the people may remove a chief executive where his behavior manifestly endangers the integrity and well-being of the nation as a whole.

Principle 5. *Individual Freedoms*. The security of the individual's life and property is mandated by God as the basis for a society that is both peaceful and prosperous, and is to be protected against arbitrary actions of the state. The ability of the nation to conduct sound policy depends on freedom of speech and debate. These and other fundamental rights and liberties are guaranteed by law, and may be infringed upon only by due process of law.

These principles serve as a summary of the Anglo-American conservative tradition that was the basis for the restoration of the English constitution in 1688 and the restoration enacted by the American Constitution of 1787. And they have continued to underpin subsequent conservative political tradition in Britain, America, and other nations down to our own time.

The crucial differences between the conservative tradition and liberalism can be understood in the following way:

Liberalism is a political doctrine based on the assumption that reason is everywhere the same and accessible, in principle, to all individuals; and that one need only consult reason to arrive at the one form of government that is everywhere the best, for all mankind. This best form of government has been given the name "liberal democracy"—a term first popularized in central Europe in the 1920s, which attained a dominant position in political discourse in the English-speaking world only in the 1990s.[3]

What is meant by this term is a form of government that borrows certain principles from the earlier Anglo-American conservative tradition, including those limiting executive power and guaranteeing individual freedoms (Principles 4 and 5 above). But liberalism regards these principles as stand-alone entities, detachable from the broader conservative tradition out of which they arose. Liberals thus tend to have few, if any, qualms about discarding the national and religious foundations of traditional Anglo-American government (Principles 2 and 3) as unnecessary, if not simply contrary to universal reason.[4]

In their effort to identify a form of government mandated by universal reason, liberals have thus confused certain historical-empirical principles of Anglo-American conservatism, painstakingly developed and inculcated over centuries (Principle 1), for universal truths that are accessible to all human beings, regardless of historical or cultural circumstances.[5]

This means that, like all rationalists, liberals are engaged in applying local truths, which hold good under certain conditions, to quite different situations and circumstances where they often go badly wrong. For conservatives, these failures—for example, the repeated collapse of liberal constitutions in places such as Mexico, France, Germany, Italy, Nigeria, Russia, and Iraq, among many others—suggest that the principles in question have been overextended, and should be regarded as true only within a narrower range of conditions. Liberals, on the other hand, tend to see such failures as resulting from "poor implementation," leaving liberal democracy as a universal truth that is untouched by experience and unassailable no matter what actually happens.

In sum, what is now called "liberal democracy" refers not to the traditional Anglo-American constitution but to a rationalist reconstruction of it that has been detached from its historical empiricism, Christian religion, and the Anglo-American nationalist tradition. Far from being a time-tested form of government, this liberal-democratic ideal is something new to both America and Britain, establishing itself as authoritative only in recent decades.

The claim that liberal-democratic regimes of this kind can be maintained for long without the conservative principles they have discarded is a hypothesis that America and other Western nations have tested for the first time in the last sixty years. Those who believed that a favorable outcome of this experiment was assured drew this conclusion not from any prior historical or empirical evidence, for there was none. Rather, their certainty came from the closed liberal-rationalist system that held their minds captive, preventing them from recognizing the other possible outcomes before us.

This experiment has run its course, and we now know that the Enlightenment-liberal hypothesis was false. A political regime founded on Enlightenment liberalism cannot sustain itself for even three generations. Enlightenment liberalism initiates a perpetual revolution that destroys its own foundations in the name of reason, opening the door to Marxism and fascism. Our concern now must be to restore, as much as possible, the Anglo-American political tradition as it existed prior to the hegemony of liberal ideas.

4. What Would Conservative Democracy Be Like?

There is, in recent Western tradition, at least one well-developed alternative to liberalism that is neither Marxist nor fascist. This is the Anglo-American conservative tradition. I do not mean to endorse every evil that was tolerated under the old republicanism in the United States—the institutionalized abuse of the African American minority being the most obvious example of something we should be very pleased to do without. But I do believe we can draw upon the resources of Anglo-American conservatism, based on the Bible and the common law, to establish an alternative political framework that can be called *conservative democracy*.

Conservative democracy does not require that changes be made in any written constitutional documents. For the truth is that neither the U.S. Constitution nor the principal constitutional documents in Britain explicitly endorse liberal doctrines, and so it must be admitted that these documents are not the source of the troubles these nations are facing today. A conservative democracy would, however, reject the axioms of the liberal-rationalist system to which American and European elites have been dogmatically committed since the

1960s. It would instead be concerned to maintain a sustainable balance between the principles of limited government and individual liberties (Principles 4 and 5) on the one hand, and the principles of religion, nationalism, and historical empiricism (Principles 1, 2, and 3) on the other.

A conservative democracy would be characterized by the following kinds of views:

1. National Identity. Like other nations, the American and British nations are characterized by their traditional language, religion, and laws, and by a history of common efforts and achievements. These particularities of the Anglo-American cultural inheritance are the basis for the unique national identities of America and Britain, for their continued cohesion, growth, and prosperity as independent nations today. The Anglo-American inheritance is to be embraced and encouraged by the national leadership and by institutions public and private. Neither America nor Britain has ever been a "creedal nation," defined primarily by an abstract formula as found, for example, in the American Declaration of Independence. Conservatives regard this as a myth promoted in the service of liberal dogma.

2. Public Religion. Conservative democracy regards biblical religion as the only firm foundation for national independence, justice, and public morals in Western nations. In America and other traditionally Christian countries, Christianity should be the basis for public life and strongly reflected in government and other institutions, wherever a majority of the public so desires. Provision should be made for Jews and other minorities to ensure that their particular traditions and way of life are not encumbered. The liberal doctrine requiring a "wall of separation between church and state" is a product of the post–Second World War period and is not an inherent feature of American political tradition. It should be discarded both with respect to majority religion and to minorities.

*3. **Law.*** The law in England and America has its basis in the Anglo-American constitutional tradition as a whole, beginning with the Bible and the common law of England. The American Constitution of 1787 is a sound expression of the English constitutional tradition, as adapted to conditions in North America beginning 150 years before independence. It is these sources of the English and American legal inheritance that a conservative democracy seeks to retrieve. The attempt to deduce particular national laws in America or Britain from theories of universal human rights is likewise a product of the post–Second World War period and should be abandoned. The Anglo-American legal tradition, with its basis in the Bible and the common law, provides ample basis for rectifying injustice, including oppression based on race.

*4. **Family and Congregation.*** Conservative democracy regards the traditional family and congregation as the most basic institutions necessary for the conduct of civilized life. Public norms in keeping with this view should be embraced and encouraged by the national leadership and by institutions public and private. Provision should be made to protect the private life of dissenting individuals or communities within their own sphere.

*5. **Education.*** Conservative democracy regards the education of children as the responsibility and prerogative of parents. Schooling in local congregational schools and homeschooling by parents should be embraced and encouraged by the national leadership and by institutions public and private. Historical education should discuss the development of the Anglo-American constitutional and religious tradition with its roots in the Bible, and the story of how this tradition gave rise to a unique family of nations whose influence has been felt by all mankind. Present conditions, wherein children are required by law to attend liberal schools, in which there is no recognition of God and no awareness of the biblical basis of civilization, are debased and dangerous, and should be ended wherever a majority of the public so desires.

6. Economy. Conservative democracy regards property rights and the free enterprise system as indispensable for the advancement of the nation in its wealth and well-being. But it also recognizes that the free market can have a corrosive effect on traditional institutions. An excessive accumulation of power by private enterprises and cartels can damage national security, national cohesion, individual liberties, and public morals. These considerations must therefore be taken into account in formulating economic policies.

7. Immigration. Conservative democracy regards large-scale immigration as possible only where the immigrants are strongly motivated to integrate and are assisted in assimilating into the national traditions of their new home country. In the absence of these conditions, the result will be chronic intercultural tension and violence. Immigration must serve the interests of the nation, not only in economic terms, but also with respect to national cohesion and the continuity of national customs.

8. Foreign Policy. Foreign policy is conducted in order to safeguard our own nation, its independence, prosperity, and welfare. Its central aim is to ensure that hostile foreign powers do not attain military and economic superiority, and thus the ability to dictate terms and curtail our national independence. Relations and commerce with other nations are to be based on the principle of respect for their independence and honor for their national and religious traditions, so long as they do not threaten the peace and stability of our own country. Independent nations reserve the right to intervene in the affairs of others in cases of manifest, large-scale criminality such as we have seen, for example, in Cambodia or Rwanda. At the same time, conservatives recognize that the imposition of liberal doctrines by means of military or economic pressure has often brought collapse and chaos, doing more harm than good.

9. International Bodies. Enlightenment liberals believe that since liberal principles are universal, there is little harm done in reassigning the powers of government to international bodies. Conservative democracy, on the other hand, recognizes that both national freedom and the tradition of individual liberties can exist only where the institution of the independent national state remains vital and firm. We see that the international organizations established since the Second World War possess no sound governing traditions and no loyalty to particular national populations that might restrain their reckless theorizing about universal rights. Such bodies inevitably tend toward imperialism, arbitrariness, and autocracy. International politics should be conducted on the basis of relations and agreements among independent national states.

5. Experiments in Conservative Democracy

The trauma of the Second World War persuaded Americans and Europeans to adopt the closed system of Enlightenment-liberal principles as the sole foundation for public life and moral obligation. But Enlightenment liberalism provides no resources for maintaining the traditional forms of public life and moral obligation that these nations had previously known. Christian and Jewish religion, the independent national state, the traditional family and congregation, and even the distinction between man and woman—all of these things have their basis in the Bible. When it displaced the biblical framework that supported these forms of life, liberalism severely damaged all of them. The current political reality of disintegrating national states, ruined families, eviscerated religious traditions, and a surging neo-Marxist cultural revolution is the direct consequence of having embraced Enlightenment liberalism as a universal, salvationist creed sixty years ago.

Many can now see that the nations of the West are hurtling toward the abyss. Conservative democracy offers us a way of backing away from it and reestablishing a traditional life based on a sustainable balance of freedom and constraint.

Conservative democracy, as I have described it, is not meant to be a political ideal or a utopia. It is a practical proposal for how historically Christian countries can restore a politics of conservation and tradition, given present conditions after six decades of liberal hegemony. I know that under these conditions, many countries and regions will not be able to muster majority support for any kind of conservative restoration at this time. In these settings, the present experiment with an ever-more destructive neo-Marxist cultural revolution will no doubt continue.

But there are also countries and regions, cities and towns—both in America and in Europe—where the framework of conservative democracy can be adopted and implemented. Conservatives must focus on what is possible in these conservative locales. We must ask what can be done in such places to pick up the thread of a conservatism that truly does regard the recovery, restoration, elaboration, and repair of national and religious traditions as the key to maintaining the nation and strengthening it through time.

Since Enlightenment liberalism is the source of the current catastrophe, biblical tradition—Christianity and Judaism—must be recovered as the normative framework and standard determining public life wherever a majority of the public is wise enough to adopt this course.

The key to such a restoration would be overturning the postwar Supreme Court decisions that imposed the principle of "separation of church and state" in America. More than anything else, these sweeping decisions delegitimized Christianity as the basis for public life in America and other Western countries, and initiated the ongoing cultural revolution with which we are familiar. Even the Reagan coalition of the 1980s, which embraced orthodox Christians and Jews and spoke explicitly of the return of religion to the public arena, was unable to slow the progress of this revolution.

But now we have come to the end of the road. We have seen the grotesque finale in which the children of Enlightenment rationalism demolish the liberal society that was established by their grandparents. Perhaps now the argument for restoring Christianity as the normative framework and standard determining public life will have greater plausibility. It is this possibility that must be considered in the coming years.

I do not believe that it is possible for such a conservative program to be advanced in America or anywhere else without extensive cooperation among Christian denominations, in coalition with orthodox Jews and other minority communities. In my proposal, the restoration of Christianity as the normative framework and standard determining public life in any particular locale should include provision for Jews and other minorities to ensure that their traditions and way of life are not encumbered; and that the private life of dissenting individuals or communities should be protected within their own sphere.

This means that I am not advocating, for example, that any part of the United States should seek to replicate conditions in the 1940s or 1950s—a return that is neither possible nor desirable. Rather, my proposal is that an alliance of factions should work together to restore Christianity as the normative framework and standard determining public life in every setting in which this aim can be attained, along with suitable carve-outs creating spheres of legitimate non-compliance. Such an alliance would be based on a negotiated settlement of the boundaries between the Christian public sphere and the sphere of minority autonomy.

Such a settlement would vary greatly from one region or state to another, establishing a series of experiments in conservative democracy. These experiments would test the ability of conservative Christians of various denominations to compromise among themselves, as well as with observant Jews, anti-Marxist liberals, and other minorities and dissenting groups.[6] A successful model in one region would open up possibilities in other regions.

Whether conservative democracy proves itself workable and succeeds in bringing about a renewed flourishing within states and regions is therefore the question of the hour.

Part Four

Personal

Chapter IX

Some Notes on Living a Conservative Life

1. Princeton Tories

In February of 1984, I took the train to New York with a young woman named Julie, who would later be my wife. We were both freshmen at Princeton, and we were on our way to Irving Kristol's Institute for Educational Affairs, where we hoped to find funding to start a conservative student magazine. Once there, we were ushered into an office where a man behind a desk was looking over the paperwork we had sent him. He smiled and said: "It looks like someone has been reading Burke." We won our first year's funding at this meeting. The first issue of our magazine, *The Princeton Tory*, appeared in October and was followed by five more issues during the academic year. The magazine is still being published at Princeton today.

Why found a magazine instead of doing schoolwork? It cannot have been the obvious thing to do. We'd been on the campus for only five months at that time, and our lives were already quite full. Julie and I had met in physics lab a few weeks after arriving on campus. It was the conservation of momentum experiment, in which you used a camera and a strobe to capture a series of images of hockey pucks colliding on an air table. If you did it right, you could measure the velocity of the two pucks before and after the collision, and show that the total velocity times mass remained the same even though the speed of the pucks had changed.

Julie had been assigned to the lab group working at the air table next to mine, and she came over to ask for help operating the camera. I recognized her immediately from the face book. In those days, before the internet, the university printed up a physical book called a face book, which had the pictures of more than a thousand incoming freshmen in it. Each photograph was accompanied by the student's name, hometown, and birthday. I had dutifully looked up every freshman who had the same birthday as mine, June 6. There were three students in my class with the same birthday, all of them women, and I had memorized their names, thinking it might be useful in starting a conversation. And so it was. When Julie brought her camera over to my table, I responded to her by name and asked if her birthday was June 6, which was my birthday as well. We ended up moving to an empty air table and doing the lab together.

The next day, we sat together in Professor Wilkinson's introductory physics course, which the students called "the magic show." We applauded as he successfully performed the experiments after describing them in chalk on the blackboard behind him. That night, we met at the student-run café under Murray-Dodge Hall, where the tables were lit with a single candle and the air was tinged with cinnamon from the cookies baking in the back room. That was the first time we really talked. A couple of weeks later, we drove up to Harvard in a car full of students to take part in the off-topic debate tournament being held over the weekend. By then, we were inseparable.

Julie was as beautiful a girl as I had ever met in my life. Her smile lit up the moody gothic halls of the campus in a way that left me in awe. But what made my attraction to her so powerful was the things she said when our conversation turned to politics and religion. She had grown up a Presbyterian in rural western Pennsylvania, and though she was no longer a Christian when we met—she was reading one of Bertrand Russell's atheist tracts at the time—she was still a Republican. The girls I had known growing up had almost all been liberals, which meant that when the conversation turned to something important, what I had to say was rarely appreciated. I still remember telling one of those high school girls that my forefathers had thought about me, just as I was thinking about my own grandchildren and their grandchildren, and that these ancestors had prayed that I would uphold and defend certain things in which they believed. She replied: "I can't believe you walk around carrying all of that!"

But Julie was carrying some burdens of her own. She had grown up with a half-brother who was born with a severe disability, and I think she always knew his death was coming soon. One evening we went to dinner in town with another couple from my college. In those days, abortion was a major issue in every election campaign, and so the conversation easily turned to abortion. Before dinner was served, the other young woman at the table had already announced that she intended to open an abortion clinic so no woman would have to bear a child she didn't want. Julie's eyes blazed with anger as she told us about her brother Kevin. When our conversation partner said such children should be aborted, Julie rose from the table and walked out. I apologized to my friends, but in my heart, I was rejoicing. I had never known this kind of woman before. I followed Julie out.

On the surface of things, Julie and I must have looked to be in the throes of a typical college romance, just like those friends of mine from the college. Princeton had only begun admitting women ten years earlier, and by now everyone understood (if there had ever been any doubt) that if you housed young men and women in the same dormitories, many of them would end up spending a considerable portion of their time this way.

But deeper things were taking place between us that only those who were very close to us could understand. Julie's father had left her mother when she was two years old, and her mother was already then on her way to divorcing a second time. Her stepfather had been abusive and neither parent had been able to protect her. When I heard these stories, it was my turn to grow angry, and Julie was comforted by my anger, as I had been comforted by hers. I knew a thing or two about this kind of shattered family myself. My father had moved out of the house the year before, leaving my violent and mentally ill mother to fend for herself. That had been his second marriage, and he married for a third time before I graduated. In fact, most of my friends in high school had been suffering through the breakup of their families. They handled these hardships badly. Many lost themselves in alcohol and drugs. Some had abortions. One took his own life. Few of them ended up married with children of their own.

Where Julie grew up, her friends decided to have the babies rather than aborting them. But they were raising them without fathers.

Between Julie and me, there sprang up a bond that reflected these depths. She was poor, but proud. When it turned out that she had only one contact lens, it took weeks of persuading before she would let me buy her a pair of glasses. I had not known the warmth of my mother's touch since I was a small child, and I experienced Julie's care for me as something akin to deliverance. Of course, neither of us had learned what a strong relationship between a man and a woman was like from our parents. But I had some idea from the year I had lived in Israel, spending sabbaths and holidays with my Uncle Isaac and Aunt Linda, Orthodox Jews living with their six children in a prefabricated home on a hillside an hour north of Jerusalem. And Julie had some idea from having lived on and off with her grandfather and her grandmother, Owen and Varda, devout Presbyterians who had raised five children in a home filled with music that was a pillar of their church.

When we spoke late into the nights, these things filled our conversations. Our schoolwork was pale and unimportant in comparison. The bond that sprang up between us was one that was full of hope and determination, although looking back on it now, I know we were also desperate. We longed for something we had seen and knew something about, although we didn't really understand it: that home in which a husband and wife remained faithful their entire lives, into which children were born and could grow strong, in which life was precious and God's blessings were tangible even in the face of tragedy and hardship. It was this that we built together in excited talk.

The bond, which we discussed in muted tones, was this: That I would be there for her—no matter what. That she would stay with me—no matter what. That we would raise children and grandchildren together. That we would not break as our own families had. Each of us wanted this more than anything else. But was it real? Can you believe in a nineteen-year-old boy? In an eighteen-year-old girl?

My father asked me what I was doing. I told him: "You need to trust me more. I won't marry a woman who isn't a Jew."

I knew how much I owed my father, and there was never a moment when I considered betraying him. My loyalty to him and to my people was firm. I had told Julie the same thing on the window seat in her dorm room in Rockefeller College a few weeks after we met. I still remember that conversation. It was hard to say because I was afraid to hurt her. But I said it. I would only marry her if she were a Jew. It didn't scare her. She had left the church long before coming to Princeton. Where she had grown up, the Old Testament was what she called "old-time religion." It had borne God's word. It had taken the Jews to the promised land. Perhaps it would take her there as well.

It is strange, now, thinking of us speaking of the promised land in that time, and in that place. In an Ivy League school, which had abandoned its Presbyterian past and was now adrift without direction. And yet, somehow, God lingered there. This was New Jersey, after all, and Bruce Springsteen's songs blared through the courtyards on stereo speakers turned outward in the windows of the dormitories. And these songs were, strangely, about Julie and me—songs of hard luck, songs of pain and a desperate hope. Songs about a young man and a young woman running away together:

Well, I ain't no hero, that's understood
All the redemption I can offer, girl, is beneath this dirty hood
With a chance to make it good somehow
Hey, what else can we do now?
Except roll down the window and let the wind blow back your hair
Well, the night's busting open, these two lanes will take us anywhere
We got one last chance to make it real
To trade in these wings on some wheels
Climb in back, heaven's waiting on down the tracks
Oh oh, come take my hand
We're riding out tonight to case the promised land
Oh oh oh oh, Thunder Road
Oh, Thunder Road, Oh Thunder Road.[1]

How many times did we hear that song about leaving for the promised land, and others that whispered similar things in our ears? The debate team sang "Thunder Road" on the way to every tournament, although it is hard to know why. What did these words mean to them?

I still don't know. But for Julie and me, these words were always about us.

2. *Ronald Reagan and the Conservative Revival at Princeton*

What did any this have to do with Ronald Reagan? Today, more than thirty-five years later, Reagan's image and legacy—like that of Margaret Thatcher in Britain—have been so thoroughly associated with economic liberalism that I know many will think the love story between Julie and me couldn't really have been shaped by his brand of politics.

But they would be wrong. The Reagan-Thatcher years sparked a broad religious and nationalist revival on the Princeton campus. It affected hundreds of Catholics, Protestants, and Jews. To understand the connection, it makes sense to start with the poster I had on my bedroom wall during the 1980 campaign, when I was still in high school.

It said: "Reagan: Let's Make America Great Again."

That's a nationalist slogan with a biblical resonance. It echoes the book of Genesis, in which God tells Abraham to take his family to Canaan, saying, "I will make of you a great nation."[2] In both its old Jewish and its modern American contexts, it calls upon individuals to take up the cause of the nation, pulling together in the face of the most daunting challenges in order to establish something of enduring importance for mankind.

And it captured the central aim of Reagan's presidency, which was to return to Americans a pride and belief in their nation after a decade of humiliation and weakness. Before Reagan, Americans had grown accustomed to using words like "malaise" and "stagflation," but what they were really describing was a once-great nation facing what seemed to be inevitable decline. In high school, I knew that the signs of this decline included the defeat in the war against Communism in Vietnam, and the subsequent Khmer Rouge genocide in Cambodia; the Watergate scandal and Nixon's resignation; the oil embargo by the petroleum-producing states that had brought gasoline rationing across America and Europe; the Soviet invasion of Afghanistan; and above all, the Iranian revolution and the endless crisis of the American hostages being held in Tehran, whose abuse I watched on Ted Koppel's nightly newscast on ABC.

Reagan's response to this series of humiliations was nationalism: the restoration of strength, pride, and self-confidence to the American nation and to the peoples allied with it. Today this nationalism is remembered primarily in the form of Reagan's massive military build-up and the deregulation and tax cuts that brought the American economy roaring back to life.

But other parts of his program were no less significant. One that especially won my admiration was his defiant stance in support of Polish Catholic nationalism. Poland had become part of the Soviet Empire when Europe was divided at the Yalta Conference at the end of the Second World War. But many Poles had maintained a posture of resistance, and one of these was Karol Józef Wojtyła—a Polish cardinal who had, astonishingly, become the first Polish pope, John Paul II, in 1978. Wojtyła had never ceased to long for a restoration of Polish national independence and self-determination, and upon becoming pope, he kept his eye fixed on this righteous aim. His nine-day tour of Poland the following year fanned the flames of what rapidly became a Catholic nationalist uprising.

Reagan became convinced that Poland's religious nationalist awakening was the key to toppling the Soviet's "evil empire,"[3] and upon entering office in January 1981, he asked to be briefed daily about Poland. Thereafter, he joined the pope and Margaret Thatcher's Britain in channeling financial and other resources to Polish

Solidarity, a nominal trade union that was, in reality, an opposition political party with several times the membership of the Polish Communist Party. That summer, Reagan proclaimed a "Captive Nations Week," specifically naming "the broken promises of the Yalta Conference" and the oppression in Poland and Afghanistan, reaffirming the American "tradition of self-rule" and "extend[ing] to the peoples of the Captive Nations a message of hope."[4] The battle to maintain the Polish independence movement in the face of martial law, which the Polish Communists imposed in December 1981, became a cornerstone of American and British foreign policy until Communism in Poland collapsed. Poland held its first free elections in the summer of 1989.

Reagan's commitment to the Polish nationalist cause was part of a broader pattern. He saw clearly that the future of democratic nations depended on restoring a willingness to fight for their independence in the face of Communism and other malign actors. If his first major step in supporting this revived democratic nationalism was in Poland, his second was directed toward Britain. Despite its glorious history, Britain seemed to have resigned itself to steep political and economic decline after the Suez debacle in 1956, never having recovered. Reagan believed the Conservative prime minister, Margaret Thatcher, who had entered office a year before him, had the potential to turn Britain into a vital partner again.

The turning point in Thatcher's prime ministership—as well as in Britain's relationship with America—was the Falklands War. The Falklands are an island archipelago three hundred miles off the coast of southern Argentina, whose population at that time consisted of 1,800 British subjects. In April 1982, the Argentine military junta placed a bet on Britain's ongoing weakness, seizing the islands and raising the Argentine flag over them. The Falklands are 8,000 miles from Britain, and military assessments suggested that it would be impossible for existing British forces to retake and hold them. Thatcher nonetheless declared that the Falklands were "our people, our islands," and assembled a flotilla of over 120 ships that arrived in the Falklands a month later.[5] The British engaged the larger Argentinian forces in air, sea, and land battles over the course of six weeks, eventually bringing about their surrender. The effect was immediate. Britons across the political spectrum rallied to support Thatcher, and the military victory against what had seemed impossible odds ended, in a stroke, the belief that British decline was irreversible.

But the Falklands War also strengthened American self-confidence. The Reagan administration, recognizing that the principle of British sovereignty was at stake—and that Thatcher's premiership was as well—threw itself into the war effort, providing Britain with weapons, intelligence, and the use of the American bases in the South Atlantic. In fact, the British victory was an American victory as well, demonstrating that the bonds of mutual loyalty binding the two great English-speaking nations were real, and that they could and would be turned against any adversary.[6]

Reagan's profound understanding of how each nation's renewed strength could inspire and build up the daring of its allies led to a breathtaking new height on March 23, 1983, a few months before Julie and I entered Princeton. Reagan had announced his Strategic Defense Initiative—the "Star Wars" program—whose aim was to deploy ground- and space-based platforms with the capacity to shoot Russian ballistic missiles out of the sky. At the time, this ambition was as far out of America's reach as the moon landing had been when Kennedy had set out to make it possible two decades earlier. And in fact, hundreds of prominent physicists and computer scientists publicly ridiculed Reagan's ambition as a technological impossibility. But I had grown up in my father's computer labs at Princeton, watching him tangle with computer scientists whose status as "experts" always seemed to be focused on explaining the impossibility of ideas proposed by others. When my father assured me that computers could be designed to track and destroy airborne missiles, I believed him. And I believed that Reagan had found a way to restore American pride and technological prowess while competing the Soviets into the ground. (In 1986, Reagan's Strategic Defense Initiative began collaborating with Israel to design the Arrow, the first operational missile defense system specifically designed to shoot incoming ballistic missiles out of the sky. The system became operational fourteen years later. Reagan—and my father—had been right.)[7]

Reagan's nationalism was closely tied to his Christianity, and he found himself naturally allied with leaders such as the pope and Thatcher, who shared a similar worldview. At home, Reagan had been elected in part thanks to the rising religious nationalism of Protestant ministers such as Billy Graham and Jerry Falwell, who understood that a love of America and a belief in its potential required reconnecting with the Christian sources of the nation's strength. Reagan was adamant that their Christianity had a crucial role to play in American public life, and built a powerful alliance with conservative Protestants and Catholics across a range of issues, including opposition to liberal policies on abortion, narcotics, and pornography, and his defense of Christian religious symbols as having a rightful and necessary place in government facilities and properties.

Perhaps the most dramatic expression of Reagan's belief in the need to ally nationalism with public religion was his 1982 proposal to amend the United States Constitution to return prayer to America's schools. Prayer had been banned from public schools by the Supreme Court twenty years earlier, but Reagan understood that this shameful suppression of America's religious inheritance had been a mistake. His message to Congress on this subject recalled the history of public religion in America going back to the country's founding, and advocated the restoration of prayer to the schools as a way of strengthening individuals and the nation as a whole. As he wrote:

> Prayer is still a powerful force in America, and our faith in God is a mighty source of strength.... The morality and values such faith implies are deeply embedded in our national character. Our country embraces those principles by design, and we abandon them at our peril....
>
> How can we hope to retain our freedom through the generations if we fail to teach our young that our liberty springs from an abiding faith in our Creator?...No one will ever convince me that a moment of voluntary prayer will harm a child or threaten a school or state. But I think it can strengthen our faith in a Creator who alone has the power to bless America....
>
> One of my favorite passages in the Bible is the promise God gives us in Second Chronicles: "If my people, which are called by my name, shall humble themselves and pray and seek my face and turn from their wicked ways, then will I hear from heaven and will forgive their sin and will heal their land."[8] That promise is the hope of America and all our people....
>
> Together let us take up the challenge to reawaken America's religious and moral heart, recognizing that a deep and abiding faith in God is the rock upon which this great nation was founded.[9]

Reagan believed deeply in individual liberty and the freedom of the market. But he was not a dogmatic libertarian. His first commitment was to the good of his nation as a whole, and when he felt that foreign steel was a threat to America's industrial capacity and to the well-being of American workers, he did not hesitate to intervene. Reagan was fond of reminding his audiences that he had voted for FDR four times, and this was a significant point. Although his views were strongly informed by *National Review*'s Cold War conservatism, he was no less the product of Roosevelt's Protestant nationalism, with its image of America as a "God-fearing democracy."[10] For Reagan, this religious underpinning was "the rock upon which this great nation was founded."

Reagan's politics came from a different era, and it spoke to conservative students at Princeton of a different world: One in which political leaders could see clearly that we were living in a time of declining nations and disintegrating families, and of the dishonorable suppression of God and religion. One in which political leaders were willing to stand against all of this, speaking plainly of a path to renewal that we really could take up.

As Julie and I shared what little we knew about a better life, we talked at length about her grandparents' strong Presbyterian household, and about the solidity and radiance of the home my Orthodox Jewish uncle and aunt had built. We could see the beauty and the goodness in a traditional family, itself taking part in the restoration of a nation and in the renewal of the thread of transmission that linked past generations to those that would come after us.

Would we have the strength and the daring to do something like that ourselves? President Reagan seemed to say that we could. We could dare to turn our backs on the decadent liberal society around us and to restore, with our own hands, what had been lost. We could make things great again.

In September 1983, Julie and I joined a thousand other students jammed into Alexander Hall at Princeton to hear Jerry Falwell speak. Though a row of students wearing armbands stood silently with their backs to him as he spoke, the things he said didn't seem so terrible to me. Falwell explained that the American constitutional tradition was intended to support "a nation under God," built upon pillars drawn from Judaism and Christianity. He proposed that these pillars included "the dignity of human life," "traditional monogamy" as the basis for a sturdy and moral nation, and a "principle of common decency" that rejected a liberal culture laced with pornography and drugs. He also called for a vigilant "pro-Americanism" that sought to build up the nation's defenses and support free nations overseas.[11]

I remember thinking that Falwell was right, but that he hadn't spoken especially well. His lengthy discussion of the Christian character of the Puritan founders of Massachusetts was historically true, but it didn't provide a compelling case for why the students at Princeton University should embrace this inheritance themselves. I thought there must be a better way to bring these ideas to Princeton students, so many of whom wanted to do something important with their lives but did not really know how.

A few months later, Julie and I gathered some friends together and proposed to support Reagan's conservative movement on the campus by publishing a magazine. We knew that through our writing and the attention it drew, we might reach other students. And that is what happened. But looking back on that prodigious effort, I know that what we were really doing was working out for ourselves what it would mean to live a conservative life.

3. Stevenson Hall

I had come back from my year in Israel with a clear understanding that the life my uncle, aunt, and cousins were leading was superior in just about every way to what my friends and I had known at Princeton High School. Life at the university only reinforced me in this view. The great stream of student life revolved around the eating clubs, where members had beer on tap twenty-four hours a day. Parties were already going on Prospect Avenue on Thursday night each week (and sometimes on Wednesday nights), so that half the week was devoted to drunkenness and dancing—and to other, darker things that appeared once the alcohol had "reduced inhibitions" enough. Students constantly used this phrase *reducing inhibitions* to explain to themselves what they were doing. It is still amazing to me that so many supposedly intelligent people, young men and young women, could think that discarding the inhibitions with which they had arrived on campus was obviously "a good thing."

I was never attracted to drinking, in high school or in college. But at Princeton, alcohol was so central to student life that the campus took on a Jekyll and Hyde character. Half the time, the students applied themselves to the rigors of problem sets and writing papers. The other half of the time, they lost themselves in staggering around the campus drunk, stripping off their clothes and shouting obscenities, and of course, vomiting (which, the older students wisely explained, they had trained themselves to do in order to make room for more beer). To be sure, there were many students who, like the circle that Julie and I befriended, were not interested in getting drunk or in getting others drunk. But the revelry completely dominated the weekends, with live bands, DJs, and dorm parties rattling every corner of the campus, while young drunks prowled around in packs, vandalizing the stately neo-gothic buildings and yelling "get raped" at the girls walking by. At times, they pounded menacingly on the doors of the girls' dorm rooms and demanded they come out. One of my larger friends carried a baseball bat when he walked the girls home. It was only after we were a little older that we began hearing the stories of actual rape from the women students.

It took me a while to understand the evil at the heart of all of this. The key to understanding Princeton in those days was that there were no responsible adults anywhere. You did find them lecturing in the classrooms from Monday morning through Thursday afternoon, and some students, at their own initiative, availed themselves of the professors' office hours. And you could meet a dean on rare occasions if you weren't keeping up with the course load or wanted the university to pay for something. But as a general matter, adults had abdicated responsibility for what was going on, so that Princeton was closer to Golding's *Lord of the Flies* than anything else.[12] Here, five thousand very young men and women had been dumped into dormitories together and given as much access to alcohol and drugs, sex, and party music as they could consume. And if they smashed the windows in their dorm rooms, broke empty beer bottles in the stairwells, or bashed in a streetlamp with their heads while they were drunk—all common occurrences—then nameless men in green uniforms would appear and repair the campus to its prior, Edenic beauty, with no questions asked.

During the daytime, everyone pretended that reason and learning were what the place was about. And in the evenings, everyone did what was right in his own eyes. My father, who had taught computers at Princeton for years, was amazed when I told him. "How can they make it to class the next morning?" he asked. But the schedule had been conveniently arranged so that three or four nights a week, they didn't have to.

When I say that we had hardly any contact with adults as undergraduates, I mean this quite literally. When I arrived on campus, I was randomly assigned a faculty advisor, a pleasant sociologist whose only advice was not to take too many courses. The only role my "advisors" played over the years was to sign my course selections. The chaplains, too, were invisible unless you went looking for them, and in any case, most were themselves quite liberal and only too pleased to demonstrate their open-mindedness by expressing displeasure over signs of orthodoxy and conservatism among the students.

No, there were no adults in our lives. Which meant, in practice, that there were no traditions of constraint and no examples of an honorable life being handed down to us—just the liberal notions ever-present in the coursework, and the barbaric behaviors that took over during the long weekend nights.

In this environment, we had to fall back on what we already knew. In my aunt and uncle's home, I had learned that a Jew should keep the sabbath and the traditional Jewish dietary laws. But upon coming back to the States, I hadn't succeeded in living this way on my own, without anyone around me doing it. This changed during the spring of my freshman year, when Julie and I began eating at Stevenson Hall, the kosher dining hall at 83 Prospect Avenue, at the far end of the street. This was a homey eating club that the university had handed over to Yavneh, the Orthodox Jewish students' group, which consisted of about forty young men and women. Besides the great dining room where the students sang traditional Hebrew songs during sabbath meals, there was also a large living room with a number of conversation pits and a pool table, a library where the students conducted Orthodox prayer services, and a computer cluster upstairs.

The Orthodox students did not have a great deal of guidance from adults on campus either.[13] But many of them brought from their homes, and from yeshiva studies in Israel, a completely different conception of student life. When these students weren't doing coursework, the leading personalities among them, both men and women, invested time and energy in infusing this odd Jewish congregation, consisting almost entirely of unmarried students, with the elements of Jewish communal life. The more knowledgeable students offered classes in Talmud and Jewish law, and everyone took turns teaching Bible from the pulpit on the sabbath. Although the university provided kitchen staff, there were daily prayer services to run and sabbath and holiday preparations that the students had to take care of. On Friday nights, there were perhaps 120 students—most of them not observant during the week—who joined to bring in the sabbath together.

As it happened, this Orthodox students' facility provided the most pronounced contrast possible to the relentlessly dissolute long weekends on campus. When Julie and I spent our first week there during the Pesah holiday in 1984, we discovered that the students at Stevenson conducted rowdy conversations about politics, philosophy, and religion as a central pastime. On Friday nights, when the rest of the campus descended into bedlam, Stevenson Hall rang with prayers, songs, and involved debates over the biblical passages that one of the students had taught from, or simply about the events of the day and the right way to live. All this continued through two additional lengthy meals on Saturday, ending with the candlelit service for concluding the sabbath when the stars came out on Saturday night.

I don't want to make this picture too dreamy. The students at Stevenson had their failings like everyone. Nevertheless, the difference between this religious life and the alternatives was so stark that after a week of Pesah at Stevenson Hall, Julie and I never went back to eating meals in the main campus dining halls. Eventually, we started keeping the sabbath and holidays and the laws of *kashrut*, and attending the prayer services with the rest of the Orthodox students. During our second year, Julie went to Israel, where she spent sabbaths with my uncle, aunt, and cousins as I had. When she came back, she began studying for conversion.

On June 1, 1987, we were married in an Orthodox wedding on campus in Prospect Gardens. The students of Stevenson, religious and non-religious alike, danced and sang down the length of Prospect Avenue, escorting us to a wedding dinner at Stevenson Hall. Our wedding procession passed between the eating clubs, silently lining the street on either side.

Ten months later, our first daughter was born in Princeton Hospital. We named her Avital, after the wife of the famous Soviet-Jewish dissident Natan Sharansky. Avital Sharansky's twelve-year public campaign to free her husband from Soviet prison had made an indelible impression on us. He had finally been released on February 11, 1986, and had joined his wife in Jerusalem.

4. George Will, Irving Kristol, and Conservative Ideas

The *Tory* was an expression of a profound conservative revival taking place on the Princeton campus in those years. This revival was both nationalist and religious. It was the project of hundreds of students, Christians and Jews, who sought to reorient their lives toward God and Scripture, family and nation. Those of us who embraced this conservative revival connected with it on two levels: We read up on *conservative ideas*, and we committed ourselves to a *conservative life.*

I've been discussing the path Julie and I took to a conservative life. I want to say a few words about the conservative ideas that helped us make sense of what we were doing.

The truth is that when we arrived at that meeting at the Institute for Educational Affairs to request support for *The Princeton Tory*, neither of us had read Burke yet. But we had read George Will's Burkean manifesto, *Statecraft as Soulcraft* (1983), and his book *The Pursuit of Virtue and Other Tory Notions* (1982) had given our magazine its name. We had also read Irving Kristol's *Reflections of a Neo-Conservative* (1983), Jeane Kirkpatrick's *Dictatorships and Double Standards* (1982), and many essays from Norman Podhoretz's *Commentary Magazine.*[14] It was largely through wrestling with these texts that the *Tory*'s nationalist conservatism was given shape.

Those who are familiar with George Will's recent writings may be surprised to learn that he was a prominent figure in launching the national conservative revival at Princeton in the 1980s. But in those days, Will's views were quite different from what they are today, and his *Statecraft as Soulcraft* seemed to be just what we needed. In it, we found an extended discussion of the basic human need for community, nation, and tradition, an awareness of which was so absent from the liberal society around us. As he wrote:

> Mankind has needs—call them spiritual, moral, emotional—that... cannot be reduced to physical needs and are ignored by society at its peril. Among those non-physical needs is a sense of social warmth, sometimes called "community."...
>
> In its quest for universals—"the rights of man and all that"—eighteenth century rationalism tried to envision humanity stripped of such inessential attributes as cultural, ethnic, and class particularities. The reaction of nineteenth century romanticism was powerful, and the twentieth century spillover was vicious. Many people found immersion in the broad, bland ocean of "humanity" akin to drowning.[15]

In passages like this one, George Will provided a theoretical framework for understanding the very things that my friends and I had been experiencing. The vacuous geometries of Enlightenment liberal political theory were everywhere in the intellectual life of the university. But during the long Princeton weekends, we could see that a great many students were drowning in the abyss that Enlightenment rationalism had created. Nor did we miss Will's warning that it was people of this kind, stripped of traditional communal attachments and moral norms, who had eventually given rise to Hitler's Germany.

Where did this recklessness and decadence come from? According to Will, the wrong turn in the road began with Hobbes and Locke, who had devised the Enlightenment rationalist myth that the individual enjoys freedom unless he is brought under government, which is itself nothing but an instrument of coercion.[16] But both parts of this Enlightenment rationalist philosophy are mistaken: Human beings are in fact shaped by the laws and customs of their society from birth. And government, as one of the most influential forces in society, shapes the character of the people, its traditions, habits, and way of life, whether it intends to or not.[17]

The belief that government can avoid influencing the public, and in fact can remain "neutral" on most substantive issues, has been prominent in the United States since the beginning. Will took particular aim at Jefferson, who had claimed that good government leaves men free to do as they wish so long as they do not injure one another.[18] This kind of talk was based on the belief that if individuals are simply left alone, their self-interestedness could be "made to do duty for public-spirited motives."[19] But, Will argued, nothing like that actually happens. Individuals who are encouraged to do whatever they like tend to become self-indulgent and reckless. And government becomes complicit in this self-indulgence and recklessness when it pretends to have no responsibility for encouraging virtue.

To be sure, there had been many public-spirited Americans in the past. But the tradition that had once tutored Americans in virtue was now being systematically destroyed, not only by liberals, but also by self-proclaimed "conservatives" who had substituted the principle of the free market for a political theory that could actually conserve something. As Will put it: "The most important human task—the one to which most people and institutions devote most energy—is transmission." But in the last two centuries, Western society had become negligent. It had turned away from philosophies of conservation, and in the end, very little of worth had been transmitted to our generation. The result was that America was living "improvidently off a dwindling legacy of cultural capital, which was accumulated in sterner, more thoughtful eras."[20]

Will, however, urged us to believe that a return to the tradition we had lost was still possible, if we would apply ourselves to reviving it. As he wrote:

> A tradition need not remain as remote as time and negligence have made it. If the wine of the Western tradition has become watery, let us pour some of the vintage that is in the old bottles. It is strong stuff and gives a bracing sense of the dignity of the political vocation, that vocation which is more than a mere partnership in low concerns and vagrant desires. It is, rather, a partnership in making the most of our finest potentialities, and doing so the only way we can: Cooperatively.[21]

A crucial complement to George Will's book was Irving Kristol's *Reflections of a Neo-Conservative*, which was also published the year Julie and I entered Princeton. At first glance, Kristol seemed a bit more positive in his assessment of liberalism. In principle, he saw himself as standing on the common ground that united Edmund Burke and Adam Smith, who had been friends and had admired one another's work: "Both of these thinkers saw no intrinsic difficulty in reconciling the commercial spirit, with its emphasis on individual liberty, to the prescriptive claims of traditional institutions and traditional modes of individual behavior."[22]

But in practice, it turned out that reconciling the free action of the market with the kinds of traditional institutions and "republican morals" needed to maintain an independent nation was harder than it looked. Considering America after two hundred years, Kristol concluded that Adam Smith, like the American founders, had been overly optimistic about the prospects of a society focused on free enterprise. There was too much they had taken for granted, which, by the 1980s, we could no longer do. In particular, what they took for granted was "organized religion, traditional moral values, and the family"—factors that had once been powerful enough to constrain the market and channel it into productive avenues. But now these things had become "unsettled, controversial, ineffectual." As Kristol wrote:

> Above all, they were able to take for granted a *coherence* in the private sector achieved through the influence of organized religion, traditional moral values, and the family. To put it another way, their confidence in the ability of men and women to live together socially and civilly under capitalism was not a fantasy; it was based on a realistic enough vision of the real world, as it then existed. But that was before the modern world was touched by the breezes of nineteenth century rationalist doctrine, and devastated by the hurricanes of twentieth century nihilism. If we today have less confidence in "natural" human sociableness, it is... because the preconditions of social life, which they imagined to be immutable, have turned out to be fragile....
>
> What they took for granted has, in the twentieth century, become unsettled, controversial, ineffectual. Bourgeois affluence has "liberated" men and women from

> these wholesome influences [of organized religion and the family], and has thereby reopened all the large questions of moral and political philosophy that Adam Smith and the Founding Fathers thought had been definitively answered.[23]

For Kristol, as for Will, political liberalism and the freedom of the market had "liberated" men and women from traditional constraints, enthroning the "sovereignty of self-centered hedonism" and destroying civic-mindedness and public-spiritedness in the process. When a people reaches this condition, "the purpose of politics becomes the maximum gratification of desires and appetites." And when, inevitably, the democratic state fails to deliver ever-increasing material goods, "it becomes possible for a great many people to think that a non-democratic state might do better."[24]

Kristol's reply to this condition was captured in a slogan he coined a few years later: "The three pillars of modern conservatism are religion, nationalism, and economic growth."[25] In a liberal society, the role of the conservative was not to inflame the self-centered hedonism that liberalism had unleashed by constantly emphasizing the freedom of the individual. It was rather to build up constraining factors—religion and nationalism—that could pull a disintegrating society back from the brink.

Nationalism appeared in Kristol's book right at the top. (George Will, too, had been writing about "the need for nationalism.")[26] Kristol told us that nationalism "arises out of hope for the nation's future, distinctive greatness," and that he welcomed the "new American nationalism" that was already being felt. President Reagan, he said, spoke "in the kind of nationalist-populist tonalities not heard since Teddy Roosevelt, appealing to large sections of the working class, to the increasingly numerous religious fundamentalists, and even to the growing, if still small, number of conservative and neoconservative intellectuals."[27]

What could nationalism do for America? Kristol believed that postwar liberalism had weakened the United States as a nation, both at home and abroad. On the one hand, American foreign policy had become internationalist. Bewitched by the "illusion" of a "world community," it was squandering precious resources on trying to serve "the interests of all," rather than responsibly looking out for what was good for Americans.[28] On the other hand, Americans had been encouraged to see themselves only as individuals, and to think only of their personal freedom and well-being. In this way, the country had been deprived of public-spirited citizens who would be able, "on critical occasions, to transcend the habitual pursuit of self-interest and devote themselves directly and disinterestedly to the common good."[29]

What these internationalist and individualist trends had in common was that they robbed America of the resources needed to preserve and strengthen itself as an independent nation. Nationalism, for Kristol, meant strengthening the United States by refocusing on the "national interest" in America's relations with other countries, and on the "public interest" in domestic affairs, which would be recognized as something distinct from the concerns of private individuals acting freely in the market.[30]

Notice, however, that Kristol was not calling on Americans to give up on private interest or personal concerns and to submerge themselves only in thoughts of the public good. Rather, his proposal was that, in addition to the interests of private individuals, there is also such a thing as the good of the nation as a whole. For example, it is possible for one part of the public to take advantage of freedoms protected under the law in a way that becomes abusive toward another part of the public. In such a case, the normal disagreements and tensions among social groups or classes may turn into hatred, dissolving the mutual loyalties that hold the nation together. Domestic peace is thereby endangered, as is the ability of the nation to mount a common defense. Remedying such threats is a legitimate public interest, which is distinct from the calculus of private interests that are to be adjudicated by the free market.

The existence of such legitimate public interests moved Kristol to insist on "the inevitable priority of politics over economics," by which he meant that the purpose of political life is to seek the good of the nation, which can never be reduced to what professional economists regard as "correct" economic policy.[31] It is because of such concerns that Kristol proposed that we give only "two cheers for capitalism" instead of three.[32]

Like George Will, Kristol believed that many conservatives—in rightly opposing socialism—had taken their hostility to government too far. A conservative cannot grant unrestrained power to private corporations, for example, because unrestrained power invariably leads to abuse. In the same way, a conservative should not be opposed to government assistance for the needy, or to government action whose purpose is to shape public morals. For such reasons, Kristol emphasized that a conservative cannot be a libertarian:

> Neo-conservatives, though respecting the market as an economic mechanism, are not libertarian in the sense that, say, Milton Friedman and Friedrich A. von Hayek are. A conservative welfare state—what was once called a "social insurance" state—is perfectly consistent with the neoconservative perspective. So is a state that takes a degree of responsibility for helping to shape the preferences that the people exercise in a free market—to "elevate" them, if you will.[33]

This last point, about the need for government to take "a degree of responsibility" in the shaping of public culture, found expression in Kristol's forceful defense of obscenity laws and the censorship of pornography. In fact, Kristol went so far as to suggest that if a government does not act to protect public morals, it forfeits its justification for existing:

> The purpose of any political regime is to achieve some version of the good life and the good society.... [The old idea of democracy] starts from the proposition that democracy is a form of self-government, and that if you want it to be a meritorious polity, you have to care about the kind of people who govern it. Indeed, it puts the matter more strongly and declares that if you want self-government, you are only entitled to it if that "self" is worthy of governing. There is no inherent right to self-government if it means that such government is vicious, mean, squalid, and debased. Only a dogmatist and a fanatic, an idolater of democratic machinery, could approve of self-government under such conditions....
>
> [The old idea of democracy] cared not merely about the machinery of democracy, but about the quality of life that this machinery might generate. And because it cared, this older idea of democracy had no problem, in principle, with pornography and/or obscenity. It censored them—and it did so with a perfect clarity of mind and perfectly clear conscience. It was not about to let people capriciously to corrupt themselves. Or, to put it more precisely: In this version of democracy, the people took some care not to let themselves be governed by the more infantile and irrational parts of themselves.[34]

In his discussion of government's responsibilities in the area of public morals, Kristol returns twice to the concept of *idolatry*, which he defines as "taking the symbolic for the real, the means for the end."[35] This is a concept drawn from Judaism, and its appearance in this crucial discussion of the legitimating grounds for a democratic regime raises the question of whether, in the end, it is at all possible to be a conservative without relying on a religious foundation for one's views.

At the end of his book, Kristol told his readers that he was "a neo-orthodox Jew, in belief at least. That is, I am non-practicing... but, in principle, very sympathetic to the spirit of orthodoxy. When I talk about religion, I talk as an insider."[36] (Kristol also slipped in a reply to those Straussians and others who had fallen into the habit of speaking of Americans as a "chosen people," and of their particular traditions as the inheritance of all mankind. "I really cannot believe that Americans are a historically unique and chosen people," he wrote. "I am a Jew and an American, and with all due respect to the Deity, I think the odds are prohibitive that he would have gone out of his way to choose me twice over.")[37]

For the most part, Kristol's orthodox sympathies remained hidden from view, so that the reader accustomed to thinking of political philosophy as something distinct and separate from religion might very well wonder why he bothered to mention his commitment to Judaism at all. But here, in his discussion of pornography and censorship, we came face to face with the religious foundation on which everything else in Kristol's politics was built: For him, there was a real difference between what is worthy of human beings and what is debased and corrupt. He was, in other words, invoking the biblical view that each of us is made in God's image. According to this view, pornography is wrong not only because it is built on enslavement and coercion. It is wrong because it reduces men and women to beasts. This is true of those who make pornography and it is true of those who consume it. And where it is allowed to spread, it swiftly reduces the entire society to one without constraint, a society of animals.

Kristol saw much good in democracy, and he was willing to go along with liberal society's emphasis on individual freedom as long as it could be kept within bounds. But beyond a certain point, Kristol recognized that the principle of individual liberty becomes, as he put it, "ridiculous" and "absurd." When Kristol wrote that the absurdity in question "is the absurdity of idolatry," he used this term exactly as the rabbis use it—to describe a principle that has become so exaggerated that it has ceased to serve its original purpose and has become an end in itself. At this point, individual liberties become detached from the good they are supposed to advance. And the regime that cares not at all whether the people choose evil or good is one that "anyone of intelligence and spirit" will no longer find reason to support.[38]

As Kristol wrote: *There is no inherent right to self-government if it means that such government is vicious, mean, squalid, and debased.*

5. A Conservative Life

The first issue of *The Princeton Tory* was published in October 1984, exactly a year after Julie and I met in the physics lab in the basement of Palmer Hall. As editor, I made sure that the nationalist and religious pillars of conservatism were at the forefront. This didn't mean we neglected the defense of free enterprise. All of us read Milton and Rose Friedman's *Free to Choose* (1980) and cheered the conservative campaign to roll back government in America and Britain.[39] But a nationalist and religious conservatism characterized Princeton's Tories—Jews, Protestants, and Catholics—from the outset.

For the first issue of the magazine, I wrote a twelve-page manifesto called "Church's Proper Place in the State," in which I sided with

President Reagan and Jerry Falwell on the question of whether religion should shape government policy. I argued that religion had been inseparable from American public life until the 1940s, when the Supreme Court had turned the liberal principle of "separation of church and state" into a centerpiece of the American Constitution, using it to progressively eliminate Christian and Jewish religion from America's schools. The result, I said, was the rise of a "churchless faith" that claimed to place reason at the center but which was, in reality, no less bigoted and intolerant than the traditional religions it sought to displace. As I put it then: "Having set about trying to remove the church from politics, we find that we leave the country to be governed by the faith of those without a church.... And is not the secular public school, having outlawed the teaching of the Bible,...of a faith even more viciously intolerant than was the Protestant public school of 1840?"[40]

By the third year, the mostly Jewish old guard handed the *Tory* over to a younger group of Protestant and Catholic students. In February 1988, they published an issue of the magazine with the words "Is God Dead? We Think Not" splashed across the cover. I was proud of them for doing it. That issue of the *Tory* made plenty of people angry. But it did something that needed to be done, directly taking on the implicit consensus that everyone and everything at Princeton had to be moving toward overthrowing received ideas and traditions, no matter how important.

At that point, Julie and I were married and about to have our first child. I was in my first year of graduate school at Rutgers. But we were still living on the Princeton campus, advising the Tories, coaching the debate team, and generally doing whatever we could to fan the fire of national and religious revival among the students. Although we still ate frequently at Stevenson Hall, we also started having sabbath meals in our tiny married students' apartment, inviting students over to be a part of our new household. There was still no orthodox rabbi on the campus, so that year Julie and I recruited Rabbi Menachem Zupnik from Passaic to teach a weekly torah class for beginners, which we called "Judaism Beyond Mother Goose." Rabbi Zupnik became a beloved teacher and a close friend, and he continued teaching his wonderfully engaging class at Princeton for thirteen years. The *Tory*, as I have said, is still being published at Princeton today.

Julie and I are in our fifties now. We live in Jerusalem. We've had nine children together, and our children are beginning to raise families of their own. Avital and her husband Eliyahu live in the neighborhood, and she brings our grandson and granddaughter over almost every day. Our son Efraim and his wife Sarah live in Jerusalem too, and they just had a baby boy. The arrival of these grandchildren means that we've now come full circle. A new chapter is beginning for us, so this may be a good time to draw a few lessons from those years of conservative revival at Princeton, which did so much for us and for so many others.

The most important thing to understand about the Reagan revolution as Julie and I and our friends experienced it is that it wasn't just about "the power of ideas"—a phrase that was ubiquitous in the Anglo-American conservative movement of those days. Conservative ideas certainly played a crucial role. George Will and Irving Kristol gave us a language we could use in resisting the liberalism around us, and helped us turn toward nationalism, religion, and tradition to establish a genuine alternative.

But looking back on it now, I can see that Princeton's conservative revival was not something that could have been inspired by these books and essays by themselves. Will's *Statecraft as Soulcraft* is as fine a manifesto for Burkean traditionalism as any published in those years. Yet it is striking that religion—which for Burke was "the first of our prejudices, . . . involving in it profound and extensive wisdom"[41]—is virtually absent from Will's account of conservatism. And though Kristol was explicitly committed to Jewish orthodoxy in principle, he and his wife, the historian Gertrude Himmelfarb, were not religiously observant themselves.

In other words, Will and the Kristols were intellectual defenders of the idea of tradition. But they didn't reach the conclusion that seemed obvious to Julie and me, as it was to dozens of other undergraduates who took part in Princeton's conservative revival of that time. These leading conservative thinkers, who did so much for us, didn't see that conservative ideas are of limited worth if they don't bring those who embrace them to lead a conservative life.

On this point, our thinking was more in line with that of Dennis Prager and Joseph Telushkin, whose *Nine Questions People Ask About Judaism* (1981) we discovered later in our years at Princeton. Prager called on us to recognize that we couldn't do without God and Scripture, and insisted that we begin keeping the sabbath and the Jewish dietary laws, going to services, and abstaining from *lashon hara* (Hebrew for "evil talk") about others.[42] His book, essays, and tape-recorded speeches argued eloquently for something Julie and I never doubted. We had always assumed that if we were going to be conservatives, there could be no evading *teshuva*—the Hebrew word for repentance, which literally means "returning" to a life of torah and keeping the Mosaic law. For a Jew, there simply is no way of conserving the ways of his people without such a personal journey of repentance and return. The fact that a prominent conservative figure such as Prager was saying this gave the Princeton revival a much-needed boost. The need for a personal "return" is something we heard from many orthodox Jewish teachers over the years, but at Princeton the one book that we bought by the box-full to hand out to students was this one.

I don't mean to suggest that Irving and Bea Kristol were unsupportive. Like almost every other conservative intellectual we got to know, they were enthusiastic about the revival of orthodoxy at Princeton and on other university campuses.[43] But their relationship with us seemed to contain a measure of wistfulness, which reminded me of Moses remaining on the far side of the Jordan River, watching the next generation enter the promised land. Many of these older conservatives talked about how it was "too late" for them to take up Jewish observance, given how they had been raised. Perhaps they also felt that their own personal *teshuva* wouldn't make much of a difference. In those days, it was commonly believed that the tide was in any case turning. Older conservatives often mentioned that the higher birth rate among the religious Christians and Jews was going to fundamentally change the character of society within a generation or two. Along the same lines, they believed that liberal ideas were quickly collapsing, and that the result would be a widespread turn to religion. Both of these trends seemed to mean that a profound conservative backlash was coming, and that the older generation could trust us younger people to lead the charge on religious issues.

In hindsight, all of this looks like a serious miscalculation on the part of Reagan-era conservatives. Liberalism has collapsed, all right, just as they said it would. But that collapse hasn't moved America, Britain, and other democratic countries toward a greater embrace of traditional ideas and norms. On the contrary, the end of hegemonic liberalism has led to an even more strident and aggressive rejection of traditional ideas by Marxists seeking to impose a hegemony of their own. Far from becoming more influential, the regions of society in which one can find the actual conservation and transmission of anything great and good from the past are rapidly shrinking. Those orthodox Christian and Jewish communities, which conservatives of a generation ago believed would soon inherit everything, are today living under siege. They, too, are having an increasingly difficult time transmitting ideas and customary norms of behavior to their children.

In light of these conditions, the emphasis of Reagan-era conservatives on the "power of ideas" looks not a little naïve. I keep thinking of George Will's suggestion that if the wine has grown weak, you could just "pour some of the vintage that is in the old bottles." This made it seem as if you could just dust off the old volumes of Aristotle or Cicero that you had on the shelves and start reading, and that would do the trick.

But if this was what Will meant, it was never true. Conservatism isn't something you can find in a book or in a whole library of books, whether old or new. The transmission of ideas, behaviors, and institutions from one generation to the next is a skill, and like all skills, it can only be learned by practice. The life of conservation and transmission is one that flourishes when people actually live it, and it dies when they do not.

Of course, there are conservative ideas, and these do have a significant role to play in the reconstruction of a conservative life. But where people talk about conservatism without actually living it, the ideas themselves are not properly understood, no genuine repentance takes place, and the transmission to the next generation is feeble, if it happens at all. In part, this is because ideas that come out of books or are heard in lectures are only vaguely grasped until they are filled out with actual experiences from lived life. Imagine reading about a mountain lion or an elephant without ever having seen one, and then spending time in proximity to the real thing. After a few minutes, you realize that you didn't understand much before. After a few days of observations, you understand that you still didn't know much after those first few minutes. And after a few years, you recognize that what you knew after a few days of observations was shallow and, in many respects, profoundly mistaken.

It is no different with the traditional family, the education of children, the life of the congregation, the revival of the nation, the study of Scripture, and service to God. Individuals can write about these things and sit on panels to discuss them, often in an odd jargon peppered with terms such as "mediating institutions," "spontaneous order," "little platoons," and "the ancestral." But without themselves having lived a life of conservation and transmission—that is, without having taken part in the renewal of the generations within the congregation and the traditional family—they still see things only in a vague and confused way, like children whose thoughts have not yet attained the clarity that comes of experience.

It is especially painful to see how conservatives imitate their liberal rivals in all of this. Liberalism is such a preposterous doctrine because it was devised by men who knew little about these subjects. Hobbes, Locke, Spinoza, and Kant never had children. Descartes's only daughter, born outside of marriage, died at the age of five. Rousseau had five children with a mistress but abandoned them all to an orphanage in infancy. In other words, Enlightenment rationalism was the construction of men who had no real experience of family life or what it takes to make it work. Enlightenment liberal political theory, which revolves around the free individual who accepts only those obligations to which he consents, was invented by men who did live in more or less this way. It is a political theory made in the image of unmarried, childless individuals, and the more people repeat its tenets, the more they act like unmarried, childless individuals.

But the freedom of unmarried, childless individuals—the freedom of the college campus—is not something that real-life families, communities, and nations can have. If they are to survive at all, and even to flourish, their thoughts and customs must be rooted in something more substantial than the fantasies of the Enlightenment's lifelong bachelors. They must uphold political and moral norms that are rooted in a life of conservation and transmission—which is to say, in a life built around securing the things that we actually need and in carrying out the obligations we really have.

The rediscovery of such a conservative life involves accepting the laws that do in fact govern a life of conservation and transmission. One of these laws is that nothing can be conserved if it is not honored in an appropriate degree. The great Anglo-American conservative inheritance was one in which a certain weight and significance were accorded to God and Scripture, congregation and nation, marriage and family, sabbaths and festivals, man and woman, honor, loyalty, and the sacred. For this inheritance to be handed on, those who have attained prominence or aspire to it must give expression to the weight and significance of these things in words and deeds. Doing so makes the revival and transmission of the tradition possible. Not doing so makes it impossible.

I think of this frequently when interacting with the new generation of conservatives, young men and women who are sharp as blades intellectually, yet frequently quite lost in everything having to do with the assignment of the proper weight and significance to things. Imagine a young man in his thirties, living with a woman year after year, deferring marriage and children, engaged in the life of no congregation, reading no Scripture, and keeping no sabbaths. I won't go so far as to say that such a person is godless and entirely without a moral compass, although one could make that argument. Rather, he is a man who has inherited no sense of what is to be honored and in what degree. Because of this, all things look good and fruitful to him, and no obligations seem especially pressing. He feels that no great harm would be done if he fails to commit to marriage and raising children, to joining a congregation and keeping the sabbath, for another ten or fifteen years. He is the kind of man who is not overly troubled by the fact that he has, in effect, left God sitting in the waiting room with a stack of conservative magazines to look at.

What does such a person know about conserving anything? He copies conservative words from others, but his life is that of a liberal. He thinks he influences others with his words. But he doesn't have enough experience in life to know that his true influence is being exerted by his deeds. Everyone around him knows how he lives. And from this they understand what is weighty and significant in his eyes and what is not. To the extent that others honor and respect him, they learn from him that they should lead a liberal life, just as he does.

What would he do differently if he were determined to bring about a change in the order of the world around him?

He would begin living a conservative life—a life that is built around the restoration and conservation of things, not just in his fantasies, but in reality. This would require locating an actual conservative community in which the tradition still lives and is being handed down to new generations. It would require presenting himself to this community as one who wishes to give honor to its institutions, and in doing so, to begin learning again. In earlier days, an alliance of families that were loyal to one another and to a shared inheritance was called a clan. Today, such an alliance of families is called a congregation, and in fact, in our time and place, there are virtually no conservative communities left outside of orthodox Christian and Jewish congregations.

The aim of the individual or of the detached couple seeking a conservative life is to find such a conservative congregation and to begin taking up its traditions. There is no liberal assumption of equality at the basis of the relationship between the congregation and the young newcomers. The congregation has an obligation to welcome and to educate them. The newcomers have a responsibility to give honor and to learn. In this way, the newcomer begins to accept his role as a part of the chain of transmission. In this way, he begins to live a conservative life.

The aim must be to do this now, not in ten or fifteen years. For as the rabbis put it, "If not now, when?" We have no control over what the world will be like in ten years. We have no control over what we ourselves will become after another ten years of drifting on the ocean of liberalism, the sea of dissolution. We must put an end to this drift. Not later, but now.

In saying this, I have in mind not only the young, but also older men and women, and married couples whose children went off to university and did not return. There is no age limit placed on rediscovery, repentance, and return. There is no knowing what inspiration and strength will be brought into the world by the example of an older man or woman, or a married couple, experienced and perhaps accomplished in many things, who are able to overcome their pride, join a congregation, and begin learning again. There is no knowing what inspiration and strength would have been brought into the world had some of the Reagan-era conservative intellectuals we admired taken this path to a conservative life in their later years.

Julie and I were more fortunate than many others. When we met as college students, we didn't just have conservative ideas to inspire us. We also knew something about what a conservative life looks like. Julie knew something about it because she had grown up near her grandparents and had often lived in their home. I knew something about it from a year of spending sabbaths and holidays with my uncle and aunt and their children. We were able to figure out that taking up the thread of our inheritance meant finding our way to Stevenson Hall, to the congregation of orthodox Jewish students at our university. There, we discovered an attractive, intimate, and inspiring congregation that welcomed us, and to which we gave honor. It was there that we took up a conservative life, and discovered that we, too, had a place in the great tradition, which still lived.

Conclusion

On Being a Conservative Person

A distinctive hardship attends the lives of men and women who have grown up in liberal societies—whose traditions, whether Christian or Jewish, were overthrown a few generations earlier. Having been told all their lives that they are "free to choose" whatever course they please, they find it increasingly difficult to choose any course at all. They find it difficult to marry, and if they do marry, they find it difficult to stay married. They evade having children. They find that religion does not speak to them. They find that work is onerous and demeaning, so that if they are employed at all, they do many things, and none of them well. They pass the time with drugs and alcohol, pornography, video games, television, social media, and similar remedies, which suppress the pain, shame, anxiety, and depression that plague them.

This condition of disorientation, dismay, and disease was described as *anomie*—literally, an existence without law or constraint—by Durkheim, in a book he wrote to try and understand the causes of suicide. We are hierarchical creatures by nature, he suggested. When we live in a hierarchy to which we are loyal, we strive to be honored by those who are important in this same hierarchy: by parents and other older relations, political figures, military commanders, employers, clergy, teachers, and so on. Through this striving, we shape ourselves, building up and refining our abilities and achieving things we hope will be worthy in their eyes, in this way becoming worthy in our own eyes as well.

The result of this striving is that certain pathways are discovered and built up through the wilderness of lawlessness, paths that lead to an honorable life in which all slipperiness and evasion ceases and one is able to make one's way with confidence and pleasure. These paths offer much more than honor. They offer purpose, meaning, direction, health, knowledge, and skill. The things that are honored by the family, tribe, and nation—varying somewhat from one to the next—are the guides that allow the individual to locate these paths and to walk upon them.

When we do away with the norms that give the individual direction and purpose, the individual is plagued by an inability to distinguish what is honorable from what is dishonorable, and what is worthy from what is unworthy. Those who live in such a society may take pleasure in a writer such as Nietzsche, who urges the depressed and demoralized individual to forge an entirely new path through this wilderness, one that is unique to him. But few, if any, have the abilities needed to do this. And so society comes to be characterized by the decadence of the individual, who is drowning in a sea of alternatives—none of which matter to anyone. And once the individual is decadent in this way, he becomes a mark for charlatans peddling easy hatreds, and for criminals who feast on damaged souls.

The suffering individual has only one honorable way out of this decadence. He must find his way to one of the traditional paths through the wilderness. This means he must find his way to a place where the traditions of our forefathers still live. As the devastation becomes more widespread, these places become fewer and more distant. Yet they do exist, and it is possible to find them in those circles that still muster under the banner of orthodox Christianity or Judaism. It is here that individuals, having found themselves among the ruins, can retrieve the lost thread of transmission. By joining himself to such a congregation and taking a direct part in the renewal and transmission of the inheritance of the past, the individual can recover a conservative life that he had thought was lost, and in so doing become a conservative person.

Political conservatism cannot be separated from such a personal conservatism. Dissolute individuals, those who are incapable of preserving and restoring traditional norms in their own lives, are not a material out of which cohesive and enduring families can be built. No tribe or nation can persist if its sons and daughters are not zealous to preserve their inheritance intact and to restore it when it has decayed or been forgotten. The private vices of individuals do not, in other words, amount to any kind of public virtue. On the contrary, the dissolute life of the individual pulls down everyone and everything around him. It is the engine driving the disintegration of every liberal society.

If a public conservatism is to have any purchase in a sick society, it must begin with *teshuva*—a personal journey of repentance and return.[1] I have in mind concrete steps undertaken by the individual to alleviate his own personal decadence, which is identical with his inability to conserve the traditions of his forefathers in his own life. It is not enough to issue fine pronouncements about "little platoons" and "mediating structures," "religion" and "the family," or to talk about government policies that are meant to encourage "family formation" or to protect "religious liberty." In the absence of a family and a congregation of one's own, all this is, in the end, mere hypocrisy and vain words.

And so, whenever we hear a conservative speaking warmly about the conservation of our national, religious, and moral inheritance, it is reasonable for those within earshot to ask what this particular person has done for the actual conservation of national and religious tradition where this is entirely within his power—which is to say, in his private life. Has he taken the necessary steps to construct a conservative life for himself and his posterity? Or is he yet another sorry example of the general dereliction that we face?

Consider the custom of setting aside a sabbath day on which to go to church or to synagogue, participate in festive communal meals, and rest from the labors of the week. I often speak to young men and women who say they are excited about "conservatism." Yet when the sabbath comes around, they have not the slightest intention of keeping the sabbath as their ancestors did for two or three thousand years, but happily tell me that they are headed for the mountains or the beach, or staying home "to finish up something for work."

Or consider the custom of reading regularly from the Bible, which is the surest mainstay of both Jewish and Christian societies, but has, in liberal society, disappeared from the lives of all but the most devoted. Often these same young men and women who talk so much about "conservatism" turn out to have only disregard for the Bible and no time for the study of Scripture. In part, this is a consequence of the fact that, having no sabbath, they know nothing of sanctifying times in which they honor the God and Scripture of their ancestors.

No doubt, many of these individuals feel free to let these customs pass into history because they see themselves as atheists or agnostics. But if they were conservatives, they would recognize that this absolves them of nothing. If they were conservatives, they could not simply shrug their shoulders and go off to the beach, saying, "Oh well, too bad I'm an atheist." For a conservative says in his heart:

> *My nation, friends and neighbors, and my family are suffering grievously from having cut themselves off from the God*

of our fathers, and from the teachings that flowed from Scripture and gave us strength. What can I do to recover and restore the old paths, and to give honor to the ideas and way of life of my ancestors who brought me here? And is it not, perhaps, my own fault that I know nothing of God, having given up the search for the wisdom and understanding of my ancestors as an adolescent? Perhaps it is my own fault, after all, if I seek to exercise my freedom by going to the seashore on the seventh day, rather than setting it aside as my ancestors did, as a day for learning Scripture and for taking my place within my congregation and family, in this way reconnecting myself to the traditions of my nation and to the God of my forefathers.

You see, a conservative understands that it is not disbelief that plagues us but dishonor: our accursed inability to give honor where it is due. A conservative knows—or at least suspects—that if he were to give honor where it is due, then knowledge of God, and of many other things, would eventually follow from this.

Where honor is possible, so too is belief. But where there is no honor given, the children who are born into these scenes of decay will believe in nothing.

Yet even among those who regard themselves as conservatives, we find an unexplained resistance to giving honor and weight to our traditions by taking up a traditional way of life. Both young and old, having been raised in a liberal society, resist giving honor where it is due. They simply prefer not to accept the constraints involved in behaving as though our inheritance in fact has something to teach us. They cannot bear the constraints on their freedom that would arise from military service; or from taking responsibility for marrying, bringing a new generation into the world, and ensuring the tradition of our fathers has been properly handed down to them; or from personally caring for their parents in their old age. They cannot see themselves shouldering the constraints involved in learning how to read and teach the Bible to others, or in keeping the sabbath, or in living a life that is clean of obscenity or immodesty.

Like adolescents, much of our generation cannot imagine weighing themselves down with the constraints cultivated by tradition. They yearn only to be free. And most of our teachers, our media, and our books cater to this sickness by valorizing freedom and only freedom, whereas next to nothing is said about the source of stability, sanity, and peace, which is constraint.

Honor and constraint are the soil in which the possibility of conserving any worthy belief and action grows. Wielding these tools, we can begin the process of healing a ravaged family and community, tribe and nation, reviving norms of behavior and a common sense that had been given up for dead.

Yet this will never happen so long as we expect others will take care of these obligations for us, while we ourselves enjoy our freedom.

Conservatism begins at home.

Acknowledgments

My father introduced me to conservative ideas. But it was in the home of my Uncle Isaac and Aunt Linda that I first learned what it meant to live a conservative life. Everything in this book is ultimately a reflection on the things I learned in my many visits to their home. This book is dedicated to them with love.

The historical and theoretical portions of the book are indebted to my close friend, the historian Ofir Haivry, who co-authored the original versions of Chapters 1–2 with me and permitted me to reprint them in revised form here. Thank you for our many years of partnership, Ofir.

Chapters 3–4 reflect conversations about loyalty with my daughter Avital Levi; and about hierarchy with my son, Hadar Ahiad Hazony. A great deal of what I have written here on these subjects reflects their scholarship and insights.

My thanks to Brad Littlejohn for assistance in understanding Hooker and much else about historical and present-day Protestantism; and to Anna Wellisz for serving as my guide to all things Catholic.

Many friends and colleagues have read and commented on parts of this book. I'm grateful for so much help, all of which I needed. I owe special thanks to those who read and commented on the entire manuscript: David Benzion, Paul Choix, Yael Hazony, N. S. Lyons, R. R. Reno, and Ben Shapiro.

Since the publication of *The Virtue of Nationalism* in 2018, I have been active in the nationalist conservative revival taking place in America and Europe. Among my close associates in this effort have been my colleagues at the Edmund Burke Foundation, Christopher DeMuth, David Brog, Anna Wellisz, Ofir Haivry, Rafi Eis, and Jim Lucier, as well as Jonathan Bronitsky, Johnny Burtka, Michael Cialdella, Josh Hammer, Brad Littlejohn, Daniel McCarthy, Joshua Mitchell, John O'Sullivan, R. R. Reno, Marion Smith, Tim Unes, Alexei Woltornist, and Elyasaf Yehuda. Alex and Cathy Cranberg, Roger Hertog, Clark Judge, Colin Moran, Tom Klingenstein, and Peter Thiel have been wonderful conversation partners and supporters through all the vicissitudes of this campaign.

The present NatCon movement is a reflection of—and a return to—another conservative revival that took place at Princeton University a long time ago. My love goes out to the Tories, to our friends at Whig-Clio, and to everyone at Stevenson Hall who made a home for Julie and me.

I am grateful to Tom Spence and Paul Choix of Regnery, and to my agent, Andrew Stuart, for bringing this book to press.

Thank you to Barry and Lainie Klein, and to Seth and Nealy Fischer, for your friendship. We couldn't have done it without you.

My wife and I have been together for almost forty years. There's nothing about the conservative life that I have not learned in conversation with her. We were almost children when we met, Julie. And here we are, having done what we set out to do. *I love you.*

Notes

Introduction: Is Conservative Revival Possible?

1. On postwar liberal democracy, see Ryszard Legutko, *The Demon in Democracy: Totalitarian Temptations in Free Societies* (New York: Encounter Books, 2016); Patrick Deneen, *Why Liberalism Failed* (New Haven, Connecticut: Yale, 2018); R. R. Reno, *Return of the Strong Gods: Nationalism, Populism, and the Future of the West* (Washington, D.C.: Regnery Gateway, 2019); Christopher Caldwell, *The Age of Entitlement: America Since the Sixties* (New York: Simon and Schuster, 2020).
2. The threat from China has been compellingly discussed in David Goldman, *You Will Be Assimilated* (New York: Bombardier Books, 2020); Michael Pillsbury, *The Hundred-Year Marathon* (New York: St. Martin's, 2016).
3. Allan Bloom predicted these developments in his *The Closing of the American Mind* (New York: Simon and Schuster, 1987).
4. Richard Current, *Daniel Webster and the Rise of National Conservatism* (Long Grove, Illinois: Waveland Press, 1992 [1955]); Michael Lind, *Hamilton's Republic* (New York: Free Press, 1997), 108.
5. Nationalist conservatism should be distinguished from the "white identity" movements of the extreme right, which seek a politics based on biological race and reject the traditional Anglo-American conception of the nation, inherited from the Bible. Here and throughout the book, I will use the term *nation* to refer to a number of tribes with a shared heritage, usually including a common language or religious traditions, and a past history of joining together against common enemies—characteristics that permit tribes so united to understand themselves as a community distinct from other such communities that are their neighbors. By *nationalism*, I mean a principled standpoint that regards the world as governed best when nations are able to chart their own independent course, cultivating their own traditions and pursuing their own interests without interference. These concepts and their uses are discussed in detail in Yoram Hazony, *The Virtue of Nationalism* (New York: Basic Books, 2018). For further reading on the Anglo-American concept of the nation, see Ofir Haivry, "What Is Anglo-American Nationalism?" *Modern Age* (Spring 2021): 7–22;

Steven Grosby, *Hebraism in Religion, History and Politics* (Oxford: Oxford University Press, 2021); Roger Scruton, *England and the Need for Nations* (London: Civitas, 2004).

6. The Abend-Offit debates began airing in 1975, when I was eleven years old, and ran for ten years. On "Point, Counterpoint," see http://www.tv.com/shows/saturday-night-live/buck-henry-the-grateful-dead-116138/trivia/.
7. Yael is Julie's Hebrew name.

Chapter 1: The English Conservative Tradition

1. The "conservative" or "traditionalist" school in English politics and law has been the subject of increasing attention in recent years. For further discussion, see, among others, Anthony Quinton, *The Politics of Imperfection* (London: Faber and Faber, 1978); J. G. A. Pocock, *The Ancient Constitution and the Feudal Law: A Study in English Historical Thought in the Seventeenth Century* (Cambridge: Cambridge University Press, 1987 edition), especially 30–55, 148–81; Harold J. Berman, "The Origins of Historical Jurisprudence: Coke, Selden, Hale," *Yale Law Journal* 103 (May 1994): 1652–1738; Ofir Haivry, *John Selden and the Western Political Tradition* (Cambridge: Cambridge University Press, 2017).
2. Jesse Norman, *Edmund Burke: The First Conservative* (New York: Basic Books, 2013) is one of many authors making this claim. However, Burke "is not historically the first of such thinkers, but . . . stands rather in the middle of an appropriately continuous tradition of thought at least from Hooker in the reign of Elizabeth I to the present day." See Quinton, *The Politics of Imperfection*, 56.
3. John Fortescue, *In Praise of the Laws of England*, in *On the Laws and Governance of England*, ed. Shelley Lockwood (Cambridge: Cambridge University Press, 1997). The theory of *dominium politicum et regale*, according to which the king is beholden to the laws of his people, and the opposition of this theory to the absolutism of Roman law in Germany and France, is the subject of this entire work. Fortescue's initial presentation of the theory is in *Praise of the Laws of England*, 1–3, 9, where it is based upon Deuteronomy 17:14–20. This conception of the supremacy of law over the king is already found in Bracton: "The king is below no man, but he is below God and the law. Law makes the king." Bracton, *On the Law of England* (Rolls Series) 1.38. Coke is said to have quoted this to James I.
4. Fortescue recalls that the Roman law, also called the "civil law," grants the king the right to rule arbitrarily in *Praise of the Laws of England*, 9, 34–35. He says

that the "civil law, by which the Holy Empire is ruled," is thought to be sufficient for the government of the whole world" in section 14. He also refers to the civil law as the law in the empire in section 19, and as the law in France in section 35. In fact, the civil law is the principal target of Fortescue's concept of "political and royal government," as becomes clear in section 34, when he refers to "kings ruling only royally... who regulate their people by the civil law... so that they change laws at their pleasure, make new ones, inflict punishments, and impose burdens on their subjects, and also determine the suits of parties, at their own will and when they wish."

5. Fortescue, *In Praise of the Laws of England*, 12–14.
6. Ibid., 20–27, 36. On torture, he writes that it will not bring out the truth but will, on the contrary, cause the judges to inflict cruelty on innocent men: "Surely such a practice is not to be called a law, but is rather a pathway to hell" (section 22).
7. John Fortescue, *The Governance of England, Otherwise Called the Difference between an Absolute and a Limited Monarchy*, in *On the Laws and Governance of England*, ed. Shelley Lockwood (Cambridge: Cambridge University Press, 1997), section 3, 88–89. Similarly, in *Praise of the Laws of England*, Fortescue repeatedly argues that the "substance" of the people needs to be protected and not diminished by the laws, which is more likely under a government in which the people must agree to the laws. See sections 9, 13–14, 36–37. The comparison with the misery of French rule appears in section 35.
8. Among other things, Fortescue speculates that the preference for herding over agriculture has had a salutary effect on the English character: "The men of that land are not very much burdened with the sweat of labor, so that they live more spiritually, as the ancient fathers did, who preferred to tend flocks rather than to distract their peace of mind with the cares of agriculture. For this reason, the men of that land are made more apt and disposed to investigate causes which require searching examination than men who, immersed in agricultural work, have contracted a rusticity of mind from familiarity with the soil." Fortescue, *In Praise of the Laws of England*, 43. This discussion is a reference to the heroes of Scripture, who avoid farming in favor of shepherding. See Yoram Hazony, *The Philosophy of Hebrew Scripture* (Cambridge: Cambridge University Press, 2012), 103–39.
9. The first printed edition is undated but appears to have been published around 1543.
10. This section is based on the work of my Edmund Burke Foundation colleague, Bradford Littlejohn, and especially his essays "The English Reformation:

England's First Brexit," *American Conservative*, January 15, 2020; "Richard Hooker: A Forgotten Father of National Conservatism," *American Conservative*, September 23, 2020.

11. Richard Hooker, *The Laws of Ecclesiastical Polity*, 4.14.1. Quotations from Hooker's *Laws*, book 14, are from *The Laws of Ecclesiastical Polity in Modern English*, ed. Bradford Littlejohn, Bradley Belschner, and Brian Marr (Landrum, South Carolina: Davenant Institute, 2019).
12. Hooker, *The Laws of Ecclesiastical Polity*, 4.14.2.
13. Ibid., 3.10.3.
14. Ibid., 3.10.7.
15. Ibid., 1.3.7.
16. Ibid., 1.3.8.
17. Ibid., 2.7.5.
18. Ibid., 5.7.1 Quotation is from *The Works of Richard Hooker*, ed. John Keble (Oxford: Oxford University Press, 1888), vol. 2.
19. Hooker, *The Laws of Ecclesiastical Polity*, 4.13.1.
20. Ibid., 4.13.10.
21. Ibid., Preface 2.2.
22. Ibid., 4.14.6.
23. Ibid.
24. Haivry, *John Selden and the Western Political Tradition*; Reid Barbour, *John Selden: Measures of the Holy Commonwealth in Seventeenth Century England* (Toronto: University of Toronto, 2003); Jason P. Rosenblatt, *Renaissance England's Chief Rabbi: John Selden* (Oxford: Oxford University Press, 2006).
25. James I, *Basilikon Doron: His Majesty's Instructions to His Dearest Son, Henry the Prince* (Edinburgh, 1603).
26. The Petition of Right, 1628. For its status in English law today, including subsequent amendments, see http://www.legislation.gov.uk//aep/Cha1/3/1/contents.
27. John Fortescue, *In Praise of the Laws of England*, with notes by John Selden (London, 1616) [Latin].
28. Hugo Grotius, *On the Law of War and Peace*, ed. Stephen Neff (Cambridge: Cambridge University Press, 2012 [1625]). On Grotius and Selden's response to him, see Ofir Haivry, "John Selden and the Early Modern Debate over the Foundations of Political Order," *Annuaire de l'Institut Michel Villey* 3 (Paris: Paris University Press, 2012), 391–416.
29. John Selden, *Natural and National Law*, book 1, chapter 7. Translations from Latin are indebted to Peter Wyetzner and Jonathan Yudelman.

30. John Selden, "Preface," *Titles of Honor* (London, 1631, second edition), not paginated.
31. Selden, *Natural and National Law*, book 1, chapter 6.
32. John Selden, dedication to *The History of Tithes* (London, 1618), not paginated.
33. Selden, *Natural and National Law*, book 1, chapter 1.
34. Jeremiah 6.16; Selden, *Natural and National Law*, book 1, chapter 1.
35. John Selden, *Table Talk*, ed. S. W. Singer (Cambrige: Cambridge University Press, 2015 [1689]), 214.
36. Selden, *Natural and National Law*, book 1, chapter 10. See also chapter 3. Matthew Hale likewise held the Talmudic Noahide law and the Mosaic Ten Precepts to be the natural law. See Richard Tuck, *Natural Rights Theories: Their Origin and Development* (Cambridge: Cambridge University Press, 1979), 163.
37. John Selden, "Notes," in John Fortescue, *In Praise of the Laws of England* (1616).
38. As he writes: "What better witness can ye expect I should produce, than one of your own now sitting in parliament, the chief of learned men reputed in this land, Mr. Selden; whose volume of natural and national laws proves, not only by great authorities brought together but by exquisite reasons and theorems almost mathematically demonstrative, that all opinions, yea, errors, known, read, and collated, are of main service and assistance toward the speedy attainment of what is truest." John Milton, *Areopagitica, A Speech of Mr. John Milton for the Liberty of Unlicensed Printing to the Parliament of England*, ed. Richard C. Jebb (Cambridge: Cambridge University Press, 1918 [1644]), 18. See also Isaiah Berlin on Selden and Hale as progenitors of a pluralistic political theory in *The Crooked Timber of Humanity* (Princeton: Princeton University Press, 1998), 53.
39. On Clarendon, see Paul Seaward, *The Cavalier Parliament and the Reconstruction of the Old Regime 1661–1665* (Cambridge: Cambridge University Press, 1989), 11–102; Anthony Quinton, *The Politics of Imperfection*, 31–34. On Hale, see Alan Cromartie, *Sir Matthew Hale, 1609–1676: Law, Religion and Natural Philosophy* (Cambridge: Cambridge University Press, 1995), 89–138.
40. "Sir Matthew Hale's Criticism on Hobbes' Dialogue on the Common Laws," reprinted in W. S. Holdsworth, *A History of English Law* (Boston: Little, Brown, 1924), vol. 5, 504–5.
41. James I, *Basilikon Doron*, ed. Daniel Fischlin and Mark Fortier (Toronto: Centre for Reformation and Renaissance Studies, 1996 [1599]); Thomas Hobbes, *Leviathan*, ed. Richard Tuck (Cambridge: Cambridge University Press, 1996 [1651]); Robert Filmer, *Patriarcha*, ed. Johann P. Sommerville (Cambridge: Cambridge University Press, 1991 [1680]), and especially Sommerville's

"Introduction"; John Locke, *Two Treatises of Government*, ed. Peter Laslett (Cambridge: Cambridge University Press, 1960 [1689]); Richard Ashcraft, *Revolutionary Politics and Locke's 'Two Treatises of Government'* (Princeton: Princeton University Press, 1986). On Hobbes and Locke as rationalist opponents of conservative political theory in seventeenth-century England, see Quinton, *The Politics of Imperfection*, 21–22, 29–30.

42. Both the later volumes of Coke's *Institutes* and Hale's *History* were published posthumously.
43. Locke's *Essay* is itself empiricist only with respect to its general theory of knowledge. It follows Descartes's rationalist method with respect to morals and politics. As Locke writes: "I doubt not, but from self-evident propositions, by necessary consequences as incontestable as those of mathematics, the measures of right and wrong might be made out to anyone that will apply himself with the same indifferency and attention to the one, as he does to the other of these sciences." John Locke, *Essay Concerning Human Understanding* (Oxford: Oxford University Press, 1975 [1789]), 4.3.18. Quinton comments: "In Locke, an empiricist account of knowledge in general is combined with a rationalist theory of our knowledge of morality, the basis of Locke's theory of self-evident natural rights.... Moral truths, like geometrical theorems, he regards as demonstrable necessities. By the time he reaches Book IV of his *Essay on Human Understanding,* in which this position is taken, and argued for in a startlingly feeble way, Locke has altogether forgotten the moral fallibilism that is intimated by his rejection in Book I of 'innate practical principles.' It is this ethical rationalism that is fundamental to Locke's political theory, being an apt support for passionately dogmatic liberalism." Quinton, *The Politics of Imperfection*, 41.
44. John Locke, *Second Treatise of Government,* sections 4, 7. See also sections 87, 95.
45. Ibid., section 6.
46. Locke, *Second Treatise of Government,* sections 14–15. On consent, see also sections 95, 119, 122. Locke also emphasizes that human beings consent to enter into government for "the preservation of their property" (s. 124), with property being defined as "their lives, liberties and estates" (s. 123). Locke recognizes the existence of no clans, tribes, or nations prior to the establishment of the state, which would contradict his claim that in the state of nature, men have "no superiority or jurisdiction of one over another" (s. 7). It is the act of establishing a government that creates the nation "wherever any number of men, in the

state of nature, enter into society *to make one people*, one body politic under one supreme government" (s. 89, emphasis mine).

47. Important early modern works of empiricist political and moral theory include David Hume, *Treatise of Human Nature*, ed. P. H. Nidditch (Oxford: Oxford University Press, 1978 [1739]); Montesquieu, *The Spirit of the Laws*, ed. and trans. Anne Cohler, Basya Carolyn Miller, and Harold Samuel Stone (Cambridge: Cambridge University Press, 1989 [1750]); Adam Smith, *The Theory of Moral Sentiments*, ed. Ryan Patrick Hanely (New York: Penguin, 2010 [1759]); Adam Ferguson, *An Essay on the History of Civil Society* (Cambridge: Cambridge University Press, 1995 [1767]); Edmund Burke, *Reflections on the Revolution in France*, ed. J. G. A. Pockock (Indianapolis: Hackett, 1987 [1790]). A famous critique of rationalist theorizing in political philosophy is Michael Oakeshott, "Rationalism in Politics," *Rationalism in Politics and Other Essays* (Indianapolis: Liberty Fund, 1991 [1962]). For comparisons of rationalism versus empiricism in political thought, see Thomas Sowell, *A Conflict of Visions: Ideological Origins of Political Struggles* (New York: Basic Books, revised edition 2007); Gertrude Himmelfarb, *The Roads to Modernity* (New York: Vintage Books, 2005); Yuval Levin, *The Great Debate: Edmund Burke, Thomas Paine, and the Birth of Right and Left* (New York: Basic Books, 2014). As Quinton emphasizes, the conservative objection to such "abstract" theorizing is not an objection to generalization from experience, without which reasoning would be impossible. The empiricist does allow "very general" principles to be derived from experience. But these are not "abstract" in that they are empirically derived, and therefore recognized as both fallible in their derivation and potentially limited in their application. Quinton, *The Politics of Imperfection*, 13.

48. Of course there is no way to derive the traditional English constitution from these axioms. Locke does write, for example, that "well-framed governments" separate between executive and legislative powers, offering as a reason that "it may be too great a temptation to human frailty" to place both powers in the hands of the same individuals, "whereby they may exempt themselves from obedience to the laws they make." Locke, *Second Treatise*, 143, 159. This is remarkably tepid support for the biblical and English constitutional tradition. The separation of powers that Fortescue considers to be the principal constitutional bulwark against tyranny in England is here presented as resulting only from a concern that otherwise rulers "may" be tempted to stray from proper government. Compare the weakness of this claim to James Madison's more forceful explanation of the traditional Anglo-American view when he writes that "experience has taught mankind the necessity of auxiliary

precautions" in controlling government through its division into competing branches in *Federalist* 51. The weakness of Locke's argument derives from his rationalist methodology. Universal reason, as conceived by Locke, cannot and does not urge the necessity of separating the executive from the legislative powers of government.

49. The enthusiasm of the French for Lockean rationalism is not surprising, given the dominance of Cartesian rationalism in France. On Descartes's rationalism and the objections of English and Scottish thinkers, see Yoram Hazony, "Newtonian Explanatory Reduction and Hume's System of the Sciences," in *Newton and Empiricism*, ed. Zvi Biener and Eric Schliesser (Oxford: Oxford University Press), 138–70.
50. Jean-Jacques Rousseau, *The Social Contract*, ed. Victor Gourevitch (Cambridge: Cambridge University Press, 1997 [1762]). See also "Declaration of the Rights of Man and the Citizen" (1789), Article I.
51. My account diverges here from that of Leo Strauss, who presents Rousseau as a critic of Locke and asserts that "the first crisis of modernity occurred in the thought of Jean-Jacques Rousseau." See *Natural Right and History* (Chicago: University of Chicago Press, 1953), 252. No doubt Strauss is right in seeing Rousseau, especially in his *Discourses*, as demanding a return to the cohesive community of classical antiquity and to the virtues that are required to maintain such social cohesion and to wage wars in defense of the community. But it is a mistake to regard this demand as initiating "the first crisis of modernity." What is now regarded as political modernity emerges from the English conservative tradition of Fortescue, Hooker, Coke, Selden, and Hale, and the first crisis of modernity is that which rationalists such as Hobbes and Locke initiate against this conservative tradition. In some ways, Rousseau does side with earlier conservative tradition, which likewise held that Lockean rationalism would make social cohesion impossible and destroy the possibility of virtue. But while Rousseau believed he could revive social cohesion and virtue while retaining Locke's liberal axioms as a point of departure, Anglo-American conservatism regards this entire effort as futile. The intractable contradictions in Rousseau's thought derive from the fact that there is no way to square this circle. Once liberal axioms are accepted, there is neither any need for, nor any possibility of, the social cohesion and virtue that Rousseau insists are necessary. Rousseau's "civil religion" and his social-contract state have no hope of playing the role that traditional religion and the nation play in conservative thought. These are ersatz creations of the rationalist universe, in which Rousseau's thought remains imprisoned.

52. Burke, *Reflections on the Revolution in France*, 28.
53. Edmund Burke, speech before the House of Commons, May 7, 1782, in *The Works of Edmund Burke* (New York: Dearborn, 1836), vol. 2, 469.
54. Burke, *Reflections on the Revolution in France*, 53–54.
55. Edmund Burke, *An Appeal from the New to the Old Whigs*, in *Further Reflections on the Revolution in France*, ed. Daniel Ritchie, *Further Reflections on the Revolution in France* (Indianapolis: Liberty Fund, 1992 [1791]), 185–87.
56. Ibid., 182.
57. Ibid.
58. Richard Price, "Preface," *Observations on the Nature of Civil Liberty* (London, 1776, fifth edition).
59. *Morning Chronicle,* April 18, 1794. Cited in Richard Bourke, *Empire and Revolution: The Political Life of Edmund Burke* (Princeton: Princeton University Press, 2015), 683. For an exhaustive investigation of Burke's relationship with Locke, see Ofir Haivry, *The Politick Personality: Edmund Burke's Political Ideas and the Lockean Inheritance,* dissertation for University College London, 2005.
60. Such nationalism is not based on race, but on the traditional Anglo-American conception of the nation, which is inherited from the Bible. See my Introduction to this book, note 5. For further discussion, see Ofir Haivry, "What Is Anglo-American Nationalism?" *Modern Age* (Spring 2021): 7–22; Yoram Hazony, *The Virtue of Nationalism* (New York: Basic Books, 2018).
61. On Anglo-American liberalism after the Second World War, see Chapter 3.1–3 and Chapter 6.
62. Selden, *Natural and National Law*, book 1, chapter 6.

Chapter II: American Nationalists

1. Remarks on May 30, 1787, cited in Robert Yates, "Notes of the Secret Debates of the Federal Convention of 1787." Or, as John Dickinson told the convention: "Experience must be our only guide. Reason may mislead us. It was not reason that discovered the singular and admirable mechanism of the English constitution.... Accidents probably produced these discoveries, and experience has given a sanction to them." Remarks on August 13, 1787, cited in James Madison, "Notes on the Debates in the Constitutional Convention." An excellent account of the activities of the conservative party during the American Revolution is David Lefer, *The Founding Conservatives* (New York: Sentinel, 2013). On Burke's influence on the founders, see Russell Kirk, *Rights and Duties*, 110–25.

2. Thomas Jefferson to William Short, January 3, 1793. Jefferson's contempt for the traditions linking one generation to another was legendary. For instance, he wrote to Madison, "By the law of nature, one generation is to another as is one independent nation to another." Jefferson to James Madison, September 6, 1789. Similarly: "Each new generation is as independent of the one preceding as that was of all which had gone before. It has, then, like them, a right to choose for itself the form of government it believes most productive of its own happiness.... It is for the peace and good of mankind, that a solemn opportunity of doing this every ten or twenty years, should be provided by the constitution." Jefferson to Samuel Kercheval, July 12, 1816. The most thorough account of Jefferson's Enlightenment liberalism, including his views on slavery, is Conor Cruise O'Brien, *The Long Affair: Thomas Jefferson and the French Revolution* (Chicago: University of Chicago Press, 1996).
3. I discuss Locke's rationalism in Chapters 1.5 and 3.3. Locke writes that the axioms of moral and political philosophy are "self-evident" in his *Essay Concerning Human Understanding.* See Chapter 1, note 43.
4. It is possible to see a shift in the views of many of the American leaders from a more conservative standpoint before the Revolution to the embrace of the language of universal rights during the war, and then tilting back to a more conservative politics by the time the Constitution was drafted. For an introduction to this topic, see Daniel T. Rodgers, "Rights Consciousness in American History," in *The Nature of Rights at the American Founding and Beyond*, ed. Barry Alan Shain (Charlottesville: University of Virginia Press, 2007), 258–79. See also John Phillip Reid, *Constitutional History of the American Revolution: The Authority of Rights* (Madison: University of Wisconsin Press, 1986), vol. 1; Daniel T. Rodgers, *Contested Truths: Keywords in American Politics Since Independence* (New York: Basic Books, 1987), especially 45–79; Russell Kirk, *Rights and Duties* (Dallas: Spencer, 1997), 95–149. An alternative, Lockean approach to the American founding is presented by Paul Rahe, *Republics Ancient and Modern: Constituting the American Regime* (University of North Carolina Press, 1994), vol. 3.; Michael Zuckert, *Natural Rights and the New Republicanism* (Princeton: Princeton University Press, 1994); Thomas West, *The Political Theory of the American Founding* (Cambridge: Cambridge University Press, 2017). It is also significant that the language of "natural rights" was often used in the eighteenth century, but these rights were rarely specified or enumerated prior to 1776. See Lynn Hunt, *Inventing Human Rights: A History* (New York: Norton, 2007), 25–26. The claim that "natural rights" exist obvious changes quite radically once it is believed that they can be known and enumerated.
5. Joseph Ellis, *The Quartet: Orchestrating the Second American Revolution: 1783–1789* (New York: Vintage, 2015), 43.

6. Thus Washington, not yet entirely committed to attending, wrote to Madison: "I am anxious to know how this matter really is, as my wish is, that the Convention may adopt no temporizing expedient, but probe the defects of the Constitution to the bottom, and provide radical cures, whether they are agreed to or not." George Washington to James Madison, March 31, 1787. The meaning of this letter would have been clear enough to anyone familiar with Washington's view, expressed repeatedly over years, that the Articles needed to be scrapped and replaced with a nationalist constitution.
7. Ellis, *The Quartet*, 140.
8. The term "federal" originated in the Latin *foederati*, denoting formally independent kingdoms, tribes, and cities that were bound to ancient Rome by a treaty or pact of mutual assistance, known as a *foedus*. Typically, the *foederati* provided military assistance to Rome in exchange for economic benefits. The term "confederal" is derived by adding the Latin prefix "con-" (meaning, "with") to the term "foedus," to refer to several entities that have been joined together by a pact.
9. The basis for the debate at the Constitutional Convention was a plan presented on May 29, 1787, drafted by James Madison and presented to the convention by the governor of Virginia, Edmund Randolph. It became known as the Virginia Plan. The smaller states drafted their own confederal proposal defending their interests two weeks later, which came to be called the New Jersey Plan. To avert drift away from a strong union, Hamilton drafted his own plan, and presented it to the convention on June 18. Modeling his proposal on the British constitution, he provocatively named it the "British plan," thus positioning the Virginia plan as the centrist, moderate option. Robert Ernst, *Rufus King, American Federalist* (Chapel Hill, North Carolina: University of North Carolina Press, 1968), 97–99.
10. Max Farrand, ed., *The Records of the Federal Convention of 1787* (New Haven, Connecticut: Yale University Press, 1911) vol. 1, 344, and also 395, 404. See also Ernst, *Rufus King*, 99–101.
11. Joseph Ellis suggests that 1789 was in fact "a second American revolution," in which the "spirit of '87" replaced the "spirit of '76." See *The Quartet*, 132, 162. It was only after this second revolution that "the American Revolution now meant not just independence but nationhood" (213).
12. On Edmund Burke's view of the Constitution of 1787 as an adaptation of the British constitution, see Ofir Haivry, "American Restoration: Edmund Burke and the American Constitution," *American Affairs*, February 17, 2020. Similarly, see Benjamin Disraeli, *Vindication of the English Constitution*, in *Whigs and*

Whiggism, ed. William Hutcheson and Christopher Briggs (Washington, D.C.: Regnery, 2006, revised edition), 104.

13. Jonathan J. Den Hartog, *Patriotism and Piety: Federalist Politics and Religious Struggle in the New American Nation* (Charlottesville, Virginia: University of Virginia Press, 2015), 16–17; David Hackett Fischer, *The Revolution of American Conservatism: The Federalist Party in the Era of American Democracy*, xviii–xix.
14. Shaw Livermore Jr., *The Twilight of Federalism: The Disintegration of the Federalist Party, 1815–1830* (Princeton, New Jersey: Princeton University Press, 1962), vii–ix.
15. Quoted in Ellis, *The Quartet*, 185.
16. *Federalist* 2. In Jay's *Address to the People of the State of New York on the Subject of the Constitution*, he warned that a habit of looking at local interests "affords one reason why so much more care was taken, and so much more wisdom displayed, in forming our State Governments, than in forming our foederal or national one."
17. Edward Millican, *One United People: The Federalist Papers and the National Idea* (Lexington, Kentucky: University Press of Kentucky, 1990), 63–67.
18. *Federalist* 12.
19. Millican, *One United People*, 209–10. Even Madison, never a fully-fledged nationalist, mentioned common Anglo-American ancestry as an argument for a Union government: "the kindred blood which flows in the veins of American citizens." *Federalist* 14.
20. George Washington, "Farewell Address," September 19, 1796.
21. Patrick Allitt, *The Conservatives* (New Haven, Connecticut: Yale University Press, 2009), 10.
22. It is impossible to understand the rise of the Supreme Court to the role of interpreter of the Constitution without the rules and principles of common law adjudication that American judges had inherited from their earlier English counterparts, and from nowhere else. Robert Lowry Clinton, *God and Man in the Law: The Foundations of Anglo-American Constitutionalism* (Lawrence, Kansas: University of Kansas Press, 1997), 94–95.
23. Lefer, *The Founding Conservatives*, 132–45, 213–25.
24. Clinton, *God and Man in the Law*, 91–92, 96–98.
25. John Adams, *A Defence of the Constitutions of Government of the United States of America* (Quincy, Massachusetts: Liberty's Lamp Books, 2015 [1787]), vol. 1, 3.
26. Ibid., 73. See also 103.

27. Ibid., 74. On the "improvements to be made" in the English constitution, see 364.
28. John Kaminski et al., eds., *The Documentary History of the Ratification of the Constitution* (Madison, Wisconsin: Wisconsin Historical Society Press, 1978), vol. 3, 145.
29. Allitt, *The Conservatives*, 12–14.
30. Rogers Smith, "Constructing American National Identity: Strategies of the Federalists," in *Federalists Reconsidered*, ed. Doron Ben-Atar and Barbara Oberg (Charlottesville, Virginia: University of Virginia Press, 2000), 28–29.
31. Allitt, *The Conservatives*, 19–20. As Jefferson described this divide in 1798: "Two political Sects have arisen within the U. S. the one believing that the executive is the branch of our government which the most needs support; the other that like the analogous branch in the English Government, it is already too strong for the republican parts of the Constitution; and therefore in equivocal cases they incline to the legislative powers. The former of these are called federalists, sometimes aristocrats or monocrats, and sometimes tories, after the corresponding sect in the English Government of exactly the same definition. The latter are stiled republicans, whigs, jacobins, anarchists, disorganizers, etc. These terms are in familiar use with most persons." Thomas Jefferson to John Wise, February 12, 1798.
32. Personal communication.
33. As Jefferson explained to Washington: "Paine's answer to Burke's pamphlet begins to produce some squibs in our public papers. In Fenno's [Hamiltonian] paper they are Burkites, in the others Painites. One of Fenno's [essays] was evidently from the author of the discourses on Davila [i.e., Adams]. I am afraid the indiscretion of a printer has committed me with my friend Mr. Adams, for whom, as one of the most honest and disinterested men alive, I have a cordial esteem, increased by long habits of concurrence in opinion in the days of his republicanism. And even since his apostacy to hereditary monarchy and nobility, tho' we differ, we differ as friends should do." Thomas Jefferson to George Washington, May 8, 1791.
34. Jefferson to Benjamin Vaughan, May 11, 1791.
35. Jefferson to William Branch Giles, April 27, 1795.
36. As Hamilton put it: "The general doctrine then of our Constitution is that the *executive power* of the nation is vested in the President, subject only to the exceptions and qualifications which are expressed in that instrument." *Pacificus* 1, June 29, 1793. The president, of course, would have to stand for election every four years, but the Constitution of 1787 did not limit the number of times he could be elected. The nationalists also supported a presidential veto on state

legislation modeled upon the British king's veto over colonial legislation. The entire Constitution, Patrick Henry said, "squints toward monarchy." Quoted in Ellis, *The Quartet*, 185.

37. *Federalist* 70, in Alexander Hamilton, James Madison, and John Jay, *The Federalist Papers*, ed. Clinton Rossiter (New York: Penguin, 1961 [1788]).
38. *Federalist* 70.
39. James Wilson, Pennsylvania Ratifying Convention, December 4, 1787, in *The Debates in the Several State Conventions on the Adoption of the Federal Constitution as Recommended by the General Convention at Philadelphia in 1787*, ed. Jonathan Elliot (New York: Burt Franklin, 1888), vol. 2, 480.
40. Jefferson to Madison, December 28, 1794.
41. Thomas Jefferson, First Inaugural Address, March 4, 1801.
42. *Federalist* 78.
43. Oliver Ellsworth was a senator from Connecticut and the main promoter of the Judiciary Act, Senate Bill No. 1, which supplemented Article III in the Constitution and established a hierarchical arrangement between federal and state courts. Section 25, the heart of the Judiciary Act, gave the Supreme Court power to veto state supreme court decisions supportive of state laws in conflict with the U.S. Constitution. All state and local laws could be appealed to the Supreme Court, which was given authority to deny them as unconstitutional. In this way, judicial review supplanted congressional review, which Madison repeatedly and unsuccessfully proposed to guarantee federal sovereignty.
44. Only in 1804 was William Johnson, the first justice who was not a Federalist, appointed to the Supreme Court by Jefferson.
45. Thomas Jefferson to Edmund Randolph, August 18, 1799.
46. In his opinion in *Chisholm*, Justice James Wilson advances a theory of nationalism consisting of three strands: a common law tradition upheld by Bracton and Coke, the nation-building of great English monarchs such as Henry IV and Elizabeth, and the origin of the United States as a unified nation under the Constitution. Chief Justice John Jay concurred with Wilson's opinion, arguing that even before independence, the Americans were a "people already united for general purposes." According to Jay, this united people, "in their collective and national capacity, established the present Constitution." Smith, "Constructing American National Identity," 28–29.
47. *Calder v. Bull* (1798).
48. Allitt, *The Conservatives*, 23–25.
49. Even in the South, many prominent Federalists such as Iredell and Marshall were lawyers from the towns rather than plantation owners.

50. Alexander Hamilton, "Opinion on the Constitutionality of a National Bank," February 23, 1791, in *The Essential Hamilton: Letters and Other Writings*, ed. Joanne Freeman (New York: Library of America, 2017), 186.
51. Doron Ben-Atar, "Alexander Hamilton's Alternative: Technology Piracy and the Report on Manufactures," in *Intellectual Property Law and History*, ed. Steven Wilf (London: Routledge, 2017), 42–44.
52. Allitt, *The Conservatives*, 15–16; Ben-Atar, "Alexander Hamilton's Alternative," 46–57.
53. See Henry Carey, *The Harmony of Interests: Agricultural, Manufacturing, and Commercial* (1851); Henry Carey, *The Way to Outdo England without Fighting Her* (1865).
54. Smith, "Constructing American National Identity," 22–23.
55. George Washington to John Adams, November 15, 1794.
56. Thomas Jefferson, *Notes on the State of Virginia, Query 8* (version of 1783).
57. Thomas Jefferson, First Annual Address to Congress, December 8, 1801.
58. Alexander Hamilton, *The Examination* 7–8, January 7, 12, 1802.
59. Smith, "Constructing American National Identity," 30–31, 36–39. Smith argues that the Jeffersonians had a Lockean view of citizenship, while the Federalists, and especially the judges among them, tended to embrace a far more coercive, duty-bound view of citizenship based on Blackstone.
60. Presidential Proclamation, October 3, 1789.
61. *Pacificus* 6. Emphasis in the original.
62. *Pacificus* 3.
63. *Pacificus* 2
64. *Americanus* 1.
65. Thomas Jefferson to James Madison, July 7, 1793.
66. *Helvidius* 1.
67. Ibid.
68. See Carl Esbeck and Jonathan Den Hartog, eds., *Disestablishment and Religious Dissent: Church-State Relations in the New American States, 1776–1833* (Columbia, Missouri: University of Missouri Press, 2019).
69. This expression comes from Thomas Jefferson to Danbury Baptist Association, January 1, 1802. On the history of this phrase and its transformation into policy, see Philip Hamburger, *Separation of Church and State* (Cambridge, Massachusetts: Harvard University Press, 2002).
70. Hartog, *Patriotism and Piety*, 6–7; Presidential Proclamation, October 3, 1789.
71. Hartog, *Patriotism and Piety*, 20–23.

72. John Adams to Massachusetts Militia, October 11, 1798; Hartog, *Patriotism and Piety*, 6–7.
73. Ankeet Ball, "Ambition and Bondage: An Inquiry on Alexander Hamilton and Slavery," Columbia University and Slavery, available at https://columbiaandslavery.columbia.edu/content/ambition-bondage-inquiry-alexander-hamilton-and-slavery#/_ftn27.
74. Alexander Hamilton to James Bayard, April 1802. A similar trajectory was followed by Noah Webster, a fierce Federalist controversialist who was one of Hamilton's closest allies, publishing the daily *American Minerva* and the semi-weekly *Herald*, both aligned with the Federalists in New York.
75. "The state of slavery is of such a nature that it is incapable of being introduced on any reasons, moral or political, but only by positive law, which preserves its force long after the reasons, occasions, and time itself from whence it was created, is erased from memory. It is so odious, that nothing can be suffered to support it, but positive law. Whatever inconveniences, therefore, may follow from the decision, I cannot say this case is allowed or approved by the law of England; and therefore the black must be discharged." Lord Mansfield in *Somerset v. Stewart* (1772). It is interesting that Burke, who was sympathetic to the cause of the American colonies, nonetheless opposed seating slaveowners in Parliament: "Common sense, nay self-preservation, seem to forbid, that those who allow themselves an unlimited right over the liberties and lives of other, should have any share in making laws for those who have long renounced such unjust and cruel distinctions." *Annual Register* (1765), 37. Quoted in Conor Cruise O'Brien, *The Great Melody: A Thematic Biography of Edmund Burke* (Chicago: University of Chicago Press, 1992), 92.
76. Massachusetts chief justice William Cushing writing in *Commonwealth v. Jennison* (1783).
77. Ernst, *Rufus King*, 372–81.
78. According to Madison's notes, edited here for clarity. In these sentiments, Morris was publicly supported by Oliver Ellsworth, a devout Calvinist and Federalist from Connecticut. But Rutledge and Charles Pinckney were both southern Federalists who defended slavery.
79. Rogers Smith, "Constructing American National Identity," 24–27; Ernst, *Rufus King*, 372–81. The opposition of nationalist officials to the expansion of slavery and to states' rights came at a steep political price for the Federalist Party and contributed to its decline.
80. Livermore, *The Twilight of Federalism*, vii–ix, 122–24.

81. Livermore, *The Twilight of Federalism*, 272–73; Allitt, *The Conservatives*, 53–55.

Chapter III: The Conservative Paradigm

1. For definitions of the terms "nation" and "nationalism," see the Introduction to this book, note 5. For further discussion, see Yoram Hazony, *The Virtue of Nationalism* (New York: Basic Books, 2018); Ofir Haivry, "What Is Anglo-American Nationalism?" *Modern Age* (Spring 2021), 7–22.
2. Hazony, *The Virtue of Nationalism*, 100.
3. These are the premises that undergird liberalism in its original Enlightenment rationalist form. At least since the nineteenth century, liberals inclined to a theoretical empiricism have sought to amend these premises. This dissent from Enlightenment rationalism has been advanced, among others, by John Stuart Mill, *Considerations on Representative Government*, ed. Geraint Williams (London: Everyman, 1993 [1861]), 188–428; Isaiah Berlin, "Two Concepts of Liberty," in *Four Essays on Liberty* (Oxford: Oxford University Press, 1969 [1958]); and Friedrich Hayek, whose ideas I discuss in Chapter 6.3. Since the 1990s, this dissent from Enlightenment liberalism has become widespread among academic advocates of liberalism. Nevertheless, a great many politicians, academics, and journalists continue to defend 1960s-style Enlightenment liberalism throughout the democratic world, often explicitly promoting it as the only viable alternative to neo-Marxism and authoritarianism.
4. There is no good word in English to replace the technical term *loyalty group*, which refers to a human community of any size whose members are bound by ties of mutual loyalty. I will at times use the terms *community* or *society*, both of which are vague and easily misunderstood, or the word *collective*, despite its historical connotations. All of these terms are to be regarded as interchangeable.
5. Descartes's "clear and distinct ideas" are the basis for his deductions. They serve the same general purpose as "self-evident principles" in later rationalist philosophy, and I will not insist on a distinction between these two formulations in this book. But when we need to be precise, we should notice that principles are relations of ideas. Thus rationalists assume (i) that the framing of certain ideas is correct and unassailable; and (ii) that two or more such clear and distinct ideas can be brought together in principles that are self-evidently correct.
6. Rene Descartes, *Principles of Philosophy* (abridged), in *Philosophical Writings of Descartes*, ed. and trans. John Cottingham (Cambridge: Cambridge

University Press, 1985 [1644]), vol. 1, 177–291; Immanuel Kant, *Metaphysical Foundations of Natural Science*, in *Theoretical Philosophy after 1781*, ed. Henry Allison and Peter Heath, trans. Michael Friedman (Cambridge: Cambridge University Press, 2002 [1786]), 183–270.

7. Isaac Newton, *Mathematical Principles of Natural Philosophy*, trans. I. Bernard Cohen and Anne Whitman (Berkeley, California: University of California Press, 1999 [1687]). Newtonian induction is not a version of the "enumerative induction" that grounds the search for statistical correlations in much of social science today. Rather, it is a method of deriving concepts that can be regarded as the "general causes" of the phenomena. On Cartesian and Newtonian science, see Yoram Hazony, "Newtonian Explanatory Reduction and Hume's System of the Sciences," in *Newton and Empiricism*, ed. Zvi Biener and Eric Schliesser (Oxford: Oxford University Press, 2014), 138–70.
8. Isaac Newton, *Opticks* (Amherst, Massachusetts: Prometheus, 2003 [fourth edition, 1730]), 404.
9. Thomas Hobbes, *Leviathan*, ed. Richard Tuck (Cambridge: Cambridge University Press, 1996 [1651]); John Locke, *Two Treatises of Government*, ed. Peter Laslett (Cambridge: Cambridge University Press, 1960 [1689]); Jean-Jacques Rousseau, *The Social Contract*, ed. Victor Gourevitch (Cambridge: Cambridge University Press, 1997 [1762]); "Idea for a Universal History with a Cosmopolitan Purpose," in Immanuel Kant, *Political Writings*, ed. Hans Reiss, trans. H. B. Nisbet (New York: Cambridge University Press, 1970 [1784]), 41–53; Immanuel Kant, "Perpetual Peace," in *Political Writings*, ed. H. S. Reiss, trans. H. N. Nisbet (Cambridge, UK: Cambridge University Press, 1991 [1795]), 93–130.
10. See Chapter 1, footnote 47.
11. Chief Justice Anthony Kennedy, with Justices David Souter and Sandra Day O'Connor, in *Planned Parenthood v. Casey* (1992).
12. A longer and more detailed version of this section appears in Hazony, *The Virtue of Nationalism*, 69–75.
13. This extension of the self is described by Hume, who argues that we feel pride and shame with respect to things that are "parts of ourselves, or something nearly related to us" (*A Treatise of Human Nature* 2.1.5), including pride in one's family and country (2.1.10). He then concludes that such pride is in fact love (2.2.1).
14. The term *cohesion* comes from John Stuart Mill, "On Representative Government," in *Utilitarianism, On Liberty, and Considerations on Representative Government*, ed. H. B. Acton (London: Everyman, 1984 [1861]),

241; Henry Sidgwick, *The Elements of Politics* (Elibron Classics, 2005 [1891]), 233, 276. As Sidgwick writes, "What is really essential... to a nation is... that the persons composing it should have a consciousness of belonging to one another, of being members of one body, over and above what they derive from the mere fact of being under one government; so that, if their government were destroyed by war or revolution, they would still hold firmly together" (202).

15. For the sake of simplicity, I have adopted a four-tier hierarchy: *Family*, *clan*, *tribe*, and *nation*. But the choice of a four-tier system is somewhat arbitrary. In actual political societies, one can often find many more layers of hierarchy before reaching the top of the political structure.
16. Exodus 20.11, 21.15, 17; Leviticus 19.3, 32, 20.9; Deuteronomy 5.15, 27.16; Proverbs 20.20, 23.22, 30.11, 17.
17. The Hebrew term for dishonoring is likewise *makleh*, or "making light." Thus we are told: "Cursed is he who dishonors [*makleh*] his father and his mother" (Deuteronomy 27.16). But this can also be translated as: "Cursed is he who makes light of his father and his mother."
18. Genesis 8.21. See discussion in Chapter 4.2–3.
19. See Chapter 3.5.
20. Enlightenment rationalist political theory did insist on maintaining certain traditional obligations, most notably the obligation to respect the life and property of others. But it was never clear why these obligations should be upheld while so many others were being cast aside. Moreover, once the theory that obligations derive from consent had gained widespread acceptance, Marx and other radicals offered reasons for withdrawing our consent from the obligation to respect property as well. I do not believe that any moral obligation that Enlightenment liberalism has left standing can survive this kind of assault. For further discussion, see Chapter 7.
21. See Chapter 3.3.
22. Academics often say that one cannot make a legitimate inference from what is to what ought to be. In the present case, the argument would be that there is no legitimate way to move from a description of relations of mutual loyalty that are the basic building blocks of all human hierarchies (what "is") to a description of the political obligations that arise from such relations (what "ought to be"). But this argument overlooks the fact that ideas or concepts are always normative in character, describing what an object ought to be if it is to be a tolerably good instance of a certain kind of object. Similarly, relations among ideas or concepts are always normative in character, describing what a relation ought to be if it is to be a tolerably good instance of a certain kind of relation. This means that

every object and every relation is known in our experience thanks to a normative standard that we use to recognize it, and that this same normative standard is also what we use to distinguish a better from a worse object or relation of its kind. This is why I say that in recognizing relations of mutual loyalty (that is, in recognizing that such relations exist), we come to have a standard against which human behavior can be judged to be better or worse.

23. But not always. I will return to the question of obligations outside of relations of mutual loyalty momentarily.
24. Exodus 1.11–22, 3.7–10.
25. Leviticus 19.18.
26. Exodus 22.21, 23.9; Leviticus 19.34; Deuteronomy 10.19.
27. The relation of mutual loyalty between God and his people appears in Genesis 17.7; Exodus 6.7; Leviticus 26.12; Deuteronomy 29.13; Jeremiah 7.23, 11.4, 24.7, 30.22, 31.1, 33, 32.38; Ezekiel 36.28; Hosea 2.23; Zechariah 13.9. This established relation with God is, in fact, the basis for the injunction not to oppress the stranger, to whom one is bound by no previous bond of loyalty: "You will have the same standard of law for the stranger and for the native, for I am the Lord your God" (Leviticus 24.22). Similarly: "When a foreigner resides with you in your land, you must not oppress him. You must treat the foreigner living among you as native-born and love him as yourself, for you were foreigners in the land of Egypt. I am the Lord your God" (Leviticus 19.33–34). See also Exodus 22.21, 23.9; Deuteronomy 24.14; Jeremiah 7.6, 22.3; Ezekiel 22.7, 29; Malachi 3.5, 9; Zechariah 7.10; Psalm 146.9.
28. See Chapter 3.8.
29. John Selden, *Natural and National Law*, book 1, chapter 7.
30. I discuss the new Marxists in Chapter 7. But "white identitarians," who seek to reconstruct the political order on the basis of their theory of biological race, make similar claims. They study the publications of academic racial science as if they were Scripture. And they are never so happy as when they are accusing liberals and conservatives of reasoning poorly, or of being ignorant of the supposedly scientific basis for their racialist political views.
31. Children do, it seems, possess certain innate ideas—namely, those kinesthetic ideas that permit every child to develop the ability to nurse, crawl, walk, and so on. But the overwhelming majority of what we know of the world is given to us by way of experience. It is thus the instruction of the child's family and society that plays the decisive role in shaping the schemes of ideas with which he approaches reality.

32. The relation to the longevity and well-being of the nation is stated explicitly in the Ten Precepts with reference to honoring one's parents: "So that your days may be lengthened, and it will go well with you, upon the land which the Lord, your God, is giving you" (Deuteronomy 5.15; Exodus 20.11). However, the books of Moses also connect observance of the law in general with the people's longevity on its land (Deuteronomy 4.40, 5.16, 29) and with its health and prosperity (Deuteronomy 4.40, 5.16, 29, 6.3, 18; Jeremiah 7.23).
33. Because the liberal paradigm assumes that adult human beings are free and equal by nature, its proponents imagine that each individual can conduct his own search for truth in a manner that is largely independent of what others believe and do. In this, their model is Descartes, who supposes that everyone can and should rethink everything he has known, seeking truth without reference to inherited ideas of any kind.
34. See Chapter 3.8.

Chapter IV: God, Scripture, Family, and Congregation

1. On the "fusion" of public liberalism and privative conservatism during the 1960s, see Chapter 6.5–6.
2. Deuteronomy 6.4.
3. See, for example, Exodus 15.26; Deuteronomy 12.8, 13.18; Judges 21.25; Samuel 1.2.3; Kings 1.11.33, 1.14.8; Jeremiah 34.15; Proverbs 12.15, 16.2, 21.2, 30.12.
4. Deuteronomy 4.6.
5. Genesis 8.21. See also 6.5.
6. Judges 17.6, 21.25; Proverbs 12.15, 16.2, 21.2, 30.12.
7. Psalms 14.1, 53.2; Proverbs 1.7.
8. Proverbs 1.7, 2.5, 9.10, 15.33, 30.3; Psalms 111.10; Job 28.28; Ecclesiastes 12.13.
9. For example, the story of Moses's birth tells us that the midwives Shifra and Pua would not murder the Israelite children at Pharaoh's command, because they "feared God" (1.17). Similarly, Nehemiah describes how the previous governors of Judah had taxed and impoverished the people, but he did not do so himself "for fear of our God" (Nehemia 5.15, and also 5.9). Other examples in which it is individuals who are said to "fear God" include Genesis 42.18; Exodus 18.21, 20.16; Jonah 1.9, 16; Psalms 36.2, 55.20, 115.11, 135.20; Proverbs 3.7, 8.13, 16.6, 24.21; Job 4.6; Ecclesiastes 5.6, 8.12–13, 12.13. Compare these examples to passages in the Mosaic law that invoke this same expression: "You will not curse the deaf, nor place a stumbling block before the blind, and you will fear your God" (Numbers 19.14). And: "Love the stranger, for you were strangers

in the land of Egypt. You will fear the Lord your God" (Deuteronomy 10.19–20). Similar verses associate the fear of God with respect for the aged, and with the refusal to engage in fraud, the abuse of one's bondsmen, or extortion from those who have taken on loans (Leviticus 19.32, 25.17, 36, 43). All these cases are the same: One may easily harm another who is dependent and weak—the deaf, the aged, the farmer, the slave. For this reason, the fear of God is considered a cornerstone of the entire structure of the law and of civilization itself.

10. As suggested by Abraham's assessment of the city of Gerar: "Surely, there is no fear of God in this place, and they will kill me to have my wife" (Genesis 20.11). Moses says that Amalek "did not fear God" in Deuteronomy 25.17.
11. See Deuteronomy 10.12–13: "And now, Israel, what does the Lord your God require of you, other than to fear the Lord your God, to walk in all his ways, and to love him, and to serve the Lord your God with all your heart and with all your soul, to follow the instructions of the Lord and his laws, which I instruct you this day for your good?" See also 14.23, 17.13, 31.12.
12. See my discussion in "Torah from Heaven: Moses and Sinai in Exodus," in *The Revelation at Sinai: What Does 'Torah from Heaven' Mean?*, ed. Yoram Hazony, Gil Student and Alex Sztuden (New York: Ktav, 2021), 1–74.
13. Exodus 20.16. Compare Deuteronomy 4.10, where God tells Moses, "Gather the people to me and I will speak my words to them, so that they may learn to fear me always."
14. Isaiah 51.4. Regarding Israel as a light and banner for the peoples, see also Isaiah 11.9–10, 12, 42.1–4, 6–7, 49.6, 51.4, 60.3; Jeremiah 3.17, 4.1–2.
15. Regarding the sins of past generations, see Exodus 20.4, 34.7; Numbers 14.18; Deuteronomy 5.8. For the sins of rulers, see Jeremiah 15.4, among others.
16. Genesis 1.27.
17. Genesis 12.3.
18. Exodus 20.1–13.
19. See Chapter 6.1.
20. The followers of Thomas Aquinas, together with some Straussians, maintain a fourth scheme in political and moral matters, which is sometimes called *Aristotelian rationalism*. This system combines a rationalist theory of knowledge with political and moral conclusions that are derived, in important respects, from the biblical tradition. This subject deserves careful treatment, which I will not be able to provide here. For now, I will say only that this system can be seen as a rationalized reconstruction of the biblical tradition, provided that the Aristotelians in question (i) recognize that their political and moral system cannot be made to function without God, (ii) seek to align its moral teaching

with Scripture, and (iii) recognize that in political matters, the traditional constitution and law of the nation is essential in securing the national interest and the common good.

21. Chapter 3.8.
22. Exodus 20.14–15, 24.1–2, 33.20–23.
23. Hugo Grotius, *The Rights of War and Peace*, ed. Richard Tuck (Indianapolis, Indiana: Liberty Fund, 2005 [1625]). See discussion in Ofir Haivry, *John Selden and the Western Political Tradition* (Cambridge: Cambridge University Press), 198–201, and especially 199, n. 26.
24. On the Bible and natural law, see "The Law of Moses as Natural Law" in Yoram Hazony, "Three Replies: On Revelation, Natural Law, and Autonomy in Jewish Theology," *Journal of Analytic Theology* 3 (2015), 184–93; Yoram Hazony, "The Bible and Leo Strauss," *Perspectives on Political Science* 45 (Summer 2016), 190–207.
25. Chapter 3.11.
26. Chapter 3.2, 4.
27. Chapter 3.5.
28. There are additional aspects of human nature that give shape to the family, which I will leave aside for now. For example, it is impossible to understand the various forms of the family life without recognizing the fundamental human desire for purification and for being cleansed from pollution—urges that find expression in traditional laws of sexuality and family life.
29. Chapter 3.5.
30. Proverbs 31.
31. Notice the assumption that wives do not need to participate in their husbands' work lives or to see them during the day, and that children do not learn much from seeing their father work every day and assisting him.
32. Deuteronomy 32.7.

Chapter V: The Purposes of Government

1. Chapter 3.2.
2. Chapter 4.3.
3. The purposes of the family that I have named are not to be confused with the idea of the *family*, which is derived from experience. No list of purposes is a substitute for such experience, because experience alone can provide an idea in which these principles are "taken together and in the right proportions," and

in which other purposes that have escaped my attention can perhaps be discerned.

4. Chapter 3.11.
5. Chapter 3.2, 8. As Montesquieu wrote concerning this subject: "Although all states have the same purpose in general, which is to maintain themselves, yet each state has a purpose that is peculiar to it: Expansion was the purpose of Rome; war, that of Lacedaemonia; religion, that of the Jewish laws; commerce, that of Marseilles; public tranquility, that of the laws of China; navigation that of the laws of Rhodians; natural liberty was the purpose of the police of the savages; in general, the delights of the prince are the purpose of despotic states; his glory and that of his state, that of monarchies; the independence of each individual is the purpose of the laws of Poland, and what results from this is the oppression of all. There is also one nation [i.e., England] whose constitution has political liberty for its direct purpose." Montesquieu, *Spirit of the Laws*, 2.5.
6. I do not mean that every tribe or party can be accorded the same degree of consideration. A ruler or statesman must maintain a ruling coalition, and in practice this is only possible if those who support him have more influence than those who do not.
7. Edmund Burke, *An Appeal from the New to the Old Whigs*, in *Further Reflections on the Revolution in France*, ed. Daniel Ritchie (Indianapolis, Indiana: Liberty Fund, 1992 [1791]), 198.
8. Samuel 1.8.20.
9. Chapter 3.5–7.
10. Chapter 2.
11. Chapter 3.9.
12. Chapter 3.10.
13. Yoram Hazony, *The Virtue of Nationalism* (New York: Basic Books, 2018).
14. Edmund Burke, *Reflections on the Revolution in France*, ed. J.G.A. Pocock (Indianapolis, Indiana: Hackett, 1987 [1790]), 80-81.
15. On the myth of the neutral state, see *The Virtue of Nationalism*, chapter 16.
16. See my discussion in Chapters 6-8.
17. On the relationship between Enlightenment liberalism and atheism, see Chapter 4.1–2.
18. Gouverneur Morris, the principal drafter of the Constitution of 1787, also delivered the most fulsome condemnation of slavery at the Constitutional Convention. See Chapter 2.10.

Chapter VI: Liberal Hegemony and Cold War Conservatism

1. On the rise of Enlightenment liberalism after the Second World War, see Christopher Caldwell, *The Age of Entitlement* (New York: Simon and Schuster, 2020); Russell Reno, *Return of the Strong Gods* (Washington, D.C.: Regnery, 2019).
2. On the appearance of the term "liberal democracy," see Chapter 8.3.
3. See, for example, Raymond Fosdick, "The League of Nations as an Instrument of Liberalism," *Atlantic Monthly*, October 1920.
4. Justice George Sutherland, *United States v. Macintosh* (1931). See also Justice David Brewer, writing for the Supreme Court in *Church of the Holy Trinity v. United States* (1892): "If we pass beyond these matters to a view of American life, as expressed by its laws, its business, its customs, and its society, we find everywhere a clear recognition of the same truth... that this is a Christian nation." Similarly, Justice Joseph Story, writing for the Supreme Court in *Vidal v. Girard's Executors* (1844), recognized that "the Christian religion is a part of the common law of Pennsylvania."
5. This phrase appears in numerous studies of Roosevelt, and it is often presented as a direct quotation. However, John Woolverton and James Bratt attribute this statement to Roosevelt without placing it in quotation marks. See *A Christian and a Democrat: A Religious Biography of Franklin Roosevelt* (Grand Rapids, Michigan: Eerdmans, 2019), 1. It is not clear to me what the original source for this remark is.
6. Radio Address on the President's Sixtieth Birthday, January 30, 1942.
7. He continued: "But when policies of nationalism—political, economic, social, and moral—are carried to such extremes as to exclude and prevent necessary policies of international cooperation, they become dangerous and deadly." Radio Address by the Secretary of State, July 23, 1942.
8. The original nationalist pledge of allegiance, adopted in 1942, did not include the words "under God." These were inserted at Eisenhower's request in 1954. Similarly, in *Zorach* v. *Clauson,* 343 U.S. 306, 313 (1952), the Supreme Court endorsed the principle that "[w]e are a religious people whose institutions presuppose a Supreme Being."
9. Franklin Delano Roosevelt, State of the Union Address, January 4, 1939.
10. Deuteronomy 25.18. See my discussion of the term "fear of God" in Chapter 4.1.

11. "Neither a state nor the Federal Government can set up a church. Neither can pass laws which aid one religion, aid all religions, or prefer one religion over another." Justice Hugo Black, *Everson v. Board of Education.* (1947)
12. Justice Hugo Black, *Everson v. Board of Education* (1947).
13. Chief Justice Earl Warren, *Brown v. Board of Education* (1954).
14. Louis Hartz, *The Liberal Tradition in America* (New York: Harcourt, 1991 [1952]); Arthur Schlesinger Jr., "The New Conservatism in America: A Liberal Comment," *Confluence*, December 1953, 61–71; Arthur Schlesinger Jr., "The New Conservatism: Politics of Nostalgia," *Reporter*, June 15, 1955, 9–12. Lionel Trilling expressed this view as well: "In the United States at this time, liberalism is not only the dominant but even the sole intellectual tradition. For it is a plain fact that nowadays there are no conservative or reactionary ideas in general circulation." Lionel Trilling, *The Liberal Imagination* (New York: New York Review of Books, 2008 [1950]), xv.
15. See George H. Nash's excellent *The Conservative Intellectual Movement in America Since 1945* (Wilmington, Delaware: Intercollegiate Studies Institute Books, 2008 [1976]).
16. Russell Kirk, *The Conservative Mind: From Burke to Eliot* (Washington, D.C.: Regnery Gateway, 1985 [1953]); Robert Nisbet, *The Quest for Community* (Wilmington, Delaware: Intercollegiate Studies Institute Books, 2010 [1953]); Peter Viereck, *Conservative Thinkers* (New York: Routledge, 1956).
17. Kirk, *The Conservative Mind*, 8–9.
18. Kirk, *The Conservative Mind*, 12–113; Russell Kirk, *America's British Culture* (New Brunswick, New Jersey: Transaction, 1993), 64–65. On the common law in America, see Russell Kirk, *America's British Culture*, 29–46.
19. Russell Kirk, *Rights and Duties: Reflections on Our Conservative Constitution* (Dallas: Spence Publishing Company, 1997), 4, 96. Kirk writes favorably not only of English conservatives, but also of the Scottish philosopher David Hume: "It was the amusement of Hume, that amiable skeptic, to puncture balloons. The biggest balloon that came his way was John Locke, whom Hume thoroughly undoes.... Reason with a capital 'R,' pure rationality as a guide to morals and politics, dominated the first half of the eighteenth century, and Locke was the grand champion of this system.... Pure reason never recovered from Hume's rapier thrust" (106).
20. Kirk, *Rights and Duties*, 95.
21. Ibid., 107.
22. Ibid., 144–45.

23. Kirk, *The Conservative Mind*, 152. It would have been helpful, for example, if Kirk had reported to his readers that Calhoun regarded slavery as a "positive good." John Calhoun, Speech on the Reception of Abolition Petitions, February 6, 1837, in *Speeches of John C. Calhoun* (New York: Harper, 1843), 222–26.
24. Kirk, *The Conservative Mind*, 169, 172.
25. Campaigning for the presidency in 1932, Roosevelt announced, "The task of government in its relation to business is to assist the development of an economic declaration of rights, an economic constitutional order. This is the common task of statesman and business man. It is the minimum requirement of a more permanently safe order of things." Commonwealth Club Address, San Francisco, September 23, 1932.
26. Franklin Roosevelt, State of the Union Address, January 11, 1944. As Roosevelt explained: "This Republic had its beginning, and grew to its present strength, under the protection of certain inalienable political rights—among them the right of free speech, free press, free worship, trial by jury, freedom from unreasonable searches and seizures. They were our rights to life and liberty. As our nation has grown in size and stature, however—as our industrial economy expanded—these political rights proved inadequate to assure us equality in the pursuit of happiness. We have come to a clear realization of the fact that true individual freedom cannot exist without economic security and independence.... People who are hungry and out of a job are the stuff of which dictatorships are made. In our day these economic truths have become accepted as self-evident. We have accepted, so to speak, a second Bill of Rights under which a new basis of security and prosperity can be established for all—regardless of station, race, or creed. Among these are: The right to a useful and remunerative job in the industries or shops or farms or mines of the nation; the right to earn enough to provide adequate food and clothing and recreation; the right of every farmer to raise and sell his products at a return which will give him and his family a decent living; the right of every businessman, large and small, to trade in an atmosphere of freedom from unfair competition and domination by monopolies at home or abroad; the right of every family to a decent home; the right to adequate medical care and the opportunity to achieve and enjoy good health; the right to adequate protection from the economic fears of old age, sickness, accident, and unemployment; the right to a good education."
27. Friedrich Hayek, *The Road to Serfdom* (Chicago: University of Chicago Press, 2007 [1944]); Friedrich Hayek, *The Constitution of Liberty* (Chicago: University of Chicago Press, 1960); Ludwig von Mises, *Human Action* (Indianapolis,

Indiana: Liberty Fund, 2007 [English, 1949; German, 1940]); Ludwig von Mises, *Liberalism* (Indianapolis, Indiana: Liberty Fund, 1985, [English, 1962; German, 1927]); Milton Friedman, *Capitalism and Freedom* (Chicago: University of Chicago Press, 2020 1962); Ayn Rand, *Atlas Shrugged* (New York: Signet, 1996 [1957]); Ayn Rand, *The Virtue of Selfishness* (New York: Signet, 1964).

28. Hayek, *The Road to Serfdom*, 58.
29. Ibid., 103.
30. Ibid., 108–9.
31. Hayek, *The Constitution of Liberty*, 54–56. Hayek emphasizes that empiricist political theory emerges from the common law tradition in *Law, Legislation, and Liberty*, which praises "the evolutionary teaching of Edward Coke, Matthew Hale, David Hume and Edmund Burke," and describes this tradition as "wholly contrary to the rationalist constructivism of Francis Bacon or Thomas Hobbes, Jeremy Bentham or John Austin." Friedrich Hayek, *Law Legislation, and Liberty* (Chicago: University of Chicago Press, 1973), vol. 1, 73–74. On the rationalism of Descartes, Hobbes, and Rousseau, see volume 1, 9–10. Hayek also says that after Descartes and Hobbes revived rationalism, it was Rousseau, Hegel, and Marx who "carried this cult of reason furthest." Friedrich Hayek, "Kinds of Rationalism," in *Studies in Philosophy, Politics, and Economics* (Chicago: University of Chicago Press, 1967), 93–94.
32. Hayek, *The Constitution of Liberty*, 56.
33. Hayek emphasizes that Darwin's theory of biological evolution appears centuries after the theory of the evolution of social institutions was advanced by the English common lawyers and the Scottish school. Hayek, *Law Legislation, and Liberty*, 22–23, 152–53 n. 33.
34. Hayek, *The Constitution of Liberty*, 57.
35. Ibid., 37. In this context of a "competition of all against all," it is possible to observe the distinction between the decision-making that takes place within organizations, which Hayek sees as characterized by conscious planning and coercive direction from above; and the kind of evolving order that arises spontaneously, in the sphere of freedom in which individuals and organizations compete with one another: "The relevant distinction... is between conditions, on the one hand, in which alternative ways based on different views or practices may be tried, and conditions, on the other, in which one agency has the exclusive right and the power to prevent others from trying.... The argument for liberty is not an argument against organization... but an argument against exclusive, privileged, monopolistic organization, against the use of coercion to prevent others from trying to do better."

36. Hayek, *The Constitution of Liberty*, 62–63.
37. Ibid., 61.
38. Ibid.
39. "Next to language, they are perhaps the most important instance of an undesigned growth, of a set of rules which govern our lives, but of which we can say neither why they are what they are, nor what they do to us: We do not know what the consequence of observing them are for us as individuals and as a group." Hayek, *The Constitution of Liberty*, 64.
40. Ibid., 67.
41. Ibid., 37.
42. Hayek, *The Road to Serfdom*, 112–18.
43. As he wrote in the foreword to the American edition of *The Road to Serfdom* in 1956: "The true liberal must sometimes make common cause with the conservative, and in some circumstances…he has hardly any other way of actively working for his ideals. But true liberalism is still distinct from conservatism, and there is danger in the two being confused. Conservatism [is] a necessary element in any stable society.… [But] in its paternalistic, nationalistic, and power-adoring tendencies, it is often closer to socialism than true liberalism; and with its traditionalistic, anti-intellectual, and often mystical propensities, it will never, except in short periods of disillusionment, appeal to the young.… A conservative movement, by its very nature, is bound to be a defender of established privilege, and to lean on the power of government for the protection of privilege. The essence of the liberal position, however, is the denial of all privilege." Hayek, *The Road to Serfdom*, 45–46.
44. Quoting Lord Acton. Friedrich Hayek, *The Road to Serfdom*, 110.
45. Hayek, *The Constitution of Liberty*, 68.
46. Hayek, *Law, Legislation, and Liberty*, vol. 1., 61.
47. Chapter 5.4–6.
48. Hayek, *The Constitution of Liberty*, 68.
49. Ibid.
50. Hayek, *Law, Legislation, and Liberty*, vol. 1., 1.
51. Hayek, *The Constitution of Liberty*, 31. Hayek writes that this dogma or axiom rests "on the belief that it will, on balance, release more forces for the good than for the bad." But he does not claim that this faith can be empirically justified.
52. Hayek concludes *The Road to Serfdom* with thirteen pages advocating a utopian rationalist scheme of world government. See 223–26. Hayek's philosophy of tradition cannot be reconciled with the centrally planned, worldwide liberal revolution that this scheme entailed.

53. As Strauss writes: "Prior to the discovery of nature, the characteristic behavior of any thing or class of things was conceived of as its custom or its way. That is, no fundamental distinction was made between customs or ways which are always and everywhere the same, and customs or ways which differ from tribe to tribe. Barking and wagging the tail is the way of dogs, menstruation is the way of women, the crazy things done by madmen are the way of madmen, just as not eating pork is the way of Jews and not drinking wine is the way of Moslems." Leo Strauss, *Natural Right and History* (Chicago: University of Chicago Press, 1953), 82–83.
54. Strauss, *Natural Right and History*, 86.
55. Ibid., 1.
56. "What was a tolerably accurate description of German thought [in the 1930s] would now appear to be true of Western thought in general.... American social science has adopted the very attitude toward natural right which, a generation ago, could still be described, with some plausibility, as characteristic of German thought." Strauss, *Natural Right and History*, 2.
57. Strauss, *Natural Right and History*, 2–3.
58. Ibid., 4–5.
59. Ibid., 3.
60. See Yoram Hazony, "The Bible and Leo Strauss," *Perspectives on Political Science* 45 (Summer 2016): 190–207; Chapter 3.11.
61. John Locke, *Essay Concerning Human Understanding* 4.3.18; Strauss, *Natural Right and History*, 202. See my discussion in Chapter 1.5, especially footnote 43; Chapter 3.3.
62. Strauss, *Natural Right and History*, 247. The quotation marks are in the original, but Strauss is not quoting Locke. The assessment is his own (borrowing a proverbial expression from German). Strauss apparently prefers a philosophy based on the virtue of the ancients, but he will accept the "low but solid" foundations provided by Enlightenment rationalism.
63. Strauss, *Natural Right and History*, 313, 316, 318.
64. Ibid., 316, 319.
65. "His 'conservatism' prepared an approach to human affairs which is even more foreign to classical thought than was the very 'radicalism' of the theorists of the French Revolution." Strauss, *Natural Right and History*, 319.
66. In 1968, fifteen years after publication of this attack on Burke, Strauss published another discussion of conservatism. This later discussion is rhetorically more restrained, reflecting the emergence of the "fusion" of liberalism and conservatism that had taken place in the preceding decade.

In these later comments, Strauss follows the liberal scholar Louis Hartz (without naming him), suggesting that the conservatism of Burke (he doesn't name him either) is "no longer politically important." According to this view, contemporary American liberalism and conservatism are, in reality, both "based here and now on liberal democracy," and "much of what goes now by the name of conservatism has, in the last analysis, a common root with present-day liberalism and even with Communism." Nevertheless, Strauss once more presses his point against Burke, writing, "Inasmuch as the universalism in politics is founded on the universalism proceeding from reason, conservatism is frequently characterized by distrust of reason or by trust in tradition, which as such is necessarily this or that tradition and hence particular. Conservatism is therefore exposed to criticism that is guided by the notion of the unity of truth." Leo Strauss, *Liberalism Ancient and Modern* (Chicago: University of Chicago, 1968), vii–ix.

67. Strauss, *Natural Right and History*, 1.
68. Strauss offers a reason for regarding Enlightenment liberalism as a matter of faith: "The fact that reason compels us to go beyond the [traditional] ideal of our society does not yet guarantee that in taking this step, we shall not be confronted with a void, or with a multiplicity of incompatible and equally justifiable principles of 'natural right.'" Perhaps to suggest that this is not merely a hypothetical statement, he observes that Enlightenment rationalism is "in the same boat" as the Aristotelian rationalism of the "disciples of Thomas Aquinas." Strauss, *Natural Right and History*, 6-7.
69. Nash, *The Conservative Intellectual Movement in America*, 176–86.
70. William F. Buckley Jr., "Our Mission Statement," *National Review*, November 19, 1955.
71. As Buckley wrote in the first clause of the *National Review* mission statement: "The growth of government (the dominant social feature of this century) must be fought relentlessly. In this great social conflict of the era, we are, without reservations, on the libertarian side." Buckley, "Our Mission Statement." See also William F. Buckley Jr., *Happy Days Were Here Again: Reflections of a Libertarian Journalist* (New York: Basic Books, 2008 [1993]). Regarding the use of the word "liberal" in postwar America, Frank Meyer writes: "Liberalism was indeed once, in the last century, the proponent and defender of freedom. But that which is called liberalism today has deserted its heritage in defense of freedom of the person to become a peculiarly American form of... democratic socialism." Frank Meyer, *In Defense of Freedom and Related Essays* (Indianapolis, Indiana: Liberty Fund, 1996 [1962]), 33.

72. In his 1959 book *Up from Liberalism*, Buckley wrote that a conservative advocates “a determined resistance to the spread of world Communism—and a belief in political non-interventionism . . . a patriotic concern for the nation and its culture—and a genuine respect for the integrity and differences of other peoples’ culture.” William F. Buckley Jr., *Up from Liberalism* (New York: McDowell, Obelensky, 1959), 193.
73. Hayek, *The Road to Serfdom*, 223–36.
74. Meyer, *In Defense of Freedom*.
75. Meyer understands that to assert that “freedom is the first criterion of the political order” is to “give primacy to principle over experience,” and that principle will have to be modified in light of experience. But the possibility that experience should be the source of our political principles rather than such a priori reasoning is not one he considers. Meyer, *In Defense of Freedom*, 85.
76. Meyer, *In Defense of Freedom*, 35.
77. Ibid., 66.
78. Ibid., 61–62. The quotation from Strauss is on 62, n. 14.
79. Meyer, *In Defense of Freedom*, 48.
80. Ibid., 84. Similarly: “The freedom of the person [is] the central and primary end of political society” (33). And: “The individual person [is] the decisive concern of political action and political theory” (39).
81. Meyer, *In Defense of Freedom*, 77.
82. Ibid., 81.
83. Ibid., 74.
84. Ibid., 80. Emphasis removed.
85. Ibid., 121.
86. Ibid., 71. Similarly: “Men are made in such a way that they can make no ends their own except through free choice. . . . To a certain extent, it is true, they can be forced to act as if they were virtuous. But virtue is the fruit of well-used freedom. And no act, to the degree that it is coerced, can partake of virtue—or vice” (78).
87. Meyer, *In Defense of Freedom*, 126. In the same way, Meyer argued that “all the prospering political ideologies—Communism and Nazism, socialism, the milder theories of the welfare state—have founded themselves upon the . . . axiom that individual men are secondary to society” (51).
88. Meyer, *In Defense of Freedom*, 99–100.
89. Ibid., 100.
90. “There exist, therefore, two problems [i.e., freedom and virtue]; but only one of them, the problem of the conditions of the good political order, is the

concern of political theory in the strict sense.... Political theory and practice, therefore, must be judged by criteria proper to the political order; and the decisive criterion for any political order is the degree to which it establishes conditions of freedom." Meyer, *In Defense of Freedom*, 81.

91. William F. Buckley Jr., "An Empiricist Theory of Conservatism," in *What is Conservatism?*, ed. Frank Meyer (Wilmington, Delaware: Intercollegiate Studies Institute Books, 2015 [1964]), 231–35. Buckley's "Empiricist Theory of Conservatism" is worth reading in this context, precisely because it presents such a stark contrast with Meyer's rationalist political theory, which is presented as a deduction from a single principle. Although Buckley frequently agreed with Meyer, he was aware that his own conservative politics was based on balancing competing principles, and he described it explicitly in this way in *Up From Liberalism*, 193.
92. Russell Kirk, "Libertarians: The Chirping Sectaries," *Modern Age* (Fall 1981), 345.
93. Ibid.
94. This alliance was formally proclaimed in a book of essays edited by Meyer, in which he declared that Cold War conservatives "share a common set of values," and that "the consensus is a great deal more fundamental than the divergence." Frank Meyer, "Consensus and Divergence," in *What is Conservatism?*, 249.
95. Chapter 5.4.
96. Meyer, *In Defense of Freedom*, 65.
97. Kirk, "Libertarians: The Chirping Sectaries," 345.
98. See my discussion of George Will and Irving Kristol in Chapter 9.4.
99. Irving Kristol, *Two Cheers for Capitalism* (New York: Basic Books, 1978).
100. Irving Kristol, "The Coming 'Conservative Century,'" in *Neo-Conservatism: Selected Essays, 1949–1995*, 364.
101. On the relationship between the liberalism of the left and the liberalism of the right, see Patrick Deneen's *How Liberalism Failed* (New Haven, Connecticut: Yale University Press, 2018).
102. Nash, *The Conservative Intellectual Movement in American*, 180.
103. Meyer, *In Defense of Freedom*, 74.

Chapter VII: The Challenge of Marxism

1. This chapter was originally published in *Quillette* on August 16, 2020, when the ideological collapse of the great liberal institutions was not yet an accomplished fact. Much of what I predicted at that time has, unfortunately, come to pass. I have edited the text accordingly.

2. On the neo-Marxist cultural revolution in America and Britain, see Douglas Murray, *The Madness of Crowds* (London: Bloomsbury, 2019); Joshua Mitchell, *American Awakening* (New York: Encounter, 2020); Rod Dreher, *Live Not By Lies* (New York: Sentinel, 2020); Michael Knowles, *Speechless* (Washington, D.C.: Regnery, 2021); Mike Gonzalez, *BLM: The Making of a New Marxist Revolution* (New York: Encounter Books, 2021).
3. Karl Marx and Friedrich Engels, "Manifesto of the Communist Party," in *The Marx-Engels Reader*, ed. Robert Tucker (New York: Norton, 1978 [1848]), 473–74, 479, 489.
4. Marx and Engels, "Manifesto of the Communist Party," 475, 486-87; Karl Marx, "The German Ideology," in *The Marx-Engels Reader*, ed. Robert Tucker (New York: Norton, 1978 [1846]), 187. "The German Ideology" is a manuscript from around 1846. It remained unpublished until 1932, when it was released by the Marx-Engels Institute in Moscow.
5. Marx and Engels, "Manifesto of the Communist Party," 486–87; Karl Marx, "The German Ideology," 154–55, 172–73. Engels first uses the term "false consciousness" in Friedrich Engels to Franz Mehring, July 14, 1893.
6. Marx and Engels, "Manifesto of the Communist Party," 474, 488; Karl Marx, "The German Ideology," 163–164.
7. Marx and Engels, "Manifesto of the Communist Party," 481.
8. Marx and Engels, "Manifesto of the Communist Party," 483–84, 490–91, 500; Karl Marx, "The German Ideology," 163.
9. Marx and Engels, "Manifesto of the Communist Party," 488–91; Karl Marx, "The Germany Ideology," 160, 174, 198.
10. By now, more than a few observers have pointed out that the present cultural revolution in America has taken on the characteristics of a class war, although in reverse: The revolution is being conducted from above by educated elites, whose aim is to re-educate a working class that is resistant to the new ideology. See Michael Lind, *The New Class War* (New York: Portfolio, 2020); Batya Ungar-Sargon, *Bad News: How Woke Media is Undermining Democracy* (New York: Encounter, 2021).
11. A compelling analysis of the structural similarities between Enlightenment liberalism and Marxism has been published by the Polish political theorist Ryszard Legutko under the title *The Demon in Democracy: Totalitarian Temptations in Free Societies* (New York: Encounter Books, 2016). A subsequent book by Christopher Caldwell has similarly documented the manner in which the American constitutional revolution of the 1960s, whose purpose was to establish the rule of liberalism, has brought about a swift transition to a

"progressive" politics that is in fact a version of Marxism. Christopher Caldwell, *The Age of Entitlement: America Since the Sixties* (New York: Simon and Schuster, 2020).

12. Chapter 2.2–3.

Chapter VIII: Conservative Democracy

1. Steven Pinker, *Enlightenment Now* (New York: Viking, 2018).
2. Quotations are from John Locke, *Second Treatise of Government,* sections 4, 6, 7, 14–15 (spelling modernized). See my discussion in Chapters 1.5, 3.2.
3. See, for example, Guido de Ruggiero, *The History of European Liberalism*, trans. R.G. Collingwood (Boston: Beacon Press 1959 [1927]), 379. Traditionally, Americans referred to their form of government as *republican government.* Indeed, insofar as usage is concerned, the term "liberal democracy" did not become more common in public discussion than the traditional term "republican government" until the 1970s. And it attained its present dominance in discourse on forms of government (overwhelming even the expression "democratic government") only in the 1990s, after the fall of the Berlin Wall.
4. Hayek argues that a "real liberalism" is one that is dissociated from nationalism, and that the time has come to end the historical error of seeing them as intertwined. Endorsing the elimination of national states and the establishment of an international federation, he writes: "That liberalism became first allied with nationalism was due to the historical coincidence that, during the Nineteenth Century, it was nationalism which in Ireland, Greece, Belgium, and Poland, and later in Italy and Austro-Hungary, fought against the same sort of oppression that liberalism opposed.... Is it too much to hope for a rebirth of real liberalism, true to its ideal of freedom and internationalism?" Friedrich Hayek, "The Economic Conditions of Interstate Federalism," *New Commonwealth Quarterly* 5 (September 1939): 131–49.
5. This is a characteristically French and German way of thinking about the constitutional freedoms inherited from the English constitution. Thus João Carlos Espada observes that "democracy in Europe is mainly perceived as an expression of a dogmatic rationalist project," which is to say that it is detached from its association with historical empiricism. For this reason, he writes, both secondary and university education in Europe largely ignores English and American tradition, seeing them as incomplete manifestations of liberal-democratic government "whose first full formulation would only occur in the 1789 French Revolution." João Carlos Espada, *The Anglo-American Tradition of*

Liberty (New York: Routledge, 2016), 10, 109, 187–88. However, this European view has in many respects been adopted in Britain and America as well.

6. On why anti-Marxist liberals should join such a coalition, see Chapter 7.

Chapter IX: Some Notes on Living a Conservative Life

1. Bruce Springsteen, "Thunder Road," *Born to Run*, 1975.
2. Genesis 12.2.
3. Speech before the National Association of Evangelicals in Orlando, Florida, March 8, 1983.
4. Ronald Reagan, "Captive Nations Proclamation," June 30, 1981.
5. Margaret Thatcher, *The Downing Street Years* (London: Harper Collins, 1993), 179; John O'Sullivan, *The President, the Pope, and the Prime Minister* (Washington, D.C.: Regnery, 2006), 148.
6. Reagan and Thatcher's nationalism could not, of course, be reconciled with the gathering clamor in Thatcher's own party to submerge Britain in a federal Europe. Thatcher had inherited this trajectory from the Heath government, and she did not challenge it so long as the battles against the Soviets and British socialism were her top priorities. But in 1988, Thatcher felt strong enough to insist that the future must be one of "willing…cooperation between independent sovereign states," as she put it in her famous Bruges speech. She continued: "To try to suppress nationhood and concentrate power at the center of a European conglomerate would be highly damaging.… Europe will be stronger precisely because it has France as France, Spain as Spain, Britain as Britain, each with its own customs, traditions and identity. It would be folly to try to fit them into some sort of identikit European personality.… We have not successfully rolled back the frontiers of the state in Britain, only to see them reimposed at a European level, with a European super-state exercising a new dominance from Brussels. Certainly, we want to see Europe more united.… But it must be in a way which preserves the different traditions, parliamentary powers and sense of national pride in one's own country." Margaret Thatcher, Speech to the College of Europe, September 20, 1988.
7. Arrow 3, deployed in 2017, reportedly has the ability to destroy incoming missiles in space. "Israel Deploys 'Star Wars' Missile Killer System," Reuters, January 18, 2017.
8. Chronicles 2.7.14.
9. Ronald Reagan, "Remarks on Prayer," May 7, 1982. The text of the proposed amendment read: "Nothing in this Constitution shall be construed to prohibit

individual or group prayer in public schools or other public institutions. No person shall be required by the United States or by any state to participate in prayer."

10. Chapters 4.1, 6.1.
11. *The Daily Princetonian*, September 21, 1983.
12. William Golding, *Lord of the Flies* (New York: Penguin, 2003 [1954]).
13. Stevenson Hall was primarily a community of students. But Stevenson did bring us into contact with older men and women who were exceptions to the generally adult-free atmosphere of the campus: The Stevenson community I have described was cultivated in all its beauty by Professor Sandra Bermann, who served as master of Stevenson Hall. Rabbi Yaakov Wasser of East Brunswick was there every few weeks to supervise the *kashrut* of the dining hall. He taught Julie for her conversion, and later conducted our wedding ceremony in Prospect Garden. Two orthodox couples from Israel, Prof. Shmuel and Zahava Elitzur, and Prof. Gideon and Moria Libson, spent a year in Princeton on sabbatical with their families and actively engaged with the students. Toby and Elaine Robison from the town of Princeton likewise contributed much to the community. Joy Roberts and the rest of the kitchen staff went out of their way to take care of us. And when Julie and I were married, they catered the wedding at Stevenson.
14. George Will, *Statecraft as Soulcraft* (New York: Simon and Schuster, 1983); George Will, *The Pursuit of Virtue and Other Tory Notions* (New York: Simon and Schuster, 1982); Irving Kristol, *Reflections of a Neo-Conservative* (New York: Basic Books, 1983); Jeane Kirkpatrick, *Dictatorships and Double Standards* (New York: Simon and Schuster, 1982).
15. Will, *Statecraft as Soulcraft*, 143.
16. Ibid., 95–96, 163.
17. Ibid., 144, 160–61.
18. Ibid., 75.
19. Ibid., 56.
20. Ibid., 163–65.
21. Ibid., 165.
22. Kristol, *Reflections of a Neo-Conservative*, 152.
23. Ibid., 168–69, 176.
24. Ibid., 168–69, 176.
25. Irving Kristol, "The Coming 'Conservative Century,'" in *Neo-Conservatism: Selected Essays, 1949–1995* (New York: Free Press, 1995 [1993]), 365.

26. In "The Need for Nationalism," an essay published in September 1980, Will praised De Gaulle's nationalism as "a model," and hinted that Reagan might have some of that in him. See Will, *The Pursuit of Virtue and Other Tory Notions*, 150–51.
27. Kristol, *Reflections of a Neo-Conservative*, xiii, 111–12, 245.
28. Kristol did not believe nations can have the same character, purposes, or interests. He therefore regarded the idea that the United States could pursue the good of the entire world to be an "illusion," which would sink America's resources into "pools of quicksand." As he wrote: "Those pools of quicksand represent the innumerable treaties, conventions, and alliances we have blandly committed ourselves to over the past four decades, under the illusion that we were moving toward an eventual 'world community.' In such a world, foreign policy—the defense of one's national interests—would cease to exist, having been completely replaced by a diplomacy aiming to reconcile the interests of all." Kristol, *Reflections of a Neo-Conservative*, 227.
29. Kristol, *Reflections of a Neo-Conservative*, 57. Writing about *The Federalist*, Kristol commented that its authors "understood that republican self-government could not exist if humanity did not possess—at some moments, and to a fair degree—the traditional 'republican virtues' of self-control, self-reliance, and disinterested concern for the public good" (81).
30. Kristol emphasized these two aspects of his nationalist political philosophy by founding two magazines, *The Public Interest*, which he edited together with Daniel Bell (first published in 1965), and *The National Interest*, which he published and was edited by Owen Harries (first published in 1985).
31. Kristol, *Reflections of a Neo-Conservative*, xiii.
32. Irving Kristol, *Two Cheers for Capitalism* (New York: Basic Books, 1978).
33. Kristol, *Reflections of a Neo-Conservative*, 76–77.
34. Ibid., 50–51.
35. Ibid.
36. Ibid., 315.
37. Ibid., 107.
38. Ibid., 50–51.
39. Milton and Rose Freedman, *Free to Choose* (New York: Harcourt, 1980).
40. Yoram Hazony, "Church's Proper Place in the State," *The Princeton Tory* (October 1984), 28–29. The following year, the Supreme Court of the United States began hearing arguments in *Wallace v. Jaffree* (1985), a church-state case in which William Rehnquist, then still an associate justice, wrote one of the most important dissents in American judicial history. Noting that the Supreme

Court's jurisprudence on the establishment of religion had been based on the Jeffersonian doctrine of a "wall of separation of church and state," he argued that this theory was historically and philosophically unsound. As he wrote: "It is impossible to build sound constitutional doctrine upon a mistaken understanding of constitutional history, but unfortunately the Establishment Clause has been expressly freighted with Jefferson's misleading metaphor for nearly 40 years." What follows is the classic legal argument for rejecting both the postwar constitutional theory of a separation of church and state applying to the states, and the entire line of decisions based on this doctrine going back to the 1940s. Justice William Rehnquist, dissenting in *Wallace v. Jaffree* (1985).

41. Edmund Burke, *Reflections on the Revolution in France*, ed. J. G. A. Pocock (Indianapolis, Indiana: Hackett, 1987 [1790]), 80–81.
42. Dennis Prager and Joseph Telushkin, *The Nine Questions People Ask about Judaism* (New York: Simon and Schuster, 1981).
43. In private conservation, Irving told me that as a matter of political theory, he thought only Christians should be able to vote in a Christian majority nation such as America; and that, by the same principle, only Jews should be able to vote in Israel. If someone wanted to be recognized as a member of a certain political community, they should adopt the public religion of the majority.

Conclusion: On Being a Conservative Person

1. See my discussion of personal *teshuva* in Chapter 9.5.

Index

S